Hitler's Hometown

Hitler's Hometown

LINZ, AUSTRIA

1908–1945

Evan Burr Bukey

Indiana University Press / BLOOMINGTON AND INDIANAPOLIS

Manufactured in the United States of America

Library of Congress Cataloging-in-Publication Data

Bukey, Evan Burr, 1940–
   Hitler's hometown.

   Bibliography: p.
   Includes index.
   1. Linz (Austria)—Politics and government.
2. National socialism. 3. Hitler, Adolf, 1889–1945.
I. Title.
DB879.L6B84   1986   943.6′2   85-45762
ISBN 0-253-32833-0

1   2   3   4   5   90   89   88   87   86

To the Memory of Andreas Dorpalen
1911–1982

Contents

ILLUSTRATIONS

TABLES

ACKNOWLEDGMENTS

This study is the product of a collaborative effort with my friend and colleague at the University of Arkansas, Kurt Tweraser. It originated during one of many discussions on recent Austrian history early in 1974 and began in earnest on a common research trip to Linz the following year. Although our specific research concerns diverged thereafter, this book could not have been written without his constant help and advice. Its pages contain so many of his insights that, while he cannot be held responsible for mistakes or shortcomings, in a significant sense it is his too.

I am also indebted to numerous others in the United States, Germany, and Austria. Among them are the staffs of the Mullins Library of the University of Arkansas, Fayetteville; the Military Archives Division of the National Archives, Washington, D.C.; the National Records Center, Suitland, Maryland; the Berlin Document Center, West Berlin; the Archiv der Stadt Linz, especially Dr. Wilhelm Rausch and Dr. Fritz Mayrhofer; the Stadtmuseum Linz; the Oberösterreichisches Landesarchiv, Linz, especially Dr. Harry Slapnicka; the Allgemeines Verwaltungsarchiv, Vienna, especially Dr. Lorenz Mikoletzky; the Dokumentationsarchiv des österreichischen Widerstandes, Vienna, especially Dr. Herbert Steiner, Dr. Jonny Moser, and the late Dr. Selma Steinmetz; and the Institut für Zeitgeschichte of the University of Vienna, especially Dr. Anton Staudinger and Dr. Gerhard Jagschitz. I should also like to extend a very special word of gratitude to the exceptionally courteous librarians of the National Bibliothek in the Hofburg.

For financial assistance I would like to thank the American Philosophical Society (the Penrose Fund) and the University of Arkansas Research Reserve Fund. I am also indebted to the University of Arkansas for an off-campus duty assignment that in 1978 enabled me to undertake the bulk of my research in Europe and to the J. William Fulbright College of Arts and Sciences for a semester leave that in 1981 helped me complete a first draft of this study.

Among the friends and colleagues who have read and criticized individual chapters I wish to thank James B. Powers, Harry Ritter, John Haag, and David Kitterman. Those who read versions of the completed manuscript and offered helpful suggestions to whom I am grateful are: my late mother Dorothy Burr Bukey, Bruce F. Pauley, Timothy P. Donovan, and James S. Chase. For a remarkably thorough and penetrating criticism that helped me rethink many of my original ideas I am beholden to Gary B. Cohen.

Other individuals who provided help and encouragement over the past decade include Edgar Walther, Irmgard Bokemeyer, Dr. Achim Weber, Gwyn Moser, Robert A. Mandel, and Suzanne Stoner. I am obliged to Gerald R. Kleinfeld for publishing a portion of my study in *German Studies Review* and to Douglas Unfug for publishing another section in *Central European History*. I also wish to thank Dr. Gerhard Botz of the University of Salzburg for bringing to my attention a number of important documents and for making copies available to me.

Finally, I owe a debt of gratitude to my family. Without the devotion of my wife Anita and the cheerful support of my children Ellen and David this project could not have been completed. For their patience and forebearance I wish to express once again my heartfelt and loving thanks.

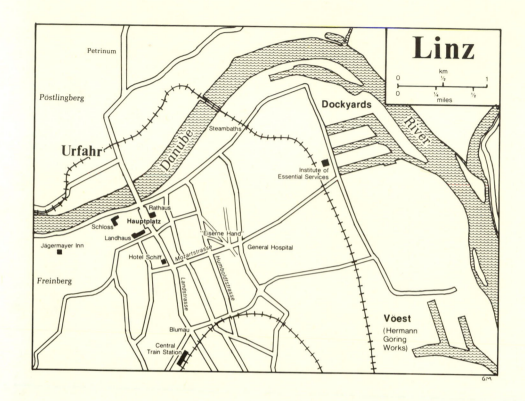

Petrinum

Pöstlingberg

Urfahr

Danube

Steambaths

Dockyards

River

Institute of
Essential Services

Rathaus

Hauptplatz

Schloss

Landhaus

Jägermayer Inn

Hotel Schiff

Mozartstrasse

"Eiserne Hand"

General Hospital

Humboldtstrasse

Freinberg

Landstrasse

Linz

km
0   ½   1

0   ¼   ½
miles

Voest
(Hermann
Goring
Works)

Blumau

Central
Train Station

GM

INTRODUCTION

Few societies have experienced greater turbulence in the first half of the twentieth century than German-speaking Austria. The core of the once-powerful Habsburg Empire, Austria west of the Leitha river was the focal point of the ethnic cleavages, social dislocation, and political disintegration that afflicted the monarchy in the last years of its existence. With the defeat and dissolution of Austria-Hungary at the end of World War I, the German remnant became a democratic republic, a small state of about six and a half million bewildered inhabitants. The new Austria was not without assets, but it was burdened with a shattered economy, an authoritarian political legacy, and, above all, a lack of national identity or cohesion. While the prospect of Anschluss, or union with Germany, seemed at first a way out of these difficulties, the refusal of the victorious allies to countenance unification without the unanimous consent of the Council of the League of Nations intensified Austria's identity crisis. In the absence of countervailing integrative forces the country fell prey to ever greater polarization and fragmentation, characterized by ideological acrimony, class division, and the rise of fascist movements.

In 1934 a brief but violent civil war put an end to what little consensus remained in Austria and laid the groundwork for the establishment of a right-authoritarian dictatorship. Since this throwback to an earlier era offered no meaningful solutions to the desperate problems of the day, the new regime unwittingly conditioned the Austrian people to welcome Hitler's incorporation of their (and his) country in 1938. Thereafter collaborative support for the Nazi dictatorship was so widespread that only persecution, suffering, and looming defeat in World War II induced public sentiment to turn against what was gradually perceived as foreign rule. Once the notion of an independent Austrian state became a viable alternative to Greater Germany, however, a patriotic consciousness developed in Austria that since 1945 has enabled the Second Republic to strike root and to flourish.

It has long been recognized that Austria's difficulties in the twentieth century, however painful and dramatic, have much in common with those of other European societies: social, economic, and ethnic division; the collapse of a vast empire and the quest for a new identity; the evolution of a participatory political culture; the transformation of a traditional social order into a modern industrial society. At the same time it is also clear that Austrian developments have manifested distinctive qualities of their own: lack of national identity, sociopolitical segmentation, intense political participation and mass party membership; consociational bargaining among leadership groups. In recent years a number of important studies have skillfully woven both the common and separate threads of Austria's recent

xiii

past into the larger fabric of Central European and European history, but there is as yet no fully integrated analysis of the historical process from the last days of the monarchy to the founding of the Second Republic.[1]

The absence of a comprehensive history of contemporary Austria can be attributed to a constellation of factors that include the lack of an integrative consensus, a reluctance to deal with the Nazi past, and until 1970 a general unavailability of archival evidence. The neglect of a longitudinal study can also be ascribed to an understandable fascination with Vienna, a city whose development is inseparable from the general framework of Austrian history but has been so unique that it cannot be regarded as paradigmatic. Before considering the mosaic of the recent Austrian past, it is necessary to learn more about the individual pieces outside Vienna. Scrutiny of provincial cities such as Linz, the capital of Upper Austria, can reveal much about the evolution of participatory politics and the process of social and economic modernization that have molded the modern Austrian community.

But why Linz? For one thing, as an entrepot on the Danube, Linz has long mirrored the sociopolitical currents and ambiguities of Central European history. The boyhood home of Hitler, Eichmann, and Ernst Kaltenbrunner, it was a center of German Nationalist agitation before World War I, a model of democratic propriety during the 1920s, and a major battlefield of the Austrian Civil War of 1934. Rapidly evolving from a bastion of Social Democracy to a stronghold of National Socialism, it was a focus of the Anschluss in 1938 and the recipient of lavish aid from its Führer-son thereafter. The record of what occurred in the Danubian city in the first half of the twentieth century thus constitutes a seismographic register of the tremors of recent Austrian experience; for the period of Nazi rule the record is useful in understanding something of Hitler's intentions, not simply for his native Linz and Austria but for much of the Greater German Reich.

Assuming a correlation between economic-technological development and political culture, examination of Linz should further provide an interesting test case of the impact of modernization. From an agricultural, commercial, and artisanal-manufacturing community of 58,791 inhabitants in 1900, the Danubian city evolved into a semi-industrial city at the end of World War I. During the interwar period, protectionist legislation and a capital shortage combined to retard growth so that after a brief period of expansion the urban economy stagnated, creating a crisis of social insecurity that led to armed violence and civil war. A subsequent attempt to stabilize the economic system through deflationary policies and a reliance on agriculture and traditional manufacturing failed utterly. Under Hitler's tutelage, however, the Upper Austrian capital underwent massive industrialization and change. Today, with a population of nearly a quarter of a million, it is one of Europe's major manufacturing centers, producing most of Austria's steel, nitrogen, fertilizers, and a host of chemical-related and finished products.

Recognizing that modernization encompasses more than industrialization and technological change, study of Linz can also illuminate the social modernizational interpretations of National Socialism proposed by David Schoenbaum, Ralf Dahrendorf, Geoffrey Barraclough, and, in the Austrian context, by Radomir Luža.[2] Despite Hitler's utopian antimodernist goals, he and his hometown retainers did more than industrialize Linz; they also established the foundation of a modern industrial society, creating thousands of jobs for the city's upwardly mobile managers, technicians, and white collar employees. More than in Germany, the Nazis were able to push aside or to destroy small-scale economic producers, to contain agricultural interests, and to curtail the power of the Church hierarchy. In church-state affairs they left a lasting impact, restricting religious instruction in schools, institutionalizing civil marriage, and separating church from state. Brutal and capricious as Hitler's rule turned out to be, it succeeded, as we shall see, in paving the way for a pluralistic order both in his hometown and in the Second Austrian Republic.

The investigation of Linz should not be regarded as a perfect microcosm of Austria's historical past. In a region as varied and complex as Central Europe no analysis of a single locality can reveal all there is to know about the society in which it is situated. Although one tessera may now be in place, the mosaic must remain incomplete until studies of Vienna and other Austrian cities become available.

ABBREVIATIONS

A St Linz	Archiv der Stadt Linz; Linz Municipal Archives
AVA	Allgemeines Verwaltungsarchiv; General Administrative Archives, Vienna
BDC	Berlin Document Center
DAF	Deutsche Arbeitsfront; German Labor Front
DAP	Deutsche Arbeiterpartei; German Workers' Party
DHV	Deutschnationaler Handlungsgehilfenverband; German Nationalist Association of Commerical Employees
DNSAP	Deutsche Nationalsozialistische Arbeiterpartei; German National Socialist Workers' Party (Austrian Nazi party before 1926)
DÖW	Dokumentationsarchiv des österreichischen Widerstandes; Documentation Archives of the Austrian Resistance, Vienna
GB	Gegenbewegung; Countermovement
GDVP	Grossdeutsche Volkspartei; Greater German Peoples' Party
HJ	Hitler Jugend; Hitler Youth
IfZ	Institut für Zeitgeschichte; Institute for Contemporary History, Vienna
KdF	Kraft durch Freude; Strength through Joy
KPÖ	Kommunistische Partei Österreichs; Communist Party of Austria
NA	National Archives, Washington, D.C.
NRC	National Records Center, Suitland, Maryland
NSDAP	Nationalsozialistische Deutsche Arbeiterpartei; National Socialist German Workers Party (Nazi party)
NSV	Nationalsozialistische Volkswohlfahrt; National Socialist Peoples' Welfare
ÖB	Österreichischer Beobachter
ÖOLA	Oberösterreichisches Landesarchiv; Upper Austrian Provincial Archives, Linz
ÖVP	Österreichische Volkspartei; Austrian Peoples' Party
PK	Parteikanzlei-Korrespondenz; Nazi party correspondence in the Berlin Document Center
RAD	Reichsarbeitsdienst; Reich Labor Service
SA	Sturmabteilung; Storm Troopers
SD	Sicherheitsdienst; Security Service of the SS
SPD	Sozialdemokratische Partei Deutschlands; Social Democratic Party of Germany
SPÖ	Sozialistische Partei Österreichs; Socialist Party of Austria
SS	Schützstaffel; elite guard of the NSDAP
UNRRA	United Nations Relief and Rehabilitation Agency
USCHLA	Untersuchungs- und Schlichtungsausschuss; Investigation and Conciliation Committee of the NSDAP
VdU	Verband der Unabhängigen; League of Independents
VdwA	Verband der deutschen weiblichen Angestellten; Association of German Women Employees
VÖEST	Vereinigte Österreichische Eisen- und Stahlwerke; United Austrian Iron and Steel Works

Hitler's Hometown

ONE

Under the Double-Eagle
1908–1918

Adolf Hitler was born in Braunau on the Inn River, but he did not consider it his hometown. That distinction fell to Linz, the capital of Upper Austria. There, at the turn of the century, the Führer of the Thousand Year Reich grew insouciantly into manhood. From the comfortable village of Leonding on the outskirts of the city he spent four years commuting to the Linz *Realschule*, where he devoted most of his time to daydreaming and sketching with colored pencils. After a brief stint at another secondary school in nearby Steyr, the sixteen-year-old Hitler moved in 1905 with his widowed mother to Humboldtstrasse 31 in the heart of Linz. "These were my happiest days,"[1] he later wrote of his carefree life in the Danubian city, days that were not forgotten after his departure in February 1908 for the outside world.

FIN-DE-SIECLE LINZ

The city of the Führer's boyhood was a town of only 60,000 inhabitants. As the capital of one of the Habsburg monarchy's smallest, least industrialized crown lands, it exuded the atmosphere of a booming rural town. Through dusty cobblestone streets farmers and peasants could be seen moving with loads of grain, potatoes, and apples; in suburban fields and pastures cattle grazed in solitude. Many of the townsfolk such as the Hitlers hailed from the surrounding countryside or were themselves children of recent arrivals. Even so, Linz was a city with a distinct urban tradition. Founded as Lentia by the Romans in the early Christian era, it originally housed a small garrison of Roman troops and provided port facilities for the empire's Danubian flotilla. As a consequence of the salt trade with the Marcomani in nearby Bohemia, a small civilian community also developed. In the fifth century Lentia was abandoned by the Romans and apparently ceased to be inhabited altogether. Three hundred years later, as part of Charlemagne's system of fortifications, a castle reputed to be the site of the composition of the *Nibelungenlied* was constructed on the spot. Under its protective walls

1

a new market town emerged, first as a toll station on the Danube and subsequently as a center of trade in salt, linen, wool, and leather. By 1140 the community had passed under the control of Leopold IV, margrave of Austria, and was accorded the status of civitas.

Although Linz never became a free city of the Holy Roman Empire, it did serve briefly as the residence first of Duke Albert VI and then of Emperor Frederick III. In 1490 it was proclaimed capital of the province above the Enns (Upper Austria) and granted municipal autonomy. Under the patronage of powerful commercial and craft guilds the town flourished. A great number of stately renaissance buildings were constructed, enclosing a broad square by the Danube, and, for a time, the city became the home of the humanist Johannes Reuchlin and later of the astronomer Johannes Kepler. During the Reformation most of the population of Linz converted to Protestantism, as did the bulk of the Upper Austrian peasantry.[2]

In 1620 the hereditary lands of Upper Austria passed temporarily to Maximilian of Bavaria, setting the stage for Linz's first appearance as a focal point of European attention. That occurred five years later, when, in reaction to Maximilian's policies of Catholicization and economic exploitation, sixteen thousand peasants rose in revolt. Under the leadership of the farmer Stephan Fadinger, they seized control of the province and besieged Linz. Throughout the summer of 1626 fighting raged back and forth between the Enns and the Danube. Finally, in November, Bavarian troops crushed the insurgents and relieved the ducal capital, though at a cost of over two hundred buildings and the exile or emigration of many of Linz's merchant families. In the course of the ensuing reaction, the townsfolk forfeited most of their municipal rights and were compelled to convert to Roman Catholicism.[3]

Over the next two centuries Linz languished and declined. Provincial commerce shifted to the rival city of Wels, and the last vestiges of communal autonomy were removed by Joseph II. On 15 August 1800 a large section of the town was devastated by fire. Considering the period as a whole, Linz's most memorable moments in the eighteenth century may have been those few days in November 1783 when Mozart paused in the city to compose his elegant thirty-sixth symphony, a work subsequently named after the Upper Austrian capital.[4]

During the French Revolution and Napoleonic Wars, Linz remained an island of tranquility; a minor battle was fought near the outskirts in 1809, but the town was spared the ravages of war and foreign occupation. Only in the decades following the Congress of Vienna did the Upper Austrian capital experience a period of sustained economic growth and change. That development did not result, however, from the general advance of industrialization, since the municipal guilds of goldsmiths, gunsmiths, printers, bakers, and candlestick makers still met the needs of the local population

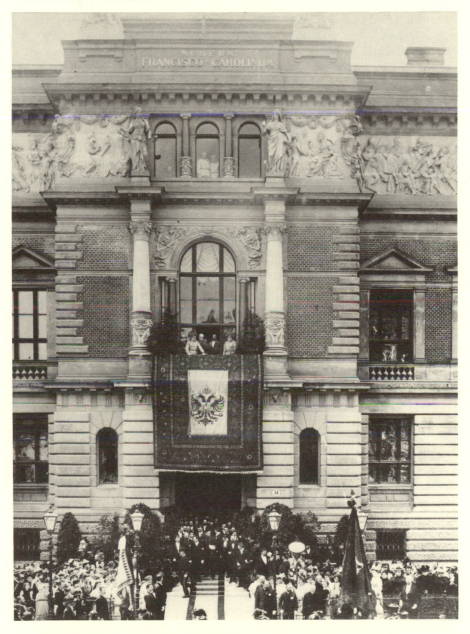

Emperor Francis Joseph dedicates the Landesmuseum in
Linz, 1892. Stadtmuseum Linz.

and for some time were able to block the introduction of merchanized manufacturing. Instead, the general expansion of trade and commerce between northwestern Europe and the eastern portions of the Danubian monarchy, including the Adriatic, put Linz in a position to take advantage of its age-old position as a bridge town.

Increasing traffic in salt, leather, iron, lumber, woollens, carpets, and linen textiles spurred the development of transportation and agriculture-related industries. Between 1827 and 1832 the first railroad line on the European continent was built between Linz and Budweis (Budejovice) inaugurating a process which by the end of the century made Linz the largest railway junction in the Austrian empire. As a result, plants were founded that manufactured locomotives, agricultural machinery, river boats, and textiles. In addition, two large breweries, a state tobacco firm, and a host of food processing industries were established.[5] By 1910 well over a third of the municipal working population was engaged in manufacturing and just under another third in trade and commerce. It should be emphasized that although some industry was mechanized—the spinning mills in the suburb of Kleinmünchen had some of the oldest power-driven machinery in Europe[6]—most production during Hitler's childhood was handicraft, requiring of workers an apprenticeship and a certificate of skill as a condition of employment.[7]

Despite its small size and rural atmosphere, the Upper Austrian capital at the turn of the century enjoyed a certain renown as one of Central Europe's minor musical cities. There between 1856 and 1869 that awkward genius Anton Bruckner wrote more than forty musical compositions including three symphonies, a fugue in D minor for organ, and three shimmeringly monumental masses. After his departure for Vienna, Bruckner's work was continued by August Göllerich, one of Wagner's last collaborators. By 1900 Göllerich was directing the Linz Conservatory, staging a respectable repertoire of operatic performances, and acquiring a reputation as a foremost interpreter of Liszt, Wagner, and Bruckner.[8] Not infrequently was he responsible for propelling the young Hitler into flights of ecstasy at the provincial opera house.

That Linz was known as a mini-Parnassus was due in part to the active support of the local Catholic hierarchy. Since the establishment of the provincial diocese in 1783, a succession of bishops had taken a keen interest in sponsoring the arts and in founding schools, seminaries, and monasteries. Bishop Francis Joseph Rudigier (1853–1884), in particular, gained renown as an ardent promoter of cultural and educational activities. He, for example, was among those most responsible for advancing Bruckner's career. So great was the bishop's zeal for parochial education that it once brought him into conflict with an anticlerical, liberal-dominated government in Vienna, thrusting Linz momentarily into the international limelight. In opposition to

The Trinity Column and Old Cathedral on Francis Joseph
Square, 1910. Stadtmuseum Linz.

the Confessional Laws of 1868 that made civil marriage possible and secularized elementary education Rudigier composed a pastoral letter so strident and shrill that he was placed under arrest, formally charged with disturbing the peace, and, before being pardoned by Emperor Francis Joseph, sentenced to fourteen days imprisonment.[9]

Although the Upper Austrian episcopate helped set the cultural tone in Linz and remained influential in the countryside, it wielded little power in the city itself. Here, as in many Austrian cities in the late nineteenth century,[10] municipal politics were dominated by the upper and middle strata of the middle classes whose socioeconomic influence helped bring it to power in the wake of the monarchy's military defeats and internal conflicts of the years 1848 to 1867. Granted a share of power by the aristocracy and the imperial bureaucracy, the well-to-do bourgeoisie sought to maintain its control of municipal affairs and to protect its economic interests by means of the restricted franchise. According to the Imperial Municipal Code of 5 March 1862, Austrian city councils were to be elected by "those paying higher taxes," while specific rules and procedures were left to the provincial diets. Since aristocratic landowners were relatively weak and thinly scattered in Upper Austria, the electoral laws adopted by the provincial diet in 1880 solidified bourgeois rule in Linz for the next four decades, as the Austro-American political scientist Kurt Tweraser has put it, "in the form of an almost naked plutocratic electoral system."[11]

The local electoral statutes divided the urban electorate into three voting classes or curiae, each of which elected one third of the city council (Gemeinderat). Those belonging to the first curia paid at least 200 gulden building or property taxes annually; those in the second paid between 11 and 199 gulden or were accorded the franchise as "intelligensia voters" (professors, clergy, physicians, civil servants, and retired army officers). The third curia consisted of all voters paying between 5 and 10 gulden in taxes. In 1904 a fourth curia of general voters was added—as well as twelve seats to the city council—but suffrage rights still remained limited to no more than 18 percent of the city's total population. In such a way a small group of bourgeois notables retained control of Linz while affirming the traditional ideals of Austrian middle-class society.[12]

Even so, bourgeois rule was not always secure. During the Liberal Era (1861–1879) those members of the middle strata (Mittelstand) who had been excluded from political participation by the liberal elite of wealthy merchants, prosperous lawyers, and tenured state officials or were adversely affected by industrialization gradually rejected the doctrines of political liberalism and laissez faire capitalism. After the financial crash of 1873, large numbers of local shopkeepers, small masters, lower officials, and handicraft workers joined extraparliamentary opposition groups throughout Austria. Their cumulative grievances found expression nine years later in the Linz Pro-

Francis Joseph Square (Hauptplatz), 1910. The view is toward the Danube. Stadtmuseum Linz.

gram of 1882. As formulated in the Upper Austrian capital, the Linz Program called for social reform, radical democracy, and ethnic-German nationalism. On its basis three mass protest movements or "camps" (*Lager*) then emerged to challenge the existing order, not just in Linz but in Cisleithania as a whole. The three "camps" were utterly divided on social, economic, and national issues, but they were united in their opposition to liberal ideology and tutelage.[13] Within a decade their uncoordinated but relentless efforts combined to force the Liberals from political power in the cities of German-speaking Austria though, given the cleavages separating the *Lager*, the ultimate outcome differed from town to town. In Vienna, for example, liberal rule gave way to a coalition of lower clericals, artisans, shopkeepers, and *Hausherren* under the flamboyant Christian Social politician, Karl Lueger.[14] In Linz—and Graz—on the other hand, the liberal order fell prey to a similar constellation united however under the aegis of anticlerical German Nationalists.[15]

The man responsible for the realignment and subsequent reunification of middle-class political forces in Upper Austria was Carl Beurle, an energetic young attorney and disciple of the uncompromising ethnic-German nationalist, Georg Ritter von Schönerer.[16] Between 1888 and 1900 Beurle forged an electoral coalition of lawyers, civil servants, teachers, independent artisans, shopkeepers, and small merchants, all of whom shared a fear of social dislocation, a contempt of liberal values, an animosity toward the Church, and a racially-based Judeophobia. In accord with the gospel of Schönerer, the German Nationalists pointed to the Jews as the root cause of societal woes and demanded their removal from the German folk community. In the hands of a skilled politician like Beurle, who also excelled in anticapitalist rhetoric, anti-Semitism proved an effective means of rallying the lower middle strata behind bourgeois rule on a basis other than that of liberalism. By 1900 even the Liberals conceded the wisdom of such an approach and threw their support to the German Nationalists rather than quarrel over the issue of anti-Semitism in a province where, as one of them put it, "there are only a handful of Jews and not a single Jew sitting in any parliamentary body."[17]

Between 1900 and 1918 Beurle's German Nationalists skillfully exercised control of the Linz city council by means of an expanded curial voting system and atavistic propaganda. As merchants, pharmacists, attorneys, teachers— men of property and education—they busied themselves with municipal administrative reforms such as the adoption of the city manager system of government, the improvement of municipal streets and utilities, the founding of vocational schools and other secondary institutions, and the incorporation within Linz of neighboring communities.[18]

Ideologically, the German Nationalists in Linz were not as radical as their compatriots in other German-speaking cities such as Innsbruck and Graz. That this was so was due to the absence of a local university with clashing nationalistic students and to Beurle's generally pragmatic leadership. Like Lueger in Vienna, the Linz political boss was more interested in stabilizing middle-class society against unwanted change than in radicalism for its own sake. Without modifying his opposition to "world Jewry," he thus refused to support Schönerer's program for the destruction of the multinational Habsburg monarchy and eventually broke with the inflexible Knight of Rosenau to join Otto Steinwender's more moderate German People's Party.[19] Even so, Beurle and his followers contributed their share of *völkisch* (populist-racial) propaganda to the community. In the uproar following the attempt by the imperial government to place the Czech language on an equal footing with German in Bohemia, for example, Beurle created a sensation by revealing that a Capucine priest, Kaspar Jurasek, was preaching at Linz's St. Martin's Church in Czech and collecting money for the construction of a Czech school.[20] Since a small number of indebted farms in the nearby Mühlviertel of Upper Austria had recently been sold to Czech peasants, Beurle's words helped incite a number of anti-Slav street demonstrations that culminated in a wild melee against the renowned Czech violinist, Jan Kubilek. In the city hall, Lord Mayor Franz Dinghofer also made no secret of his anti-Czech, anti-Semitic sentiments and was fond of concluding his speeches with a reference to the "German watch on the Danube."[21] At the same time, less sophisticated, more xenophobic agitation was being undertaken by local gymnastic societies, teachers organizations, and the *völkisch* press. *Der Scherer, Linzer Fliegende Blätter,* and *Deutscher Michl,* for example, were all German Nationalist-sponsored papers published in Linz at the turn of the century. Exalting the aryan race while excoriating the Habsburg monarchy, the Roman Catholic Church, and the Jews, they were presumably read, or at least seen, by the young Hitler.[22]

Opposition to German Nationalist hegemony in Linz came primarily from the Roman Catholic People's Association (*Volksverein*), a movement founded in 1870 as part of a widespread European counteroffensive against modernism. The People's Association was originally a traditional conservative party pledged to resist the anticlerical measures of liberalism. Under the guidance of Rudigier it expanded into a mass organization of peasants and priests that sought to protect the interests of local agriculture against both foreign competition and domestic laissez faire legislation aimed at the repeal of usury laws or the subdivision of family farms. The People's Association thus sponsored the founding of agricultural cooperatives, savings banks, and mortgage institutions in Upper Austria. It also advocated such projects as rural electrification, the extension of rural telephone service, and the construction of an interurban tramway network. Since the Catholic movement increasingly depended on mass participation, especially in the cooperatives, it gradually adopted democratic procedures and goals; by the turn of the century it was also demanding the abolition of the curial franchise even though its own dominance of the provincial diet was based on a mastery of indirect elections. As a mass party, however, it had little to fear from democratization. Furthermore, so long as the restricted electoral system remained in force and the German Nationalists retained the allegiance of the anticlerical *Mittelstand,* the Catholic party stood little chance of winning municipal power in Linz.[23]

That Catholic politics experienced a separate and independent development in Linz as against Vienna must be stressed. In the imperial capital the Christian Social movement that emerged in the 1890s was an aggregation of diocesan priests, artisanal procedures, shopkeepers, schoolteachers, and—later—peasants united against both liberalism and the Austrian episcopate; it was a coalition that relished radical rhetoric and high-tension behaviour but which aimed at the maintenance of middle-bourgeois privilege in the face of participatory demands by the lower orders of society. By 1907 the movement that began as a party of the masses was becoming a conservative coalition of petty bourgeoisie and peasants. In Linz and Upper Austria, on the other hand, Catholic political life evolved in harmony with the Church hierarchy. Although pledged to Catholic Conservative values, the People's Association developed into an organization of self–confident farmers and priests who refused to eschew democratic means to strengthen its position. In contrast to Lueger's party in Vienna, the Upper Austrian movement even advocated universal suffrage as the best way of wresting power from the hated Liberals and German Nationalists. When the People's Association formally joined the Christian Social caucus in 1907, it thus represented a tradition substantially more democratic and eudaemonistic than the mainstream movement.[24]

In its resistance to German Nationalist hegemony the Catholic party was joined by Linz's Social Democrats, a group generally less militant than political compatriots in other Austrian cities at the turn of the century, especially in Vienna. Organized from the ranks of journeymen printers, tailors, carpenters, bakers, and cobblers shortly after the Austro-Prussian War of 1866, working-class associations in Linz fully endorsed the unique emphasis on education and self-help that was rapidly becoming a distinctive feature of Austrian socialism; as in Graz they also received the support of some of Upper Austria's more enlightened upper-middle-class families. After an imperial crackdown in July 1870, labor organizations in the Habsburg monarchy faced nearly two decades of governmental harassment and persecution. In Upper Austria their hardships were aggravated by bickering between a moderate majority and a small group of Anarchists, largely from Bohemia, who advocated revolutionary action. Since most labor leaders in Linz were primarily displaced artisans, however, they focused their principal resentments on reactionary guild masters, demanding such measures as the prohibition of Sunday work and prepaid health insurance. Given the persistence of handicraft industry in Upper Austria, craftsmen also took the lead in organizing trade unions. They were particularly susceptible to the teachings of Ferdinand Lassalle and appear to have been only dimly aware of the works of Marx and Engels. When a provincial branch of the Austrian Social Democratic party was founded on 22 November 1891, it too was dominated by artisans and semiskilled workers.

In the two decades before World War I Social Democracy experienced a rapid growth in Linz, developing a local press and running candidates for political office. With the introduction of universal (though not equal) suffrage in the city in 1905 and in Cisleithania two years later, two Social Democrats were elected to the *Reichsrat* in Vienna, one to the provincial diet, and ten to the city council. During this period of expansion the labor movement began to manifest tendencies divergent from the norm in Vienna. For one

The fashionable Landstrasse in 1910. Stadtmuseum Linz.

thing, most of the leaders of the local party remained craftsmen, whereas the leadership of the Austrian party fell more and more into the hands of professional party managers or (frequently Jewish) intellectuals such as Viktor Adler. For another, while the rank and file of the party in Vienna, Prague, and other major cities of the empire consisted increasingly of industrial workers, those in Linz remained largely craftsmen or wage earners in small firms. Inevitably, little of a Marxian working class consciousness developed in Linz, so that, with the general extension of the franchise after 1905, local Social Democratic leaders eschewed radicalism and set their sights on achieving the eight-hour day or other specific, limited demands through the existing system.[25]

The Linz of Hitler's childhood and youth, then, was an ancient town located in the rural heartland of the Upper Danube, a region sometimes called the orchard of Austria. With a balanced economy and a well-established middle class, it could at times seem bucolic. In the years after Königgrätz, moreover, the provincial capital largely avoided the nationality struggles that were tearing the Habsburg monarchy to pieces; indeed Francis Joseph once referred to the Upper Austrian diet as a "model parliament."[26] Yet Linz was not a very exciting or stimulating place in which to live. It had no university, little industry, and not much opportunity for advancement. Moderate in tone, its relative social harmony and political tranquility had evolved from ethnic homogeniety, rural prosperity, and industrial backwardness. Alone these were insufficient underpinnings for a moderate political culture to withstand the convulsions of war and revolution. But the town's moderate institutions and traditions would survive World War I and the collapse of the Habsburg monarchy both intact and enhanced. That this was possible was due in large part to the wise and generous leadership of the provincial governor, Johann Nepomuk Hauser.

HAUSER AND REFORM

Hauser was a diocesan priest who had stumbled into provincial politics in 1891 as the consequence of a severe case of laryngitis. Unable to perform his pastoral duties, he had been relieved of his parish at Wels and appointed secretary of the Catholic Credit Institute. In that capacity he rose rapidly through the ranks of the People's Association and in 1899 was elected to the Upper Austrian diet. There he distanced himself from the representatives of large landed estates and championed the cause of the province's small farmers and peasants. By means of a colorful populist delivery he advocated military deferments for peasants, agricultural subsidies for small producers, and other measures designed to aid Upper Austria's rural population. With equal vigor he assailed Beurle's German Nationalists, partly for their anticlericalism but more fundamentally for their economic avarice and refusal to extend the political franchise beyond the ranks of the propertied middle classes. Within just a few years of his election, Hauser had established a reputation as one of the most forceful advocates of political democracy in Upper Austria.[27]

Appointed provincial governor (*Landeshauptmann*) in 1908, Hauser threw himself into his work with energy and determination. His principal goals were to balance the provincial budget and to expand the dietal and municipal franchise in accordance with reform legislation that in 1907 had extended the right to vote in *Reichsrat* elections to virtually all adult males in Cisleithania. The first task was accomplished by persuading the diet to raise taxes on beer, wine, hunting licenses, bicycles, and automobiles. The second proved more formidable as the German Nationalists under Beurle adamantly opposed the introduction of equal suffrage on the regional level, demanding instead the retention of the curial system upon which their local power was based.[28] According to a reform bill adopted by the diet in 1909, the curial franchise was retained, but a fifth class of general voters was added to the rolls and the number of mandates increased from fifty to sixty-nine. In elections held in May of that year the Catholic party strengthened its absolute majority in the diet, the Social Democrats won their first mandate, and the German Nationalists declined from 40 percent of the seats to less than a third.[29]

Under these circumstances the Chambers of Commerce and Trade and the cities of Upper Austria, especially Linz, remained the last stronghold of the German Nationalists. Despite the addition in 1904 of a fourth class of voters encompassing nearly all males over age twenty-four, the survival of the curial franchise on the communal level enabled Beurle and his followers to maintain their hammerlock of muncipal control. This voting system the Social Democrats on the Linz city council proposed sweeping away in favor of direct and equal suffrage; further they demanded the introduction of proportional representation. Given the entrenched power of the German Nationalists, the labor movement would have stood little chance of success were it not for the support of Hauser and the Catholic party.[30]

The son of a rural innkeeper, Hauser shared little of the romantic, patronizing view of the social question held by so many Austrian Catholics who followed the teachings of Baron Karl von Vogelsang. Nor did the prelate indulge in the anti-Semitism of Karl Lueger or, more importantly, in the studied contempt of "atheistic" Marxism shown later by the authoritarian head of the First Austrian Republic, Ignaz Seipel. Hauser was rather willing to accept Social Democratic control of Linz and Steyr as a natural consequence of the extension of democratic voting rights, just as he anticipated Catholic control of the countryside as the result of the same process. For these reasons he established contact with Social Democratic leaders early in his career and, as governor, worked closely with them to achieve his ends.[31]

Largely as a consequence of Catholic and Social Democratic pressure the curial voting system in Linz underwent substantial modification in the years immediately preceding World War I. In 1909, for example, when the German Nationalists reluctantly agreed to the introduction of election by proportional representation in the third and fourth curia of voters, Linz became the first city in the Habsburg monarchy to institute such electoral methods. (That the reform would also enable Beurle's followers to capture three seats in the fourth curia from the Social Democrats two years later was, needless to say, not foreseen).[32] Also, all parties agreed in February 1914, after much debate, to what amounted to an expansion of the second class of voters by its division into two subgroups and the creation of an executive committee (*Stadtrat*) to administer the city with the mayor and the city manager. Although these measures did not go into effect due to the outbreak of war five months later, they were nonetheless indicative of a grassroots movement of slow but steady democratization.[33] Without making too much of these changes, they clearly demonstrate that much of what would occur during the revolution of 1918–19 in Linz and Upper Austria was merely the ratification of a process well under way for many years.

WAR AND UNREST

The acceleration of that process, however, definitely began on 28 June 1914 with the assassination of Archduke Francis Ferdinand in faraway Sarajevo. Since Emperor Francis Joseph was then residing in nearby Bad Ischl (he left for Vienna the next day but returned on 7 July), the eyes of the world were focused fleetingly yet with rising intensity on Upper Austria. When the imperial government declared war on Serbia at the end of July, Linz found itself one of the first European cities to experience that wave of climactic enthusiasm that would sweep across the continent until it was engulfed in devastation. At mid-morning on 30 July the emperor's train pulled into the station south of the Danube to be met by the massed formations and regimental bands of the Linz garrison. Francis Joseph emerged briefly to express his confidence in the army and then chugged off to Vienna. From the station the troops marched north over the Landstrasse through cheering throngs of men, women, and children to a retreat on the broad square by the banks of the Danube.

The next day the announcement of general mobilization, posted at four in the afternoon, unleashed an even greater torrent of excitement. As in Vienna, Paris, Berlin, St. Petersburg, and London, ordinary people in Linz pushed and shoved each other in front of newspaper offices for word of further developments. Strangers engaged in conversations, students and gymnasts sang patriotic songs, bands played the national anthems of the Triple Alliance, and crowds cheered soldiers and officers. Even a few Czechs were seen joining in the celebration. For several days the holiday mood continued unabated, though with the arrival of troops on the way to the front, an air of confusion set in. Rumors, for example, spread that the tsar had been assassinated in Geneva and that enemy spies were moving through western Austria disguised as nuns. In a few places foreigners were roughed up and, in one unfortunate case, several Serbs were lynched. By the middle of August with the departure of local units of infantry, artillery, engineers, and sappers for Galicia, municipal life calmed and seemed to return to normal. That it was not in fact normal could be gauged by one ironic twist of fate: the reserve units now manning the Linz garrison—what Lord Mayor Dinghofer called the "German watch on the Danube"—were Czech.[34]

For the first year of the war conditions in the Upper Austrian capital were probably better than in most regions of the Austro-Hungarian Empire. Far removed from the fighting fronts and living in the heart of an agriculturally balanced province, most townsfolk in Linz were able to go about their business with a minimum of hardship or suffering. To be sure, hard money grew scarce as small change virtually disappeared from circulation, the price of milk, cheese, and other dairy products skyrocketed, and, toward winter, shortages of coal developed. But, for a while, these price rises and shortages were offset by an increase of eggs and poultry products, by a barely perceptible switch from coal to wood (of which Upper Austria had abundant supplies), and by the general availability of sufficient amounts of grain, potatoes, and fat. In fact, because the Linz municipal government had purchased eighty car loads of Hungarian wheat and rye before the outbreak of hostilities, local bakers and consumers scarcely felt the impact of the military requisition of substantial stocks of Upper Austrian grain. Under these conditions, it is not surprising that public morale remained comparatively high in Linz, particularly throughout the summer of 1915 as news arrived of great victories in Russian Poland.[35]

Not until the following winter did the war at last come home to the province above the Enns. With lists of casualties mounting and letters of hometown soldiers circulating, people began to get a clearer picture of the grim and desperate nature of the conflict. Simultaneously, prices lurched uncontrollably upward, and, for the first time, serious shortages of meat, sugar, and potatoes developed. To cope with the inevitable problems of supply and distribution the city government had created a provisioning committee soon after the beginning of the war. The committee possessed little real power, however, and was forced to compete with provincial, imperial, and military authorities so that it failed to establish effective control over local foodstuffs. Nor did Vienna create a centralized agency until late 1916 designed to regulate food prices and distribution or to allocate scarce resources in a meaningful way. Instead, ration stamps were issued by the Habsburg government to provincial authorities, who allocated and distributed them at their own discretion. Virtually no attempt was made by the competing authorities to institute direct controls over the actual production of food or agricultural produce. The result was a haphazard system of overlapping, sometimes conflicting, regulations that bred hardships, class hatred, and ultimately greater shortages.[36]

In Upper Austria, as elsewhere, peasants found their grain and draft animals subject to requisition by the Habsburg army. As a consequence, they curtailed the planting of wheat, barley, and oats, fed their livestock sugar beets, and substantially increased their flocks of poultry. Under these circumstances a flour shortage developed in Linz while the price of sugar, meat, and dairy products soared beyond the reach of the average city dweller. In order to assure adequate supplies of bread and milk, in particular, ration cards were introduced in 1915; unfortunately, the major effect of the measure was to reduce milk production by 60 percent, since farmers and peasants soon found it more profitable to make butter and cheese. The agricultural producers also discovered that they could sell fruit, vegetables, eggs, meat, and dairy products in Vienna at higher prices than in the towns and cities of Upper Austria. By 1916, therefore, serious food shortages were developing in the heart of one of the monarchy's richest agricultural provinces.[37]

In Linz itself the municipal government found it increasingly difficult to provide sufficient supplies of food for the town. With most provincial produce increasingly earmarked for Vienna or available only at extortionist prices, wheat had to be purchased from as far away as Rumania, salted fish from Scandinavia, and even fresh vegetables from Hungary. Within the city limits vacant lots and open spaces were turned into victory gardens, eggs stockpiled, and chicken houses opened to produce even more eggs. In some respects these ad hoc measures were quite successful, as the number of hens, for example, rose from less than six thousand in 1914 to over fifteen thousand two years later. By 1917 such a surplus of eggs existed in Linz (over twenty-five thousand) that they were offered for sale on the open market. Yet, without effective controls, eggs and poultry disappeared almost overnight and remained in short supply for the duration of the war.[38]

As scarcities intensified, public pressure in Linz and throughout Austria-Hungary grew for the adoption of a more equitable, unified system for the distribution and control of foodstuffs. In response, the imperial government in 1915 and 1916 created Nutritional Control Stations in the cities and towns of Cisleithania. In Linz and Upper Austria the control stations for fodder, grain, meat, vegetables, fruit, sugar, and alcohol were usually administered by local businessmen and merchants. Given the already chaotic, overlapping system of rationing and the inability of government agencies to control the distribution of food except for forced requisitions, the control stations in Linz were unable to improve the situation. Indeed, the results of their efforts were largely counter-productive because their ineffective program of centralization led to a good deal of food spoilage without, at the same time, increasing distribution. This, in turn, only fired rural resentment of Vienna and reinforced working-class hatred of the Linz business elite, since, as we have seen, the control stations were in the hands of local bankers and entrepreneurs.[39]

Just as the war caused major problems in the provisioning and distribution of food in Linz, so did it create difficulties in the town's plants and manufacturing sites. These difficulties, however, were of a different kind, since industry was regimented and not subject to the wild speculations of the agricultural market. The War Services Act of 1912 effectively put a number of firms under imperial control, so that they were assured of raw materials and their employees subject to military discipline and frozen wages. Under these conditions, relatively high levels of production were maintained throughout the war, but the increasingly harsh regulation of workers in factories under military control or in those considered vital to the war effort coupled with near starvation rations and a staggering rise in the cost of living provoked bitterness and class hatred.[40]

Working class resentment in Linz appears not to have been as great initially as in Vienna or in other large cities of the monarchy. Manufacturing in the Upper Austrian capital remained comparatively small in scale and underwent no major structural changes as it would during World War II. Nevertheless, by 1917 alienation and bitterness over short rations, long hours, and managerial discipline had spread from the important armaments factory in nearby Steyr to the few large concerns in Linz itself. The imperial viceroy (*Statthalter*) in the provincial capital reported to his superiors in August that public morale was slipping badly and that the laboring population had "nearly reached the limits of its capacity for performance and patience."[41] In early 1918, therefore, many Linz wage earners were ready to support the wave of strikes that swept through the western monarchy in response to Vienna's curtailment of the flour quota in Cisleithania. In the marshalling yards and heating plant of the imperial railroads, in the Krauss locomotive factory, at the Linz dockyards, in the state tobacco plant, and in several other local firms some 5,800 workers downed tools on 19 and 20 January 1918 not to return to work until two days later.[42]

As in Germany and other industrial centers of Austria-Hungary, growing labor unrest in Linz coupled with the general disruption of life itself was at first spontaneous and nondirected. For the first several years of the war local political leaders had observed a kind of unofficial civic truce, confining their grievances to complaints about the inefficiencies of the Vienna government or to problems of day-to-day life. With both the imperial parliament and the provincial diet standing adjourned until 1917, moreover, little opportunity existed for airing and debating views in public. It is true that the city council continued to meet, but its proceedings were confined primarily to local matters. On the few occasions when the war did become a subject of discussion, all parties agreed—somewhat in the mode of characters in a Robert Musil novel—not to let the matter disturb or interrupt their deliberations. Social Democratic leader Josef Gruber, for example, repeatedly voiced strong opposition to the war, but until December 1917 he routinely voted credits to support it.[43]

Not until the outbreak of serious disturbances in 1917 and the convening of the imperial parliament in Vienna did the contending political factions in Linz become ensnarled in the threads of the disintegrating social fabric. Yet once this actually occurred, the rhetoric of all three parties escalated to a radical, sometimes revolutionary level. The Social Democrats predictably denounced war profiteers, greedy peasants, and food speculators. They called for the lifting of censorship, the introduction of women's suffrage and taxes on wealth, and the adoption of a more coherent system of rationing. On 5 April 1917 party leader Gruber proclaimed his solidarity with the revolutionary masses in Russia. Across the aisle the German Nationalists also railed against the inefficiencies of central planning, blaming the Habsburgs for local woes and demanding autonomy for Upper Austria. Lord Mayor Dinghofer, in particular, did not hesitate to voice middle-class fear and resentment of the growing power of the Czechs in neighboring Bohemia and to demand Anschluss with the German Reich. That this could only be accomplished with the dissolution of Austria-Hungary seemed a price he was willing to pay. As for the Christian Socials, not even they stood steadfastly behind the policies of the Habsburg government. Admittedly, few considered open insurrection, but Governor Hauser on numerous occasions emphasized the necessity of transforming the monarchy into a genuine democratic state. This was a demand he no doubt knew had clear revolutionary overtones.[44]

To what extent the political parties in Linz might react to the confused and ever growing bitter feelings of the town population was at first not clear. Throughout 1918 public morale slipped badly as part of a general wave of antiwar feeling sweeping through Central Europe. During the summer, cases of tuberculosis and venereal disease rose sharply, and by autumn an average of eighteen townspeople were dying daily of Spanish influenza. Similarly, the number of violent crimes, especially among juveniles, increased with the pattern of crime itself shifting from hoarding, theft, and price manipulation to mugging, rape, and murder. As if these problems were not enough, a growing housing shortage focused xenophobic attention on the eighteen thousand refugees in the province (many from Galicia), leading to repeated calls for the expulsion of Jews.[45]

For those Linzers, primarily of the working classes, who were reluctant to take their cues from prewar political leaders—even Social Democratic ones—but who were politically conscious enough to reject inchoate or random violence, entirely new organizations came into being to redress their grievances. These were the workers' councils, first founded in Linz on 12 December 1917 by Richard Strasser, a lathe operator and shop steward in the Linz dockyards. Representing the more radical elements of the labor movement and unabashedly inspired by the Soviets in revolutionary Russia, the workers' councils in Linz, Steyr, Vienna, and the other cities of the monarchy helped direct the January strikes and sought to mobilize the masses against the Habsburgs. In Linz itself Strasser expressed a willingness to cooperate with local Social Democratic leaders but emphasized that their goals had to be more wide-ranging than a mere end to the war, as Gruber, for example, had always insisted should come first. After the January strikes, Strasser's council movement declined and throughout the summer of 1918 did not engage in political agitation. By late September, however, it began to show signs of revival, particularly among the exhausted and angry workers of the Krauss locomotive factory and Linz dockyards.[46]

Despite growing labor unrest, despite increasingly massive food shortages, despite suffering and death from influenza, and despite the almost ubiquitous disenchantment with the Habsburg dynasty, only a few individuals or groups in Linz or Upper Austria seriously considered revolutionary violence as a way out of the problems unleased by the war and its hardships. Indeed, so long as the Austro-Hungarian army stood intact in the field, concern that its troops could be redeployed to maintain domestic order was a serious and realistic one.[47] With the collapse of the army on the Piave and the simultaneous disintegration of the monarchy in October 1918, this attitude might be expected to change. Yet in the coming months of upheaval and turmoil most of the population looked for leadership not to Richard Strasser but to existing municipal and provincial authorities, particularly to Governor Hauser. Democratic change was now the order of the day, but it was to be achieved with local leaders primarily through established institutions. In this sense, the Austrian Revolution of 1918–1919 in Linz and its rural hinterland represented the continuation or completion of a process begun many years before.

TWO

Revolution by Consensus
1918–1920

The revolutionary turmoil that swept through German-speaking Austria as a consequence of the defeat and disintegration of the Habsburg monarchy was a bewildering affair. Almost overnight a Provisional National Assembly convened in Vienna, the Austro-Hungarian army ceased to exist, and the masses took to the streets. Through months of debate and demonstrations the core of the Habsburg Hereditary Lands was transformed into a parliamentary state in which the forces of political and social democracy seemed to hold sway. Yet the Austrian revolution of 1918–19 was more a revolution of appearance than of substance. Accompanied by surprisingly little violence, it was carried out by respectable politicians of Austria's three major political parties who joined hands in a moment of crisis and desperation. They succeeded in forging a moderate constitutional order largely because the forces of reaction had been decisively broken by the war and collapse. The new state thus enjoyed advantages not possessed by the Weimar Republic and other successor states, including grassroots support of many independent farmers in the provinces and of the workers in Vienna and other industrial centers. Nevertheless, the structure of society remained unchanged, and the government was faced with economic difficulties that precluded sweeping social and political reforms. Largely dependent on the victorious Allies, the First Austrian Republic could neither completely put its house in order nor, according to the Treaties of St. Germain and Versailles, join Weimar Germany in a larger union. As a consequence, a sense of demoralization set in that ultimately undermined the cause of democracy and national independence.[1]

To what extent conditions for a genuine revolutionary upheaval existed in Vienna after October 1918 remains a matter of historical controversy.[2] That such conditions were not present in Linz and Upper Austria is beyond doubt. There the masses turned toward local leaders and institutions, expressing a kind of natural instinct to fall back on regional loyalties in times of crisis.[3] Their sense of attachment to the dynasty had never been very great, and whatever good will that existed before 1914 was shattered during the war by imperial requisitions and centralized controls.[4] In Governor

Hauser, on the other hand, they perceived a man who was respected by virtually all local parties and interest groups, and who had behind him a solid record of democratic achievement. On 30 October 1918 Hauser was elected second president of the Provisional National Assembly in Vienna, the body pledged to transforming German Austria into a democratic republic. Under these circumstances the advice and counsel of radical revolutionaries, except in moments of turmoil, hardly seemed necessary.[5]

Actually, it was the sudden collapse of the Austro-Hungarian army in Italy that spurred local authorities into action. With hundreds of thousands of mutinous troops beginning to move through Linz on their way home to Bohemia or Hungary and in view of the pending collapse of discipline in the local garrison, representatives of the three major parties met to preserve law and order. Insofar as possible, they sought to get control of the many demonstrations now spreading through the town. That they had to move quickly became chillingly clear on 31 October when Strasser's dockworkers paraded by the *Rathaus* under scarlet banners in support of the Russian revolution. The politicians thus scheduled a mass rally in support of the Republic for the next day to be followed by the organization of a provincial soldiers' council.[6]

As elsewhere in German Austria, the Linz demonstration of 1 November was primarily a Socialist affair. Even so, it was actively supported by the Christian Socials and German Nationalists.[7] Under streamers carrying Schiller's inspiring words "Der Freiheit eine Gasse" teams of Socialist youth and gymnasts, worker choirs, the railwaymen's band, and thousands of soldiers and officers wearing red cockades assembled in the Francis Joseph Square by the Danube. There they were addressed by Josef Dametz, editor of the Social Democratic *Tagblatt*, Georg Pischitz, head of the Christian trade unions, and Franz Langoth, leader of the provincial German Nationalists. All three men welcomed the end of the war, the creation of German Austria, and the establishment of civil liberties. They promised an end to hunger, and they appealed to the crowd for law and order. After singing several stanzas of Josef Stein's powerful "Das Lied der Arbeit," the rally came to an end around noon.[8]

FORMATION OF THE SOLDIERS' COUNCIL

Few people, however, left the grounds of the huge public square for very long. Three hours later a Linz Soldiers' Council was constituted from the thousands of soldiers and officers still congregating outside the town hall. With each military unit represented by two enlisted men and one officer, the Soldiers' Council was charged with maintenance of discipline, the granting of leaves, and the "protection of the Republic." The man elected head of the Soldiers' Council was a certain Eduard Euller, a sergeant-major just back

from the front and well-known Socialist politician who had served on the
Linz city council since 1909. He was to work with the soldiers' representatives and with a kind of ad hoc committee of notables consisting of the
provisional lord mayor, Karl Sadleder, Major General Baron Durfeld, and
Field Marshal Stipek. Significantly, the Soldiers' Council was to be under
the command of a provincial security committee headed by the German
Nationalist politician, Franz Langoth.[9]

Although an institutional structure now existed capable theoretically of
restoring order, it had some difficulty doing so. By evening a wave of looting
and plundering had broken out that would not be contained for several days.
Around six o'clock, in a pale imitation of the storming of the Bastille, a large
mob of soldiers opened the gates of the Castle Barracks and freed its political
prisoners as well as, allegedly, nearly two hundred criminals. With crowds
of tattered, hungry people roaming the streets of the city, the Linz garrison
rapidly dissolved. Some of its soldiers left town by foot, some tried to catch
the next train home, and some—indeed a great many—joined the growing
crowd of looters. By morning the plunderers, who now included women and
children, were moving like hungry locusts from one military installation to
another taking shoes, coats, underwear, canned meat, bread, rifles, pistols,
ammunition, and, in one barracks, saddles, bridles, and cavalry blankets.
Attempts to disperse the crowds on the part of isolated platoons of the
Soldiers' Council met with little success.[10]

In those tense and confusing hours community notables moved swiftly to
shore up their authority by founding a provisional state government. On that
very day (2 November) the executive committee of the old provincial regime
met in the Upper Austrian state house to receive Baron Erasmus von
Handel's formal resignation as imperial viceroy. After accepting on behalf of
the province, Prelate Hauser summoned party leaders to a meeting on the
following day for the purpose of hammering out a new constitutional order.
In that constituent gathering Hauser and the politicians agreed to convene
the Upper Austrian diet on the basis of the *Reichsrat* elections of 1911. In
the diet the parties would be represented by the actual number of votes cast
rather than by mandates allocated under the prewar curial system. This
meant that the Christian Socials would have sixty-three deputies, the
German Nationalists twenty-three, and the Social Democrats fifteen. It also
meant that the bishop of Linz, the Upper Austrian Chamber of Commerce,
and the provincial landowning nobility lost their seats in the diet. The party
leaders also agreed on 3 November to the formation of a provisional cabinet
of seven Christian Socials, three German Nationalists, and two Social
Democrats. The cabinet was to advise the governor, who, in turn, was to be
elected by the diet. He was to administer the province with the aid of three
deputies, one each from the three parties.[11]

Once these arrangements were completed, Hauser was unanimously elected or "confirmed" governor by the party leaders, an affirmation that was repeated in the first meeting of the provisional assembly of 18 November. So far as the prelate was concerned, these proceedings constituted a kind of "half seizure of power," as he once jestingly remarked. Sovereignty had reverted from the Habsburg monarchy to provincial institutions and newly-founded soldiers' and workers' councils, at least until elections could be held and a new Austrian state system created. As second president of the Provisional National Assembly in Vienna, the prelate did not insist (as did many particularists in the Alpine provinces) that Upper Austria's ties with Vienna had been completely dissolved, but he made it abundantly clear that in the future the province should enjoy the same degree of democratic self-government and independence as a Swiss canton or an American state.[12]

Whatever Hauser's constitutional plans or scruples, he did not hesitate to assume and then to delegate virtually autonomous power in order to overcome the province's growing lawlessness and serious nutritional problems. Tied down by administrative duties and suffering from gout, the governor placed his German Nationalist deputy Franz Langoth in charge of police and military affairs, Social Democratic deputy Joseph Gruber in charge of nutrition and supplies, and Christian Social deputy Max Mayr in charge of administration and finance.[13]

The weather-wrinkled Langoth, in particular, moved with considerable skill and dispatch to restore order. This was no easy task with thirty thousand riotous soldiers moving daily through Linz and in light of now undefined lines of jurisdiction in town and province. Since, however, the security director's power derived from both traditional and revolutionary sources (in the sense that he had been appointed before 30 October and was subsequently confirmed by the provisional assembly), he was able to bridge the gap between imperial and revolutionary authorities and to command respect in both camps. As a founder of the Linz Soldiers' Council, for example, he created armed contingents willing to enforce the peace before elections were actually held in local garrisons. Thus, as early as 5 November, Langoth was able to order a general curfew and to demand the withdrawal from Linz of all nonresidents within twenty-four hours. On the same day, he also sent an order to the Steyr Works for ten thousand rifles, thirty machine guns, and one thousand service revolvers.[14]

The weapons (of which less than half actually arrived) were earmarked for an armed force called the *Volkswehr*, organized by the Soldiers' Council in support of the republic. Langoth, however, saw to it that the guns were issued to the rural constabulary (*Gendarmerie*), whose officers and men had been appointed by the imperial regime and who were generally still loyal to the Habsburgs. In so doing the security director acted from a realistic appraisal of the situation rather than out of a desire to subvert the revolution.

He knew that the largely urban *Volkswehr* would be resented in the countryside and in all likelihood would fail to establish order there without violence. By supporting the existing constabulary he hoped to head off the arming of the peasants and the formation of paramilitary groups, as was occurring in neighboring Bavaria. As for the *Volkswehr*, it would be used mainly in the towns of Linz, Steyr, and Wels. Significantly, on 8 November, constabulary, *Volkswehr*, police, and all other units in Upper Austria were declared under the jurisdiction of the provincial government.[15]

Generally speaking, Langoth's policy of reliance on both rural constabulary and urban *Volkswehr* to maintain order proved successful. His approach coupled with appeals from Governor Hauser and Bishop Gföllner to the peasants for "calm and self-discipline"[16] met with a favorable response in the countryside, so much so in fact that Upper Austria was one of the few regions of Central Europe in which bands of "military desperadoes" never emerged in sufficiently large numbers to challenge the postwar status quo. In Linz itself the security director kept a tight rein on the *Volkswehr* without simultaneously alienating its Socialist supporters. He recruited its formations from those members of the Soldiers' Council who demonstrated a willingness to assume police duties in the town. They were to wear red-white-red arm bands, to retain military courtesy, and to obey the municipal Soldiers' Council. At the same time, each platoon was given the right to elect one commissioned and one noncommissioned officer.[17]

By the time the first *Volkswehr* were deployed in Linz after a lethal exchange of gunfire (on 10 November) at the central train station, most of the riotous, nonindigenous troops had departed the city.[18] Large numbers of Italian and Russian prisoners of war still remained in nearby compounds, but Italian officers had assumed command of all Entente troops in Upper Austria and saw to it that the Russians, who were perceived as a danger, remained under guard.[19] With a relatively diminishing threat to public security, therefore, and with an overwhelming majority of the local population standing behind the provisional Upper Austrian government, the *Volkswehr* along with a crack Tyrolean rifle batallion was able to restore order in Linz with a minimum of difficulty. Furthermore, as municipal police regained their authority, the *Volkswehr* was relieved of many of its initial tasks and was used primarily to patrol train stations, to control black marketeers, or to distribute food supplies. Under these circumstances the *Volkswehr* in Linz never evolved into a quasi-professional force, as it did in Vienna; nor did it come to be regarded as the exclusive party army of the Socialists, as it did elsewhere in the country. On the few occasions when the *Volkswehr* was used to quell disturbances, few complaints were heard about poor discipline or "red terror."[20]

After the official proclamation of the Austrian Republic in Vienna on 12 November and the meeting of the Upper Austrian provisional assembly six days later, it became clear that power in Linz and its hinterland resided primarily in the provincial "government of the three deputies" supported by the regional Soldiers' Council. As if to underline this reality, a retired colonel, Arthur von Poeschmann, was appointed commander of military forces in Upper Austria (including the soldiers' councils and *Volkswehr*), apparently on orders from Langoth. The elderly colonel strongly objected to the power of the soldiers' councils in the first place, and his appointment was vigorously opposed by the Socialist-dominated war ministry in Vienna. The Linz Soldiers' Council approved the command, however, without dissent. Whatever power that body possessed in theory was thus being wielded ultimately by Langoth and his associates.[21]

ROLE OF THE WORKERS' COUNCIL

Just as Upper Austrian authorities were able to assume control of local affairs during the fall of the Habsburg monarchy by instituting democratic reform and by co-opting the functions of the Soldiers' Council, so were they able to harness working class support by sponsoring the formation of a Workers' Council. In Germany such organizations sprang up spontaneously in late 1918 and quickly gained enough strength to compete with the majority Social Democrats for control of the German Revolution. This was generally not the case in German Austria. The Austrian Social Democrats were more to the ideological left than their German compatriots and already possessed a tightly knit organization of trustees (*Vertrauensmänner*) in shops and factories.[22] When workers' councils, therefore, did emerge in German-Austrian industrial towns, they usually came quickly under the control of the local party and remained separate from the soldiers' councils. In Linz, as we have seen, such a workers' council had come into being as part of the strike movement in January 1918 and appeared to be reviving nine months later under the leadership of Richard Strasser. It was this still amorphous organization that local authorities now sought to control. Thus, on 11 November 1918, the first full meeting of the Linz Soldiers' Council resolved to commission the Social Democratic party "to create workers' councils at once and to have them establish the closest contact with the soldiers' councils without delay."[23]

In light of their party-sponsored origins, the revived workers' councils in Linz got off to a slow start. Eduard Euller assumed the chairmanship of the movement, relinquishing the chair of the Soldiers' Council to Franz Kelischek, a former student of philosophy at the University of Vienna.[24] For the next two months the workers' councils stayed in the shadow of the provincial government, routinely accepting orders to help in the distribution of food or to engage in other comparatively menial duties. By mid-January 1919, however, the membership had grown sufficiently strong to pass a resolution against the "rightist tendencies" of the Socialist party and to elect Richard Strasser chairman. In assuming this office Strasser argued that, although the *Volkswehr* would enjoy his support in maintaining law and order, the revolution was by no means complete and that the workers' councils should take a leading role in the transformation of the state.[25]

In coming months the Upper Austrian Workers' Council acquired a reputation as the largest and most independent in the entire country.[26] Under Strasser's leadership it negotiated increased unemployment benefits with the provincial government, successfully pressured local peasants to maintain milk deliveries to Linz, and issued a call for the formation of an all-Austrian workers' council in Vienna. On one occasion Strasser even went so far as to claim that the Linz city council would never decide any matter of concern to labor without the consent of his organization.[27]

Yet, despite this outward show of independence and strength, the Linz workers' councils never severed their ties with the Social Democratic leadership nor declined an order of the provincial government. Indeed, Strasser adamantly refused to claim legislative authority for the workers' councils (as happened in Germany). He remained, despite his rhetoric, a good Social Democrat and would not permit members of Christian or yellow trade unions to join the councils. In fact, out of 310 council members in Linz, 299 were Social Democrats and eleven were Communists.[28] As if to underline his dependence on the provincial government, Strasser willingly cooperated with the "three deputies" in containing radicalism, especially in early 1919 when fears arose that the German Spartacist movement might somehow spread into Upper Austria.[29] All in all, the Linz Workers' Council seems to have been a kind of umbrella organization for nonskilled workers and Socialist malcontents. To be sure, considerable lip service was paid to the notion of "making things Russian" or to complaining about Socialist "betrayal" of the revolution, but as one outside observer shrewdly noted, the resentments of the Workers' Council were more social than ideological. The members hated "intellectuals" of all stripes, by which they meant their own Social Democratic leaders, who were primarily craftsmen and artisans. They carried this attitude to the extreme of refusing to conduct any business over the telephone, arguing, not illogically from the standpoint of the untutored and inarticulate, that personal contact was a more effective means of making their position known.[30]

That the Linz workers' councils appeared to wield more power than they actually did was due to their highly visible role in the collection and distribution of foodstuffs. As the Austrian historian Harry Slapnicka has recently noted, virtually all activity in Linz and its hinterland during the grim and desperate winter of 1918–19 was determined by hunger and need.[31] Because Upper Austria had the most abundant supplies of grain in the new Austrian republic, the Vienna government had turned to it when the food trains stopped rolling from Bohemia and Hungary.[32] Grain and cereal production in the province, however, stood at only about two-thirds of 1913 levels (although that of barley had doubled), while the peasants, having welcomed the end of imperial regulations, had no desire to exchange them for new controls from "Red Vienna" or "Red Linz." Nevertheless, within weeks after the end of the war, teams of rural constables and *Volkswehr* were requisitioning food and cattle in the province. After the first of the year they were joined by members of the workers' councils.[33]

THE PROBLEM OF FOOD DISTRIBUTION

Generally speaking, Upper Austrian authorities maintained the flow of foodstuffs to urban areas with a minimum of violence. By relying on the *Gendarmerie* in outlying regions, by appealing to the peasants' religious sensibilities through Bishop Gföllner, by providing leather, refined sugar, and petroleum in exchange for food, and by promising to stimulate agricultural production by means of subsidies, Governor Hauser and his deputies for a time kept a lid on the simmering resentments between town and country. Yet not even the resourceful Hauser could prevent increasing demands by Vienna for provisions from leading to local food shortages that soon exceeded those of the war. Just how serious these shortages were became clear in mid-January when a food riot near Steyr provoked a firefight between *Volkswehr* and constables in which a civilian bystander was killed and several others were wounded. Within less than a month, an even more desperate outburst occurred in Linz.[34]

Early in the morning of Tuesday, 4 February 1919, approximately a thousand workers from the Krauss locomotive factory, the state tobacco plant, and the Linz dockyards congregated in the Reichsstrasse district of the provincial capital to protest a reduction of the weekly meat ration to a mere ten grams. From there they marched into the city, surrounded the *Landhaus*, and sent a delegation of dock workers to meet with Hauser. The prelate was able to calm the swarthy roustabouts and riveters by offering them fresh cigars and by promising them the immediate distribution of stocks of canned meat.[35] At this point most of the organized workers seem to have gone home, but the crowd itself, egged on by numerous angry women and hot-headed youngsters, stormed into an adjoining *Gasthaus* and cleaned out its kitchen. From there they swept through the Archduke Charles Hotel into various inns, delicatessens, and restaurants, devouring food and breaking china in their path.

As the rioteers paused at a specialty shop on the Landstrasse to feed on spiced ham, brightly colored easter eggs, candy, and other delicacies, the municipal police arrived on the scene. Reinforced within minutes by units of *Gendarmerie* and a few *Volkswehr*, these forces tried to restore order. The presence of rural constabulary, however, infuriated the mob. Women charged into their ranks, spitting and calling them "white guards" or "troops of reaction," shots rang out from inside the crowd, and the outnumbered forces of law and order, rather than retaliate, beat a hasty retreat. After the withdrawal of the police, widespread plundering broke out that eventually damaged sixty-six shops and stores. Only toward evening with the arrival of squads of *Volkswehr*, supported by armored cars and equipped with machine guns, could the streets finally be cleared. Yet, quiet lasted only overnight. In the morning the looting errupted once again and continued unabated until 6 February, when proclamation of martial law threatening summary execution at last brought it to an end.[36]

Backed by some twelve hundred reinforcements from Vienna and supported by the Linz soldiers' and workers' councils, Upper Austrian authorities thus managed to contain anarchy without appealing to the forces of reaction as was then happening in Germany.[37] It was clear to all that the hunger riots were spontaneous and nonpolitical, so that little pressure arose for punitive action.[38] On the other hand, the government's police formations were strained to the limit and could not be expected to maintain domestic order without additional help, let alone requisition grain and livestock from the ever recalcitrant peasantry. To make matters worse, the Italian armistice commission in Vienna suddenly demanded a reduction of the *Volkswehr*, an order that Colonel Poeschmann announced simply could not be carried out.[39]

Only with much effort and skill did the production and distribution of food improve in the summer of 1919. It was during this period that the workers' councils assumed the primary task of food collection in the province, and although great difficulties persisted in dealing with local farmers and peasants, council leaders acquired a certain knack for doing so. In May 1919, to cite one instance, the Linz council managed to dissuade dairy producers from doubling the price of milk in exchange for a guaranteed rate increase of 50 percent. Prodded by the *Volkswehr* and by the (sometimes passive) rural constabulary, food deliveries were thus continued. The deliveries were also stimulated by what amounted to an independent and particularist foreign policy on the part of provincial authorities. With much fanfare Hauser, for example, negotiated a barter agreement with Rome to import stocks of Italian rice, vegetable oil, and fat in exchange for Upper Austrian grain. To ensure payment his government levied export duties to other parts of German Austria and even established a military cordon on the Lower Austrian frontier.[40]

Although Hauser's acts of interposition were effectively called into question by the federal government and although food shortages and serious economic difficulties lasted well into 1921, overall agricultural output in Upper Austria did gradually improve. The elimination of competition from

Hungary, in fact, so stimulated grain and sugar beet production that slight surplusses occurred as early as the autumn of 1920. Six months later controls on milk and eggs were lifted; shortly thereafter those on fruit and vegetables were removed; and in July meatless days came to an end. With the resumption of trade in livestock in October 1921 and the simultaneous removal of the potato ration, hunger at last ceased to be a problem in Linz.[41]

ELECTORAL RATIFICATION

In the bone-chilling winter of 1918–19, however, few people anywhere in German Austria escaped the torment of Tantalus. Numb with cold and hunger, they traipsed to the polls on 16 February 1919 to elect delegates to the Constituent National Assembly. For the first time men and women participated in equal, direct elections, sending 159 representatives to the parliament on the Ringstrasse. As a rule, the results tended to favor the Social Democrats with that party winning 41 percent of the votes, the Christian Socials 36 percent, and the German Nationalists 18 percent. In Linz the outcome was similar: the Social Democrats captured 52 percent of the ballots, the Christian Socials 21 percent, and the German Nationalists 27 percent. In the provincial balloting, however, it was the Christian Socials who emerged as the victors with a plurality of 46 percent of the votes; by contrast the Social Democrats won 28 percent, the German Nationalists 26 percent (table 1).

The elections to the National Assembly constituted a formal ratification of the changes of the past few months. That the Social Democrats did especially well in Linz was a consequence of winning a large number of protest votes directed in some cases against the war and in others against the well-fed Catholic peasants.[42] The referendum did not reveal the Upper Austrian political landscape with quite the clarity of provincial and municipal elections held three months later. By 18 May sufficient time had passed for the revised political parties to formulate their goals and programs in a more coherent manner and for the masses to digest—if not food—at least the great international and national events of the day. After all, between 16 February and 18 May 1919 the radical left was crushed with appalling brutality in Berlin and Munich, a Communist bid for power was foiled in Vienna, Bela Kun's Soviet Republic was proclaimed in Budapest, and the terms of the Paris peace agreements became generally known. Of even greater significance, however, was a feeling among voters in Linz and Upper Austria that the February elections were for a *Provisorum et Transitorium* (inasmuch as few people identified with the new Alpine Republic),[43] whereas the May balloting had a more immediate impact on their own personal lives.[44]

Generally speaking, the February elections served to legitimate the new

TABLE 1   Elections in Linz, Upper Austria, and Austria 1919–1920
(percentages in parentheses)

Party	Social Democrat	Christian Social	German Nationalist	Other	Total
(a) Linz only					
Constituent National Assembly 16.2.1919	20,915 (51.6)	8,666 (21.4)	10,970 (27.0)		40,551
Landtag/Gemeinderat 18.5.1919	24,600 (55.3)	12,555 (28.2)	7,358 (16.5)		44,513
National Assembly 17.10.1920	23,792 (46.1)	13,476 (26.1)	13,389 (26.0)	911 (1.8)	51,568
(b) Linz and Surroundings (Wahlkreis Linz)					
Constituent National Assembly 16.2.1919	34,217 (46.0)	23,137 (31.1)	16,977 (22.8)		74,331
Landtag/Gemeinderat 18.5.1919	27,673 (56.2)	13,750 (27.8)	7,827 (16.0)		49,250
National Assembly 17.10.1920	31,188 (41.4)	27,067 (36)	15,878 (21.1)	1,099 (1.5)	75,232
(c) Upper Austria					
Constituent National Assembly 16.2.1919	115,761 (28.0)	191,182 (46.2)	106,859 (25.8)		413,802
Landtag/Gemeinderat 18.5.1919	111.026 (27.5)	196,982 (52.0)	77,372 (20.5)		385,380
National Assembly 17.10.1920	104,552 (26.7)	216,281 (55.3)	67,811 (17.3)	2,527 (0.7)	391,171
(d) Austria					
Constituent National Assembly 16.2.1919	1,211,814 (40.8)	1,068,382 (35.9)	545,938 (18.4)	147,320 (4.9)	2,973,454
National Assembly 17.10.1920	1,072,709 (36.0)	1,245,531 (41.8)	514,127 (17.3)	147,019 (4.9)	2,850,426

SOURCE: Tweraser, "Linzer Gemeinderat 1914–1934," p. 219 and *Statistisches Handbuch für die Republik Österreich*, vol. 1, pp. 2–7; vol. 2, pp. 2–5.

order in Upper Austria including the cities of Linz and Steyr.[45] We have already seen that the changes introduced by Hauser and his three deputies tended to ratify a regional process under way since 1908. That meant the formal adoption and modification of new rules for parliamentary procedure worked out in 1914, the establishment of eight electoral districts (reduced to five in 1925) in place of the curial system, and the election of *Landtag* deputies by proportional representation. Henceforth the governor was to be elected by a plurality of the provincial parliament, while his three deputies would be selected from each of the three parties.[46] This last feature was of particular importance, since it constitutionalized a proportional system (*Proporz*) in which cabinet positions were appointed according to the parliamentary strength of the three parties. Such a system was in effect in Vienna at that time, but it was abandoned in October 1920 not to be resumed until after World War II by the Second Austrian Republic. In the case of Upper Austria, however, Hauser's *Proporz* would survive until 1934 and, as we shall see, prove remarkably resilient in regulating political conflict and in preserving the regional democratic order.

In Linz itself the constitutional changes instituted after the collapse of the Habsburg monarchy were similar though operationally somewhat more wide-ranging. In November 1918 Mayor Dinghofer and the entire city council resigned from office; they were replaced by a provisional government under the German Nationalist Karl Sadleder, consisting of thirty-one German Nationalists, nineteen Social Democrats, and seven Christian Socials. Technically, the statute of 1904 remained in place, but expectations were that it would be replaced by a more liberal document, as indeed it was in 1920. In the meantime, everyone anticipated (and the German Nationalists feared) major political changes to result simply from the introduction of universal, direct, and equal suffrage on the municipal level.[47]

As we have seen, the political parties did not campaign with much verve or vigor for the elections to the Constituent National Assembly. Rallies were kept to a minimum, while in view of the near total breakdown of normal social and economic activity, party leaders actually agreed to refrain from interrupting or heckling their opponents' meetings. Not until spring did political lines begin to be drawn and conventional agitation resume. Of the three major parties the Social Democrats stood to gain the most from the revolution, particularly, though not exclusively, in the towns of Linz and Steyr. They were, in a sense, the principal founders of the republic and therefore advocated the complete democratization of existing institutions. In keeping with the pronouncements of party leaders in Vienna, local Socialists also demanded state centralism, the nationalization of industry, and, above all, a rigid separation of church and state. Significantly, the principal politicians in Linz, Josef Gruber and Josef Dametz, downplayed the more radical features of the Socialist program (such as centralization and nationalization) and supported Governor Hauser's efforts at political and constitutional reform. The same was not entirely true of the anticlerical rank and file Social Democrats, however, many of whom regarded the Christian Socials as deadly opponents and charged them with cryptic intentions of transforming Upper Austria into a province of the Vatican.[48]

In point of fact, the dissolution of the Austro-Hungarian monarchy placed the Christian Socials in an awkward and ambivalent position. As heirs of the old Catholic Conservative movement some of them, such as Bishop Gföllner, retained their loyalty to the Habsburg dynasty and refused to countenance the idea of living either in a German-Austrian republic or—in case of Anschluss—in a Protestant Germany.[49] Their ideas and feelings closely paralleled those of the Jesuit Ignaz Seipel and what would soon be a majority of party members throughout German-Austria. Yet, as we have seen, political Catholicism in Upper Austria resided on a peasant-democratic base. Prelate Hauser, as second president of the Provisional National Assembly, was a founder of the republic and as such refused to compromise on democratic principles. To his political credit he astutely maintained party unity, however, by advocating particularist economic measures designed to appeal to the peasants and by adopting the electoral slogan "Upper Austria to the Upper Austrians."[50]

Nevertheless, Hauser encountered great difficulty in justifying to all factions of his party his conciliatory and cooperative policies toward the "atheistic" Social Democrats. As he eloquently explained to an assembly of Christian Social trustees:

> We are not yet a state; we do not yet exist; we have nothing but debts. From that you have to consider why we reluctantly decided to form a coalition with the Social Democrats in Vienna. Not for amusement, not for love of the Social Democrats, not because we betrayed the Christian, good Catholic cause; no, rather because together in common effort we are helping our impoverished state-substance on to its legs. On the other hand, have you ever heard that the Social Democrats are happy with us? Of course not! When we are suspended in midair we cannot fight each other. We have no floor under our feet. If a house catches fire igniting another house, and the entire neighborhood begins to burn, the fire department will come. The Socialists and the Christian Socials are coming. Why? To save what is to save![51]

Hauser did not significantly include the urban middle-class parties in his remarks. The German Nationalists had enthusiastically welcomed the collapse of the Danubian Empire, believing that the opportunity to join the German Reich was at hand. They demanded immediate union of all ethnic Germans in Central Europe, primarily for ideological reasons but also, as Langoth later put it, to free Upper Austria from the "Viennese great capitalists and Jewish press."[52] In the February elections the bourgeois parties, under the banner of the German Peoples' Party, acquitted themselves rather well in Upper Austria, winning approximately a quarter of the votes cast and therefore a larger percentage than in German Austria as a whole. Carl Beurle's earlier warnings of electoral disaster following the removal of property qualifications and the elimination of the four class voting system hardly seemed warranted. Indeed, as the local press was wont to point out, the election results could be interpreted as a victory over clericalism, since the Christian Socials had failed to muster a majority of the votes cast.[53]

This sanguine illusion was dispelled by the provincial election of 18 May 1919 in which the German Nationalists, the remnants of the German Liberals, and the largely Protestant Rural League (*Landbund*)—united as the Freedom and Order Party—slipped five percentage points and gave up eleven seats in the diet. More ominously, in the municipal balloting of the same day the German Nationalists lost some 3,612 votes, declined from 27 percent to 17 percent, and fell from thirty-one seats to a mere ten on the Linz city council (See table 1). Beurle's worst fears were indeed realized, and the clubby middle strata of Linz's physicians, attorneys, pharmacists, merchants, and entrepreneurs were compelled to relinquish control of the Upper Austrian capital. Not until 1938 would they and their sons regain what they had lost.

What constituted a debacle for the German Nationalists represented a triumph for the Christian Socials and the Social Democrats: in the province Hauser's party won a clear majority of the votes (52 percent), gaining control of thirty-eight seats (out of seventy-two) in the diet; in Linz the Socialists, for the first time able to draw on the working-class votes of recently annexed Urfahr, obtained an absolute majority of 55 percent and captured thirty-three seats (out of sixty) on the city council. It could not be foreseen at the time, but the pattern for the future was now set. In the next fifteen years politics in the villages, cloisters, and farms of Upper Austria would be dominated by the Christian Socials and in the shops, homes, and streets of Linz by the Social Democrats.

In one sense, the lugubrious history of the First Austrian Republic would be replicated in Upper Austria with the Catholic party in charge of the rural hinterland and the labor movement controlling the industrial islands of Linz and Steyr, just as in the larger sea the Christian Socials dominated the countryside of the Alpine republic and the Social Democrats "Red Vienna." Yet the land between the Enns and the Danube was not a perfect mirror of the larger Austrian milieu, for the pluralistic political culture being forged by Governor Hauser and his three deputies would prove more resilient and less given to polarization and fragmentation than that of the country as a whole. Admittedly, what was wrought at the ballot box in 1919 was eventually shattered by violence in *both* Linz and Vienna on 12 February 1934, but, as we shall see, the paths to the tragic day were by no means as parallel as might meet the eye.

Once the May ballots were counted, provincial and municipal authorities completed the work of reform begun at the turn of the century. In the provincial diet the continuity of events was emphasized by the implementation (with slight modification) of the 1914 rules of procedure (*Geschäftsordnung*) and the passage of two laws regulating elections and parliamentary representation. Significantly, those clauses of the Imperial Patent of 1861 pertaining to Upper Austria were declared still valid, insofar as they did not violate the provisions of the then pending federal constitution.[54] In the Linz *Rathaus*, meanwhile, similar reforms were enacted in the months after the May elections, though in this case an entirely new statute was created. That had not really been possible until the Social Democrats came to power in the city council, because the German Nationalists impeded meaningful change even during the provisional period. Yet as finally promulgated on 31 May 1920, the new municipal constitution represented little break with the past. The statute's principal features foresaw the establishment of an executive committee (agreed upon in 1914) with control over most administrative appointments and jobs, election of the lord mayor by a simple majority of the city council, and the duplication of the *Proporz* system on the municipal level.[55] All things considered, the most radical characteristic of the new municipal order was the institutionalization of the democratic and equal franchise—something of course now hardly unique to Linz and Upper Austria.

A SPATE OF RADICALISM

The completion of the "revolution by consensus" in the spring of 1919 was accompanied by a leftist upsurge in Linz that did not abate for another year. The radical wave emanated not from local disillusionment with the failure or inability of the Social Democrats to socialize the means of production nor from a feeling (so widespread among German radicals) that a "revolution from above had pre-empted the revolution from below."[56] Nor was any perceptible impetus provided by the Spartacist risings in the Reich or by the Communist Maundy Thursday putsch in Vienna.[57] The origins lay instead in repeated demands of the Italian armistice commission in Vienna to reduce the size of the *Volkswehr* in Linz by several thousand men. While bringing fiscal relief to federal and local authorities, these reductions also cut the strength of the city's hard-pressed police forces and widened the ranks of the unemployed. For about seven months the Linz *Volkswehr* was able to stave off the mandated dismissals, but in mid-July 1919, after two Italian officers had been roughed up by returning prisoners of war at the central train station, the reductions at last went into effect.[58]

As we have already seen, the task of food requisitioning had been undertaken by the Upper Austrian workers' councils, perhaps the largest and most influential in German Austria. Although these councils never assumed the importance they did in Germany and although they remained firmly under the control of the Social Democrat Richard Strasser, they did become a gathering place in the summer and fall of 1919 for the unemployed and malcontented. Stimulated by the Bavarian and Hungarian soviet republics as well as by what appeared to be the growing power of the council movement following the summer reductions of the *Volkswehr*, a small group of Communists within the workers' councils resolved to use these organizations as a means of radicalizing Linz society and through "putschist tactics" contribute to the establishment of an Austrian soviet republic.

The Communist party (KP) itself was organized in Upper Austria between December 1918 and February 1919 by Heinrich Reisecker, a twenty-seven-year-old journeyman artist from Schärding with extensive contact among German radicals.[59] Having spent the war in Switzerland, where he was exposed to the teachings of Lenin, Reisecker returned to his hometown shortly after the armistice. Here he tried unsuccessfully to mobilize the peasants, attracting instead (according to the police) only a handful of discharged soldiers and unemployed ruffians. Nevertheless, he set up a party secretariat in Linz in March 1919, renewed contact with party leaders in Vienna, and apparently became the KP's major contact man on the Austro-Bavarian frontier. Throughout the spring and summer of 1919 Reisecker's Communists played virtually no role in Linz politics, comprising only a tiny fraction of the local workers' council and being compelled to cancel scheduled meetings due to poor attendance.[60]

With the onset of winter, a sharp rise in prices, and a renewed tightening of food supplies, the KP in Linz began to make inroads among the town's truly desperate classes. In February 1920, for example, a nasty riot of disabled veterans, war widows, and unemployed pick-and-shovel workers was provoked by local Communists. Unrest and agitation, continued into the spring, moreover, as the Kapp putsch in Germany unleashed a revival of the radical left. By the end of April over six hundred ragged, disabled veterans were pleading daily to provincial officials for new clothes, better vacations, and cost of living adjustments, while over three hundred laborers, armed with spades and shovels, marched in support to the tune of Communist songs and music.[61]

Local authorities, including Security Director Langoth, were hard put to deal with this latest threat to domestic tranquility. They did not have the means or the will to meet the demands of the hopeless poor, but if they proceeded with force, they knew they would incur the wrath of Strasser and his followers, not to mention that of the Social Democrats who also refused to break with the Communists.[62] After several weeks of rising tensions, events came to a head on the afternoon of 10 May 1920, when a crowd of one thousand street and construction workers assembled first by a tavern and then on the Francis Joseph Square. Inspired by Communist agitators, they were joined by a large number of onlookers, including several hundred juveniles, to shout for the resignation of Socialist Deputy Governor Gruber. To contain the growing mob the security director rushed contingents of police, *Volkswehr*, and some sixty rural constables to the scene. In the meantime, teams of Socialists tried to calm tensions as best they could. The arrival of the hated *Gendarmerie*, however, played into the Communists' hands for it drove the crowd into a frenzy. As if by perfect calculation, the Communists incited the masses to disarm the peacekeeping forces and, in line with putschist tactics devised earlier in Vienna, to storm the Castle Barracks and other centers of municipal power. At this point gun shots rang out, fired either by a sniper or by a nervous security man. That prompted the police to clear the square with a burst of rifle fire of their own, killing seven demonstrators and wounding twenty-one others.[63]

Without doubt, Linz's worst outbreak of violence in the immediate postwar period affected Upper Austrian affairs more than any other single local event at that time. Earlier disturbances, such as the hunger riots of February 1919, had been clearly spontaneous outbursts of desperation. But the fracas of May 1920 was quite literally Communist inspired. The middle classes pointed with some justification to a clear-cut example of "red terror" and closed ranks to demand the federalization of the municipal police and the total dissolution of what they considered to be the unreliable *Volkswehr*. Right-wing paramilitary groups such as the Front Fighters Association (*Frontkämpfervereinigung*) came into being for the first time in Linz, and, judging from police reports, they appear to have won some following.[64] As for the workers' councils, their members were so shaken by the May riots that resolutions were introduced calling for the expulsion of Bolsheviks from the councils on a countrywide basis. The motions were defeated at a subsequent meeting in Vienna in the interests of "proletarian solidarity," but within the Linz Workers' Council individuals now came to the fore who questioned continued cooperation with the extreme left.[65]

It should not be imagined of course that the May violence was the sole cause of what appeared to be a rapid polarization of Upper Austrian politics. Disillusionment with the Treaty of St. Germain, accelerating inflation, and psychological uncertainty were countrywide concerns shared between the Enns and the Danube that were just as responsible for a hardening of political lines. It was therefore no coincidence that elections to the National Assembly on 17 October 1920 produced a general swing to the right in Upper Austria as elsewhere in the Alpine republic. (The provincial and municipal power structure of course remained unaffected.) The Christian Socials increased their majority in the province to a whopping 55 percent and rose in the country from 36 to 42 percent. Both the German Nationalists and Social Democrats lost votes on the provincial and national level, although in Linz itself the German Nationalists staged an electoral comeback by doubling the number of votes received over the *Landtag* elections of May 1919. To what extent this bourgeois victory was part of an antisocialist backlash is difficult to determine, however, since it clearly was won with the help of several thousand new voters on the municipal rolls. The Social Democrats indeed did not do all that badly and actually picked up three thousand new votes themselves; on the other hand their share of the total was considerably less than the year before (table 1).

In a general sense, therefore, societal and political developments in Linz and Upper Austria after World War I paralleled those on the larger Central European stage. Military defeat, uprisings in the armed forces, hunger and deprivation, spontaneous working class demonstrations and hasty constitutional reforms combined to transform an authoritarian political structure into a parliamentary democracy. At the same time, continued economic hardship, disillusionment with a seemingly punitive peace, and an awakening of entrenched elites—such as the urban middle classes, the bureaucracy, and the episcopate—conspired to prevent the democratization of society itself. The revolution was left dead in the water and the forces of the old order given a chance to stage a comeback. In the case of Germany, of course, the army, the bureaucracy, and the agrarian-industrial complex accomplished this with greater brutality than their counterparts south of the border. Yet even in diminutive Austria with the old army in ruins, the bankers and industrialists enjoying comparatively little power, and the church shaken to the bone, the outcome of events was similar to that in Germany.

In a more specific sense, the configuration in Linz and Upper Austria was different from the whole. All parties joined forces in the "revolution by consensus," continuing to cooperate with each other long after the polarizing Communist riots of May 1920. By way of contrast, all such cooperation ceased on the federal level in October 1920. The Social Democrats thus controlled the towns of Linz and Steyr, the local trade unions, most personnel of the transportation and communications network, and, for a while, the Linz army garrison. The Christian Socials commanded a majority in the provincial parliament and generally held sway in the villages and estates of the countryside. Even the German Nationalists or Greater Germans as they called themselves after 1920, though significantly reduced in power and influence, were well represented in the local bureaucracy and administration. What kept this equilibrium in balance was the mandating of the *Proporz* system in the provincial and municipal governments as well as the personality and behavior of Governor Hauser. For over a decade the "red prelate" had fought to democratize Upper Austrian politics and would not countenance a return to a more authoritarian order. As early as

September 1919 he warned against the formation of reactionary, paramilitary formations in Upper Austria and generally succeeded in keeping them out of the province. Hauser therefore accepted the dissolution of the monarchy, the establishment of the republic, the separation of church and state, and even some of the social changes wrought by the revolution. Under his leadership democracy and fair play would flourish both in Upper Austria and in the more polarized provincial capital.

THREE

A Moderate Political Culture
1920–1927

The First Austrian Republic has been characterized as a centrifugal democracy, an unstable order marred by little real consensus, intense societal cleavage, and a highly polarized party system. The regime's identity crisis was so severe that its predominant leaders tended to place allegiance to their subcultures above allegiance to the state. They preferred confrontation to cooperation, and, after the breakup of the Great Coalition in 1920, they generally refused to bargain on basic issues. Their behavior intensified the instability of the political culture and contributed to its ultimate breakdown. Yet the republic did not collapse overnight: it was prone to political violence and civil war, but it prevailed for over a decade, managing change and demonstrating considerable vitality. Given the centrifugal drives of the system, historians have been hard put to explain its relative durability.[1]

A shift of focus from the abnormal environment of Vienna to other localities provides one way of better understanding Austrian democracy in the interwar period. In Linz and Upper Austria, for example, there existed a pluralistic system that lent strength and vitality to the federal order while prefiguring the consociational democracy of the Second Republic. In contrast to the federal regime, the local political culture was imbued with a sense of legitimacy, a commitment to democratic procedures, and a willingness of elites to engage in dialogue and cooperation. It was a fragile, limited system, but it succeeded in regulating local conflict, in thwarting federal bureaucratic interference, and in fending off fascist bands of *Heimwehren* and National Socialists. To what extent the provincial order helped forestall the ultimate breakdown of democratic politics in the First Republic is impossible to determine. Yet the fact that the Austrian Civil War of 1934 began not in radical Vienna but in moderate Linz must be seen as more than a coincidence.

Any analysis of the moderate political structure of Linz and its hinterland must first take into account the region's underlying substructure. As elsewhere in Austria, the population of Upper Austria remained fragmented and polarized throughout the interwar period: workers and wage earners flocked to the Social Democrats; farmers, retailers, small producers, and

39

TABLE 2   Principal Occupation of Linz Politicians 1918–1934 (percentages)

	Social Democrat	German Nationalist	Christian Social
Nobility	—	—	2.8
Clergy	0.8	—	6.5
Farmer/Peasant	—	7.8	16.8
Civil Servant/Public Employee	31.5	29.8	26.1
Professional (self-employed)	3.8	12.8	5.6
Self-employed	8.5	20.5	21.5
Private Employee	12.3	15.6	4.7
Workers:			
Skilled	26.9	0.9	4.7
Unskilled	6.2	2.0	5.6
Apprentice	1.5	0.9	—
Military	—	0.9	1.0
Other (including housewives)	8.5	8.8	4.7
(Sample Size)	(130)	(102)	(107)

SOURCE: Linz *Tagespost* (1918–1934) and Bart and Puffer, *Die Gemeindevertretung der Stadt Linz* (see note 2, chapter 3).

craftsmen threw their support to the Christian Socials; professionals, civil servants, and teachers coalesced around the German Nationalists (table 2).[2] The three *Lager* responded by representing the socioeconomic interests of their members while demanding a high degree of ideological conformity. At the same time, moderate elements within the subcultures also encouraged interelite cooperation as a means of regulating conflict and achieving stability.

The best evidence of political fragmentation in Upper Austria can be found in relatively unchanging election results (tables 1, 3–5). Between 1919 and 1931 roughly one-half of the provincial voters normally cast their votes for the Christian Socials, one third for the Social Democrats, and the rest for the Greater Germans or for other German Nationalist parties. In Linz itself the electoral strength of the two major parties was in inverse proportion to their position in the province. The Social Democrats won absolute majorities in the elections of 1919, fluctuated between 46 and 49 percent of the vote in four electoral contests between 1919 and 1925, and recaptured an absolute majority of 52 percent in the important federal and municipal elections of 24 April 1927. In voting for the National Assembly in November 1930 they fell to a plurality of 49 percent, but rebounded with an absolute majority in the municipal balloting of 19 April 1931. For their part, the Christian Socials

TABLE 3   Elections in Linz, 1923–1931 (percentages in parentheses)

	Social Democrat	Christian Social	German Nationalist	Landbund	Schober	Heimat	Nazi	Communist	Other	Total
Gemeinderat 26.6.1923	28,038 (48.5)	15,155 (26.2)	9,159 (15.9)				4,533 (7.9)	854 (1.5)		57,739 (100.0)
National Assembly 21.10.1923	29,168 (49.7)	17,356 (29.5)	12,202 (20.8)							58,726 (100.0)
Landtag 17.5.1925	26,450 (46.3)	24,463* (42.8)					4,380 (7.7)	1,201 (2.1)	645 (1.1)	57,139 (100.0)
National Assembly 24.4.1927	34,015 (52.3)	27,712* (42.6)		1,927 (3.0)			46 (0.1)	242 (0.4)	1,048 (1.6)	64,990 (100.0)
Gemeinderat 24.4.1927	33,776 (52.7)	30,116* (47.0)						230 (0.3)		64,122 (100.0)
National Assembly 10.11.1930	32,482 (48.6)	12,436 (18.6)		660 (1.0)	9,697 (14.5)	7,623 (11.4)	3,145 (4.7)	383 (0.6)	371 (0.6)	66,797 (100.0)
Landtag 19.4.1931	32,322 (50.8)	14,799 (23.2)		6,037 (9.5)		6,022 (9.4)	3,882 (6.1)	634 (1.0)		63,696 (100.0)
Gemeinderat 19.4.1931	32,140 (51.0)	14,285 (22.6)		5,922 (9.4)		5,794 (9.2)	4,202 (6.7)	700 (1.1)		63,043 (100.0)

*Bourgeois Unity List

SOURCE: A St Linz: Statistische Vierteljahresberichte der Stadt Linz, 1922–1932 and Tweraser, "Linzer Gemeinderat 1914–1934," p. 241.

TABLE 4 Elections in Linz and Surroundings (Wahlkreis Linz), 1923–1931 (percentages in parentheses)

	Social Democrat	Christian Social	German Nationalist	Landbund	Schober	Heimat	Nazi	Communist	Other	Total
National Assembly 21.10.1923	35,498 (43.5)	31,268 (38.3)	14,868 (18.2)							81,634 (100.0)
Landtag 17.5.1925	32,445 (40.2)	41,018* (50.8)					4,856 (6.0)	1,186 (1.5)	1,262 (1.5)	80,767 (100.0)
National Assembly 24.4.1927	41,143 (46.3)	42,886 (48.2)		3,449 (3.9)			62 (0.1)	276 (0.3)	1,075 (1.2)	88,891 (100.0)
National Assembly 10.11.1930	39,977 (43.7)	23,881 (26.1)		1,923 (2.1)	10,906 (11.9)	10,520 (11.5)	3,418 (3.7)	421 (0.5)	415 (0.5)	91,461 (100.0)
Landtag 19.4.1931	39,558 (45.1)	27,976 (31.9)		7,945 (9.1)		7,110 (8.1)	4,412 (5.0)	736 (0.8)		87,737 (100.0)

*Bourgeois Unity List

SOURCE: *Statistisches Handbuch für die Republik Österreich*, vol. 4, pp. 140–42, vol. 7, pp. 189–92, vol. 12, pp. 207–10 and *Oberösterreichische Arbeiterzeitung*, 11 April 1931.

TABLE 5 Elections in Upper Austria and Austria 1923–1931 (percentages in parentheses)

a) Upper Austria	Social Democrat	Christian Social	German Nationalist	Landbund	Schober	Heimat	Nazi	Communist	Other	Total
National Assembly 21.10.1923	122,189 (27.5)	254,822 (57.2)	67,895 (15.2)						270 (0.1)	445,176 (100.0)
Landtag 17.5.1925	113,456 (26.0)	305,471* (70.0)					12,127 (2.8)	2,416 (0.6)	2,996 (0.7)	436,466 (100.1)
National Assembly 24.4.1927	141,113 (29.5)	290,018* (60.7)		42,065 (8.8)					4,465 (0.9)	477,661 (99.9)
National Assembly 10.11.1930	135,933 (28.4)	217,674 (45.4)		36,931 (7.7)	34,964 (7.3)	39,724 (8.3)	11,562 (2.4)	1,193 (0.2)	1,293 (0.3)	479,274 (100.0)
Landtag 19.4.1931	128,374 (28.0)	239,923 (52.4)		50,836 (11.1)		18,818 (4.1)	15,770 (3.5)	3,431 (0.8)	411 (0.1)	457,563 (100.0)
b) Austria										
National Assembly 21.10.1923	1,311,870 (39.6)	1,490,870 (45.0)	422,600 (12.8)						87,266 (2.6)	3,312,606 (100.0)
National Assembly 24.4.1927	1,539,635 (42.3)	1,756,761* (48.2)		230,157 (6.3)					114,973 (3.2)	3,641,526 (100.0)
National Assembly 10.11.1930	1,516,913 (41.1)	1,314,468 (35.7)			427,962 (11.6)	227,197 (6.2)			200,542 (5.4)	3,687,082 (100.0)

*Bourgeois Unity List
SOURCE: *Statistisches Handbuch für die Republik Österreich*, vol. 4, pp. 140–42, vol. 7, pp. 189–92, vol. 12, pp. 207–10 and *Oberösterreichische Arbeiterzeitung*, 11 April 1931.

never controlled the Upper Austrian capital, but they saw their urban
consitutency rise from 21 percent of the electorate in February 1919 to just
under 30 percent in October 1923. Joining the Greater Germans for the next
several years on Seipel's Unity List, the Catholics did not run a separate
slate of candidates until November 1930, at which time they lost votes to the
extremist *Heimwehr*. Six months later, however, the Christian Socials
recaptured their normal share of the electorate.

As for the German Nationalists, their position in Linz oscillated errati-
cally. Their Freedom and Order Party captured 27 percent of the urban vote
in February 1919, but failed to attract more than 17 percent of the electorate
a mere three months later. The following year the Greater German People's
Party (GDVP) rebounded with 26 percent of the town's votes, fell to 16
percent in municipal balloting on 26 June 1923, but rose once again to nearly
21 percent in October. Exactly seven years later, with Seipel's anti-Marxist
unity lists a thing of the past, the German Nationalists could still muster
about 15 percent of the vote in Linz; by April 1931, however, their electoral
strength was down to 9 percent and showed every sign of falling still further.
The seemingly erratic fluctuations in German Nationalist electoral performance were largely produced by Linz's tiny Nazi party: when the town's four
thousand National Socialists failed to run a separate slate of candidates, they
usually cast their ballots for the *völkisch* Greater Germans.

THE SOCIAL DEMOCRATS

It was of course the Social Democrats who dominated political life in Linz
after World War I. As a result of the introduction of equal adult suffrage
based upon proportional representation, the labor movement controlled the
city hall and extended municipal patronage. The party's electoral victories
were always smaller in Linz than in Vienna, but until 1934 the Socialists
commanded a majority of the votes cast and consequently administered the
city. In addition to their electoral strength of roughly 30,000 voters, the
Social Democrats maintained an extensive network of trade union organizations, social and cultural associations, and after 1923 a paramilitary formation. Socialist influence thus permeated the city and until 1927 extended
into the military barracks of the federal army as well.

Of the three *Lager* in Linz, the Social Democrats were by far the most
homogenous and internally integrated. In the confusion accompanying the
collapse of the monarchy, for example, thousands of local workers demonstrated their social solidarity by rushing to join distinctly proletarian
associations. One participant recalled that

> the workers no longer wished to remain in "bourgeois" clubs. They dropped out
> and founded their own organizations. The class-conscious expression "labor"

even had to appear in the title. Very soon there were Labor Waterballers, Labor Skiers, Labor Broadjumpers, . . . Labor Soccer Players, . . . Labor Boxers, . . . Labor Esperantoists, . . . even Labor Mushroom Collectors. . . . [3]

Although the working rank and file may have dreamed of a Marxist order in Linz, their leaders realized from the start that economic hardship necessitated cooperation with the other political parties. They were acutely aware of the city's financial dependence upon the agriculturally dominated diet and therefore ruled out radical experimentation as a purely practical matter. Since a decade of mutual collaboration with the Catholic Peoples' Association had contributed to the democratization of local institutions, they concluded that continued cooperation offered the best prospect of further reform. It was for these reasons that Socialist elites deemphasized anticlericalism, class struggle, state centralism, and the nationalization of industry in favor of gradual change.

Despite the objection of party militants to this reformist approach, the social structure of the local Socialist movement itself militated against Jacobin behavior. Composed in many cases of wage earners in small firms, the Social Democrats in Linz could not draw on the sense of mass alienation and laboring solidarity that motivated workers in large, impersonal factories. It is true that substantial numbers of radical activists did play a role on the municipal revolutionary stage between 1918 and 1920, but precisely because most of them worked in the town's few large-scale enterprises they seem to have been unable to appeal to (often better educated) workers in the more numerous smaller establishments. With the formation in 1921 of a municipal Chamber of Labor having the legal right to represent the interests of working men in government agencies and to express opinions on pieces of legislation, Socialist leaders found the means of co-opting the more militant elements of their movement. It was thus no coincidence that throughout the history of the First Republic most leaders of the municipal Chamber of Labor were drawn primarily from the ranks of the postwar workers' councils. [4]

In considering the occupational profile of those Linz Social Democrats who ran for public office or played active roles in the party bureaucracy between 1918 and 1934 few surprises are to be encountered (table 2). Approximately one-third were public employees, one-third were skilled workers, one-seventh were office clerks, and the rest belonged to various categories including, in one case, the clergy. Conspicuously absent were professionals, academics, and managers. Narrowing the focus on the Socialist elite sitting in the chambers of the city hall, a similar but more revealing pattern emerges. Of that group, as indicated by table 6, most began their careers as manual workers. In keeping with prewar tendencies, however, few were unskilled laborers, having been trained rather as printers, locksmiths, butchers, carpenters, masons, bakers or in other preindustrial

TABLE 6   Learned Occupations of Social Democratic City Councillors,
1919–1931 (percentages)

	1919	1923	1927	1931
Self-employed	—	—	—	—
Professionals	7.1	5.9	8.1	5.4
Public Service (officials, employees)	19.1	20.6	16.2	16.2
Public Service (workers)	14.3	8.8	13.5	8.1
Private Employees	2.4	8.8	8.1	8.1
Workers	57.1	55.9	54.1	62.2

Computed from Bart and Puffer, *Die Gemeindevertretung der Stadt Linz.*

occupations. Given the fact that roughly one half of the Socialist councillors were also trade union functionaries, it can be seen how a Lassallean, reformist cast of mind, more reminiscent of Friedrich Ebert's German SPD than Otto Bauer's SDAP, characterized much of the party.[5]

Among the top leaders of the municipal Social Democrats, moderate, pragmatic tendencies predominated. Josef Dametz, lord mayor of Linz from 1919 to 1927, for example, won respect within all three camps for his acute sense of responsibility and conciliatory behavior. The son of a shoemaker, he was apprenticed as a printer in Linz but spent his journeyman years in southwestern Germany. There, in Ravensburg and Stuttgart, he experienced the resurgence of the SPD at the end of the 1880s and was greatly impressed by the organizational techniques and cultural affiliations of the German party. On returning to Linz, he helped found the Upper Austrian branch of the SDAP, was instrumental in organizing provincial trade unions, and in 1898 established a party press and publishing house. A handsome man with long, flowing moustaches, Dametz was elected to the Linz city council in 1905, edited the Socialist daily *Tagblatt* between 1911 and 1918, and was elected mayor of the Upper Austrian capital in June 1919. As such he worked closely with the Christian Socials in instituting a program of urban reconstruction that embraced public housing, unemployment relief, and tax reform. Because Linz suffered from a shortage of capital and depended on the provincial diet for financial outlays, Dametz's municipal accomplishments hardly matched those of "Red Vienna." Furthermore, the mayor always proceeded with Ebert-like caution. He proudly modeled his attitudes and behavior on the German SPD and went out of his way to avoid Viennese leaders, such as Otto Bauer, Robert Danneberg, and Friedrich Austerlitz whom he dubbed the "wandering Jews." Just how little importance Dametz attached to the doctrines of Austromarxism was revealed during the famous party convention of 1926 that produced the radical Linz program. As the majority of delegates rallied behind Otto Bauer's fiery rhetoric justifying the use of dictatorial force, Dametz sat by impassively eating plums. Turning to an astonished colleague, he remarked, "Nothing is more important than a good bowel movement."[6]

Even more conciliatory than Dametz was the Socialist *Landtag* deputy Josef Hafner. Originally a school teacher, Hafner was in 1909 the first Social Democrat elected to the provincial diet. Here he developed close ties to Governor Hauser, with whom he collaborated in the struggle for equal suffrage. As a personal friend of the governor, Hafner viewed his role as that of intermediary between Hauser and the ideological wing of the Socialist establishment. Foremost among that group was Josef Gruber, provincial lieutenant governor from 1918 to 1930 and lord mayor of Linz from 1930 to 1934. Also a onetime teacher, Gruber was known for his sarcastic barbs and sour disposition. Since he was partially deaf, he often assumed an aggressive stance with others as a means of concealing his handicap. Gruber did not get along with Hauser or, for that matter, with a number of party comrades. Once dismissed from a teaching post for refusing to kneel during mass, he was an irascible anticlerical who relished assailing the Christian Socials in the chambers of the city hall and on the floor of the provincial diet. In other political matters, however, he behaved more phlegmatically, regularly joining his opponents in fruitful collaboration.[7]

Given the autodidactic, reformist quality of Socialist leadership in Linz, Austromarxist ideology never assumed much importance in the life of the local party. Forced to govern with moderate Christian Socials, who, like Hauser, stood closer to the Viennese Socialist Karl Renner than to the Christian Social party chief Ignaz Seipel, Upper Austrian Socialists played down such burning issues as the "socialization of the means of production," the "conquest of state power," or the necessity of breaking "the resistance of the bourgeoisie by means of dictatorship." They placed heavy emphasis on political harmony and continued cooperation with the Catholic Peoples' Association. As late as December 1927—five months after the burning of the Viennese Palace of Justice had radically polarized Austrian politics—the official annual report of the provincial party noted: "We have no particular reason in Upper Austria to complain about an attitude of hostility on the part of the Christian Socials such is manifest in other provinces. The autonomy of both Social Democratic cities [Linz and Steyr] is respected even when resolutions are passed contrary to the interests of the Christian Socials."[8]

In only one respect did Socialist ideology seriously threaten to disturb amicable relations with the Christian Socials in Linz. Nearly all Social Democrats subscribed in some measure to a strong local tradition of anticlericalism, dating in Linz from the days of the Counter-Reformation. They remembered the patronizing pronouncements of Bishop Rudigier in the nineteenth century and could not refrain from heaping abuse on his successor, Johannes Maria Gföllner. In the weeks immediately following the collapse of the Habsburg monarchy, for example, mobs of workers assailed the monarchist bishop for his denunciations of the "atheistic" workers' councils. They accused him (unfairly) of inciting farmers and peasants against them and did not hesitate to attack his residence on Christmas Eve 1918 or during the food riots six weeks later. On 9 November 1921, scores of workers, screaming catcalls and obscenities, also broke into St. Ignatius church in the midst of the solemn high mass that was sponsored by a legitimist paramilitary group.[9] Although these confrontations posed no serious threat to the political order in Linz, Socialist elites felt compelled to tone down anticlericalism in the press. The editor of the Social Democratic *Tagblatt* thus focused his attacks almost exclusively against Gföllner while deliberately sparing Hauser and his moderate Christian Social associates. Since the "red prelate" frequently found himself at odds with Gföllner anyway, this approach bolstered Hauser's position within the Catholic establishment while placating anticlerical extremism within the Socialist camp. All the same, anticlericalism continued to fester in the labor movement, always threatening to poison relations with the Christian Socials.[10]

THE CHRISTIAN SOCIALS

The Christian Socials in Linz were a heterogeneous, highly diversified group that found shelter under the umbrella of Roman Catholicism. They possessed a strong party organization in the Peoples' Association, but were divided into three identifiable factions. Each of these vied for leadership of the movement, while pursuing separate ideological and tactical goals. For all this diversity, however, the Christian Social *Lager* in Linz and Upper Austria was a more eudaemonistic, pluralistic movement than the larger conservative party of Ignaz Seipel and his adherents in Vienna.

Long before joining the Christian Social caucus in 1907, the Catholic movement in Upper Austria was dominated by the rural Peoples' Association. While the association exercised near total control of the provincial diet, it played a secondary role in Linz itself. Here the Christian Socials regularly received only about a fourth of the ballots cast between 1919 and 1931, although this was a decided improvement over prewar days, when Catholic politicians ran far behind Liberals and German Nationalists. Like the Social Democrats, the Christian Socials maintained an extensive subcultural network of clubs and associations that reinforced and buttressed the philosophical-religious ideology of political Catholicism. Unlike the Socialists, however, these auxiliary organizations often stood at loggerheads with each other and, at times, with the provincial leadership.

The social structure of the Christian Social party in Linz was not markedly different from that elsewhere in Austria. Of those candidates running for elective office during the First Republic almost a fifth came from agricultural backgrounds, another fifth were master artisans or handicraftsmen, and over a fourth worked as intermediate civil officials or employees for the railroad, the post office, or the provincial government (table 2). Nearly 7 percent of the candidates belonged to the clergy. Relatively underrepresented were professionals, office clerks, and manual workers. Compared to the party in Vienna after the First World War, the Christian Social movement in Linz seems to have included virtually no industrialists or large landowners, fewer white collar employees, but, because of the city's dependence on the railroad, more public officials.[11] Indeed, a close examination of the Christian Social elite on the Linz city council reveals a fairly wide spectrum of occupations that included attorneys, public officials, teachers, trade union functionaries, a foreman, a leather merchant, a book dealer, a private contractor, a grocer, and an apartment building owner (*Hausbesitzer*) (table 7). Interestingly, almost a third of the councillors came from working-class backgrounds, but unlike their Socialist counterparts, most had become self-employed artisans or craftsmen (table 8). As a group, despite a wide variety of vocations, the Christian Socials in Linz clearly represented the loyal Catholic elements of the old *Mittelstand* of shopkeepers, artisans, small producers, lower clergy, and peasants that characterized the party as a whole. Decidedly *bürgerlich und kleinbürgerlich*, the local movement virtually replicated Karl Lueger's Viennese party of a generation before.[12]

However much the social basis of the Christian Socials in Linz approximated that of the larger movement in Austria, the ideological goals and behavior of the regional party stood at variance with those of the leadership in Vienna. In contrast to Seipel, to the Roman Catholic hierarchy, and to a majority of proclerical conservatives in the First Republic, the Catholic Peoples' Association of Upper Austria accepted the fall of the Habsburg dynasty, the establishment of a democratic republic, and the notion of a pluralistic distribution of power on a geographical basis. While it would be a mistake to exaggerate the intensity of intraparty differences or to dwell on the "split" between Vienna and the provinces, it was nonetheless true that the key elements of the Upper Austrian party remained generally committed to moderate, conciliatory principles that at times transcended the class-based secularism of the larger Christian Social movement.

That political Catholicism in Linz differed from the proclerical conservative norm of the First Republic can best be explained by its agricultural character. Originally founded by the clergy of the Linz diocese to protect the interests of the Church, the Peoples' Association of Upper Austria had evolved into a mass movement of independent farmers and peasants. Aside from Roman Catholicism, the association had little in common with the urban middle class Christian Social party in Vienna or, for that matter, in

TABLE 7   Principal Occupations of Christian Social City Councillors,
1919–1931 (percentages)

	1919	1923	1927	1931
Self-employed	27.8	25.0	43.7	33.3
Professionals	11.0	12.5	18.8	13.3
Public Service (*Beamte*, employees)	50.0	56.2	31.2	46.7
Public Service (workers)	5.6	—	6.3	—
Private Employees	5.6	6.3	—	6.7
Workers	—	—	—	—

Computed from Bart and Puffer, *Die Gemeindevertretung der Stadt Linz.*

TABLE 8   Learned Occupations of Christian Social City Councillors,
1919–1931 (percentages)

	1919	1923	1927	1931
Self-employed	10	11.0	17.6	13.3
Professionals	10	5.6	11.8	13.3
Public Service (*Beamte*, employees)	20	44.4	29.4	20.0
Public Service (workers)	20	5.6	5.9	13.3
Private Employees	5	5.6	11.8	6.8
Workers	35	27.8	23.5	33.3

Computed from Bart and Puffer, *Die Gemeindevertretung der Stadt Linz.*

Linz itself. It was concerned primarily with maintaining its position of
dominance in the countryside and was therefore willing to cooperate
informally with the Social Democrats so long as the workers confined their
activities to Linz and Steyr.[13] Under the aegis of Hauser and a number of
like-minded lower clergy, the Peoples' Association had superseded the
Catholic Conservatives long before 1907, instituted important administrative reforms, and guided the province through difficult days of war and
revolution. Once conditions returned to normal, Hauser and his associates
managed to retain the support of their peasant constitutents through the
establishment of agricultural extension services, the acceleration of rural
electrification, and the sponsoring of other patronage projects in the Upper
Austrian diet. In such a way the democratically inclined governor strengthened the base of the Peoples' Association and kept its adherents from
succumbing to that siege mentality so characteristic of political Catholicism
in the interwar period. That he remained an ordained priest may also have

played a role in mobilizing support and in countering authoritarian, corporatist appeals of the Austrian episcopate.[14]

In light of German Nationalist and Austromarxist propaganda, it is ironic that the most conciliatory elements of the Christian Social movement in Linz and Upper Austria were principally clergymen. Besides Hauser, these included Monsignor Heinrich Binder, editor of the daily *Volksblatt,* Ernst Hirsch, moderator of the Catholic Parents' Association, Josef Pfeneberger, director of the Linz Normal School, and Josef Moser, general secretary of the Peoples' Association. In contrast to Hauser, these men were deeply suspicious of the Social Democrats. They especially resented Socialist support of nonsectarian schools and rarely refrained from heaping rhetorical abuse on the ever-grumpy Josef Gruber in the provincial diet.[15] Nevertheless, the cassocked politicians always took pains to preserve the government coalition and to reaffirm their commitment to democracy. As early as 1924, for example, they cautioned their constituents against Mussolini's brand of fascism. Thereafter they opposed (with some equivocation) the emergence of the *Heimwehr* in Upper Austria, while taking a generally jaundiced view of pleas to reconstruct Austria along corporate lines.[16] Like Hauser, the priest-politicians also resisted the tight control of the reactionary bishop of Linz, Johannes Maria Gföllner.[17]

Gföllner was the orphaned son of a harness maker and a peasant girl, who had been one of those bright boys groomed by the Church over the centuries to rejuvenate its ranks. Like Hauser, he aspired to a political career, but after ordination and advanced study in Rome, he became a professor of pastoral theology in the Linz Petrinum. In 1915 Gföllner was unexpectedly elevated from his academic chair to the diocesan throne by Emperor Francis Joseph. Although the bishop was known as a dogmatic spokesman of Catholic Conservatism in Upper Austria, his appointment was welcomed by Prelate Hauser, who secretly suggested it to Cardinal Piffl in the vain hope of deflecting Gföllner's interests away from politics toward weightier theological matters. Hauser soon had reason to regret his judgement. Within just a few years the Linz bishop had carved out a place as one of the most reactionary members of the Austrian hierarchy.[18]

Like many Austrian Catholics, Gföllner viewed the disintegration of the Habsburg monarchy as an incredible calamity. In an almost catatonic state he received Cardinal Piffl's letter of 25 November 1918 urging support of the emperor's "voluntary" transfer of political power to his people. The bishop attempted to conceal his true feelings by issuing a pastoral letter that appealed for calm and expressed a willingness to cooperate with the new authorities. Yet, as helpful as he was over the next several months in easing tensions between Linz and the countryside, Gföllner could not bring himself to accept the departure of the dynasty. He lent his support to monarchist groups plotting Charles's restoration and established contact with scattered paramilitary bands that were trying to find a foothold in Upper Austria. Genuinely shocked by attacks on his residence by rioting mobs in 1919, the bishop was even more appalled as he gradually comprehended the extent of Hauser's commitment to the democratic republic. He determined to throttle his "red prelate" regardless of the consequences, going as far as to countermand a papal dispensation allowing cloistered clergy to vote in federal elections.[19]

These differences notwithstanding, relations between bishop and priest remained generally cordial until the summer of 1920. At that time a small coterie of legitimists in Linz devised a plan to overthrow Hauser and to subordinate the Christian Social movement in Upper Austria to the majority party under Seipel. Their tool was Gföllner. Apparently at the request of the exiled Charles himself, the bishop wrote Hauser in early August urging him not to run for another term in the National Assembly. Ignoring the request, the prelate-governor countered Gföllner by securing a unanimous vote of confidence from the party faithful (*Vertrauensmänner*). The bishop responded by ordering party secretary Ernst Hirsch and two of his colleagues transferred temporarily to pastoral duties, in effect dismissing Hauser's chief administrative subordinates.[20]

By the spring of 1921 Gföllner's dilettante political behavior was becoming a threat to the moderate wing of the Christian Social movement. In the wake of Charles's abortive attempt to regain the crown of St. Stephan in Budapest, any evidence of Christian Social complicity in Habsburg exile politics stood to damage the Catholic cause in Austria and to undermine the federal government in its relations with neighboring countries. In Upper Austria fear was expressed that Gföllner's activities might play into the hands of the Social Democrats. To check the bishop, Hauser entered into an unholy pact with the editor of the Socialist *Tagblatt*, Dr. Franz Jetzinger, former priest and excommunicant. The two agreed to exchange information on Gföllner and by means of carefully orchestrated newspaper policies to dilute his political influence as much as possible. In late 1921, therefore, the Christian Social *Volksblatt* rejected what its editor termed "clerical interference" in politics by refusing to publish a blistering letter from the bishop assailing the Social Democrats for the disturbances of 9 November in St. Ignatius Church. By the same token, as we have seen, the Socialist *Tagblatt* took pains to separate Gföllner's activities from the mainstream of provincial Christian Social politics: in numerous editorials it emphasized the bishop's "medieval mind-set" and stressed his ideological commitment to the Seipel wing of the party in Vienna. In such clandestine ways cooperation between Socialist and Catholic camps survived in Linz long after it had ceased on the Ringstrasse in the federal capital.[21]

In 1924 Hauser and Gföllner reconciled their differences on a pilgrimage to the Vatican. By then the prelate-governor was in frail health, and the bishop was inclined to forgive earlier "transgressions." More importantly, Pius XI expressed his personal approval of Hauser's behavior in 1918–19. For the next several years Gföllner felt compelled to keep a lower political profile, although he in no way modified his opposition to the democratic republic.[22] He continued to encourage rightists within the Christian Social movement such as Princess Franziska Starhemberg, president of the Austrian Catholic Women's Association and mother of the playboy fascist Ernst Rüdiger von Starhemberg; Count Heinrich Clam-Martinic, former imperial minister president; and Balthasar Gierlinger, landed aristocrat and provincial *Heimwehr* chieftain.[23] Unlike Hauser and his followers, these clerical conservatives espoused the authoritarian corporatist values of official Austrian Catholicism. In the pages of the monthly diocesan newsletter, Gföllner, in particular, kept up a drumfire of denunciations of "atheistic" Social Democrats, Freemasons, Liberals, Methodists, Jehovah's Witnesses, Adventists, Jews, the YMCA, and even Rotary clubs. The attacks failed to garner much public support in Linz, where the bishop was frequently ridiculed for his pronouncements against contemporary women's fashions, immorality, nudity, and modern dances, specifically the "foxtrot, tango, one-step and shimmy."[24] Still, the bishop's words could not be blithely dismissed by pious Catholics and clearly exerted some influence, particularly after Hauser's death in 1927.

Although the Christian Social movement in Linz and its hinterland was divided into democratic and authoritarian wings, many individuals and some groups in the Catholic camp did not fit consistently into either category. The provincial Catholic trade unions, for example, espoused the cause of democracy in principle, but after the burning of the Viennese Palace of Justice in 1927, they lent their support to the *Heimwehr*.[25] Three years later they withdrew their approval and joined federal chief Leopold Kunschak in denouncing the *Heimwehr's* fascistic Korneuburg oath "because it contradicts in essential points the social and political principles of the Catholic workers' and employees' movement."[26] Much the same observation could be made of the workers' employers, as represented in the Linz Chamber of Commerce. Deploring rent control, high taxes, and especially social insurance, local merchants and small producers at first praised the *Heimwehr* and called for the constitutional reorganization of the state along corporatist lines. As their official newsletter put in in September 1929: "The demand for the abolition of the federal council and its replacement by a chamber of estates is the most effective way of reestablishing in Austria legislative work that focuses on the well-being of the economy."[27] Yet within just a year, some businessmen expressed second thoughts. In endorsing the Christian Social ticket in the National Assembly elections of November 1930, the Upper Austrian Trade and Commercial Association observed that "the struggle of different occupational estates against each other and class hatred will not save our economy."[28] Nevertheless, when a corporatist, authoritarian system became a reality three years later, most members of the local *Mittelstand* welcomed it with open arms.

However complex and multifaceted the Christian Social movement in Linz and Upper Austria actually was, it remained generally pledged to moderate, democratic values throughout the 1920s. This was one reason that local Catholics often felt uncomfortable joining in anti-Marxist unity lists with German Nationalists, as they were required to do by Seipel between 1925 and 1927. After all, the German Nationalists had been Hauser's principal adversaries before 1918 and had repeatedly blocked plans for electoral reform.

THE GERMAN NATIONALISTS

Like their compatriots elsewhere in Austria, the German Nationalists in Linz survived the collapse of the monarchy as a sociologically cohesive but ideologically fragmented group. Approximately one-third of the candidates for public office in the town were civil servants, one-fifth self-employed merchants or shopkeepers, one-sixth private white-collar employees, and another sixth academically trained professionals (table 2). Strikingly underrepresented were small producers and workers, although a number of individuals did hail originally from working-class backgrounds. The German Nationalists, in other words, remained the party of professionals, civil servants, and merchants, particularly as represented on the Linz city council (tables 9 and 10).

As opposed to the other two parties in Upper Austria, the German Nationalists rarely pursued independent policies on the local level, especially since their chairman, Franz Dinghofer, first as vice chancellor and then as chief justice of the Austrian Supreme Court, played such a prominent role in federal politics. Welcoming the collapse of the multinational Habsburg monarchy, they initially advocated regional autonomy as the best means of achieving the cherished goal of Anschluss with the German Reich.[29] Forced to postpone that objective by the Treaty of St. Germain, they shared portfolios in the provincial cabinet and on the Linz city council, although their influence in those deliberative bodies was never as great as in Vienna, where they participated as members of various federal coalitions. In ideological matters the German Nationalists retained their prewar anticlericalism while endorsing a particularly rabid brand of anti-Semitism. Their all-Austrian program adopted in 1920, for example, stated that the party would "provide enlightenment about the pernicious influence of the Jewish spirit and the necessity of racial anti-Semitism caused by it. It will oppose the Jewish influence in all spheres of public and private life; the immigration of foreign Jews to be curtailed; the eastern Jews to be expelled."[30]

55

TABLE 9   Principal Occupations of German Nationalist City Councillors, 1919–1931 (percentages)

	1919	1923	1927	1931
Self-employed	20	25	18.2	25
Professionals	10	—	9.1	50
Public Service (*Beamte*, employees)	40	50	63.6	25
Public Service (workers)	—	8.3	—	—
Private Employees	30	16.7	9.1	—
Workers	—	—	—	—

Computed from Bart and Puffer, *Die Gemeindevertretung der Stadt Linz.*

TABLE 10   Learned Occupations of German Nationalist City Councillors, 1919–1931 (percentages)

	1919	1923	1927	1931
Self-employed	—	—	9.1	20
Professionals	9.1	7.7	18.2	20
Public Service (*Beamte*, employees)	27.2	30.8	27.2	40
Public Service (workers)	9.1	7.7	18.2	—
Private Employees	27.3	15.4	9.1	—
Workers	27.3	38.4	18.2	20

Computed from Bart and Puffer, *Die Gemeindevertretung der Stadt Linz.*

By resorting to anti-Semitism the German Nationalists tried to reconcile the conflicting interests of their constituents without creating a tight-knit party organization. Their bourgeois elitist predelictions, in fact, prevented them from forming a united party at all. While several attempts were thus made immediately after the war to unify the anticlerical bourgeoisie, the best that could be achieved was the Greater German Peoples' Party (GDVP), a loose federation of German Liberals, German Nationalists, and several smaller groups including for a time the National Socialists.[31] In Linz and Upper Austria the GDVP usually combined with the *Landbund* of Protestant, more democratically oriented farmers in electoral contests while excluding the Nazis or other socially unacceptable fringe groups. German Nationalist behavior at times thus tended to be more moderate than in other regions of Austria—such as Styria—although ideological goals remained the same. In terms of electoral performance, however, there were virtually no differences from the federal norm. Local German Nationalist candidates usually garnered 15 to 20 percent of the votes cast in municipal, provincial, and federal elections in the early years of the republic. They suffered a major setback in 1923, and joined the Christian Socials in fusion tickets between 1924 and 1927. Thereafter, as in Austria as a whole, the GDVP splintered and disintegrated, eventually to be swallowed by the Nazis in 1933.[32]

Although the German Nationalists in Linz, as elsewhere, refused to become a mass party, their chairman, Franz Dinghofer, tried to expand their influence by organizing gymnastic and sports clubs to disseminate *völkisch* propaganda or to act as shock troops against the "Marxists." In such a way he presumably hoped to mobilize public opinion without sacrificing bourgeois control to working-class adherents or to outsiders like the Nazis. Refusing to make the compromises necessary to sustain a modern party, the German Nationalists remained wedded to outmoded nineteenth-century liberal procedures. They were an *Honoratioren* party, unable to develop a coherent political organization supported by dedicated, disciplined, dues-paying members. At the same time, their gymnastic and sports clubs as well as their affiliated teachers organizations provided an associational link to the masses that for a while offered the means of mobilizing some support.

Within Linz the most prominent German Nationalist athletic clubs appear to have been the German Gymnastic Society of 1919 (*Deutscher Turnerbund 1919*), the Jahn Gymnastic Council (*Turngemeinde Jahn*), and the German Populist Gymnastic Association (*Deutschvölkischer Turnverein*). As a rule, each of these associations consisted of several hundred members who had joined to compete in swimming, rowing, canoeing, soccer, and volleyball or simply to keep in condition. They were patterned after the nineteenth-century Prussian clubs, founded by *Turnvater* Jahn to train youth in the struggle against Napoleon, and consequently often had a paramilitary character. More importantly, the German Nationalist athletic clubs accepted only "Aryans," preached the virtues of good grooming, and regularly denounced Jews, Socialists, and the Church. Judging from the newsletter of the German Populist Gymnastic Association of Urfahr, most of the rank and file seem to have been young commercial clerks, bookkeepers, or middle-level civil servants, many of whom were already Nazis. The officers, on the other hand, belonged to the respectable German Nationalist establishment.[33]

In terms of occupational categories, the German Nationalists exercised considerable influence among Linz schoolteachers. Secular education had long been a bourgeois concern, and as a result of the Imperial Elementary School Law of 1869 local German Liberals were able to establish a network of public primary and secondary schools in town and province.[34] By 1914 a later generation of German Nationalists had turned these into hotbeds of anticlerical, *völkisch* agitation through their control of the provincial school board and hence of most teaching appointments. Elementary teachers and gymnasial professors thus had a vested interest in the German Nationalist cause, whose elitist values they inclined to endorse. With the collapse of the monarchy and the introduction of equal suffrage, the German Nationalists lost control of the Linz city council but not of the provincial board of education. Backed by an overwhelming majority of provincial teachers organized in the Teachers Association of 1867 (*Lehrerverein 1867*), they stood firm in their determination to maintain the locally hard-won Central European two-track system of education: on the one hand they resisted Christian Social attempts to reinstitute compulsory parochial education; on the other, they opposed Socialist demands for egalitarian, comprehensive schools.[35]

Given this reservoir of relatively articulate men and women, it was not unusual that teachers played an important part in local Greater German politics. Of those individuals, the most prominent was the Upper Austrian Security Director, Franz Langoth. Aloof, ambitious, and level-headed, he had been the hand-picked successor of Schönerer's one-time associate and local political boss, Dr. Carl Beurle. Elected to the provincial parliament in 1909 as a Libertarian (*freiheitlich*), Langoth rose rapidly to the top of the German Nationalist heap. In late 1918 he was appointed one of Hauser's "three deputies," and entrusted with the maintenance of regional law and order. In that capacity he demonstrated great skill throughout months of turmoil in deploying rural constabulary and urban *Volkswehr* against rioting and anarchy.[36] As a result he won the respect of Hauser, who did not especially like him, and of the more conservative Princess Franziska von Starhemberg, who introduced him to respectable reactionary circles. At the same time, the security director managed to retain the friendship of his Social Democratic colleague in the provincial diet, Josef Gruber, and through him to mollify militant elements of the local labor movement.[37] In 1920, Langoth became a principal founder of the Austrian GDVP, succeeding Franz Dinghofer as its provincial chairman. Working closely with another German Nationalist schoolteacher in Linz, Hermann Foppa—who after 1930 rose to head the federal GDVP—Langoth eventually used his extensive social and political connections in leading the Greater Germans to the swastika banner. Throughout the 1920s however, he worked closely with Hauser, enjoying his position as security director to dabble in federal politics.[38] With a stake in the system, neither Langoth nor his Greater German associates saw much point at that time in sweeping it away. Despite a greater sense of ideological alienation than the other two *Lager* and a passionate commitment to Anschluss with Germany, the German Nationalists in Linz and Upper Austria, in other words, also inclined toward operational moderation and cooperation.

The Red Prelate. Johann Nepomuk Hauser, Governor of
Upper Austria, 1908–1927. Stadtmuseum Linz.

CONSOCIATIONAL OR CONCORDANT DEMOCRACY

The relative flexibility and tolerance of Linz's tripartisan political system in the 1920s should give pause to accepted notions of Austria's unbending *Lager*. Rather than representing irreconcilable military camps, the three local parties resembled vertical columns supporting a common entablature. The three columns coexisted separately, but together they were indispensable in maintaining the local political order. In this respect Upper Austria's governmental system displayed many of the characteristics of the consociational or concordant democracy of modern Holland and the Second Austrian Republic. Under the consociational system, elites of a highly fragmented society join forces to regulate the social and political conflict of their subcultures. They achieve stability through the process of constant bargaining—frequently outside elected deliberative bodies—and through their own moderate, cooperative behavior. Since external force or immobilism may threaten to upset their consensual applecart, they often seek to institutionalize their informal arrangements under law. While these procedures admittedly violate the principle of majority rule, they do not deviate from accepted democratic behavior when the stakes are high. In addition, they provide an example of conciliation for the competitive subcultures while offering a pluralistic means of achieving consensus.[39]

Without doubt, the most striking feature of Upper Austria's political order between 1918 and 1934 was the ongoing cooperation of its subcultural elites. Whereas political leaders in Vienna regularly exchanged insults on the floor of the National Assembly, those in Linz daily engaged in collaboration in the Upper Austrian diet and, somewhat more reluctantly, in the Linz City Hall. However much the local elites differed on social and economic issues, they all concurred in a pluralistic distribution of power (at least on a geographical basis), in the principle of majority rule, and in the peaceful regulation of conflict. What made cooperation possible on the local level were several factors, including especially a continuity of personnel and institutions.

Alone among Austrian provinces, Upper Austria was governed in the First Republic by essentially the same men who had controlled local affairs under the Habsburgs. Hauser, for example, was the only prewar governor to continue in office after 1918;[40] his hand-picked successor, Josef Schlegel, had been a member of the provincial cabinet since 1909. By the same token the Socialist and German Nationalist politicians, Josef Hafner and Franz Langoth, while not holding portfolios until 1918, had also acquired parliamentary experience before the collapse of the monarchy.[41] United by shared experience and personal contact, Hauser, Schlegel, Dametz, Hafner, Gruber, and Langoth were able to pilot Upper Austria through difficult days of war and revolution and, more importantly, to retain control of local affairs throughout the 1920s. During the sixteen years of the First Austrian Republic only two men sat in the governor's mansion in Linz. By way of contrast, eleven chancellors presided over the rise and fall of twelve separate federal cabinets at the *Ballhausplatz* in Vienna. Elsewhere on the provincial level numerous changes of government also occurred in Styria and Carinthia, regions well known for widespread radicalism.[42]

Interelite cooperation in Linz was also facilitated by a strong sense of cultural homogeneity. In contrast to their federal counterparts in the National Assembly, Upper Austrian political leaders shared certain common values, especially a high regard for German culture and civilization. Hauser was known for his love of German classical and romantic literature, Schlegel for his role as a founder of the anti-Czech *Schutzverein Ostmark*, and Dametz for his penchant for quoting Goethe and Schiller over Marx and Engels. The elites of all three camps also professed feelings of regional patriotism, but always within a German rather than an Austrian context. Manifesting various degrees of political and racial anti-Semitism, they all concurred in the necessity of Anschluss with Germany.[43]

A final factor encouraging collaborative politics in Upper Austria was tight party discipline, especially in the Christian Social and Social Democratic movements. Although the rank and file of both parties seem to have recognized the necessity of coalescent behavior in provincial and municipal affairs, only firm control at the top made its continuation possible beyond 1920. Hauser could not have contained Gföllner's disruptive activities or cooperated with the Social Democrats without a firm hold on the Catholic Peoples' Association. Nor could the Socialists have responded effectively without coopting the militant elements of the labor movement, first in the workers' councils and later in the Chamber of Labor. That the elite cartel in Upper Austria and Linz would experience difficulties after the deaths of Hauser and Dametz in 1927 was due in part to the inability of their successors to establish effective dominance over their respective organizations.

By means of constant bargaining and collaboration, elites of all three *Lager* were generally able to regulate conflict and to achieve a measure of stability between 1918 and 1934. As a result, they reinforced the consociational order and enhanced a local tradition of democratic moderation. Tenuous or imperfect as the tradition might have been, it was nonetheless real, as manifested by the relatively low level of regional violence and by the refusal of local politicans to lend aid or support to disloyal opposition groups such as the *Heimwehr*.[44] Unencumbered by the disadvantage of newness, such as that crippling the federal government, provincial leaders could point with pride to a record of democratic achievement over two decades. While Upper Austrians might refuse to give loyalty to the "state nobody wanted," they could not afford to ignore their own local government by pledging absolute allegiance to individual political parties.[45] As Dametz's successor in the Linz City Hall, Robert Mehr, proudly emphasized to a Socialist rally in 1928, "Upper Austria has the only democratically inclined provincial government in the Republic."[46] Given such a sense of democratic legitimacy, it was possible for local politicians to eschew violence and to seek changes by constitutional means. In retrospect, this was really quite remarkable considering the attenuated powers of provincial government in general and the fact that Upper Austria enjoyed neither the comparative autonomy of neighboring Bavaria nor the political cohesion of "Red Vienna." It should also not be forgotten that the province suffered its share of economic distress and general unrest as well.

Decisive in the establishment of consociational democracy in Upper Austria was Prelate Hauser. Willing to share power with the Social Democrats and, to a lesser degree, with the German Nationalists, it was Hauser who founded a political system of enforced cooperation by guaranteeing each major party at least one seat in the provincial cabinet. Since this coalition, or *Arbeitsgemeinschaft* as the "red prelate" called it, left final decisions in the hands of the majority party, it could not be compared to the great coalitions that twice assumed power in the Weimar Republic or, in this sense, even in Austria after World War II. Nevertheless, the consociational system worked so well in establishing personal and institutional relationships, that Upper Austria was generally spared the sort of acrimonious debate and extended political fragmentation characteristic of both Weimar and the First Austrian Republic. Without downplaying powerful social and economic forces, Hauser's political order bore a strong resemblance to that once described by Aristotle in which stability was achieved not so much by a constitutional system as "by the good relations in which officers stand alike with the unenfranchised and with the members of the civic body" and by the fact that "the officers and other members of the governing class behave towards one another in a democratic spirit of equality."[47]

In contrast to the province, in Linz itself the collapse of the monarchy and the introduction of universal suffrage brought about a fundamental change. With the establishment of Social Democratic rule in 1919, a more radical break with the past could hardly be imagined. Nevertheless, a sense of continuity was preserved in municipal government through the institutionalization of consociational procedures in the City Statute of 1920. Under this document, the lord mayor was elected by a simple majority of the city council, just as the governor was chosen by a majority of the Upper Austrian diet. The mayor then administered the muncipality with the assistance of an Executive Committee (*Stadtrat*) consisting of three vice-mayors from each of the major parties and eight senators (*Stadträte*) chosen proportionately. While this system virtually precluded radical social experimentation (unlikely in any case, given the reformist mentality of the majority of Social Democrats), its tripartisan character gave the town the same sort of stability found in the provincial government. City councillors could thus transcend cleavages and concentrate on problems common to all. Through collaboration they helped forestall further fragmentation and contained, for example, the electoral ambitions of extremist groups like the *Heimwehr* and the National Socialists. Those fascist parties would win seats on the city council, but never garner enough votes for representation on the executive committee.[48] As in the province, enforced participation by the three major parties also helped establish feelings of mutual respect among the participants. When Mayor Josef Dametz died unexpectedly in September 1927, for example, the genuine outpouring of grief on the part of Christian Social and German Nationalist politicians provided a clear demonstration of the esteem he had won among the opposition. While such tributes are not unusual in a healthy parliamentary system, they were certainly notable in interwar Austria, where politicians normally looked upon their opponents as hated enemies rather than competitors in the political arena.[49]

Just how well Hauser's consociational system worked in maintaining democratic stability in Linz can be discerned by an examination of the debates of the city council in the 1920s. In the Renaissance City Hall by the Danube, municipal politicians regularly grappled with issues confronting the First Republic such as currency reform, unemployment, rent control, and private-versus-public ownership of property. Because the councillors were acutely aware of Linz's dependence on the Upper Austrian diet for appropriations and felt driven by economic hardship to cooperate, they sought consensus on budgetary matters while confining their verbal clashes to ideology. As a consequence, their arguments sometimes approached the bitterness and intensity of the war of words in the National Assembly. But, in the end, they invariably resolved their differences in a fruitful and productive way.

During the revolutionary turmoil of 1918 and 1919 the Christian Socials and German Nationalists on the city council raised few objections to changes proposed by the Social Democrats. The middle class parties endorsed the repeal of regressive excise taxes and municipal surcharges on rents. They also voted for the communalization of the gas and water works, the general hospital, and several other essential services. Beginning in the spring of 1920, however, the two bourgeois parties started provoking quarrels over seemingly trivial but highly symbolic issues. They rejected funds for the municipal bakery, accused the Socialist trade unions of instituting a reign of terror in the general hospital, and charged the workers' councils with inciting the riots of May 1920. So incensed were the German Nationalists by a proposal leasing city property to the Social Democratic Workers Gymnastic Association, that they stalked out of City Hall in a rage and boycotted the next meeting of the city council.[50]

After the collapse of the Great Coalition in Vienna and a general swing to the right in the federal elections of 1920, the political lines hardened in Linz just as elsewhere in the troubled Alpine republic. It was, in fact, only with great difficulty that municipal party leaders were able to persuade their followers to continue collaborating with their adversaries in the city hall until the return of more prosperous times. Christian Social and German Nationalist city councillors therefore still ratified Social Democratic municipal budgets, but they did so labeling their opponents disloyal Bolsheviks. As for the Social Democrats, they replied with charges of monarchism and antirepublicanism. After Charles's ill-fated attempt to regain his throne in Budapest in March 1921, the Social Democratic leadership, in the face of determined middle-class opposition, deliberately flouted consensual procedures by passing a resolution changing the name of Francis Joseph Square to the Square of the 12th of November.[51]

For the next two years the growing radicalization of German and Austrian political life spilled over into the chambers of the Linz City Hall. In March 1922, members of the Workers' Council uncovered stocks of weapons that belonged to the German Populist Gymnastic Association in the store rooms of the Kraus and Schober department store.[52] On the city council Socialist spokesman Hermann Schneeweiss denounced the German Nationalists for their part in purchasing the arms and demanded the resignation of Greater German Vice-Mayor Karl Sadleder. Responding with laughter, Sadleder openly acknowledged his links to the gymnastic association. German Nationalist and Christian Social councillors then defended the right of Linz businessmen to protect themselves from armed workers and "shop terror." With tempers rising, the Social Democrats accused the bourgeois parties of fostering class hatred and poisoning the political atmosphere of Linz.[53]

In 1923 tensions reached a kind of high point in Upper Austria as throughout most of Central Europe. Early in the year the Social Democrats organized their own paramilitary formation, the Republican Defense Corps (*Republikanischer Schutzbund*), and rammed a bill through the city council annexing the working-class suburb of Kleinmünchen. Although the annexation was vigorously opposed by the Christian Socials and German Nationalists, it was approved by Hauser's provincial government without comment. On 24 June the Socialists were able to draw on their new electoral reservoir to win a plurality of the votes cast in the municipal elections of that day. With only thirty seats on the new city council, Dametz's administration faced a hostile coalition of sixteen Christian Socials, ten Greater Germans, and, for the first time, four National Socialists. Out of respect for Dametz the middle-class parties concurred in the unanimous reelection of the lord mayor, but they also took advantage of their newly won strength to obstruct proceedings, demanding, for example, a change in the composition of the executive committee. Thereafter, they delayed the election of a Socialist vice-mayor for two months and blocked proposals raising taxes on real estate, housing, and personal property.[54] In short, consociational politics in Linz appeared to have reached a dead end.

Paradoxically, the Social Democrats were able to break the stalemate in City Hall with the help of the National Socialists. The Austrian Nazis before 1926 were a quasi-independent, social-reform party with only tenuous links to Hitler. Although violently anti-Marxist in outlook, they were willing to vote with the Socialists in raising taxes to alleviate housing shortages and unemployment.[55] The severity of these problems was recognized by the other parties as well, but neither the Christian Socials nor the Greater Germans would allocate public funds for their solution, proposing instead the sale of municipal bonds and construction by the private sector. At times, the parties did reach consensus by awarding one contract to a trade union cooperative and the next to a private firm. More often than not, however, they refused to bury their differences in interest-group compromises.

In early 1925 the housing issue provoked a stormy confrontation between the Social Democrats and the National Socialists on the one side and the Christian Socials and Greater Germans on the other. Having joined the Socialists eleven months before in legislating a property appreciation tax (*Bodenwertabgabe*), the Nazis now lent their support to a bill for the municipal construction of 130 small apartments. In response, Christian Social Councillor Georg Stempfer bitterly accused the Social Democrats of plotting the abolition of all private property in Linz and denounced the Nazis for conniving with Jews and Marxists. So vitriolic did the ensuing debate become, that the city council adjourned for fifteen minutes to let the councillors recover their composure. After reconvening, the bill carried by a margin of 32 to 26 votes.[56]

The acrimony of the debates on the Linz city council in 1923 and 1925 reflected more than the ideological cleavages separating Austria's political *Lager*. Between 1922 and 1925 the National Assembly had passed legislation curtailing federal subsidies to provincial and municipal employees and restricting the right of municipalities to impose surtaxes on federal levies. Faced with a loss of revenue, the contending forces in Linz could not agree on local taxes to meet municipal expenses. Compounding their disagreement was the expiration on 31 December 1925 of a federal law permitting expropriation of unused rental property for temporary housing. As a result, the city government found itself unable to house 3,000 needy families at a time when 300 apartments were standing vacant.[57]

Eventually economic hardship drove the city councillors to resume cooperation. In 1926 Mayor Dametz accepted a tripartisan package, according to which the city would build 160 apartments and 90 single-family homes. As part of the financial settlement, the Social Democrats assented to a reduction of real estate taxes and to the repeal of the annual property appreciation tax; in return the middle-class parties voted for the passage of a real estate transaction tax. Since expenditures still outran revenue, the parties agreed the following year to apply for a substantial loan from the Central Savings Bank in Vienna. Throughout these deliberations bargaining proceeded in a surprisingly moderate and rational way. Between 1926 and 1930, in fact, few outbursts marred the routine business of the Linz city council.[58]

The resumption of consociational politics in the city hall represented something of a calculated risk on the part of the Social Democratic administration. Hoping to avoid renewed deadlock, Socialist leaders in Linz extended an olive branch to the middle-class parties on the future of the municipal police force. Ever since 1919 the Christian Socials and German Nationalists had insisted on bringing the Linz police under the control of the federal government, but had made little headway against Socialist resistance. Because the peacekeeping forces consumed nearly 10 percent of the municipal budget, however, Social Democratic aldermen and councillors gradually modified their opposition to federalization. In May 1926, they voted to initiate negotiations transferring police control to the Ministry of the Interior, rationalizing to the party faithful that the Republican Defense Corps could safeguard the hard won gains of 1918–19. For their part, the Christian Socials and Greater Germans accepted this critical Socialist concession, but, at first, spurned further cooperation. They combined instead with the National Socialists in an anti-Marxist Unity List in an all-out effort to win control of City Hall. In the elections of 24 April 1927, however, the bourgeois parties suffered a serious setback, losing four seats on the city council to the Social Democrats. In order to retain some say in municipal affairs the Christian Socials and Greater Germans sheepishly reverted to more conciliatory habits. During the budgetary debates of December 1929, in fact, the Christian Social spokesman acknowledged an obligation for unanimity in the municipal proposals for the following year.[59]

Between 1918 and 1930, then, interelite cooperation in the chambers of the Linz City Hall was generally more strained than on the floor of the nearby Upper Austrian diet. While party leaders concurred in the principle of majority rule and the moderate regulation of conflict, they found the socioeconomic barriers dividing their subcultures nearly insurmountable. Out of desperation they did compromise on the municipal budget, but not in such a way as to put the city on a sound financial footing either by raising the requisite taxes or by agreeing on strategies of economic growth. That consensual procedures prevailed on the Linz city council can be attributed to economic necessity, to habits of cooperation, and, above all, to the tutelage of the provincial government. Without the supervisory goodwill of Hauser's regime, the constitutional entablature in Linz might have collapsed onto its shaking political columns long before 1930. That it did not stands as a tribute to the "red prelate" and to the flexibility of the Catholic Peoples' Association.

THE ECONOMIC REALITIES

Although political conflict in Linz appeared to be ideological, the underlying issues of contention were, more often than not, economic. The Christian Socials and, to a lesser extent, the German Nationalists supported the democratic order in Upper Austria. They accepted a pluralistic distribution of power. They collaborated with the Social Democrats in the provincial diet and on the Linz city council. Some middle class elites even sympathized with Socialist municipalization schemes, especially public housing. But what social services should receive priority? Who should pay for them? What indeed were the distributive capabilities of local government? These were questions that were addressed but not satisfactorily answered in Linz during the 1920s. The fact was that the municipal order rested on an outmoded economic base, dependent on agriculture and hostile to industrial development. With the town's middle strata accustomed to protection against modernization, the local economy stagnated. As a result, societal conflicts intensified, and consociational democracy eventually collapsed.

In the years immediately after World War I, economic prospects did not appear so bleak. While groups of middle-class civil servants, teachers, and shopkeepers suffered severely from inflation and currency devaluation, a number of local bankers and commerical entrepreneurs at first viewed the future with some optimism. They saw that Linz, with one hundred thousand inhabitants, had emerged as the third largest city in the Austrian state. Given an annual growth rate of 1 or 2 percent, this seemed the kind of population capable of supporting sustained—if modest—economic growth. Forlorn about Austria's economic future, the business leaders were strangely sanguine about that of Linz. They regarded their town as an Alpine funnel through which flowed the trade of the Atlantic, Adriatic, and Black Seas. Freed from the shackles of Habsburg protective tariffs, located a stone's throw from the vast German market, and in possession of well-developed dock and rail facilities, there seemed little reason why the Upper Austrian capital should not develop into a major inland port and commercial center. The city fathers accordingly poured enough capital into Linz's port facilities to double capacity by 1924.[60]

In retrospect, economic conditions in Linz after World War I were indeed more favorable than in Austria as a whole—at least on paper. The town had access to abundant supplies of food, comparatively cheap sources of electrical energy, and a well-developed, low-cost transportation network. Compared to Vienna with its vast population imbalance vis-à-vis the rest of the country or to Graz its most approximate counterpart, the Upper Austrian

capital faced few insurmountable problems.[61] Expectations of future prosperity were therefore by no means uncalled for and may well have colored
the generally cordial deliberations of the Linz city council between 1919 and
1924.

All the same, Linz failed to become the entrepot envisaged by its
commercial elites. Local trends, in fact, closely paralleled those in Austria
itself. During the first years of peace, the Danubian city thus experienced
intitial dislocation from a loss of markets, especially in southern Bohemia,
shortages of coal and capital, and persistent inflation. Merchants and
tradesmen grumbled about unfair competition from peddlers or war-surplus
dealers, and ordinary people tried to find permanent jobs. During this
period of high inflation and wild speculation a number of new businesses,
particularly construction firms, were founded and employment remained
full. With the stabilization of the currency in late 1922, many of the newer
establishments went bankrupt, and unemployment, especially among machine and metal workers, reappeared. Thereafter, shortages of capital
combined with high interest rates, growing dependence on foreign loans,
and local habits of investing in commerce over industry to keep overall
production relatively stagnant. Those few industries and trades that did
show measurable growth in Linz between 1922 and 1933 were related to
housing and construction, wood finishing of all types, and food processing.[62]

Actually, a retrospective examination of the Linz economy in the 1920s
reveals structural weaknesses that inhibited growth and undermined the
cause of political democracy. Despite the impression of an expanding
population, for example, the city's birth rate actually declined between 1923
and 1939 (table 11). While several thousand newcomers did move to the
Upper Austrian capital, many did so on a seasonal basis, often retaining
domiciles in the nearby countryside. Demographically, therefore, Linz's
population remained comparatively stagnant throughout the interwar
period.[63]

Much the same generalization can be made about the city's occupational
structure (tables 12 and 13). In the three decades between 1910 and 1939 the
percentages of individuals employed in local farms, factories, shops, and
governmental agencies remained virtually constant. Although the number of
salaried employees trebled and the percentage of small producers declined,
no major sectoral shifts occurred paralleling developments in more advanced
industrial cities.[64]

Linz thus remained a city of small-scale, largely nonmechanical enterprises with well over 60 percent of its work force (in 1937) employed in
handicrafts.[65] The size of these firms averaged less than five employees, a
fact helping to account for a municipal average of all enterprises (in 1930) of
only 7.7 employees per establishment.[66] A substantial number of these
businesses, moreover, were family-owned as were most of the local trade

TABLE 11   Population of Linz 1890–1945

1890	47,685
1900	58,791
1910	67,817
1915	75,186

(growth through incorporation)

1923	102,081

(growth through incorporation)

1930	106,700
1935	108,993
1937	111,545
1939	121,071
1945	194,186

(growth through incorporation and industrialization)

SOURCE: *Statistisches Jahrbuch der Stadt Linz* (1946), p. 23, 38 and Otruba "Der gesell-schaftliche und wirtschaftliche Strukturwandel der Stadt Linz," p. 21.

and commercial interests. Indeed, somewhere between 60 and 80 percent of all productive and commercial establishments in Linz during the interwar period could be categorized as owned and operated by families.[67]

By way of contrast, the remaining enterprises were relatively large but often state- or municipally-owned. By far, the most important were the headquarters, switchyards, and repair shops of the Austrian federal railways. As the largest rail junction in Austria, the railroad in Linz employed several hundred officials and over a thousand wage earners. In the province its employees numbered over seven thousand. The importance of the railroad in the life of Linz was underscored by the sizeable number of municipal politicians who worked for it, especially those belonging to the Social Democratic and, to a lesser degree, to the Nazi parties. Much the same can be said of the municipal branch of the federal post and telegraph service, although its employees were not nearly so numerous. Another large, federally owned establishment was the state tobacco plant with approximately a thousand wage earners.[68] As for the municipal enterprises, they were generally large but less numerous than in Vienna, where a more extensive system of public services reposed on Karl Lueger's prewar foundations. All told, perhaps as many as two thousand people worked for the city.[69]

Private large-scale manufacturing in Linz comprised only a fraction of the town's interwar productive economy. Nevertheless, the few large industries provided several thousand jobs, contributing substantially to the life of the community. The largest private enterprise was the combine of cotton and

TABLE 12   Occupational Structure of Linz in Percentages of Total Persons with Regular Incomes

Year	Total Persons with Income	Agriculture and Forestry	Industry and Handicrafts	Trade and Commerce	Public Service and Free Professions	Rentiers, Pensioners, et al.
1910	37,372	1.7	31.6	25.1	19.5	22.1
1934	—	1.7	31.7	25.3	—	—
1939	79,238	2.8	32.2	23.2	16.8	25.0

SOURCES: Otruba and Möller, "Der Wandel des Wirtschaftsgefüges der Städte Wien, Linz, Innsbruck und Graz," p. 55; Otruba, "Der gesellschaftliche und wirtschaftliche Strukturwandel der Stadt Linz," p. 22; and *Statistisches Jahrbuch der Stadt Linz* (1946), p. 79.

TABLE 13   Employed Persons in Linz

Year	Independent Producers	Assisting Family Members	Civil Servants/ Public Officials	Employees	Workers
1910	4,705 (11.7)	304 (0.7)	8,599 (21.4)	4,545 (11.3)	22,077* (54.9)
1939	5,555 (8.9)	1,943 (3.1)	8,577 (13.7)	14,511 (23.1)	32,148 (51.2)

*Includes domestics.

SOURCE: Linz *Tagblatt*, 26 April 1919 and *Statistisches Jahrbuch der Stadt Linz* (1946), p. 87.

woolen mills located in the suburb of Kleinmünchen. Founded early in the nineteenth century, the mills possessed nearly one hundred thousand spindles and employed over twelve hundred carders, spinners, winders, warpers, and weavers of whom nearly 60 percent were women. Having enjoyed tariff protection before the collapse of the monarchy, the Linz textile industries faced an uncertain future in the 1920s. Cut off from traditional markets in the underdeveloped regions of the former empire and with a productive capacity exceeding domestic demand, their antiquated, water-driven machinery made them inefficient and unprofitable. The mills remained operative between the wars but declined steadily in output and numbers of employees.[70]

A seemingly healthier economic atmosphere prevailed at Linz's next largest industrial firm, the Krauss locomotive works. With some five hundred employees and substantial capital investment, the Krauss firm manufactured specialty equipment, railroad carriages, and electric locomotives. It prospered and expanded production in the 1920s but collapsed quite unexpectedly in August 1930. Other important industries were the dockyards, whose two hundred wage earners had supplied the shock troops of the revolutionary workers' councils, the Essef saccharine plant, the Posselt machine shops, and a group of other enterprises manufacturing fire extinguishers, electrical appliances, and hardware.[71]

The manufacturing and industrial structure of Linz, then, remained outmoded and largely unprofitable. While some consolidation did occur in brewing and distilling plants, the town's merchants and traditional producers continued to favor older manufacturers over technologically advanced industries. Since the business elites also endorsed the deflationary policies of the federal government, it is difficult to imagine that sustained growth could have occurred under the best of circumstances. Without such growth, however, it was virtually impossible to overcome problems of unemployment, housing, health care, or social welfare in general. As for Linz's laboring classes, they were able to make headway in advancing their interests in the early 1920s, but primarily as the consequence of the introduction of universal suffrage in 1919. Faced with increasing economic hardship, they could never fully mobilize their forces in the hundreds of family-owned workshops of the city. It was probably unavoidable that they were eventually driven to make political as well as economic concessions, notably on the future of the Linz police force.

GRADUAL SOCIALIST ECLIPSE

The undermanned Linz police department had experienced considerable difficulty dealing with the unrest of the immediate postwar period. Only by combining with rural constables and newly established *Volkswehr* units on an ad hoc basis had order been maintained. After the Communist-inspired riots of May 1920, provincial Security Director Langoth and the municipal chief of police, Dr. Anton Zöttl urged the federalization of the Linz police as the best means of eliminating overlapping authority and of strengthening the town's peacekeeping forces. Since, however, this proposal would have placed the municipal police under the jurisdiction of the bourgeois-controlled Ministry of the Interior, it was rejected by the Socialist city government. Instead, some forty-nine officers—including Zöttl—were permitted to remain on the force, but 172 others were recruited from the *Volkswehr*. With over two-thirds of all municipal policemen owing their jobs to the Socialist city hall, the bourgeois cry for "reform" and the "depoliticization" of public security—the elimination of Social Democratic influence—

became louder and more intense. Nevertheless, the Linz police department was able to retain its autonomy until 1926, when, as we have seen, it became too expensive for the city to maintain.[72]

In early 1927 control of the municipal police passed to the federal Ministry of the Interior. Almost immediately pressure was put on patrolmen and officers to withdraw from the Socialist Free Trade Union. Those who refused or were considered incorrigible were compelled to undergo rigorous medical examinations which usually found them unfit and therefore subject to dismissal from the force. By the same token, applicants with a Socialist background, such as membership in the Soldiers' Union (*Militärverband*), were not accepted as recruits. Within just a few years, the Linz police force was thus purged of "unreliable" elements and made into a reliable instrument of the increasingly authoritarian federal government. In February 1934, few local patrolmen had second thoughts about opening fire on bands of Socialist workers.[73]

On the parade grounds and in the barracks of the federal army a similar "depolitization" also occurred. In contrast to Germany, where the *Reichswehr* retained its prewar command structure and rigid social hierarchy, the *Bundesheer* of interwar Austria was at first an entirely new formation of democratically inclined officers and men. The Constitution of 1920 even permitted Austrian soldiers to organize military unions and to engage in political agitation. Because the Treaty of St. Germain limited the army's size to thirty thousand long-term volunteers, however, a succession of conservative coalition governments in Vienna was able to transform the *Bundesheer* gradually into their notion of a "nonpartisan" force. For a while, War Minister Vaugoin's measures, including the mandatory recommendation of a parish priest as a condition of recruitment, met only limited success. The Socialist Soldiers' Union maintained the loyalty of most enlisted men and sometimes blocked aribtrary changes in policy and personnel.[74] Nevertheless, as the following table of elections of military shop stewards demonstrates (table 14), the process of "depoliticization" was well under way by 1927.

In Linz itself the growing pressure from Vaugoin's army ministry was felt acutely in the local garrison of elite Alpine troops. Here a Lieutenant Colonel Fischer, aided by a Nazi subordinate, harassed working-class soldiers by breaking up their meetings, impounding their mail, denying them promotions, and confining them to barracks for the most trivial infractions. Against these outrageous procedures the Soldiers' Union held its ground for some time; in fact, during the tense days following the burning of the Viennese Palace of Justice in July 1927, union stewards actually persuaded large numbers of troops in Linz's Castle Barracks to refuse firing on unarmed workers if ordered to do so. Such acts of resistance usually did more harm than good, however, since they only accelerated the dismissal of

Table 14   Military Shop Steward Elections in Upper Austria (percentages in parentheses)

	Militärverband (Social Democrat)	Wehrbund (Christian Social)	Nationalverband/ Deutsche Soldatengewerkschaft (German Nationalist/ National Socialist)
1923	2058 (97.4)	51 (2.4)	5 (0.2)
1926	1567 (75.4)	511 (24.6)	—
1927	1201 (52.8)	1028 (45.2)	46 (2.0)
1928	652 (32.0)	1189 (58.3)	197 (9.7)

Source: AVA, Militärverband der Republik Österreich, Box 4; Slapnicka, *Von Hauser*, pp. 193–96 and idem, *Oberösterreich von Bürgerkrieg zum Anschluss*, pp. 230–31.

"disloyal" soldiers. Within less than a year, union leaders wrote the party executive in Vienna that the Linz garrison was no longer a Socialist stronghold.[75]

The gradual exclusion of Socialist influence from the Linz police and from the military forces stationed in Upper Austria constituted a serious shift in the local balance of power. For all their anti-Marxist rhetoric, not even the most conservative Christian Socials could rejoice at what was clearly a revival of Viennese bureaucratic absolutism. More ominously, the Social Democrats were forced back on a much narrower power base than before. Henceforth, their major strength would have to come from success at the polls, an advantage which was substantial as late as 1931. Yet in the face of an increasingly authoritarian federal government willing to encourage disloyal, right-wing opposition groups and to countenance antidemocratic procedures, electoral performance, no matter how impressive, would become hollow and meaningless. The Socialists ultimately had to rely on their organizations in the shops, factories, and workplaces of Linz, Steyr, and a handful of other manufacturing sites in the province to protect their interests. Since, however, local industry was largely family-owned, small-scale, and underdeveloped, the opportunities for party patronage, for the full mobilization of Linz's work force, and even for the training and arming of a party militia were severely restricted. As the following tables (15 and 16) demonstrate, moreover, the Socialists actually lost some ground among Upper Austria's workers during the comparatively quiet years of the later Hauser era.[76]

Table 15   Elections to the Chamber of Labor in Upper Austria
(percentages in parentheses)

	Social Democrat	Christian Social	Völkisch
(a) Workers' Sector			
1921	33,887 (92.1)	2,908 (7.9)	—
1926	27,800 (81.1)	5,200 (15.2)	1,293 (3.5)
(b) Transport Sector			
1926	9,304 (78.3)	957 (8.1)	1,618 (13.6)
1931	7,522 (75.3)	733 (7.3)	1,736 (17.4)
(c) Employee Sector			
1921	3,182 (58.8)	2,233 (41.2)	—
1926	2,610 (46.7)	822 (14.7)	2,155 (38.6)

Source: Linz *Volksstimme*, 21 August 1926 and Slapnicka, *Von Hauser*, p. 192.

Table 16   Trade Union Membership in Upper Austria

	Social Democrat	Christian Social
1913	15,152	4,687
1922	98,912	7,974
1926	63,229	8,574
1930	55,151	18,577

Source: *Oberösterreichische Arbeiterzeitung*, vol. 37, no. 33 (15 August 1931).

On the other hand, when Hauser died on 8 February 1927, few could see that Socialist influence was on the wane, either in Linz, or in Upper Austria. The new Christian Social governor, Josef Schlegel, in glaring contrast to Chancellor Seipel, graciously emphasized, "So long as there are Social Democrats, I shall talk to them."[77] With a sense of legitimacy, a commitment to democratic procedures, and a continuity of personnel and institutions, the local consociational order remained intact. It was not a social partnership, as frequent clashes in the city hall made all too clear. All the same, it would succeed both in thwarting violence and in containing a rising tide of right-wing radicalism.

Holding the Fascist Tide
1927–1932

On the morning of 15 July 1927 a massive riot errupted in Vienna. The upheaval was provoked by the acquittal by a Viennese jury of three right-wing freebooters charged with killing a crippled war veteran and a child. An enraged crowd that had assembled on the Ringstrasse to protest the verdict stormed the Palace of Justice and set it ablaze. Socialist leaders tried to calm the mob without success. Finally toward evening, heavily armed police arrived and opened fire with military carbines. The result was eighty-nine dead and nearly five hundred wounded. In reaction, Socialist leaders proclaimed a general strike that brought all economic activity and traffic throughout Austria to a standstill. The government of Monsignor Seipel refused, however, to resign and appealed to reactionary *Heimwehr* forces in the provinces for aid. In less than a week the strike was broken, and the Socialists for the first time since 1918 were put on the defensive.[1]

The Palace of Justice affair ushered in a period of reaction in Austria that was marked by an upsurge of fascist violence, increasing bureaucratic authoritarianism, and the eventual collapse of the First Republic. Throughout the country groups of bankers, industrialists, and estate owners contributed substantial sums to right-wing paramilitary formations in hopes of paving the way for the return of an authoritarian order. Even before the advent of the Great Depression, their efforts met with widespread success, especially in Styria, Lower Austria, and Carinthia.[2] This was not the case, however, in Linz and Upper Austria, where the local civic culture proved sufficiently resilient to withstand fascist pressure and infiltration. Though not immune to bureaucratic penetration by the federal government, the consociational order in Upper Austria held firm against the depradations of the radical right.

THE HEIMWEHR

In the years immediately following World War I, Linz experienced little right-wing violence. Wedged between Bavaria and Styria, two regions plagued by paramilitary bands, Upper Austria did not have quite the right environment for the growth of such movements. It was not an area of ethnic contention like Styria or Carinthia; it did not undergo a period of postwar extremism like Munich; it had not lost territory like the Tyrol. There was admittedly widespread resentment in the countryside against Vienna and its seemingly inexhaustable need for food as well as against the workers' councils in Linz and Steyr. But the peasants, who for centuries had exercised the right to bear arms, felt that they could defend their homes and farms without resorting to collective action. So for that matter did Security Director Langoth, who saw to it that weapons were issued only to legally constituted *Volkswehr*, to police, or to constabulary.[3] Most important of all, Governor Hauser and the Catholic Peoples' Association opposed the establishment of self-defense groups or home guards as a threat to the hard-won local democratic order in Linz and Upper Austria. As early as June 1919 Hauser took issue with Seipel on the *Heimwehr*, pointedly telling the Christian Social parliamentary club in Vienna that order in Upper Austria could be maintained "only through the Social Democrats and through the *Gendarmerie*."[4] For the rest of his life the prelate did not deviate from that policy.

This is not to say that attempts were not made to found home guard contingents in Linz or its hinterland. Numerous individuals felt threatened by the collapse of the monarchy. They saw their savings devoured by inflation, their incomes suddenly thrown into a tailspin, and their status seriously endangered. Fearful of socialism and democracy, they were all too ready to defend their interests with force. In the summer of 1919 the twenty-year-old Starhemberg organized his father's employees and agricultural laborers into a private guard to protect his ancestoral castle, now the University of Linz, against would-be plunderers and thieves.[5] Similarly, in remote hills and valleys, especially in the Mühlviertel north of the Danube, a number of local groups sprang up differing from each other in goals and effectiveness. As a rule, most of these bands seem to have had a vague sense of loyalty to the Habsburg dynasty. They were united theoretically under the command of the estate owner and former Austro-Hungarian prime minister, Heinrich Clam-Matinic. Because of their legitimist character, however, these early *Heimwehren* were unable to rally much support among the democratically inclined peasants or among the anti-Habsburg Greater Germans.[6]

In the meantime, a host of paramilitary political organizations seeking the overthrow of the Weimar Republic had grown up in neighboring Bavaria. One of these, the *Orgesch* (*Organisation Escherich* after its founder, Georg Escherich), set up a branch to establish contact with right-wing home guard units in Austria. Under the direction of a certain Rudolf Kanzler, the branch was appropriately called *Orka*, or *Organisation Kanzler*. It possessed substantial stocks of infantry rifles, machine guns, howitzers, and over two dozen airplanes.[7] On 24 April 1920 a Bavarian First Lieutenant Krazer representing *Orka* showed up in Linz. He met with Deputy Governor Schlegel, who expressed considerable interest in the activities of the *Orgesch* in Bavaria but registered official disapproval of the *Heimwehr* on his own turf. The next day Krazer consulted Dr. Franz Reisetbauer, a Linz attorney, who claimed to head a local bourgeois *Heimwehr* group. According to Reisetbauer, the home guards were well organized in the eastern districts of Upper Austria but were considerably short of ammunition. Krazer promised help and invited Reisetbauer to meet him on 5 May in Rosenheim near Munich.[8]

Some weeks later, a representative of the legitimist bands in the Mühlviertel also got in touch with Krazer. In return for four thousand rifles, the monarchists offered to place their units under command of the *Orgesch*. Krazer agreed on condition that Clam-Matinic suspend plans for a Danubian Confederation (i.e. a revised Habsburg Empire) until the fight against Bolshevism was won. Otherwise, the lieutenant explained, German National- ist paramilitary groups could not be brought into the fold. Accordingly, an agreement was reached at the end of June, and Bavarian officers were posted to Upper Austria.[9] From the beginning the Reich Germans caused more problems than they solved. They failed to provide promised arms and ammunition; they schemed with the Greater Germans against the legiti- mists; and they trained their formations to support operations in Germany rather than in Upper Austria. Only in the Innviertel next to Bavaria does there seem to have been at least a modicum of cooperation.[10]

With the failure of Charles's attempted restoration in Budapest in March 1921, the monarchist home guards in Upper Austria dissolved almost as rapidly as they had arisen. By July only one significant group under Count Peter Revertera at Helfenberg remained in the province.[11] In Linz itself, meanwhile, Reisetbauer's paramilitary unit kept a shadowy and low profile. Except for the *Frontkämpfervereinigung*, it seems to have been the only rightist paramilitary contingent in the city. On 15 March 1921 a so-called Technical Emergency Auxiliary (*technische Nothilfe*) was established to intervene in strikes on behalf of management.[12] Affiliated with the German Populist Gymnastic Association, this group created a stir in March 1922 when a cache of blackjacks and glass cannisters containing a primitive form of tear gas was uncovered by the Linz Workers' Council.[13] On 19 November the formation made a show of force during a speech in Linz by Chancellor Seipel. In face of massive Socialist resistance and local Christian Social disapproval, however, the Technical Emergency Auxiliary made no more impact in the provincial capital than other *Heimwehr* groups before it.[14]

Between 1921 and 1925 the position of the *Heimwehr* in Upper Austria remained in the words of one historian, "most confused."[15] Generally speaking, the armed adventurers in the province consisted of small separate groups which were at times mutually antagonistic. In 1921, apparently at the behest of *Orka*, thirty-four-year-old Captain Friedrich Mayer was designated head of the Upper Austrian *Heimwehren*. For the next several years he tried to unify and coordinate their activities without success. The legitimist bands resented the interference of the Germans with their pro-Anschluss "radicalism," while the urban middle-class groups could not abide the pro-Habsburg monarchists. Nor in the face of opposition by most Christian Social politicians was it possible to mobilize much popular support. Often homeguard units were founded in a town or village only to dissolve in a month or two. This was not, however, for lack of trying. Impoverished though Austria was, a number of wealthy Upper Austrian estate owners and industrialists made substantial sums of money available to fight the "Marxists." Encouragement also came from Greater German politicians such as Karl Sadleder, former mayor of Linz, Franz Slama, a prominent Wels attorney, and, occasionally, Franz Langoth.[16]

Perhaps the most influential *Heimwehr* advocate in Upper Austria was Princess Franziska Starhemberg. Wife of a local grand seigneur, member of the upper house of the Austrian parliament (*Bundesrat*), and confidant of Ignaz Seipel, she also maintained close contact with the more liberal wing of the provincial Christian Social party. On 18 July 1925 she met with Governor Hauser at her villa in Bad Ischl, and, as she later claimed, convinced the ailing "red prelate" to withdraw his opposition to the home guards.[17] Although it seems unlikely that Hauser actually made such a volte face, a subsequent meeting of right-wing Christian Socials and Greater Germans at the Starhemberg villa two months later did produce a formal agreement on a provincial *Heimwehr* organization.[18] A unified command structure was established under a wealthy farmer and Christian Social politician, Balthasar Gierlinger, with Friedrich Mayer and Franz Slama as deputies.[19] United at long last—at least in theory—the various defense groups in Upper Austria could look forward to more coherent and more coordinated operations.

For the next two years, the *Heimwehr* in Upper Austria did not, however, undergo any marked expansion. Perhaps as many as 8,000 men actually belonged to it, but they appear to have been poorly trained, poorly equipped, and nowhere as powerful as their compatriots in neighboring Styria.[20] Although under the umbrella of the Christian Social movement, the formation was still opposed by most provincial Catholic politicians and dared not venture en masse into Linz or Steyr, where the Social Democrats controlled not only City Hall but, until 1927, the local police and military forces as well.

News of the bloody Viennese riots of 15 July 1927 aroused the full fury of the well-to-do in Linz. Many middle-class groups were incensed that Hauser's successor, Josef Schlegel, cooperated with Socialist leaders as the disturbances spread to Upper Austria in the form of a one-day general strike and the seizure of key roads and intersections by teams of armed workers.[21] Local *Heimwehr* leaders were especially outraged that the Socialists actually extended their control into the countryside and offered the provincial government 20,000 *unarmed* men to break the strike. They also threatened to take action on their own, and in parts of their stronghold in the Mühlviertel they did, in fact, succeed in getting the telephones into operation before the strike was over. In so doing they attracted a great deal of rural support, for the first time enrolling substantial numbers of new recruits. Within seven months ninety-five new detachments were founded in Upper Austria.[22]

The spontaneous counterrevolutionary uprising of many Upper Austrian peasants in the wake of the July days was only one reason for the sudden change of local *Heimwehr* fortunes. The other was the dramatic appearance of Ernst Rüdiger Starhemberg. Descended from the famous Count Rüdiger Starhemberg, who helped save Vienna from the Turks in 1683, Ernst Rüdiger was a born adventurer. Handsome, jovial, plain-spoken, and charismatic, he had served as an officer candidate with the renowned Green Dragoons during World War I. Only nineteen years old at the collapse of the monarchy, he had organized a private guard in early 1919 to protect his father's estate from wandering soldiers and looters. Moving from Linz to Innsbruck, he matriculated at the university, where he spent more time freebooting with the Tyrolean *Heimwehr* than studying. In 1921 he fought with a German Free Corps against Polish irregulars in Upper Silesia. Thereafter, he moved to Munich where he participated in Hitler's Beer Hall putsch and enlisted as a private in the *Reichswehr*. Aristocratic in lineage and deportment—he was a notorious womanizer—Starhemberg was at heart an ethnic German nationalist. He admired Hitler and dreamed of returning Central Europe to a more authoritarian order in which Austrians like himself (and presumably Hitler) would play a leading role.[23]

In 1926 Starhemberg returned from Bavaria to his ancestral home in Upper Austria. Immediately, he became involved with the *Heimwehren* in the countryside north of the Danube. Enlisting as a private, he rose to command the home guards first in Rohrbach, then in the Mühlviertel, and in July 1929 in all Upper Austria. His rapid ascent aroused the jealousy and envy of Balthasar Gierlinger and other provincial chieftains. But as a young seigneur, Starhemberg possessed the confidence, experience, and resources they did not. On the basis of his patrician personality and oratorical skill, for example, he was able to win over a number of peasants to the anti-Marxist cause. More importantly, after the death of his father on 16 November 1927, the playboy fascist inherited a vast fortune to outfit and arm his followers as he chose.[24]

Using the German Free Corps as a model, Starhemberg trained and

equipped eighteen *Jäger* battalions of 550 men each.[25] These were true
military formations consisting usually of unemployed agricultural workers,
adventurers, and a handful of right-wing middle-class youngsters. Dressed
in windbreakers, leather shorts, knee stockings, and Alpine hats, the
Jäger were divided into four rifle companies of 200 men. Detached to each
company was a machine gun unit, a motorized group, and a medical branch.
In the Mühlviertel, according to the testimony of Count Peter Revertera,
there was even "a whole *Jäger* brigade of six battalions, with forty-eight
machine guns, an artillery detachment, and a staff company for special
purposes."[26] Well trained and combat ready, Starhemberg's *Jäger* represented a serious challenge to the democratic order of Upper Austria.

In Linz itself, according to police reports, the *Heimwehr* expanded after
1927 to five companies of roughly three to four hundred rifles each. The
exact strength of the contingents kept shifting, however, so that at one time
only thirty men were counted in one of the municipal companies. Given the
strong position of the Socialists in the town as well as Starhemberg's
preference for rural volunteers, the *Heimwehr* in the provincial capital and
apparently also in Steyr did not amount to much of a paramilitary formation.
It consisted instead of auxiliary organizations, such as a youth group, a
women's association, and a veterans' club. These groups established contact
with the German Nationalist German Gymnastic Association whose members volunteered to combine forces in the event of "Marxist disturbances."[27]
Even so, few German Nationalists actually joined the *Heimwehr* whose
municipal adherents, according to the police, came "almost without exception from the Christian [Social] population."[28]

Exactly what social groups comprised the rank and file of the *Heimwehr* in
Linz is not entirely clear. Many may have been peasants, small holders, or
agricultural laborers as elsewhere in Austria. The fact that Starhemberg's
ticket in the federal elections of 1930 did better on the outskirts of Linz than
in the city or in Upper Austria in general suggests that the immediate
adjacent countryside was a particularly fruitful recruiting ground for the
Heimwehr.[29] As for the middle and upper strata of the movement, most
were, in the tendentious but insightful words of Ernst Fischer, "provincial
lawyers, master butchers, embittered failures, a middle class in which dry
rot had set in."[30] In the suburb of Kleinmünchen, for example, the local
Heimwehr leader was the executive vice president of the woollen mills. His
staff consisted of other company managers and men, who openly sought to
use armed force in intimidating organized labor.[31]

Considering the principal occupations of local *Heimwehr* activists and
politicians (table 17), it is clear that the movement was indeed an extremist
offshoot of the old *Mittelstand*. In Linz, for instance, the *Heimwehr*'s social
profile generally resembled that of the municipal Christian Socials: approximately a fifth were self employed, a third were civil servants, and a tenth

TABLE 17   Principal Occupations of Christian Social and *Heimwehr* Activists, 1927–1931 (percentages)

	Linz CSP (1918–1934)	Linz Heimwehr (1927–1931)	Upper Austrian Heimwehr (1930)	Upper Austrian Heimwehr (1931)
Nobility/Landowner	2.8	2.5	3	—
Farmer/Peasant	16.8	2.5	32	21
Clergy	6.5	—	—	—
Civil Servant/ Public Employee	26.2	29.6	14	24
Professional	5.6	4.9	3	7
Self-employed	21.5	18.5	24	21
Private Employee	4.7	13.5	3	3
Workers:			21	21
Skilled	4.7	2.5	—	—
Unskilled	5.6	4.9	—	—
Apprentice	—	3.7	—	—
Military	0.9	11.1	—	—
Other	4.7	6.3	—	3
(Sample Size)	(107)	(81)	(29)	(29)

SOURCE: AVA Vienna and Botz, "Faschismus und Lohnabhängige in der Ersten Republik" (see note 32, chapter 4).

were manual workers. In contrast to the Christian Social movement, however, there were a disproportionate number of military officers and white collar employees. In the province of Upper Austria, on the other hand, a third of the activists were farmer-peasants, while only 3 percent were salaried employees. Given the natural differences between town and country, it can readily be seen that those individuals and groups leading the *Heimwehr* in Upper Austria constituted the displaced ruling classes of the Habsburg monarchy.[32]

It has often been noted that one of the hallmarks of the *Heimwehr* in interwar Austria was the lack of a coherent ideology.[33] Before the adoption of the fascistic Korneuburg oath in 1930, numerous self-defense bands throughout the land advocated goals ranging all the way from greater local autonomy to a total restructuring of society along corporatist, elitist lines. As a rule, the groups were united only by a strong aversion to democracy and to Marxism. In Upper Austria this lack of a positive ideology proved useful for a while in mobilizing popular support. After the burning of the Palace of Justice, numerous individuals joined self-defense contingents as a kind of

spontaneous gesture of protest. They were supported by the bishop of Linz
and, for some two years, managed to coordinate their activities under the
supervision of previously skeptical Christian Social authorities. The eleva-
tion of Starhemberg to provincial leader in 1929, however, changed things
once again. Within the *Heimwehr* quasi-democratic procedures were abandoned in favor of a hierarchial structure. The change was welcomed by many
local officials who felt it essential to a winning cause, but it was questioned
by others. The German Nationalist *Landbund*, in particular, grew uneasy
with Starhemberg's autocratic ways. More importantly, priests and politicians of the provincial Christian Social movement resented his attempts to
infiltrate Catholic unions. As a result, the Catholic Peoples' Association
broke completely with the *Heimwehr* on 7 September 1929 and reaffirmed
its commitment to democracy.[34]

The *Heimwehr* in Upper Austria thus found itself in an anomalous
position. On the one hand, it was a well-equipped paramilitary formation that
enabled Starhemberg to embark on his reckless career in federal politics. It
was especially strong in the hamlets of the Mühlviertel, where it received
the aid of county lieutenants (*Bezirkshauptmänner*) and rural constabulary.
In Upper Austria as a whole the movement was encouraged by Bishop
Gföllner and the clerical hierarchy. On the other hand, Starhemberg's *Jäger*
did not really enjoy all that much grassroots support. In many parts of the
countryside sizeable numbers of independently armed peasants and farmers
continued to remain aloof as did many clergy, especially those who became
aware of the prince's numerous infidelities. After an initial burst of enthusiasm, they and the Christian Social leadership—albeit for different reasons—turned against the *Heimwehr*.[35] Governor Josef Schlegel, in particular, objected to the movement and categorically rejected Chancellor Seipel's
demands to use the home guards as auxiliary police. "Under no circumstances," the governor repeatedly emphasized, "do I want a civil war."[36]

THE SOCIALIST SCHUTZBUND

The reluctance of the Catholic Peoples' Association to back Starhemberg's
cause was one reason for the *Heimwehr's* failure to win decisive influence in
Linz or its hinterland. Another was the active resistance of the Socialist
militia or Republican Defense Corps as it was called. Immediately after
World War I, the Social Democrats had hoped to create an army of
short-term conscripts as the best means of maintaining their hard-won gains.
Since a conscript army was forbidden by the Treaty of Saint Germain, the
Socialist Party Executive decided in 1923 to establish a paramilitary
formation in hopes of countering the *Heimwehr* and of protecting the labor
movement from Seipel's anti-Marxist coalition government. Exactly how the
new Republican Defense Corps (*Schutzbund*) was to be organized and

deployed or under what circumstances it should act were not matters that at first aroused much concern. Party leaders believed that the formation itself would act as a deterrent and preferred to leave operational details to provincial lieutenants. In Linz the man chosen to do that was Richard Bernaschek.[37]

Bernaschek was a militant shop steward who had once quit his job at the Linz dockyards rather than be bought off by management. As deputy chairman of the Upper Austrian workers' councils he played a key role in representing the demands of nonskilled labor to the Social Democratic leadership during the last outburst of revolutionary violence in early 1920. At that time he also organized a kind of party guard, called the "workers' battalions"; it was to fight black marketeering, to resist threats from armed peasants, and to protect Socialist party meetings.[38]

In founding the Upper Austrian *Schutzbund*, Bernaschek turned predictably to the remnants of the postwar workers' councils. Using the "workers' battalions" as a base, he built up an organization that by 1927 consisted of 6,452 men in thirty-seven localities. With over two thousand men in Linz alone, the Defense Corps was also strong in Steyr and in the coal mining districts of the province. For a while, Bernaschek did not pay much attention to military theory or to Marxist doctrine. He assumed that his forces would be deployed as they were in 1919–20, that is as security for Socialist party meetings or in conjunction with mass demonstrations or a general strike. He therefore showed little concern for the maintenance or use of firearms beyond registering and storing existing war surplus stocks. He placed emphasis instead on physical fitness, discipline, and rapid mobilization. In times of crisis the *Schutzbund* was to occupy factories, municipal institutions, workers' cooperatives, the railways, and other key intersections in town and country. In all cases the Defense Corps was to act in support of the Social Democratic party and to cooperate with the local police.[39]

Until the upsurge of the *Heimwehr* in 1927, Bernaschek's *Schutzbund* devoted most of its energy to organizational matters and occasionally to fighting local bands of Nazis. The "swastika fellows" (described below) were not numerous at that time and consisted primarily of Sudeten German immigrants who played only a marginal role in regional politics. Because they did, however, elicit the sympathy of some employers—notably the management of the Epple and Buxbaum agricultural implements factory in Wels—and of the Association of Manufacturers of Upper Austria and Salzburg,[40] Bernaschek did not hesitate to deploy the *Schutzbund* against them. During the abortive Hitler putsch of November 1923 in neighboring Bavaria, for example, the *Schutzbund* was placed on full alert with the result that several Nazis were roughed up when they tried to disturb the annual Republic Day celebration of 12 November in Linz. Soon after that, club-wielding *Schutzbündler* stormed a Nazi tavern and broke up a small rally.[41]

We have already seen that the turbulence of July 1927 provoked a resurgence of the *Heimwehr* in Upper Austria. For the first time since 1919 Socialist authority faced serious challenges in Linz and Steyr as well as in "Red Vienna." The *Heimwehr* threat coupled with the gradual exclusion of Social Democratic influence from the police and military caused the Party Executive in Vienna to place greater emphasis on its party militia. The Republican Defense Corps was, therefore, reorganized as a uniformed, hierarchical military force, theoretically capable of meeting the *Heimwehr* in open battle. Military advisor General Theodor Körner warned at the time, however, that this was a mistake. It was unrealistic, he argued, to believe that the Defense Corps could ever be a match for the more experienced *Heimwehr* and the increasingly authoritarian police. Worse, the division of political and military functions undercut working class unity and weakened self-reliance.[42] Just how correct Körner was became all too clear in February 1934. But beforehand, in the twilight war of maneuvers, threats, marches, and countermarches that flickered between 1927 and 1933, the militarized *Schutzbund*, in Upper Austria at least, more than held its own against the "military desperadoes" of the radical right.

In Linz the reorganization of the Republican Defense Corps was undertaken as a routine matter. By 1930 Bernaschek could field a highly disciplined formation of forty to fifty thousand men, which in the Upper Austrian capital alone consisted of seven detachments of 7,610 men organized into seventeen platoons possessing eighteen machine guns, seven to eight hundred Mannlicher rifles, and over three hundred Walther pistols.[43] In terms of military experience, weapons, and financial resources the Defense Corps was probably no match for Starhemberg's largely motorised *Jäger*. The Socialists sensed, however, the weaknesses of the *Heimwehr* and remained confident that even in a shooting confrontation their more numerous forces would carry the day. Bernaschek, in particular, never lost sight of the political goal of preserving the democratic order, despite his authoritarian instincts. For that reason he always planned and coordinated operations with Socialist politicians such as Deputy Governor Gruber and Lord Mayor Robert Mehr.[44]

Meanwhile, Starhemberg and the *Heimwehr* sought to provoke the Socialists by means of mass marches through Linz and Steyr so as to reveal the inability of the Social Democrats to protect their followers and of the local authorities to maintain law and order.[45] While this technique worked well in other parts of Austria, inciting violence and fueling rightist demands for the establishment of a more authoritarian system, it generally did not meet with success in Upper Austria. On 14 October 1928, for example, when nearly six thousand uniformed activists paraded through the streets of Linz, they predictably received the acclamation of many noisy burghers, but in the working-class districts of the town they encountered only stony silence. In

Richard Bernaschek's workers-in-arms. The Republican
Defense Corps in Linz. DÖW.

the judgement of Bernaschek and Lord Mayor Robert Mehr such marches posed "no danger for the Republic" in view of Upper Austria's democratic order. The *Schutzbund*, therefore, was not mobilized except to keep its adherents sober and away from the *Heimwehr*. As a consequence, incidents were avoided and the few arrests made for public disorder were of Starhemberg's men, that is of the putative guardians of public morality.[46]

Over the next several years Bernaschek's Defense Corps generally avoided direct confrontation with the *Heimwehr* in Linz and Steyr, though in compliance with orders from the party executive, his men mobilized during all such marches.[47] Accordingly, Starhemberg's feudal army tended to stay away from the Upper Austrian capital in large numbers, although small scale marches and countermarches did become more and more frequent. In 1930 alone they averaged one every other weekend. In almost all cases, however, five to six hundred *Heimwehr* men would assemble in Linz only to proceed from there into the more receptive countryside.[48] Nor was Bernaschek content to keep the *Heimwehr* merely at bay. In a number of instances he personally led the Defense Corps into hostile territory, such as on 20 October 1929 when 2,600 *Schutzbündler* were driven to Starhemberg's estate at Waxenberg. There as Bernaschek's men paraded around the castle, Deputy Governor Josef Gruber, pointedly reminded a group of onlookers that the Mühlviertel could be occupied by the Defense Corps within hours.[49]

While it should not be imagined that Bernaschek's Republican Defense Corps in any way impeded Starhemberg's reckless career on the federal level, by 1931 it was clearly playing a significant role in keeping the *Heimwehr* at bay in Upper Austria. According to police reports, Bernaschek's men kept up relentless pressure by countering *Heimwehr* demonstrations and by harassing or ridiculing individual activists in the streets and taverns of Linz and Steyr. Jeering the *Heimwehr* as "snotty kids," "traitors," or "murderers," they ripped cock feathers from their Alpine hats and tore medals from their tunics. When the "green fascists" tried to fight back or to retaliate, they were usually surrounded by teams of brawny workers who showed great skill in disappearing just before the arrival of the police.[50] Just how little popular support the *Heimwehr* actually enjoyed in Upper Austria was made abundantly clear in the National Assembly elections of November 1930 in which Starhemberg's *Heimatblock* won only 8.2 percent of the provincial vote and 11.5 percent in Linz. Five months later in *Landtag* elections of 19 April 1931 the percentages slipped to 4.1 and 8.1 respectively.[51] As late as February 1932, in fact, the police estimated that *Heimwehr* membership in Linz stood at just over a thousand, while the *Schutzbund* could rely on four times that number backed by 32,000 Social Democratic supporters.[52]

THE NATIONAL SOCIALISTS

The relative failure of the *Heimwehr* to dominate the political life of Linz and its hinterland as it did in neighboring Styria and elsewhere was matched only by the lame and impotent efforts of another local extremist movement, the National Socialists. A party of Sudeten German malcontents, the Nazi party in Hitler's home town, won fewer adherents between 1927 and 1933 than Starhemberg's *Jäger*.

The Nazi party, as is now generally known, originated not in the Weimar Republic but in the Austro-Hungarian monarchy. Founded in 1903 in Bohemia as the German Workers' Party (DAP),[53] it was a *völkisch*, "semifascist" movement[54] of ethnic-German apprentices, journeymen, and laborers. Interested primarily in combatting the competition of "unskilled" Czech workers, the DAP established its own trade unions—especially of railwaymen and white collar employees—and adopted a democratic internal structure. In its early stages the party was not particularly anti-Semitic (by Austrian standards), but during the First World War it became more rabidly *völkisch* and widened its net to attract more middle-class adherents. In August 1918 in Vienna the party changed its name to the German National Socialist Workers' party (DNSAP).[55]

Although the prewar DAP maintained chapters in Vienna, Graz, and Klagenfurt, it was primarily a Bohemian movement. In 1913 a branch was established in Salzburg,[56] but, with the exception of a few itinerant railway men, the DAP was not represented in Linz or Upper Austria at that time. During the desperate summer and autumn of 1918 a number of *völkisch* unionists appeared in Linz and scored some success recruiting women employees of the Titze coffee processing plant and the state tobacco factory. A number of transport workers also were won over.[57] Since the *völkisch* unionists were concerned primarily with job security, it was not until 13 May 1919 that an Upper Austrian branch of the DNSAP was actually organized in Linz. The founder was Alfred Proksch, a Sudeten German accountant with the Austrian railways and a longtime member of the DAP.[58] Initially, the new party attracted little attention in the provincial capital, although on 20 October 1920 a local newspaper did report the arrival in town of "party comrade Adolf Hitler, the leader of the National Socialist German Workers' Party of Bavaria."[59] The following year (13–14 August 1921) an "interstate" meeting of over two hundred National Socialists from German-Austria, Czechoslovakia, and Bavaria convened in Linz. One of the principal speakers was Hitler's Munich associate, Gottfried Feder, who discussed "the Breaking of the Shackles of Interest."[60]

Aside from one or two clashes with local Socialists, the DNSAP aroused little interest in Linz until March 1923. At that time, Alfred Proksch began

TABLE 18   Nazi Party Occupational Composition (percentages)

	Linz, 1923–1930	Linz, 1923–1933	Vienna, 1923–1925	Austria, 1923–1933	Bavaria, 1923
Farmer/Peasant	—	—	—	—	2
Private Employee	24.2	24.7	32	26	24
Civil Servant/					
Public Employee	27.3	30.8	8	9	14.8
Professional	16.7	8.9	—	2	8.4
Self-employed	4.5	5.5	5	8	3.5
Workers:					
Skilled	18.2	13.7	32	32	21.5
Unskilled	—	0.7	1	4	4.5
Apprentice	—	4.8	4	8	1.9
Students	—	2.7	14	9	10.7
Military	9.1	6.8	—	2	—
Other	—	1.4	4	—	8.7
(Sample Size)	(66)	(146)	(73)	(167)	(1,126)

SOURCE: AVA Vienna; BDC Berlin; NRC Suitland, Md.; *Linzer Volksstimme* 1923–1931; Bart and Puffer, *Die Gemeindevertretung der Stadt Linz;* and J. Linz, "Fascism in Sociological Historical Perspective" (see notes 62–64, chapter 4).

publication of a newspaper, the *Linzer Volksstimme,* and entered a slate of candidates in the municipal elections of 26 June 1923. In the balloting of that day his movement won a surprising 7.85 percent of the votes and four seats (out of sixty) on the city council. For the next decade it played a small but active role in Linz municipal politics.[61]

In terms of geographic origin and social composition, the Nazi party in Linz before 1931 was a party of outsiders.[62] One-third of its activists came from Bohemia-Moravia, another third from elsewhere in German-Austria, and only one-fourth from the provincial capital. Of the eleven Nazis to serve as city councillors between 1923 and 1933, five had been born in Bohemia-Moravia, one in Galicia, and only three in or near Linz.[63] Occupationally, most activists were accountants, station masters, or conductors of the Austria federal railroads, officials in the post and telegraph service, soldiers in the local garrison, teachers, or white collar employees. As a group they were clearly middle-class (see table 18).[64]

Few Nazis, however, belonged to the traditional urban bourgeoisie dependent on the ownership of property or the rendering of professional services for a livelihood. Rather, nearly three-fourths of them drew wages or salaries, and at least half received their incomes from the state. The Linz DNSAP, in other words, consisted of recent urban immigrants, and other individuals standing outside the economic life of the city who were not involved with local producing, retailing, or municipal services.[65] The movement, therefore, would have difficulty winning local acceptance, and the other political parties were indeed quick to cast aspersions on its members as "foreign born" or "Bohemian." Perhaps Adolf Eichmann may have had all this in mind years later when he recalled, "the Nazi Party in Linz at that time consisted mainly of frustrated people or half-wits."[66]

Although clearly petite bourgeois in composition, the DNSAP in Linz retained the leftist ideology of the prewar German Workers' Party. With an interest in trade union matters and a commitment to the parliamentary process, it preached a reformist—sometimes radical—program stressing anti-Semitism and social equality. In the municipal campaign of 1923, for instance, the party attacked unearned increment of all kinds. It demanded the confiscation of local war profits and advocated the introduction of capital gains and property taxes, subsidized housing and a general improvement of municipal services in the fields of health, water, and streets. Once in the *Rathaus*, the DNSAP did not hesitate, as we have seen, to vote with the hated Socialist majority to achieve these goals.[67]

The working-class ideology of the Nazi party in Linz should not be regarded as inconsistent with its bourgeois social profile. Not only did a fourth of the Nazis have proletarian origins, but most belonged only marginally to the bourgeoisie. Dependent on salaries and wages, owning little or no property, excluded from the traditional Linz middle class, their self-perception was not yet that of the petite bourgeoisie, that is of a separate group standing between the propertied middle class at the top and the wage earning working class at the bottom. Rather, they sympathized with the proletarians, while at the same time they realized dimly that their interests did not really coincide with those of most manual laborers. This bifurcated consciousness, therefore, helps to explain Nazi contempt for Social Democracy as well as a reluctance to engage in any fundamental criticism of the capitalist system. What they objected to in capitalism, in other words, was its excesses and superficial contradictions such as unearned increment and finance capital.[68]

Although the DNSAP in Linz remained ideologically to the left until 1926, its attempts to win industrial workers to its cause were half-hearted and generally unsuccessful. Some effort was made again in 1923 to mobilize workers in the Titze coffee processing plant and in the Redtenbacher cutlery firm. The party also founded a local chapter of the German Workers' Union (*Deutsche Arbeitergewerkschaft*), a *völkisch* union of private wage earners. But with the exception of about 17 percent of the railwaymen in the city who voted regularly for representatives of the *völkisch* German Transport Union (*Deutsche Verkehrsgewerkschaft*), few workers responded to these organizational activities. In national Chamber of Labor Elections in 1926, for example, only 3.5 percent of the industrial proletariat in Linz indicated affiliation with Nazi unions.

Much more successful were Nazi attempts to organize local white-collar employees (*Angestellten*). Working through the Linz branch of the German Nationalist Association of Commercial Employees (DHV) and the Association of German Women Employees (VdwA), the party by 1926 came to enjoy the support of between 40 and 50 percent of the local white-collar employees. In elections to the Clerks' Medical Cooperative Board (*Leitung des Handlungs-Kranken-Vereins*) on 16 September 1925, for example, 2,825 retail clerks cast their votes for pro-Nazi candidates giving them an absolute majority of 54 percent. Similarly, in Chamber of Labor elections held nine months later, 41 percent of the salaried employees in Linz voted for Nazi unions. Shortly thereafter, on 27 November 1926, National Socialist Josef Renner was elected chairman of the *Angestellten* section of the municipal Chamber of Labor.[69]

Another group from which the Nazi party sought recruits was the Fourth Infantry Brigade of the Federal Army stationed at Linz. Since the Austrian constitution of 1920 permitted soldiers to organize military unions and to engage in political agitation, seven Nazi soldiers under Cadet Leopold Leberbauer on 1 July 1924 were able to found a *völkisch* Soldiers League in the Upper Austrian capital. The group at first attracted the allegiance of over one hundred local servicemen but expanded little thereafter. Even in the early 1930s it did not increase its membership significantly and, in fact, on 15 October 1932 in the last military shop steward elections held in the First Republic it garnered only 13 percent of the votes cast in the Linz barracks.[70]

Although women were banned in 1921 from the party leadership through-out Austria and Germany, they too played a visible role in Nazi affairs in Linz. In municipal and national balloting in 1923 and 1927 and in the provincial election of 1925, they were included on the official slate of candidates. Among them was the particularly outspoken Marie Werbik (1890–1970), a regular columnist of the *Linzer Volksstimme*. She chaired the Upper Austrian "*völkisch* Women and Maidens' Society," and between 1929 and 1931 served as a councillor in City Hall. Although hardly a militant feminist, Werbik constantly demonstrated in her editorials and activities an obdurate refusal to conform to the submissive role demanded at least theoretically by National Socialism. In 1925 she wrote that working women were a necessity in an indebted state like Austria and that professional women in particular had an obligation to enter politics and spread *völkisch* ideas. So outspoken did Marie Werbik become in her belief that women should actively engage in politics that in 1931 she was disciplined and, much against her will, forced to resign her seat on the Linz city council.[71]

In summarizing the social composition, ideology, and support of the early Nazi party in Linz, it is clear that the party was organized and led primarily by middle-class outsiders, most of whom came from Bohemia and had been affiliated with the prewar German Workers' Party. In its propaganda it attacked capitalism, Jews, and Social Democracy, and promised to eradicate class barriers by creating a racial community of Germans. Within Linz it was supported primarily by private and public white-collar employees and by 17 percent of the local railroad workers. The party was in its early stages, therefore, very much a "class party" (though not in the Marxist-Leninist sense)[72] in that it represented almost exclusively the interests of the salaried petite bourgeoisie and was unable for many years to attract other groups of Linz society. Indeed, as late as 1929 only 297 party members were officially registered in Linz and 867 in all Upper Austria.[73]

Despite its populist rhetoric and petite bourgeois constituency, the Nazi party in Linz shared much in common with the more respectable German Nationalist GDVP. Both movements were anti-Marxist, anti-clerical, and anti-Semitic; both preached *völkisch* nationalism, and both drew recruits from the same gymnastic and sports clubs. Yet for many years examples of Greater German-Nazi cooperation in Linz were rare. The Greater Germans shared an ideological affinity with the National Socialists, to be sure, but as men of property and education they were disturbed by the Nazi party's petty bourgeois social composition, its concern for trade union matters, and its fierce independence. Furthermore, as participants in the federal, provincial, and municipal governments of Austria, the Greater Germans had a vested interest in the system and could not quite accept the Nazis' insistence on eliminating it altogether.[74]

By 1924, however, the Greater Germans felt driven into a more radical rightist position. Not only did they suffer from the cumulative effects of popular discontent with the Treaty of Saint Germain, inflation, and declining fortunes at the ballot box, but many saw their careers threatened or ruined by the mass dismissal of civil servants resulting from Seipel's stabilization of the currency. Above all, the appearance of Bernaschek's Republican Defense Corps aroused memories of postwar looting and stirred fears of expropriations of property.[75] Under these circumstances Greater Germans and Nazis occasionally put aside social and factional differences to engage in mutual operations.

One such occasion was a violent anti-Czech demonstration reminiscent of those at the turn of the century. On 29 March 1924 before the provincial theater where Hitler had once swooned to Wagner's *Rienzi*, stormtroopers joined well-dressed youngsters from Linz's respectable gymnastic clubs to protest a celebration honoring the nineteenth-century Czech composer, Bedřich Smetana. One hundred twenty policemen on the scene provided protection for the Czech consul, but they could not prevent a clash with the nearly two thousand demonstrators, many of whom were armed with blackjacks, knives, and clubs. Because several people, including Greater

German city councillor (and former mayor) Karl Sadleder, were injured in the melee, Nazis and Greater Germans on the city council joined forces in charging the Social Democrats with police brutality. They demanded the immediate suspension of the chief of police, the introduction of badge numbers for individual patrolmen, an investigation of the entire force, and, above all, the federalization of the municipal police. What they really hoped to do, of course, was weaken the power of the Social Democrats.[76]

These events notwithstanding, Greater German-Nazi collaboration in Linz was infrequent. The German Nationalists continued to be alienated by the socially unacceptable "swastika fellows," while the Nazis recalled that the issue of cooperation with the GDVP once nearly destroyed Austrian National Socialism altogether. In August 1923 at a heated party congress in Salzburg, representatives of the Munich National Socialists had gained temporary control of the Austrian DNSAP. Anticipating a quick seizure of power in Germany, Hitler and Göring convinced the party to renounce an electoral alliance with the Greater Germans, to abstain from elections and parliamentarianism, and to accept the dictatorial control of Hitler himself. The Salzburg conference coupled with the dismal failure of the Beer Hall putsch three months later split the Austrian Nazis into two factions: one, a splinter group under the former party chairman Dr. Walter Riehl, called itself the German Social Association and favored cooperation with the Greater Germans; the other, comprising a majority of the party, chose as its leader Karl Schulz, a skilled worker pledged to democratic procedures and trade union politics. Adding to the confusion were regional rivalries, particularly between Vienna and the provinces.[77] In Linz, for example, Proksch sympathized with Riehl but in the interests of party unity supported Schulz.[78]

In February 1926 an all-Austrian meeting of 110 National Socialist delegates in Linz led to deeper party fragmentation. A group of impatient stormtroopers, nearly fifteen years younger than the majority rank and file, charged the leadership with corruption and demanded the adoption of the German leadership principle. For the moment, Schulz retained control of the proceedings, but in April at a convention in Vienna the hot heads seceded from the DNSAP altogether and organized the NSDAP (Hitler Movement). After some months of confusion, the factions reassembled at Passau in Germany. There, after a lengthy harangue by Hitler, a majority of the delegates sided with the dissenters and affirmed their loyalty to the German Party. Among them was Alfred Proksch, who signed a declaration of personal allegiance to Hitler.[79] In return, he was promoted from chairman (*Obmann*) to *Gauleiter* of Upper Austria.[80]

Almost immediately Proksch began to steer the Linz party away from its "leftist" position. He secured a provincial party resolution condemning *völkisch* trade union interference in party affairs and demanding total submission to the NSDAP (Hitler Movement). He saw to it that verbal assaults on Jews and Socialists were stepped up, and during municipal elections of April 1927 he joined the Greater Germans and Christian Socials in an anti-Marxist Unity List.[81]

Although Proksch did not ingratiate himself with middle-class voters and failed to strengthen the Nazi cause in Upper Austria, he did succeed in bolstering his own position within the larger NSDAP. On 7 September 1927 his newspaper, the *Linzer Volksstimme*, received Hitler's blessing as the official Austrian Nazi daily. The next year the Linz *Gauleiter* was promoted to business manager of the Austrian party and shortly thereafter to its administrative head (*Geschäftsführender Landesleiter*).[82] As a rather color-less figure without the power to make major political decisions, Proksch aroused the envy and hatred of other provincial leaders who could not comprehend his control of the Austrian NSDAP.[83] In fact, his authority was due primarily to his own business acumen as well as to the financial and administrative incompetence of his competitors in Vienna and Graz. Be-tween 1927 and 1931, according to his own testimony, Proksch was able to liquidate a party debt of 30,000 schillings, while his rivals blustered about leadership but could not even collect dues from their members.[84]

Proksch also aroused the opposition of the stormtroopers (SA) and the Hitler Youth (HJ). Although the Austrian SA (also called the *vaterländischer Schutzbund*) often behaved independently and had spearheaded the revolt against Karl Schulz in 1926, the few stormtroopers in Linz remained under control of Proksch's close friend and fellow city councillor, Andreas Bolek. When Bolek in 1929 became *Gauleiter* of Upper Austria, he was succeeded by another Sudeten German who demanded greater autonomy for the brown battalions. The new leader, Alois Zellner, formed a *fronde* with other stormtroopers and balked at Proksch's orders, objecting to what Zellner called the democratic organization of the party. He repeatedly complained about Proksch's overtures to the Greater Germans and even assailed him for sitting at the same table in the Linz City Hall with Social Democrats.[85]

As for the Hitler Youth, by 1930 it comprised some twenty-four groups in Upper Austria with a membership of over five hundred.[86] Always more independent than other Nazi organizations, the HJ was controlled from Vienna by a certain Rolf West. Like Zellner, he protested Proksch's "bourgeois-democratic" inclinations, by which he meant the *Landesleiter*'s overtures to the more democratic Schulz faction and apparent willingness to compromise on the leadership principle.[87]

Given Proksch's limited powers, the Nazi leadership in Linz was hard put to deal with the SA/HJ resistance. The *Landesleiter* did not have full control over the Austrian party and was expressly forbidden by Hitler from interferring in stormtrooper affairs. Nevertheless, Proksch was able to cope with the challenge by mobilizing the other *Gauleiter* against West and by instituting expulsion proceedings against Zellner in the Nazi party court (USCHLA). Since the court was controlled by Walter Nadler, a Linz attorney personally loyal to Proksch, Zellner was found guilty of insubordination and, after numerous appeals to Munich, expelled in early 1932 from the party.[88]

Having dealt with the internal threat, Proksch turned his full attention to other matters. His primary aim, as he wrote Gregor Strasser in Munich, was to woo the Schulz and Riehl groups back into the party in order to "absorb" them—that is, to consolidate the entire Austrian Nazi movement under his aegis.[89] At the same time he undertook negotiations with Prince Starhemberg and with Dr. Heinrich Steinsky, a prominent Linz *Heimwehr* attorney, in hopes of creating a rightist coalition. The results of the efforts were mixed: Riehl dissolved his German Social Association and joined the Hitler movement, but Schulz and his followers refused to give up their *völkisch* trade unions or to abandon their democratic ways. In addition, neither the *Heimwehr* nor the Greater Germans expressed interest in collaborating with the Nazis in upcoming elections.[90]

Although Proksch demonstrated little of the ruthlessness required of a Nazi leader during his tenure, he did manage to restore a limited measure of unity to the party and to improve its finances considerably. Hitler's movement still remained small in Austria, but by the autumn of 1930 it seemed to face a brighter future. In September the Schober government fell in Vienna, and new federal elections were scheduled for 9 November. In the wake of the Nazi electoral upsurge in Germany, Proksch and his followers entered the campaign with considerable enthusiasm and confidence. In Linz throughout October they held mass meetings in the municipal auditorium (*Volksgartensaal*), in the Hotel Achleitner, and in numerous taverns scattered throughout the city. According to police records, these assemblies were well attended by between seven hundred and a thousand participants. Most of them were federal white-collar employees, but a few came from the city's "better classes," especially "businessmen and officials." Almost all were male. Aside from the usual vitriolic attacks on the Jews, the meetings were marked by speeches of prominent German Nazis such as Gregor Strasser, who spoke on 1 October, Heinrich Himmler (23 October), and Hermann Göring (5 November).[91]

Despite this hard campaigning, the results of the November 1930 elections were disappointing from the Nazi point of view. Throughout Austria the party garnered only 11,638 votes, or a miserable 3 percent of the total; in Linz the figure was 3,418, or 3.8 percent.[92] The balloting clearly indicated that despite the arrival of the Great Depression and the spectacular success of Hitler's party in Germany, the Austrian NSDAP had not expanded from its urban base, had not yet disengaged middle-class voters from the German Nationalist parties or the *Heimwehr*, and had made no inroads in the Social Democratic or Christian Social camps. Above all, the failure revealed the party's shaky organization, it internal squabbling, and its ineffective leadership. Challenges to Proksch's authority now welled up all over the country.[93]

Austrian Nazi leaders were virtually unanimous in their appeals to Munich for new leadership. Even before the November elections, some of them, such as *Gauleiter* Josef Leopold of Lower Austria and Heinrich Suske of Tyrol, had suggested the appointment of a German leader as the best means of resolving the party's divisions.[94] Others, backed by Gregor Strasser and Baldur von Schirach at German party headquarters in Munich favored the brash new *Gauleiter* in Vienna, Alfred Frauenfeld. In March 1931 Schirach took it upon himself to nominate Frauenfeld to Hitler. The Führer, however, reacted with scorn, saying:

> The population of Vienna amounts to some 1,800,000 human beings, of whom only 800,000 [are] German. The rest are Czechs, Jews and Polacks. Even if Frauenfeld succeeds in winning a majority of the 800,000, mastery of Vienna is by no means assured. In this case the conquest of Vienna is simply not possible. The hydrocele [*Wasserkopf*] is to be eliminated only by bringing the provinces with their good racial material into the movement so as to secure foodstuffs. The notion of a headquarters in Linz is therefore correct. If this city can be made into a N[ational] S[ocialist] fortress, more will be done for the conquest of Vienna than winning the majority in Vienna itself.[95]

In favoring his hometown over Vienna Hitler provided a glimpse of Nazi strategy in Austria after 1938, but for the time being, he was too caught up in feverish developments in Germany to intervene any further. Three months later, however, he suddenly "reconfirmed" Proksch as *Landesleiter*, officially established Linz as the seat of the Austrian Nazi party, and appointed Theo Habicht, a former Communist and Nazi Reichstag deputy, State Business Leader (*Landesgeschäftsführer*). (In 1932 the title was raised to Inspector General [*Landesinspekteur*].)[96] The Führer thus ostensibly permitted the Austrian party to retain its autonomy, resolved the leadership problem to the satisfaction of the Austrian *Gauleiter*, and of course strengthened his own control by dispatching Habicht to Linz as his special agent.

In the meantime, these labyrinthine maneuvers and internecine quarrels went scarcely noticed outside the Nazi camp. The Upper Austrian party remained a movement of Sudeten German outsiders and was still not taken seriously by the local population. As late as 1933, in fact, there were only 690 registered members in the entire province.[97] Of much greater concern was the economic distress brought on by the Great Depression.

IMPACT OF THE DEPRESSION

So much has been written about the catastrophic impact of the world economic crisis in strife-torn Central Europe, that little can be added here. Austria suffered from structural economic problems and a high rate of unemployment. Dependent on foreign trade and foreign loans, the country was particularly hard hit by the depression. Between 1929 and 1932 production fell by 39 percent, foreign trade by 47 percent, and wholesale prices by 17 percent. During the same period unemployment—subject to seasonal variations and therefore difficult to plot precisely—rose some 97 percent. By 1933 approximately one-third of the laboring population was out of work. In the words of one authority, "in Austria the industrial depression was more acute and lasted longer than in other countries."[98]

Nevertheless, the *initial* impact of the economic crisis in the Alpine republic was not as devastating as one might conclude. Compared to Germany, the unemployment rate until 1933 was actually lower[99] and the psychological atmosphere much calmer. The normal seasonal fluctuation of employment tended to postpone feelings of desperation and kept alive some hope of economic improvement. Above all, the fact that nearly 90 percent of the Austrian electorate regularly voted and had strong existing party affiliations meant that only a small reservoir of nonvoters existed to be mobilized by extremist movements.[100] While the long-range impact of the Great Depression in Austria was certainly disastrous, its immediate effect was to produce a curious relaxation of political tensions. In the parliamentary elections of 9 November 1930 the Socialists actually increased their share of the vote, while the *Heimwehr* polled only 6 percent and the Nazis less than 3 percent.[101]

In Upper Austria economic conditions were generally better than in other parts of the country. As a region relatively self-sufficient in foodstuffs and not particularly dependent on foreign trade, the province generally experienced lower unemployment than elsewhere (in 1937, 7.13 percent vs. 20.3 percent federally—see table 19).[102] In summer months the rate declined even further as seasonal jobs opened up in fields and forests. For a while, unemployment also remained comparatively steady in Upper Austria. The number of jobless in the province, for example, rose from 44,185 in January 1931 to 44,346 at the beginning of January 1932, an increase of only 0.36 percent; for the same period unemployment in Vienna climbed from 141,667 to 155,164 or 8.69 percent.[103] Under these circumstances, it was not all that clear just how grave economic conditions actually were. At the end of August 1931, in fact, with over 5,000 unemployed in Linz, the police reported a feeling of cautious optimism.[104] Given the moderate political culture of Upper Austria and the willingness of Governor Schlegel to use the prov-

TABLE 19   Registered Unemployed in Linz, Upper Austria, and Austria

a. Linz/Urfahr

	1921	1922	1923	1924	1925	1926	1927
Maxima	1,783	3,077	6,168	7,209	9,268	8,654	9,077
Minima		938	3,322	3,589	6,061	5,483	4,891

	1928*	1929*	1930	1931*	1932*	1933*	1934*
Maxima	9,483	5,374	n.a.	9,398	9,632	10,888	9,285
Minima	3,240	2,906	n.a.	4,569	6,821	7,304	7,406

b. Upper Austria

	1918*	1919*	1920*	1921*	1922*	1923*	1924*
Maxima	7,400	14,060	5,666	2,072	14,132	18,250	19,581
Minima	n.a.	4,960	651	264	932	6,098	5,510

	1925	1926	1927	1928	1929	1930	1931
Maxima	28,905	31,216	31,671	32,088	37,592	39,631	44,446
Minima	11,458	17,341	15,637	12,058	9,756	16,396	21,516
Employed	n.a.	n.a.	n.a.	n.a.	n.a.	n.a.	61,071

	1932	1933	1934	1935	1936	1937	
Maxima	46,297	48,466	42,955	40,161	38,270	37,919	
Minima	29,755	33,695	28,057	23,410	21,300*	19,456	
Employed	49,894	39,496	n.a.	n.a.	n.a.	n.a.	

c. Austria

	1918*	1919*	1920*	1921*	1922*	1923*	1924*
Maxima	46,263	186,030	69,247	16,713	117,144	167,417	125,783
Minima		87,266	14,733	8,709	30,967	75,810	63,556

	1925	1926	1927	1928	1929	1930	1931
Maxima	243,376	250,859	275,984	260,018	275,407	341,073	395,981
Minima	149,415	149,209	153,987	135,609	124,031	179,610	230,766

	1932	1933	1934	1935	1936	1937	
Maxima	449,899	480,063	440,345	424,487	415,863	407,475	
Minima	327,531	307,873	325,547	289,944	303,891	261,840	

*Unemployed receiving assistance

SOURCE: Tweraser, "Der Linzer Gemeinderat, 1914–1934," p. 231; Statistisches Handbuch für die Republik Österreich, vols. 1–18; and others (see note 102, chapter 4).

ince's balanced budget for modest tax credits and the like, radicalism remained at bay.[105]

In February 1932 the local unemployment rate started, however, to accelerate. There were no signs of abating in the spring. Both town and country at last felt the full weight of the world economic crisis and, more particularly, the devasting collapse of the Viennese Credit Anstalt of the year before (11 May 1931). The deterioration of the Austrian banking system thereafter led to the flight of one billion schillings of foreign capital, the devaluation of the currency, the introduction of exchange regulations, and drastic cuts of salaries and wages.[106] In Linz the municipal government for some time managed to find summer jobs for a number of the unemployed or supplemental incomes for others. Between 7 August and 9 September 1931, however, the welfare rolls were slashed 20 percent on orders from Vienna and notice was given of additional cuts in the future.[107] These measures, combined with rising unemployment after the first of the year, severely undermined local morale and set the stage for renewed political unrest.

Not surprisingly, organized labor in Linz was especially hard hit by the depression. Free Trade Union membership fell sharply as members could no longer pay dues (table 16), while active Socialist strength during 1932 declined some 10 to 15 percent.[108] In desperation Linz workingmen increasingly vented their anger at their own Social Democratic leaders. They assailed elected officials such as National Assembly deputy Ernst Koref and Lord Mayor (after 1930) Josef Gruber for cooperating with the establishment in Vienna or for failing to do more to block federal budgetary cuts.[109] In January 1932 the rank and file reacted with particularly bitter scorn to revelations that City Manager Josef Stöger and former Lord Mayor Robert Mehr, both Social Democrats, had renovated their apartments with 20,000 schillings of municipal funds. Although the two men resigned their positions in disgrace, the memory of their behavior continued to rankle the masses who, more and more, questioned the Party Executive's insistence on "iron patience."[110]

Meanwhile, many civil and police officials feared a resurgence of the diminutive Communist Party of Austria (KP). In the early days of the Republic the Communists had stirred up a good deal of trouble in Vienna, Linz, and elsewhere with their "putschist" tactics, only to be neutralized by the left wing of the Social Democrats. In elections the KP normally attracted less than 1 percent of the vote in Austria and only slightly more than that in Linz. As a tiny band of disputatious Viennese intellectuals, the party was further weakened by intraparty purges that eventually led to the triumph of a Stalinist leadership in 1928 under Johann Koplenig.[111] In Upper Austria the KP normally confined its activities to organizing the unemployed in Linz and Steyr or to passing out leaflets against "fascism." On paper it maintained an extensive network of affiliated organizations such as the "Red Auxiliary," the "Antifascist Action Committee," and the "Workers' Guard." But in fact the party had only 309 members in the Upper Austrian capital at the end of 1929.[112]

With the advent of the Great Depression the Communists in Linz redoubled their efforts, so that by July 1930 as many as 800 participants were

TABLE 20   Principal Occupations of Communist Activists in Linz
1929–1933 (percentages)

Nobility	—
Clergy	—
Civil Servant/Public Employee	1.6
Professional (self-employed)	—
Self-employed	4.8
Private Employees	8.1
Workers:	
Skilled	37.1
Unskilled	21.0
Apprentice	22.6
Military	—
Other	4.8
(Sample Size)	(62)

SOURCE: AVA Vienna (see note 117, chapter 4).

attending party meetings.[113] Actual membership remained low, with about 300 adherents in Linz, 120 in Kleinmünchen,[114] and 191 in Steyr.[115] By the end of 1932, according to the police, unfavorable reports from Soviet Russia, constant squabbling with the Central Committee in Vienna, and determined resistance from local Social Democrats combined to induce a slight decline in KP ranks.[116] In short, the great fear of a Communist revival in the midst of economic crisis simply did not materialize.

Who were the Communists in Linz? In one respect they were a genuine proletarian party, much more so than other European Communist parties at this time. Over 80 percent of the known activists were manual workers, primarily unskilled laborers or apprentices (table 20).[117] According to the police, many worked at the dockyards, the state tobacco plant, the post office, and the central railroad station.[118] The chairman of the party, Johann Kerschbauer, was a skilled machinist. Significantly absent were peasants, public officials, intellectuals, merchants, businessmen, and white-collar employees. The party was not particularly a youthful movement, at least compared to the local Nazis, nearly half of whom were in their late twenties or early thirties. By contrast, the Communists were usually in their late thirties or early forties. The most striking aspect of the KP in Linz, however, had little to do with these matters. The party's greatest distinction was that it was a movement of the unemployed. Between 1929 and 1933 nearly half of the KP's activists were on the welfare rolls. They devoted most of their energies to organizing hunger marches or to demanding greater unemployment relief.[119] Aside from their inflammatory rhetoric, they were a rather passive group.

HEIMWEHR COLLAPSE
AND NAZI SURGE

Much as the worsening depression troubled the inhabitants of Linz and Upper Austria, nothing quite so shocked or upset them as an unexpected revival of the *Heimwehr*, punctuated by an attempt in September 1931 to seize power in neighboring Styria.[120] As we have seen, the cockfeather fascists had not had much success in Upper Austria. Outside the rural Mühlviertel their appeal was tempered by internal feuding, by erratic and vague ideology, and, above all, by the resistance of Socialist and Christian Social politicians. Even within the proclerical conservative camp a sufficient number of individuals remained pledged to moderate, democratic values to limit the spread of the fascistic movement. It was thus paradoxical that the leader of the Upper Austrian *Heimwehr*, Prince Starhemberg, came to play such an influential role in Austrian politics. With ties to Chancellor Johannes Schober, to Ignaz Seipel, to Premier Istvan Bethlen of Hungary, and to Benito Mussolini of Italy (from whom he received subsidies), the prince cleverly steered a course between the proclerical and pro-Hitler wings of the *Heimwehr* to emerge as federal leader on 1 September 1930. Several weeks later, he was appointed minister of the interior by Chancellor Carl Vaugoin. As a politician the glamorous Starhemberg turned out, however, to be woefully inept. By participating in the federal cabinet he antagonized those radical *Heimwehr* putschists needed to establish an extraparliamentary regime; by entering a separate slate of candidates in National Assembly elections on 9 November 1930, he infuriated his more moderate backers in the Christian Social and German Nationalist camps. The failure of the prince's candidates to garner more than 6.2 percent of the vote, moreover, demonstrated that the *Heimwehr* was hardly the irresistible force it claimed to be.[121]

Largely as a consequence of Starhemberg's incompetence, the *Heimwehr* fell into disarray all over Austria. Rent by rivalries, fissures, and the lack of a common ideology, the movement could not take advantage of the deepening depression to achieve its authoritarian goals.[122] This was one reason that political passions temporarily cooled in the summer of 1931. In Linz and Upper Austria the results of municipal and provincial elections on 19 April 1931 were particularly discouraging for the *Heimwehr*. Not only did the movement's share of the vote fall substantially from the previous autumn,[123] but the Social Democrats recovered their absolute majority on the Linz city council. In the provincial diet the moderate Christian Socials strengthened their hold by obtaining 52.4 percent of the vote.[124] Under these circumstances, it came as a great shock on 13 September 1931 to learn that armed *Heimwehr* units had occupied the town of Kirchdorf south of Linz. As part of a coup staged by Dr. Walter Pfrimer in Graz and Styria, the contingents planned to arrest Governor Schlegel, to incarcerate local Socialist leaders, and to "march on Vienna."[125]

As events transpired, the ludicrous "Pfrimer putsch" collapsed within twenty-four hours. The principal conspirators were allowed to escape or were treated with kid gloves by sympathetic federal authorities. In Linz Starhemberg was detained with a number of his lieutenants but released after four days. The coup deserved to be forgotten as bad farce. Psychologically, however, it injected a new dose of toxin into Austrian politics, especially in Styria and Upper Austria, where enraged Social Democrats demanded judicial retribution. Even more damaging was the effect on the *Heimwehr* itself. Once again the blustering leaders of Austrofascism were revealed as incompetent or, at the very least, incapable of concerted action. Yearning for disciplined, inspired leadership, many of Starhemberg's followers began gravitating toward the National Socialists.[126] That this was the case was due not simply to the ineptitude of their playboy commander or even to the inconsistencies of the *Heimwehr* movement as a whole. Just as important was the organizational skill of Hitler's new deputy in Austria, Theo Habicht.

Habicht had been posted to Linz in July 1931 as the de facto head of the Austrian Nazi party. Within a matter of months he was able to forge a degree of unity virtually unknown before and to reorganize the party structure along German lines.[127] He divided the central administration (*Landesleitung*) into eight agencies for the determination of economic, agricultural, and labor policy and for the management of party leadership, finance, recruitment, propaganda, and legal affairs. This organization he duplicated in the seven Austrian *Gaue*, 110 *Bezirksleitungen*, and in numerous *Ortsgruppen*, *Sprengl*, and *Zellen* throughout the country. Backed by Hitler, he also moved the central offices of the often rebellious Hitler Youth, Storm Troopers, and SS from Vienna to Linz.[128]

Like Proksch, Habicht aimed at winning the Austrian middle strata to the swastika banner. But instead of continuing Proksch's technique of seeking electoral alliances with the Greater Germans or other bourgeois groups, he set his sights squarely on the disintegrating *Heimwehr*. In August 1931 the State Business Leader ordered his followers to refrain from assailing *Heimwehr* leaders by name in the press or at public meetings but not from criticizing their "wrong policies."[129] Apparently hoping to capture the *Heimwehr*'s German Nationalist wing, Habicht hardly needed to point to the failure of the Pfrimer putsch a month later as an example of ideological incoherence and flaccid organization. On 31 October 1931 the Nazi leader thus concluded a "fighting alliance" with the pro-German, anti-Semitic Styrian *Heimatschutz* in Graz.[130] Although the pact aimed at creating a common front "to radicalize the great mass of the discontented in town and country and to incite them against the government and parliament,"[131] its actual effect was to win large numbers of *Heimwehr* men for the Nazi cause. By year's end, somewhere between 80 and 90 percent of the *völkisch* gymnasts had changed sides and were joining the SA or the SS.[132] More dramatically, on 24 April 1932 in provincial and municipal elections in Lower Austria, Salzburg, and Vienna, Habicht's Nazis won stunning victories largely at the expense of the *Heimwehr*. The fact that nearly 90 percent of the urban Greater Germans also voted National Socialist indicated that Hitler's party at long last was becoming a mass movement in the Austrian Republic.[133]

In Linz and Upper Austria the decline of the *Heimwehr* and the rise of the Nazis was not quite as apparent as elsewhere. Starhemberg's provincial adherents were more legitimist, more pro-Italian, and certainly more rural than the larger Styrian *Heimatschutz*. As we have seen, they tended to represent the interests of the preindustrial old *Mittelstand*, while the Nazis and the Styrian *Heimatschutz* were more secular, more urban, and more modern, constituting two radical shock troops of the industrial new *Mittelstand*. Starhemberg himself had been badly compromised in the Pfrimer putsch and lost face among his rank and file through his blundering and constant equivocation. With ties to Seipel and Mussolini, however, the prince retained considerable independence and elbowroom, so that in November 1931 he was able to break with the Styrian *Heimatschutz* and reassume command of the remaining contingents. What that meant in Upper Austria with its moderate political culture was a slow retreat into the Mühlviertel. There the *Heimwehr* continued to enjoy local support and to wait in comparative solitude for new orders from its reckless commander.

In Linz itself police observers in the winter of 1931–32 reported a decline of the *Heimwehr* followed by a National Socialist groundswell. By April 1932 urban Nazi membership was estimated at 1,100 with a reservoir of 7,000 supporters.[134] In actual fact, fewer than seven hundred members were registered in all Upper Austria, but their fervid propaganda and political agitation conveyed the impression of greater strength than actually existed. On 7–8 November 1931, for example, thirty-seven mass meetings were staged in and around Linz,[135] while in the city hall National Socialist councillors stepped up charges of incompetence and corruption in high places. In January 1932 when Josef Stöger and Robert Mehr, faced censure for financial irregularities, Hitler's representatives had a field day charging the Socialist administration with obstructing justice. Their verbal abuse of Hermann Schneeweiss, the one Jew on the city council, was even more lurid.[136]

After the electoral victories of 24 April 1932 in Lower Austria, Salzburg, and Vienna, the Upper Austrian capital became the scene of a mass propaganda rally similar to the annual party congress in Nuremberg. Convinced that the key to victory in Austria lay in the conquest of the streets,[137] over five thousand Nazis assembled in their Führer's hometown on the weekend of 4–5 June 1932.[138] Under swastika banners four thousand stormtroopers, 343 black-shirted SS, and 627 Hitler Youth, accompanied by six marching bands, paraded through the city to cheer Hermann Göring and former Bavarian *Freikorps* commander, Ritter von Epp. The police confiscated fourteen pistols, sixty-five hunting knives, ten black jacks, seven whips, and three crow bars. Nevertheless, the Nazis proclaimed that the "red dictatorship" had been broken in Linz and joined the dimunitive local wing of the Styrian *Heimatschutz* in calling for new municipal elections.[139] In rejecting that petition Social Democratic Mayor Gruber cleverly took advantage of Nazi racial mythology by emphasizing *Gauleiter* Andreas Bolek's own Silesian background. "Mr. Bolek," Gruber sarcastically observed, "confuses the German city of Linz with some kind of corporate entity in his Polish homeland. One would really like to know how you have the right to speak in the name of the German way of life."[140]

Gruber's stiff resistance throughout 1932 to intense Nazi-*Heimatschutz* pressure for new elections in the face of Hitler's rising fortunes elsewhere in Austria and Germany was only one part of a concerted Social Democratic effort to stem the Nazi tide in Linz and its hinterland. Another part was played by Richard Bernaschek's Republican Defense Corps. Against the brown battalions the Socialist commander deployed his workers-in-arms much as he had against the *Heimwehr*: he mobilized the *Schutzbund* during Nazi rallies, intimidated individual stormtroopers, and regularly patrolled the streets of the Upper Austrian capital,[141] where his men were more than a match for the town's three SA battalions and single SS brigade.[142] Violent clashes were usually avoided, but when they did occur, the workers carried the day. Just a week before the mass rally of 4–5 June 1932, for example, Linz Socialists brashly occupied a Nazi meeting hall just minutes before the arrival of Hitler's uniformed followers. When the police tried to intervene against the "Marxists," fists began to fly. In the ensuing melee three *Schutzbündler* were hurt, but nine Nazis, including future SD security chief Ernst Kaltenbrunner, were sent to the hospital. In the judgement of Inspector General Habicht, National Socialism suffered an embarrassing setback.[143]

Determined working class opposition to the rise of fascism in Upper Austria between 1927 and 1934 was by no means an isolated phenomenon as the record of many bloody clashes between Socialists and rightists throughout Austria at that time makes clear. Unlike their German counterparts, Austrian Social Democrats did not at first shrink from fear of civil war. What was unusual in the case of Linz was that the Socialists were joined in opposition (albeit tacitly) by their Christian Social rivals, and in the autumn of 1932 by their most inveterate foe, Bishop Josef Maria Gföllner.

Linz Nazis welcome Bavarian Freikorps leader Ritter von
Epp, 1932. Standing in the front row center is Epp. Next to
him are Alfred Proksch and Fritz Werbik. In the rear on
the extreme right is the youthful Ernst Kaltenbrunner. DÖW.

    We have already seen that many priests and politicians of the provincial
Christian Social establishment lent their visceral support to the *Heimwehr*
movement after the July riots of 1927 and heartily approved of efforts to
weaken the Socialists. As late as the autumn of 1930 the *Linzer Volksblatt*
applauded a *Heimwehr* march through Steyr as a victory in the "last bulwark
of Marxist terror."[144] The authoritarian behavior of Prince Starhemberg,
however, coupled with his attempts to infiltrate Catholic unions, impelled
the Upper Austrian Peoples' Association to break with the Austrofascists in
September 1929 and to reaffirm its commitment to democracy. Thereafter
the Catholic political establishment in Upper Austria moved increasingly
away from the *Heimwehr*, on 22 February 1931 formally demanding the
withdrawal of all party members from Starhemberg's feudal army.[145]
Possible lingering doubts about the wisdom of that order surely were

dispelled seven months later with the revelation that Governor Schlegel was a chief target for arrest by the Pfrimer putschists.

The flirtation of Bishop Gföllner with the *Heimwehr* lasted much longer than that of most Christian Socials in Upper Austria and, to a degree, never ceased. The authoritarian bishop encouraged the formation of rightist paramilitary contingents long before 1927, sponsored field masses in advance of street battles or marches, and remained close to the Starhemberg family throughout his life. The creation of a *Heimwehr* women's association, however, offended Gföllner. Consequently, he issued guidelines in pastoral letters restricting clerical participation in *Heimwehr* activities and prohibiting the display of political banners or regalia in churches. On 19 September 1932 he publicly forbade priests from supporting either the Styrian *Heimatschutz* or the NSDAP; four months later he issued a blistering pastoral letter denouncing Nazi racial anti-Semitism.[146]

The relative unity of the Social Democrats and the Christian Socials in the face of the Nazi menace was generally consistent with Upper Austria's long tradition of informal, reciprocal cooperation. The spread of fascism to the province was not without impact as it deepened subcultural cleavages, poisoned the political atmosphere—especially in the chambers of the Linz City Hall—and led to the penetration of the German Nationalist *Lager* by the NSDAP. Even so, Socialist and Christian Social elites continued to collaborate against what they perceived as a common danger. As in the days before World War I, they remained committed to moderate democratic values and to consociational procedures. In an hour of extreme crisis they honored Hauser's legacy by providing a sense of regional stability, continuity, and fair play. Elsewhere their Nazi opponents could look back on a year of impressive gains, while in Germany they stood on the very threshold of power. But in Hitler's hometown the brownshirts were no closer to their goal than a decade before. In elections for military shop stewards on 15 October 1932, for example, the National Socialists obtained only 13 percent of the votes cast;[147] two months later their leaders could report no more than 690 party members in all Upper Austria. It is possible, of course, that the NSDAP might have polled substantial votes had parliamentary elections been held in 1932 or 1933, but judging from police reports, a strong majority of the local population still stood firm against the National Socialists.[148] Indeed, police reports from the period take pains to emphasize declining party membership and pending financial bankruptcy.[149] Within just a matter of months, however, events changed dramatically in favor of the Nazis.

THE SECOND NAZI WAVE

In December 1932 news broke of a financial scandal that was tailor-made for Nazi propaganda. Between 1925 and 1928 a Viennese Jewish banker, Hans

Alma, had negotiated $16 million worth of American loans for the Upper Austrian government. Shortly thereafter he moved to New York where he founded his own firm, the Austrian and American Securities Company, illegally using as collateral $2 million worth of Upper Austrian bonds. In the world banking crisis of 1931 Alma's securities scheme collapsed, leaving the Upper Austrian government with $700,000 in immediate short-term debts to various New York and London brokerage houses. It took some time to unravel the full scale of Alma's fraudulent manipulations, but by December 1932 it appeared that the provincial government had lost $5 million or 40 million schillings.[150]

The Alma affair unleashed a torrent of abuse in Linz. In the diet Franz Langoth demanded a vote of no confidence in Christian Social governor Schlegel for his part in negotiating the American loans, while several blocks away in the city hall Nazi councillors assailed what they called the "black bourgeois Alma front for the red counterfeiters of millions." Since Upper Austria's financial woes were clearly the result of proven Jewish fraud, they argued, so the municipal deficit, unemployment, and general economic misery should be attributed not to the depression but to a worldwide Jewish conspiracy. The very fact that the Linz budget with its deficit and large outlays for relief was the work of Hermann Schneeweiss, a Jew, offered, they claimed, the indisputable proof.[151]

Much more ominous for the political life of Linz than the Alma affair was Hitler's appointment as German chancellor on 30 January 1933, followed by Reichstag elections five weeks later. Overnight, personalities long regarded as crackpots or outsiders became important people. Alfred Proksch, for example, received a personal invitation from Hitler to attend the festive opening of the new Reichstag on 21 March at the Garrison Church in Potsdam, while Theo Habicht, as inspector general of the Austrian NSDAP, became a sort of second German ambassador to Austria. Constantly moving back and forth between Linz, Vienna, and Berlin, Habicht conveyed the impression that the formation of a National Socialist government in Vienna was simply a matter of time. In the face of such activity, as well as growing German pressure and declining economic conditions in Austria, grassroots resistance, such as existed in Linz, now appeared futile.[152]

Of the three major political groups in Linz, the most susceptible to Nazi propaganda was the German Nationalist bourgeoisie. By 1931 their share of the municipal vote still stood at between 22 and 25 percent, but instead of uniting in one party, the GDVP, their loyalties were split among four mutually contentious factions: the urban GDVP, the rural *Landbund*, the pro-Nazi Styrian *Heimatschutz*, and to a lesser extent the NSDAP.

In the winter of 1932–33 many Greater Germans began to pay more serious attention to the National Socialists. Long attracted by Nazi anti-Semitism, anticlericalism, and *völkisch* chauvinism, the respectable Greater

German elite in Linz for years could not stomach the anticapitalist rhetoric and seemingly plebeian quality of the Nazi party. Now with the GDVP's disintegrating political fortunes and Hitler's rise to power in Germany, the Nazis suddenly became a viable alternative to the moribund bourgeois parties. Above all, the NSDAP was seen as the one group capable of realizing the cherished German Nationalist dream of Anschluss with Germany.[153]

Ideological questions aside, the Nazi party was certainly more socially acceptable than it had been in the previous decade. Of 84 individuals who joined the NSDAP in Linz between 1931 and 1933, for instance, nearly half (43 percent) were engineers, lawyers, pharmacists, bankers, manufacturers, skilled workers, or shopkeepers—that is, members of the professional and entrepreneurial middle class. Before 1931, it will be recalled, only 21.5 percent of the Linz NSDAP belonged to this category. Similarly, the percentage of those dependent on wages or salaries for a livelihood declined from 72 to 49 percent, while those receiving income from the state as public officials and white-collar employees, teachers, soldiers, policemen, and the like now constituted only 31 percent of the new converts (compared to 49 percent in the 1920s). Occupationally, then, the municipal NSDAP was more closely attuned to Linz's property-owning classes than before.[154]

To what extent the Nazis in Linz succeeded in winning the respectable bourgeoisie to their cause cannot be, in the absence of municipal, provincial, or federal election statistics, determined with precision. The evidence available suggests however that, as in other parts of Austria, the incursion into the German Nationalist camp was considerable. As early as July 1932 all five members of the local branch of the Styrian *Heimatschutz* and one Greater German councillor in the *Rathaus* were voting regularly with the Nazis. Led by Dr. Heinrich Steinsky, a prominent Linz attorney and head of the municipal *Heimwehr*, the rightists broke with Starhemberg and agreed to the formation of a so-called National Socialist *Gemeinderatsfrak-tion*.[155] With the revelations of the Alma affair, growing municipal debts, and the Nazi seizure of power in Germany, cooperation between Greater Germans and Nazis became closer and more frequent. Throughout December and January both groups joined forces in attacking the provincial government over the Alma affair; on 2 March 1933 they held Anschluss rallies simultaneously in Linz and Wels; and on 15 May they negotiated a federal political alliance calling for new elections and mutual parliamentary cooperation.[156]

No doubt many Greater Germans hoped to strengthen the Styrian *Heimatschutz*, the GDVP or the *Landbund*, or otherwise to use the Nazis for their own ends. The actual result of their activities was the defection of their most prominent leaders to the Nazis. Franz Slama, a Greater German attorney in Wels and former federal minister of justice, pledged his allegiance to Hitler's cause on 27 March, as did Heinrich Steinsky and most of the *Heimatschutz* a month later.[157] The most important bourgeois politician to become a National Socialist however was the provincial head of the GDVP, Franz Langoth, who apparently joined the party and the SS in March 1933.[158]

The disintegration of the Greater German party and the absorption of its members in Linz by the Nazis was, of course, only part of a similar phenomenon occurring all over Austria. In the Innsbruck municipal elections of 2 April 1933 the NSDAP won 40 percent of the vote almost entirely at the expense of the GDVP. Drawing on this new-won strength, the Austrian Nazis in coordination with Hitler in Berlin demanded new federal elections in the hopes of winning cabinet seats for themselves and of penetrating the Christian Social and legitimist *Heimwehr* camp.[159] Once this was accomplished, they believed it possible to employ tactics used the previous year in Germany and, in their Führer's opinion at least, to establish a Nazi government in Vienna by the end of the summer.[160]

Despite these awesome circumstances, the Austrian federal government, like the city council and provincial diet in Linz, was determined to resist Nazi pressure. Backed by the Roman Catholic church and by much of the Austrian peasantry, Chancellor Engelbert Dollfuss passed a number of repressive measures designed primarily to strengthen his own power at the expense of the Socialists but also to crush the Nazis and preserve Austrian independence. On 4 March 1933 he prorogued the federal parliament, instituted press censorship, forbade political parades and assemblies, and prohibited the wearing of uniforms by political paramilitary groups. The Nazis responded by a series of riots in Vienna and Graz, while on 26 May, Hitler, seeking to cripple the nearly moribund Austrian economy, proclaimed a thousand mark fee on German tourists visiting Austria. Two weeks later, after an unprecedented wave of Nazi terror, Dollfuss outlawed the NSDAP altogether.[161]

In Linz Nazi violence and brutality was contained not by Dollfuss's repressive measures but once again by local authorities. Here, despite the chancellor's dissolution order, Richard Bernaschek mobilized the Republican *Schutzbund* and began patrolling the streets of the city.[162] In terms of numbers, as we have seen, his formations were more than a match for the town's brownshirts.[163] To be sure, the Nazis might also rely on the bourgeois *Heimatschutz*, but that group was not very large. Furthermore, the one man capable of neutralizing local police forces in a clash with the Nazis, provincial Security Director Franz Langoth, was dismissed from his post by federal authorities in May 1933. Under these circumstances, Linz experienced no street fighting such as occurred in Vienna, Innsbruck, Graz, and other parts of Austria, and the municipal SA and SS confined their activities to passing out pamphlets on street corners, haranguing pedestrians, or other forms of relatively tepid political agitation.[164]

Since Dollfuss's dictatorial measures were directed more against the Social Democrats than the Nazis, the Socialist show of force in Linz and Upper Austria would not have succeeded without the continued resistance to the brownshirts by the Roman Catholic church. On 22 January 1933 Bishop Gföllner issued an angry pastoral letter that had an impact far beyond his diocese. While sophistically holding the Jews responsible for such evils as capitalism, free masonry, socialism, and bolshevism, the letter emphatically drew the line at Nazi *racial* (or biological) anti-Semitism. As parishioners heard that Sunday morning:

> The racial materialism of the NSDAP, the "blood myth" that places exclusive emphasis on physical peculiarities, is colossal racial madness. Miscegenation is not the fall of man nor a sign against blood and race. The National Socialist notion of race is totally incompatible with Christianity and must therefore be rejected categorically. Racial anti-Semitism is also inhuman and un-Christian. The Catholic Church has always prayed for the Jewish people, who until Jesus were the bearers of divine revelation. The Holy See disapproves of anti-Semitism as hatred of the Chosen People.[165]

Although the Socialist *Tagblatt* sardonically chortled that Gföllner's pronouncement reassured the faithful that they could remain anti-Semites without becoming Nazis,[166] the bishop's letter was widely read and caused considerable consternation among Hitler's followers. Numerous public meetings were thus held in Linz on the topic "Can a Catholic also be a National Socialist?"[167] Just when these meetings seemed to be having some effect, a group of Nazi rowdies provoked an even greater stir on Maundy Thursday 1933 by posting a crude drawing on the walls of the Catholic publishing house in Linz. The drawing was of Jesus hanging from a Swastika with the scurrilous inscription:

> Once taken from Jewish hands
> To be crucified by Aryan Romans
> The Savior has now fallen prey to Hitler.
> On a hooked cross we are hanging Christ.
>
> Heil Hitler!
> Death to the Jew Christ![168]

So great was public outrage at this blasphemous—albeit harmless—act, that the German consul in Linz reported a new surge of support for the Catholic cause in Upper Austria. More importantly, the provincial Christian Social establishment publicly refused to back the Dollfuss government's plans for an anti-Marxist coalition. Instead, the Catholic Peoples' Association and its organ the *Linzer Volksblatt* concentrated their venom against the Nazis, resolving that "for the Catholic People's Association there is no cause to depart from its absolutely negative view of National Socialism for religious, cultural, and patriotic reasons."[169] The provincial Christian Social party, in other words, maintained its tacit alliance with the Social Democrats, putting up, in the judgement of the German consul, a formidable roadblock to the further development of Nazism in the region.[170]

The initial failure of fascism to strike deep roots in Linz and Upper Austria, it must be admitted, was of little consequence for the future. What happened in the region could not keep Dollfuss from his repressive policies nor Hitler from his aggressive plans. The record of that failure, however, provides a rare example of a political culture in Central Europe that actually withstood fascist pressure and infiltration, first by the *Heimwehr* and then by the Nazis. At the time of Hitler's appointment as German chancellor in 1933, Starhemberg's *Heimwehr* stood in disarray north of the Danube, while the Nazis had yet to make a breakthrough in the towns and villages of Upper Austria. In Linz, unlike other major Austrian cities including "Red Vienna," Hitler's minions could claim little substantial progress toward the realization of their goals.

For this state of affairs both fascist groups were partially to blame, since for many years incompetent leadership and internal squabbling prevented them from winning a wide following. It is difficult to disagree with F.L. Carsten's assessment that "the story of the Austrian fascist movement is really a story of their failure to achieve power by their own efforts."[171] Nevertheless, it would be a mistake to attribute the failure of the *Heimwehr* and the Nazis in Upper Austria solely to their own ineptitude. The extremist movements foundered because they met opposition from the Social Democrats, the Catholic People's Association, and the Roman Catholic hierarchy. It is true that the *Heimwehr* appealed to segments of the Catholic population, including for some time the bishop of Linz, but the rightist movement never won the support of the local Christian Social establishment. After some hesitation and equivocation, the Catholic People's Association disavowed it altogether. As for the National Socialists, they succeeded in capturing the German Nationalist *Lager* but were unable to expand their base beyond that, encountering instead stiff resistance from organized labor as well as from the provincial peasantry, the Catholic People's Association, and the higher clergy. In contrast to Vienna and Salzburg, Hitler's movement won few followers in Linz among the Christian Social electorate.

That fascism faltered in Upper Austria was, finally, due in some measure to the moderate political culture of the region. So long as Social Democratic and Christian Social notables continued to follow consociational procedures in the Upper Austrian diet and the Linz City Hall, extended political fragmentation and radicalization could not occur. Eventually, their elite cartel was shattered during the slow motion crisis of 1932–34 as the moderate Christian Socials were driven from office and the Social Democrats crushed in the Austrian Civil War. Conditions were then completed in Linz and its hinterland for fascism to take root and to flourish, so that within four short years Hitler's hometown would become a stronghold of his movement.

FIVE

Crisis and Civil War
1932–1934

While the moderate institutions of Linz and Upper Austria held firm against the onslaught of disloyal opposition forces, those of the larger Austrian polity did not. Beginning in 1927 the balance of power in Vienna shifted to the right as Seipel's proclerical conservatives secured control of the military and police, and openly encouraged the extralegal behavior of the *Heimwehr*. Three years later the minority government of Carl Vaugoin arbitrarily curtailed parliamentary control of the army, ended Socialist influence in the railways, and placed restrictions on the press. Although substantial numbers of peasants, craftsmen, and lower clergy within the Christian Social *Lager* disapproved these antidemocratic measures and opposed collaboration with the *Heimwehr*, the rank and file of the Catholic party generally supported the movement for the establishment of an authoritarian order in Austria. In the meantime, the Social Democrats looked on in paralysis. Unwilling to use force, they could delay but not prevent their opponents from exploiting the insoluble problems of national identity and economic hardship to narrow the arena of debate, to undermine the rule of law, and to transfer state authority to bureaucratic structures not dependent on the electorate.[1]

The breakdown of democracy in Austria was a gradual process, but the establishment of a bureaucratic authoritarian regime occurred in little over six months. In October 1932 the government of Chancellor Engelbert Dollfuss, in alliance with the *Heimwehr*, initiated a series of random measures seeking to strengthen its own power at the expense of parliament. On 1 October Minister of Justice Kurt Schuschnigg issued a decree under the War Economy Emergency Act of 1917 attaching the personal assets of the Credit Anstalt bank and ordering other disclosures. Although the action required parliamentary approval, the cabinet managed to ignore protests in the National Assembly. On 19 October, Dollfuss appointed the ruthless *Heimwehr* leader Emil Fey, state secretary of public security. The new security chief one-sidedly used his power to prohibit public meetings and to set up arms searches in workers' cooperatives, public housing projects, and other Social Democratic strongholds. On 1 March 1933 the Dollfuss regime

112

violated the constitution by arresting striking railway workers and instituting disciplinary proceedings against them.

Three days later, the National Assembly met to deal with the incipient constitutional crisis. Unable to reach agreement, the three parliamentary presidents resigned their positions, two of them in order to vote against the government. Dollfuss responded not with his resignation but with a proclamation that the parliament had "committed suicide." He then prorogued the National Assembly and fell back on the War Economy Emergency Act to legislate by decree. Thereafter, the diminutive chancellor ordered the police to bar access to the parliament building, instituted press censorship, prohibited political parades and assemblies, suspended the Constitutional Court, and proclaimed his intention of creating a Christian Corporative state. On 18–19 August 1933 he won foreign support for his quasi dictatorship by meeting Benito Mussolini at Riccone in Italy.[2]

The breakdown of representative government in Austria paralleled the collapse of democracy in Germany. In both countries a small group of traditional conservatives took advantage of the Great Depression and widespread fear of Marxism to topple a seemingly incompetent pluralistic order.[3] In both cases they were aided by powerful fascist movements that had already undermined democratic values, incited violence, and radicalized society. In both instances traditional conservatives tried to harness fascist energies for their own ends. In Austria, unlike Germany, however, no transfer of power to the fascists took place, partly because the Austrofascists—whether *Heimwehr* or Nazi—could not appeal to nationalist ideology as an integrating, galvanizing force and partly because Dollfuss for some time managed to deflect the ambitions of both his rivals and collaborators. He and his successor, Kurt Schuschnigg, thus succeeded in playing the *Heimwehr* off against the Nazis, in deploying it against the Social Democrats, and eventually in absorbing it into the bureaucratic, absolutist Patriotic Front. In a sense, the two Austrians concluded a process that Hindenburg, Brüning, Papen, and Germany's aristocratic conservatives attempted but could not complete.

THE IMPACT IN LINZ

At first glance, it would seem that the moderate political culture of Upper Austria was ideally suited to resist the usurpation of executive power in Vienna. For years local leaders and institutions had effectively withstood challenges from militant workers' councils, *Heimwehr* freebooters, Nazi rowdies, and proclerical conservatives. The shared experience of that success fostered a sense of confidence among many Social Democrats and some Christian Socials, including Governor Schlegel, so that the establishment of the Dollfuss regime and its violation of states' rights presented a new

challenge to be resisted, if need be by force. It was thus hardly by chance
that the Austrian Civil War erupted not in the highly charged atmosphere of
Vienna but in the streets of moderate Linz. All the same, the Dollfuss
government experienced little real difficulty extending its control to Upper
Austria. For that reason detailed examination of events in Linz and its
hinterland can reveal how such an unpopular dictatorship consolidated its
power outside Vienna with such relative impunity.

Generally speaking, the combination of fascist agitation, economic distress, and Hitler's rise to power in Germany exacerbated tensions in Linz
long before Dollfuss's grasp for extraconstitutional power. As early as 1931
the consociational order in City Hall began to buckle as subcultural
cleavages widened and conflicts *within* the three *Lager* began to intensify.
For the first time since 1925 ideological outbursts impeded the proceedings
of the city council and placed a serious strain on the elite cartel. Gradually,
political leaders lost control of their party organizations, making it increasingly difficult to bargain on basic issues. By 1933 the process of internal
disintegration had proceeded so far that the Greater Germans had lost nearly
all their followers to the National Socialists, the Christian Socials inclined to
heed the authoritarian appeals of the Austrian episcopate, and the Social
Democrats were divided once again between parliamentary moderates and
labor militants. Elites of all three *Lager* remained committed in some
measure to moderate pluralistic values, but isolation from their subcultures
as well as disagreement among themselves made it impossible to pursue
democratic policies, let alone to resist the quasi-legal measures of the
Dollfuss regime.

The first serious fissures in Linz's consociational entablature appeared in
early 1931 during the course of a sectarian dispute between clerical and
anticlerical forces on the city council. Despite the danger posed by the
emergence of fascist movements in Upper Austria, the Social Democrats
could not resist joining the National Socialists in denying a modest Christian
Social request for municipal funds to renovate several local churches. It was
clearly in the interest of the labor movement to be conciliatory at this critical
juncture, but the Social Democratic councillors continued to needle their
Catholic opponents by refusing aid to parochial schools or by combining with
the Greater Germans or Nazis in anticlerical invective.[4] For their part, the
Christian Socials demonstrated greater rhetorical restraint than the Social
Democrats but were themselves not above verbal abuse. After the failure of
the Pfrimer putsch in late 1931, for example, the Catholic *Volksblatt*
fecklessly compared the right-wing revolt to the Palace of Justice affair four
years before. Likening Social Democratic mayor Josef Gruber to Walter
Pfrimer, the newspaper accused the municipal chief executive of links to
"arsonists and plunderers" as well as incitement to riot during the tense July
days of 1927.[5]

Contributing to the deterioration of consensual behavior in Linz was the election in April 1931 of five *Heimwehr* members to the city council. The rightists did not win enough votes to participate on the executive committee, but they and the four National Socialist councillors possessed sufficient strength to disrupt proceedings and debase the general level of debate. Without regard to established procedures, the fascists used their position in City Hall as a propaganda forum to assail the existing order. They regularly interrupted the deliberations of the municipal body with catcalls and anti-Semitic epithets; in July 1932 they demanded the dissolution of city council and the holding of new elections; five months later they took advantage of the Alma scandal, as we have seen, to bring municipal government to a standstill.[6] It is true that the two fascist parties continued to meet stiff opposition from the majority Social Democrats and the Christian Socials, but, with the final desertion of the Greater Germans to the Nazis in May 1933, one of the three pillars supporting the consociational order in Linz had clearly collapsed.

By contrast, divisive behavior did not mar the proceedings of the Upper Austrian government at this time. Neither the *Heimwehr* nor the National Socialists had won a seat in the provincial diet, and Christian Social governor Schlegel continued to seek tripartisan consensus for his policies. When the provincial constitution was revised under federal pressure in 1930, in fact, he had insisted on the retention of Hauser's proportional administrative system and the grant of parliamentary immunity to members of the diet. Resisting antidemocratic tendencies within his own camp, Schlegel persisted in collaborating with both the Social Democrats and the Greater Germans. Nevertheless, when the Upper Austrian diet met to consider Dollfuss's suspension of the National Assembly, the debate revealed bitter and widespread disagreement: the Social Democrats and Greater Germans proposed separate motions of urgency (*Dringlichkeitsantrag*) calling for the resumption of parliamentary business, but the Christian Socials supported the chancellor's measures as "necessary safeguards for the maintenance of calm, order, and peace as well as the preservation of goods and chattels and life and limb of the citizens of our state."[7]

STRAINS IN THE CATHOLIC CAMP

The sudden acceptance of Dollfuss's ordinances by the Catholic Peoples' Association of Upper Austria reflected both a growing susceptibility to authoritarian propaganda and a naive trust in the word of the federal chancellor. Schlegel and the local party leadership had long resisted pressure from within the Christian Social *Lager*—especially on the part of Bishop Gföllner—to abandon democratic institutions in favor of a reactionary, bureaucratic order. In 1931 the governor's chief advisor,

Fr. Josef Pfeneberger, even took issue with the Austrian episcopate, arguing that the bishops' antidemocratic interpretation of the encyclical *Quadragesimo Anno* constituted a deliberate distortion of Pope Pius XI's call for the reorganization of European society along corporate lines.[8] Despite anti-Marxist hostility, the rank and file of the Catholic peasantry also continued to support Schlegel's policies and remained deeply suspicious of the *Heimwehr*. In October 1932 during initial discussions on the use of the War Economy Emergency Act, for example, the president of the Peoples' Association, Josef Aigner, warned Dollfuss that the rural population of Upper Austria would not tolerate the establishment of a Brüning-like dictatorship in Vienna.[9]

But the commitment of the Peoples' Association to democracy was, at best, marginal. Even during the Hauser era relations with the Social Democrats remained strained, being limited primarily to cooperation on a territorial or consociational basis. In Linz and its hinterland a genuine democratic consensus as such did not exist. What Aigner and his associates thus found objectionable in the Dollfuss cabinet was not its intention of excluding the Social Democrats extralegally from power but rather its reliance on the *Heimwehr*. Just how far the Peoples' Association was actually prepared to go in support of Dollfuss was revealed during a critical meeting of the Christian Social parliamentary club that took place in Vienna on 9 March 1933. At that time the chancellor asked the party caucus to agree to censorship of the press, a ban on political demonstrations, and suspension of the National Assembly until the Social Democrats accepted certain constitutional modifications. In response, Schlegel and Aigner expressed minor constitutional and procedural reservations, but readily joined the party caucus in voting assent.[10]

Paradoxically, the decision to support Dollfuss's antiparliamentary course in the interests of party unity had the effect of intensifying fragmentation within the Christian Social movement of Upper Austria. Although Aigner managed to rally considerable numbers of the party faithful to the government's cause, neither he nor Schlegel won the trust of local proclerical conservatives or the Church hierarchy. The party's peasant association (*Bauernbund*) reluctantly endorsed the party line, but more out of admiration of Dollfuss than agreement with his policies.[11] On the other hand, the anti-Marxist consensus among the rank and file of the Catholic movement seems to have hardened to the point of seeking an end to collaborative politics with the Social Democrats altogether.[12] While it would not be correct to say that the initiative now lay with the extremists of the *Lager*, those elites like Schlegel who still hoped to govern with some help from organized labor found themselves stymied. Without control of the party organization, the provincial governor could not enforce the compromises necessary to avoid violence.

THE DISMISSAL OF LANGOTH

By May 1933, the consociational order in Linz and Upper Austria had severely deteriorated. As a consequence, the Dollfuss regime encountered only sporadic, piecemeal opposition as it moved to extend its extraconstitutional authority to the region. An initial foray, however, did bring resistance from an unexpected quarter. In November 1932 Dollfuss had offered Franz Langoth the post of federal minister of public security, clearly seeking the support of an important figure of the German Nationalist *Lager*. Langoth, however, declined, expressing strong disapproval of the federal government's authoritarian behavior. Four months later, moreover, he backed Governor Schlegel in refusing to accept twenty-six hundred *Heimwehr* men as auxiliary police in Upper Austria. Langoth followed the refusal with a proposal prohibiting local *Heimwehr* marches and demonstrations altogether.[13]

These obstructionist tactics infuriated Dollfuss's *Heimwehr* supporters. Starhemberg had long regarded Schlegel with undisguised malevolence, remarking on one occasion that he "would rather die than ask a favor of Mr. Schlegel."[14] Federal Minister of Security Fey was equally contemptuous. Enraged by Langoth's effrontery, he resolved to subordinate all provincial security directors to his office. Because Dollfuss was engaged in negotiations with the National Socialists at that time, however, Fey was not quite in a position to act. Indeed, it was not until the collapse of negotiations in the spring following a renewed wave of Nazi terror and the imposition of Hitler's "thousand-mark blockade" that Fey had an opportunity to exploit Langoth's Nazi sympathies.

On 31 May 1933 Fey wrote Schlegel demanding Langoth's dismissal on the grounds of disloyalty. To Schlegel's credit, he refused to act without consulting the provincial cabinet. Much as he despised National Socialism, he argued that the real issue was not Langoth's involvement with Hitler's movement but rather his continued support of the existing political order in Upper Austria and his refusal to grant the *Heimwehr* special favors. As the Social Democrat Franz Jetzinger concurred, Fey's demand was only a pretext for further unconstitutional behavior. Although backed by his cabinet, Schlegel unfortunately had no choice but to accept Langoth's forced resignation and to assume the portfolio for security himself. This, however, was not enough for Fey: on 21 June 1933 a federal decree placed all provincial peacekeeping forces in Austria under his jurisdiction.[15]

COLLAPSE OF THE CATHOLIC PEOPLE'S ASSOCIATION

The new security director in Upper Austria was a professional soldier, Major Johann Kubena. During his brief tenure in office, 21 June to 22 December

1933, he conducted affairs in a nonideological, businesslike manner. With
Langoth out of the way, however, the Dollfuss regime was free to concentrate its fire more directly on Schlegel and the democratic wing of the
People's Association. This time the attack was led not by the heavy-handed
Heimwehr chief but by the keeper of sacerdotal truth in Upper Austria,
Johannes Maria Gföllner. As we have seen, the inflexible bishop never
accepted the democratic republic. Much as he abhorred National Socialism
or the excesses of the *Heimwehr*, he probably did more than any other figure
in authority to undermine representative government in Upper Austria.
Like most members of the Roman Catholic hierarchy in Italy, Germany, and
Austria, his share of the responsibility for the eventual triumph of fascism
was substantial.

Ever since the collapse of the Habsburg monarchy, Gföllner had been at
loggerheads with the People's Association, and at various times he had tried
to get control of it. So long as Hauser lived, the bishop's often clumsy
attempts met with little success, primarily due to the priest-governor's tight
control of the party organization. After Hauser's death, Gföllner kept a
somewhat lower political profile in his dealings with Schlegel, though he
could not abide the governor's constitutional fastidiousness and his readiness
to cooperate with "atheistic" Social Democrats. The bishop also disapproved
of Schlegel's diocesan clerical advisers, Ernst Hirsch and Josef Pfeneberger.
What the bishop must have found most galling, however, was the People's
Association's lukewarm endorsement of the Dollfuss regime. While he saw
that the provincial party leadership agreed to the chancellor's emergency
ordinances, he knew that Schlegel did so halfheartedly, even recommending
that Dollfuss seek reconciliation with the Social Democrats lest they join the
Nazis in an opposition front.[16]

It is not clear to what extent the bishop of Linz actively connived with the
Dollfuss government, but there can be no doubt that he and the Austrian
episcopate rendered it great service.[17] After the chancellor's ringing con-
demnation of political parties and parliamentarianism on 11 September
1933, the regime and the church hierarchy shared a common interest in
reducing the Christian Social party to a propaganda organ of the Christian
Corporative state. On 3 October Dollfuss skillfully won the support of the
party caucus for the new course, although a minority, including the
authoritarian Vaugoin, opposed him. By late November, however, voices
began to be raised in several western provinces, including Upper Austria,
against dispensing with the party organization.[18] It was at this point that
Gföllner forced a resolution through the Austrian bishops' conference
ordering the resignation of Catholic clergy from the National Assembly, from
provincial parliaments, and from municipal councils.[19] A Christmas pastoral
letter justified the elimination of the clergy from politics as a means of easing
tensions; it also endorsed the Dollfuss dictatorship "with grateful recognition

of the outspoken Christian course which our government charts and holds, and gladly lend it our moral help and support for its Christian efforts."[20]

The barring of priests from public service had a greater impact in Austria than has been commonly recognized. Gföllner's order not only severely crippled the Christian Social coalition by displacing the party bureaucracy, but it enabled the Church hierarchy to reassert the control of Catholic affairs that it had lost to the diocesan clergy nearly a half century before.[21] In provincial diets and municipal chambers the departure of numerous independent-minded priests weakened the hand of moderate Catholic officials while undermining local autonomy. This was especially true in Upper Austria, where the dismissal of Hirsch and Pfeneberger completely isolated Schlegel within his own party. The fact that Gföllner later appointed two other clergymen to Upper Austria's "estates" parliament suggests that disciplinary control lay at the heart of the bishops' decree.[22]

Aside from Schlegel, the most influential Christian Social moderate remaining in Upper Austria was Aigner. As president of the People's Association, Aigner had lent his support to the establishment of a Christian Corporative order; at the meeting of the party caucus on 3 October he even expressed his belief that Dollfuss was fulfilling the wishes of the Holy Father. Nevertheless, Aigner had a long record of opposition to the proclerical conservative wing of the Christian Social *Lager* and had, in fact, threatened at various times before 1931 to withdraw from the national movement. While he supported Dollfuss, he did so conditionally, questioning, for example, the establishment in Upper Austria of the rival government-sponsored Patriotic Front. Under these circumstances it was not unusual that Bishop Gföllner eventually turned his wrath on Aigner. On 8 January 1934 the bishop wrote demanding his immediate resignation as head of the People's Association. Aigner begged for time, as he put it, to consult his conscience and Governor Schlegel. Gföllner responded that the judgement of one's bishop carried more weight than one's conscience or one's ruler. As a good Catholic Aigner had no choice but to yield.[23]

In retrospect, the relative autonomy of the Catholic People's Association of Upper Austria had been maintained in the First Republic so long as the party organization was controlled by the lower clergy. Under Hauser, Binder, and to a lesser extent, Hirsch and Pfeneberger, personal lines of communication always existed to higher apostolic authorities. During the revolution of 1918–19, for example, Hauser regularly solicited the aid of Cardinal Piffl, himself a former diocesan priest, in containing the political ambitions of Bishop Gföllner. As a layman, Schlegel did not have as many ecclesiastical wires to pull. While technically immune to the bishop's blandishments in a way that Hauser was not, he gradually lost control of the Catholic press, the party's associational network, and eventually the People's Association itself. More and more, he was forced to rely on his working relationship with the Social Democrats, an organization which by 1933 was in an increasingly desperate position.

DIVISION AMONG THE SOCIALISTS

Theoretically this should not have been the case. Unlike their German counterparts, the Austrian Social Democrats acknowledged the possible need to use force to preserve their position in state and society. Through their rhetoric, their tightly knit party organization, and their Republican Defense Corps, they actually prepared their followers for armed struggle. At the first breach of the constitution they stood ready, in Otto Bauer's words, "either to defend themselves by force or to be enslaved."[24] In Upper Austria the Social Democrats had generally matched their words with deeds. Tacitly backed by Schlegel's moderate Christian Social establishment, their ragged contingents had helped maintain order during the turmoil of July 1927 and played a key role thereafter in countering the paramilitary operations of the radical right.

In March 1933, with a confidence born of success, many Upper Austrian Social Democrats simply did not shudder at the thought of civil war. To them the struggle would be primarily with the local *Heimwehr* in which the army and police forces would remain neutral—a naive but not entirely illogical assumption in the still unclear situation. When Dollfuss acted to prevent an "unconstitutional" meeting of the National Assembly in Vienna on 15 March, the Republican Defense Corps went on full alert. In the streets and intersections of Linz and Steyr, in the Wolfsegger coal mines, in the smallest villages of Upper Austria, pistols, handgrenades, carbines, and machine guns were readied, trucks assembled, and men sent on patrol. With emotions at a fever pitch, the workers stood fully mobilized to resist the government.[25] Then at the moment of extreme crisis, Otto Bauer balked. Placing his hopes in a peaceful solution, he called off the alert. The Dollfuss government responded not with a gesture of compromise, but with an order for the dissolution of the Republican Defense Corps. Refusing to resist, the Social Democrats forfeited their last chance of saving Austrian democracy.[26]

The failure of the Social Democrats to use force against the Dollfuss regime reopened the rifts in the Austromarxist *Lager*. Overnight the movement was split between parliamentary moderates and labor militants. In Linz as well as Vienna, party leaders recoiled from taking action, partly as a consequence of their deterministic ideology and partly for fear of losing constitutional safeguards still in place. After nearly two decades of parliamentary experience, they misjudged both the historical situation and the determination of their opponents. Like the moderates in the Christian Social camp, the Social Democrats took Dollfuss at his word, mistakenly regarding the suspension of parliamentary government as a heavy-handed method of effecting constitutional change. As a consequence, they did not consider means other than established procedures to bring the chancellor to account or, at the very least, to find a basis for compromise.[27] In Linz during a special session of the city council on 12 May 1933, for example, party spokesman Ernst Koref demonstrated little understanding of the gravity of the crisis. Koref shrewdly argued that Dollfuss's principal goal was the establishment of an anti-Marxist dictatorship, but in the next breath he offered the chancellor support against the National Socialists, expressing the hope that intervention by the federal president would produce a peaceful resolution of the crisis.[28]

In the meantime, the rank and file of the labor movement, especially in Tyrol and Upper Austria, reacted with shock and disbelief. In Linz the commander of the Republican Defense Corps, Richard Bernaschek, could not comprehend the Hamlet-like paralysis of Otto Bauer's Party Executive in the face of relentless pressure from the Dollfuss regime. At a meeting of provincial representatives in Vienna on 16 April 1933, Bernaschek proposed an ultimatum to the federal president. "Behind my recommendation," he emphasized, "stands the iron will to run the risk. Should the opponent not yield, we shall wait no longer."[29] Bernaschek's proposal was rejected, but it reflected the frustrations of many provincial Social Democrats and of his own men. The Upper Austrian leader shared the view of the Socialist left that the Social Democratic party functioned effectively within the parliamentary system only so long as the bourgeoisie could afford to make concessions to organized labor. Since concessions were no longer possible in the depths of the depression, the Party Executive's insistence on preserving the parliamentary party structure made no sense. Rather, the labor movement should revert to something like the workers' councils of the postwar period and use mass force to resist its opponents. Since this strategy, or something like it, had worked in Upper Austria, Bernaschek believed that it might succeed in Austria as a whole. It was thus imperative to define party goals more realistically and to take a stand against the government.[30]

In the eyes of Koref and other Upper Austrian elites, Bernaschek's suggestions smacked of the radicalism of the immediate postwar period. With thousands of unemployed workers spoiling for a fight, the Social Democratic leaders apparently decided to coopt the rank and file by promoting Bernaschek to provincial party secretary.[31] The stubborn labor leader refused, however, to play the role once assigned to Richard Strasser and now to him. Assuming office on 1 July, Bernaschek took personal control of the provincial party apparatus, a move made possible by the inability of parliamentary Social Democrats like Koref to grapple with the quasi-legal behavior of the Dollfuss regime. To what extent Bernaschek acted out of ambition, contempt for wrongheaded policies, genuine concern for his fellow workers, or a whole host of other motives is not clear. He made no secret of his disdain for the members of the national Party Executive, whom he called "brakemen" (*Bremser*).[32] For years he had been exposed to virtually all segments of working-class opinion; in contrast to his comrades in Vienna he was aware of the widespread resentment raging against party leaders for swallowing every abuse. Given the traditional division of political and paramilitary functions as well as Bauer's insistence on waiting for the right moment to resist, Bernaschek realized—as General Körner had warned—that meaningful opposition was becoming increasingly difficult. He also saw that the growing attraction of National Socialism for younger militants further undercut what little Socialist unity remained. Under these circumstances, Bernaschek repeatedly pleaded for a firmer stand against the Dollfuss regime. At the same time, he demanded absolute obedience from his followers in Upper Austria and kept all knowledge of local weapon stores to himself.[33]

REACTION TO RENEWED GOVERNMENT PRESSURE

In the meantime, Dollfuss prepared to renew the offensive against the hard-pressed Social Democrats. In August 1933 he paid a third visit to Mussolini and shortly thereafter proclaimed his intention of creating a "social Christian, German state of Austria on the basis of estates and under strong authoritarian leadership." The announcement was followed by a demand from Starhemberg for the dissolution of Vienna's Social Democratic city government and, soon after that, by the withdrawal of the German Nationalist *Landbund* from the federal cabinet.[34] Confronted with growing government terror and provocation, Social Democratic leaders called two extraordinary conferences in the autumn to formulate strategy and tactics. At the first, held at Salzburg on 15–16 September, western provincial leaders tried to appease Dollfuss by offering aid against the Nazis; at the second, held at Vienna one month later, the Party Executive threatened to take up arms if the government proclaimed a fascist constitution, seized control of the Viennese municipal government, suppressed the trade unions, or dissolved the party.[35]

By defining precisely the conditions under which organized labor would act, Otto Bauer's Party Executive once again handed the initiative to the Dollfuss regime and the *Heimwehr*. Sensing this, Bernaschek demanded at both party conferences a policy of organized resistance that went beyond Austromarxist rhetoric. What he had in mind was not an armed uprising but first and foremost a change in official Socialist policy from one of wait-and-see to massive resistance like that between 1918 and 1920. From his own experience he knew that the *Heimwehr* in Upper Austria rested more on bluster than bullets and that the local Christian Social government of Josef Schlegel remained opposed to it. A political mass strike, therefore, would receive the support of more than the working classes and could be backed up by the underground Republican Defense Corps, whose members had access to weapons and were being kept in a state of readiness through constant meetings and athletic contests.[36]

Bernaschek's insistence on a change in Bauer's policy of waiting for the right occasion to resist the Dollfuss dictatorship struck regular Social Democratic leaders as insubordinate and radical. In December 1933 Ernst Koref intercepted General Theodor Körner in the Social Democratic parliamentary club at Vienna, imploring him to use his authority in the *Schutzbund* to "curb" the Linz commander.[37] Yet stubborn and impetuous as Bernaschek may have been, he was normally not the sort of person to break party ranks and take action on his own. Virtually untrained in political theory, his trade union background made him a practical man, willing to heed orders from above and to execute them without question. Lacking experience in the party bureaucracy, he remained more closely attuned to the working class rank and file than did the Social Democratic leadership in either Linz or Vienna. As such, his reputation as a radical stemmed primarily from his refusal to ignore the demands of his desperate followers for action. Bernaschek simply confronted the party "bosses" with a reality they refused to acknowledge. Among Socialist leaders he was, in the words of Anson Rabinbach, "the only one who faced the inevitability of a final conflict."[38]

THE SITUATION AT NEW YEAR

By the beginning of 1934, the consociational order in Upper Austria lay nearly in ruins. While Schlegel continued to go through the motions of consulting German Nationalist and Social Democratic elites, including Langoth and Bernaschek, the widening fissures within all three *Lager* made it impossible for him and other party leaders to accommodate the conflicting demands of their followers, let alone join in a common effort. Persistent extralegal pressure from Dollfuss and the *Heimwehr* intensified the process of fragmentation, further weakening local institutions and undermining local autonomy. Judging from police reports, much of the local population resented these developments and registered disapproval of neo-absolutist control by refusing to join Dollfuss's Patriotic Front or, in some border areas, by actively supporting the outlawed Nazi party.[39] In Linz, Steyr, and the other industrial regions of the province the working class was especially embittered. Suffering from low wages and high unemployment, many workers, particularly the young and unemployed, urged Social Democratic leaders to take action before it was too late. Among older, regularly employed workers of the stations, shops, and switchyards of the federal railways, however, a more fearful, cautious attitude prevailed.[40] Just as federal authorities hoped, a process of gradual fragmentation was setting in that undermined working-class unity and found expression in the growing rivalry between Bernaschek and the regular party leadership. As provincial Security Director Kubena reported from Linz on 30 December 1933:

> The propaganda activity of the SDP is now being conducted through the distribution of fliers. The party has not declined numerically since early in the year, but it has suffered grievously. It is no longer capable of offensive action, although it may be expected to act passively with strikes and sabotage. Under existing circumstances, such means of resistance should not be underestimated.[41]

The security director's report was received in Vienna during the Christmas Peace, a government-ordered political hiatus that lasted through January. Despite official assurances to the contrary, the armistice heightened public anxiety and gave the Dollfuss regime an uncontested opportunity to whittle away additional constitutional rights. On 8 January 1934 martial law was proclaimed for an indefinite period. Under increasing pressure from Starhemberg, Fey, and Mussolini, Dollfuss resolved to dissolve the political parties and to occupy remaining Social Democratic strongholds in Austria. How much of a specific plan or timetable he had in mind is unclear. What does seem certain is that Fey decided to force the issue by instigating a *Heimwehr* coup in the provinces. On 2 February the Tyrolean *Heimwehr* trooped into Innsbruck and demanded the transformation of the provincial government into an estates system under authoritarian leadership.[42]

HEIMWEHR PUTSCH IN LINZ

Four days later, Prince Starhemberg's Mühlviertel bullyboys marched into Linz with a set of similar demands. A delegation of fifteen *Heimwehr* functionaries under Heinrich Wenninger forced its way into the governor's mansion, insisting with "justified impatience" that "the obstacles blocking the implementation of the chancellor's policies in the province be removed." A "nonpartisan" provincial cabinet composed of members of the *Heimwehr* and Patriotic Front was to be established, the office of security director entrusted to the *Heimwehr*, and government commissioners assigned to the autonomous towns of Linz and Steyr as well as to municipalities where "the administration is endangered politically or economically." In the countryside, county magistrates were to be replaced by *Heimwehr* men and all schools and offices cleansed "of enemies of the state." In an outburst of naked self-interest rare even for fascists, the landowning *Heimwehr* functionaries also demanded the reduction of property taxes, especially those on forests. Their spokesman, Wenninger, reiterated his "discouragement and bitterness" over the slow progress of Dollfuss's "reform program," concluding that the population might otherwise go over to the Nazis.[43]

In his reply, Schlegel coldly told the Austrofascists that he could not give them a definite answer. "I have been elected by the diet," he said, "and have sworn an oath to the federal president. . . . You gentlemen should not expect that I will break an oath." When pressed by Wenninger that such inhibitions could be cast aside during parlous times, Schlegel stated, "a German man does not break his word, certainly not when he has invoked God as his witness."[44]

The next day (7 February 1934) Schlegel consulted his cabinet and made a proposal strikingly similar to that of the militant Bernaschek. Recalling that legal institutions eventually prevailed in the workers' and soldiers' councils of the immediate postwar period, the governor declared: "My conviction is that if we now assume the title of such a council, legal bodies will sooner or later be attracted to it."[45] Without disagreeing, former security director Langoth suggested convening the provincial diet. Backed by a unanimous declaration of support, Schlegel then dismissed the meeting without formulating a precise plan of action.[46]

BERNASCHEK'S REACTION

In the meantime, the Heimwehr's "rolling putsch" was being followed with intense interest by Bernaschek. A good month before, squads of *Heimwehr* men had appeared on the streets of Linz, boasting of a forthcoming coup.[47] That they and the federal government intended to resume a general offensive against the Socialists after the Christmas Peace was no secret. With frenetic energy Bernaschek tried to rally his men for what he believed a final reckoning. On 3–4 February, the weekend that federal *Schutzbund* commanders Alexander Eifler and Rudolf Löw were taken into custody at Vienna, Bernaschek staged forty-eight rallies in Upper Austria, including three in Linz. To his dismay the meetings were attended by dispirited, dejected men who saw little sense in resisting the inevitable. As Bernaschek expressed it in a report to the Party Executive:

> Some comrades do not believe that they have the strength to fight; others have lost the will to resist. Out of protest a not inconsiderable number are formally resigning from the party and joining the KP.[48]

Having filed his report, Bernaschek learned from confidential *Heimwehr* sources that the Tyrolean coup presaged a comprehensive seizure of power in the provinces. The *Heimwehr*'s ultimatum to Schlegel the following day did not, therefore, come as a surprise. On Thursday morning, 8 February, Bernaschek and a delegation of Socialists met with Schlegel. The group included Franz Jetzinger, Ferdinanda Flossmann, and four other prominent members of the provincial party caucus. Bernaschek acted as spokesman. To emphasize the gravity of the situation, the *Schutzbund* commander presented a memorandum to the effect that acceptance of the *Heimwehr* demands would provoke armed Socialist resistance. Although those present, especially Jetzinger, subsequently expressed shock at the actual outbreak of hostilities four days later, Bernaschek made it unmistakably clear on that Thursday morning that he intended to fight. Numbed by years of Austromarxist rhetoric, none of the others took him seriously. As for Schlegel, he thanked the Socialists for their advice and offered assurances of constitutional probity.[49]

In the afternoon Bernaschek solicited the advice of his lieutenants in the underground Republican Defense Corps. After some discussion, they agreed that since the police and executive forces no longer opposed the *Heimwehr*, a mass strike had to be accompanied by armed Socialist resistance. In view of the *Heimwehr*'s reluctance to engage in open battle, violence might, however, be avoided. What was critical was to ascertain if one of the four "occasions" for taking up arms, as defined by the Party Executive in October, had actually arrived. To that end Bernaschek's brother, Ludwig, and a unit commander, Otto Huschka, were dispatched to Vienna. They were to sound out Socialist trustees in shops and factories and to consult Dr. Adolf Schärf and General Theodor Körner.[50]

The two Upper Austrian Socialists spent less than a day in the capital. They readily learned that working-class frustration and rage there were just as great as in Linz and Steyr. The hotheaded Huschka pushed for an immediate showdown but was dissuaded, at least for the moment, by the more sober Körner. Returning to Linz, the two emissaries suggested that the time for armed struggle was not quite at hand. Bernaschek, according to the later testimony of his brother, greeted the news with some relief.[51] That very afternoon, however, he acquired a purloined copy of a directive from the provincial security director's office. The top secret order called for the immediate registration and detention of Upper Austria's leading Socialists. From that moment, Bernaschek believed there was no turning back. He placed his men on alert and ordered his chief subordinates to his headquarters in the Hotel Schiff on the Landstrasse.[52]

On Saturday Bernaschek's preparations were confirmed by a telephone directive from Vienna: "Advanced readiness! Orders imminent!" Throughout the rest of the day and into Sunday morning the Linz command worked feverishly, taking stock of its resources and waiting for final orders. On Sunday unconfirmed reports arrived that the Linz police were deploying in a search for Socialist weapons and that heavily armed *Heimwehr* contingents were encircling Wiener Neustadt south of Vienna. After days of waiting and alerts, the news only heightened the atmosphere of tension and confusion. Most unbearable was the silence of the telephone. Shortly before noon,

Bernaschek consulted his lieutenants. He told them a *Heimwehr* putsch was imminent, if not already under way; he was prepared to take the necessary "countermeasures" but did not want to assume the sole responsibility for starting a civil war.[53] The party "bosses" in Vienna, therefore, should be put on notice and, if possible, prodded into action. Bernaschek then drafted an ultimatum to Bauer warning that

> if tomorrow, Monday, an arms search is started in any of the towns of Upper Austria or if any key men, either of the party or of the *Schutzbund*, are arrested, these acts will be met by armed resistance followed by offensive action.[54]

Bernaschek's ultimatum was more than a call to arms. Through a decade of experience fighting fascism and clerical conservatism on his home turf, the Linz commander believed that he knew when and under what conditions to resist tyranny with armed force. Since large numbers of peasants and ordinary people as well as important Christian Social politicians like Schlegel still refused to countenance the *Heimwehr*, Bernaschek thought that the workers-in-arms might possibly hold their own in an armed confrontation. A hard-bitten militant whose entire life was devoted to the cause of Socialism, he was simply not the sort of man to surrender without a fight.[55]

Yet while Bernaschek did not shy away from armed struggle, the major purpose of his letter was to pry Bauer from the party's bankrupt policies of appeasement. The fact that the Linz commander explained in his note that he intended to plead his case in person to Bauer the next day suggests that he did not expect hostilities to commence when they actually did. In this sense, Bernaschek was neither guilty of igniting an armed insurrection as alleged by the Dollfuss-Schuschnigg regime, nor of behaving in a "stupid and irresponsible" manner as subsequently charged by Otto Bauer.[56] However, in drafting the ultimatum, Bernaschek acted on his own authority. He deliberately neglected Lord Mayor Josef Gruber, then recuperating from major surgery in Vienna, and flagrantly bypassed the provincial party caucus.[57] Bernaschek did contact unit commanders in Linz, Steyr, Vöcklabruck, and Wels; he also penned a postscript explaining his intention of bringing Koref with him to Vienna. Nevertheless, by taking matters into his own hands Bernaschek violated party discipline. In all probability, he regarded the Upper Austrian leadership as too fainthearted and too cautious, thinking that only by one last, desperate gesture could he persuade the Viennese brahmins to reverse course. What remains unexplained is the fact that Bernaschek believed a showdown with the Dollfuss regime and the *Heimwehr* might be postponed until Tuesday or Wednesday.[58] Did he have access to privileged information? Had he not really thought things through? Whatever the reason, his miscalculation was fatal.

CIVIL WAR IN LINZ

Around 5:30 that Sunday afternoon, two emissaries carrying copies of Bernaschek's ultimatum boarded the train for Vienna. One of them was Alois Jalkotzy, a Viennese city councillor who had been in Linz on party business and who, as a moderate, reluctantly agreed to carry Bernaschek's letter to Bauer. At the Hotel Schiff, meanwhile, orders were issued to uncover arms and prepare for action. Most Socialist weapons in Linz and its vicinity had been acquired gradually over the years: some were obtained from war surplus supplies, some bought from peasants, and a few surreptitiously secured from the *Heimwehr*. In one case, three hundred service revolvers were purchased in Germany by Bernaschek himself.[59] Since a police raid in 1930 had netted nine machine guns, 190 rifles, and a number of handgrenades, the Linz commander regularly moved his arsenals from one location to another. In the Hotel Schiff, behind the cinema marquee he hid four machine guns, fifty-three Steyr '95 rifles, 2,300 rounds of ammunition, eighty sticks of dynamite, and a disparate assortment of bayonets, blackjacks, and pistols. Now, in the bitter, cold evening of 11 February 1934, these weapons were fetched and brought into the Dametz Hall of the complex.[60]

Approximately forty men spent the night in the Hotel Schiff. Some were ordnance and intelligence specialists, but most were unemployed workers with little better to do.[61] At 3:30 A.M. the telephone rang in one of the back offices. Otto Huschka picked up the receiver and heard Jalkotzy's voice: "Uncle Otto's and Auntie's condition will be decided tomorrow. The latter says wait. Don't do anything for the time being."[62] A short time later the telephone message was confirmed by the return of Bernaschek's second courier. The two men had not reached Bauer until midnight, when he and his wife arrived home from a Greta Garbo film. Reading the ultimatum, Bauer conceded the imminence of a putsch, but characteristically and angrily claimed that countermeasures had to await a *Heimwehr* razzia in Vienna. Resistance in the provinces was to be postponed at all costs and Bernaschek to report to him personally. In the shabby rooms of the Hotel Schiff Bernaschek accepted the news with bewildered apprehension. Perhaps hoping that the Party Executive was at last ready to hear his case, he retired for two hours of sleep. Rising around 6:00, he allowed the *Schutzbündler* still holding jobs to go to work. As he prepared to receive a consignment of weapons due at any moment, police were spotted in the street below. It was just before 7:00.[63]

Precisely because Bernaschek's security normally was so watertight, he had been under police surveillance for some time. As part of the government's program of accelerated arms searches, the Upper Austrian security director, Baron Hans Hammerstein-Equord, had ordered a raid at a suspected arsenal in the municipal steam baths on 9 February. Because of the Madri Gras season, the search was postponed until Monday morning.[64] Knowledge of this action as well as a directive for his own arrest, of course, had prompted Bernaschek to place his men on armed alert. What the Linz commander did not know was that his telephone was under wiretap. Jalkotzy's call about "Uncle Otto" and "Auntie" was overheard by a telephone girl in the post office. She relayed the message to Hammerstein, and he decided to act.[65] Before daybreak, some twenty-three policemen were rounded up under Chief Commissioner Josef Hofer at police head-quarters in the Mozartstrasse. At 6:45 he left for the Hotel Schiff.[66]

The arrival of the police took Bernaschek and his men by complete surprise. They did not expect a search before 9:00 A.M., that is before regular working hours, and were busy assembling their weapons for deployment elsewhere. No thought had been given to defending the Schiff complex.[67] At the first sight of the police Bernaschek locked himself in his office and grabbed the telephone. In a last act of desperation, he called Governor Schlegel and begged for help. The sleepy but ever decorous governor acknowledged the "gravity of the situation," promising to do what he could. By this time the police had broken into the hotel and were climbing a flight of stairs to Bernaschek's office. Crouched on the floor, the Socialist leader called his contact men in Linz. With security officers beating on his door, he ordered a general strike, the full mobilization of the *Schutzbund*, and the notification of Steyr and Vienna. Immediately after that, the door gave way and Bernaschek was taken prisoner.[68]

In the three-quarters of an hour that elapsed between the arrival of the police and Bernaschek's arrest, the hard-pressed *Schutzbündler* made their way to the central cinema on the top floor of the building and strapped on their guns. The militant Otto Huschka urged them not to give up without a fight before himself disappearing out a side door.[69] By 7:45 a machine gun was fixed in place on a small wooden table with its sights trained on the courtyard below. Seeing Bernaschek being dragged away in handcuffs, a nervous cabinetmaker pulled the trigger. The police returned his fire immediately.[70] Scrambling to take cover, Chief Commissioner Hofer sought to call up reinforcements before the fighting spread elsewhere. Within an hour, however, Austria was engulfed in civil war.

The hostilities that erupted in Linz at dawn on 12 February 1934 bore little resemblance to the sort of confrontation previously imagined by either the authorities or the Republican Defense Corps. With 3,700 officers and men of the Austrian army, nearly 1,000 police, and perhaps as many as 9,000 *Heimwehr* irregulars, the government forces in Upper Austria clearly had the advantage—at least on paper. In terms of leadership, discipline, and equipment, the army's 4th Brigade alone was probably a match for Bernaschek's tattered workers-in-arms. Most military officers, for example, were combat veterans of World War I, with a clearer grasp of strategy and tactics than their Socialist counterparts, who were often former sergeants and corporals. In addition, the military could draw on stocks of howitzers, trench mortars, and armored cars, whereas the *Schutzbund* had only limited supplies of repeating rifles, machine guns, and homemade grenades. Reeling from the effects of the depression, from constant arms searches, and from internal bickering, the debilitated Republican Defense Corps could mobilize no more than 10 or 20 percent of its once-confident rank and file. Yet, on balance, the situation was not all that clear cut. The army had a shortage of troops in Linz and initially faced serious problems transporting men and materiel over the icy roads of Upper Austria. As for the *Heimwehr*, its ranks were so depleted by 1934 that no more than 1,800 men actually took up arms on 12 February. In the one firefight that occurred in Linz between *Heimwehr* and *Schutzbund*, in fact, Bernaschek's men easily carried the day.[71]

Without doubt, the fatal weakness of the Republican Defense Corps in Upper Austria was its lack of a coherent strategic objective. As a good party soldier, Bernaschek never questioned the militarization of the *Schutzbund* after the Palace of Justice affair of 1927, blindly succumbing to Eifler's insistence on "proletarian discipline" and "iron patience." In the twilight war of marches and countermarches lasting from 1927 to 1933, that approach proved highly successful in Upper Austria, primarily because Bernaschek planned and coordinated operations with the provincial party leadership. Despite his authoritarian instincts, moreover, he never lost sight of the political goal of preserving the local democratic order, as his last hopeless call to Governor Schlegel made pathetically clear. Given the refusal of Otto Bauer and the party executive to use armed force in the parliamentary crisis of 1933–34, however, the *Schutzbund* became an army without a general staff—a multitude of angry, confused, and bewildered men. In Linz and its hinterland Bernaschek admittedly managed to preserve the underground Defense Corps as a relatively tight-knit apparatus, perhaps more success-fully than his compatriots elsewhere in Austria. Nevertheless, his exclusive control of Socialist weapons, his reluctance to delegate authority, and his insistence on iron discipline undermined his men's self-reliance and hence their effectiveness as a military formation. While Bernaschek's men may have sensed they were taking up arms on 12 February in defense of something more than their own personal lives, they had little idea of how to proceed once the barricades were in place.

Bernaschek and his subordinates had developed an operational plan for Linz and Upper Austria, but its contours are not entirely clear. Judging from a police report of October 1932, the plan seems to have paralleled the muddled Eifler scheme for the defense of Vienna.[72] In conjunction with a general strike the Linz *Schutzbund* was to mobilize within two hours. Each man was to proceed to a predetermined alarm station with a rucksack and one day's provisions. Once the *Schutzbund* was in control of local factories, housing projects, and communal enterprises, the gas and electricity was to be turned off and economic activity brought to a halt. Patrols of workers were to seal off roads leading into the countryside and presumably to take control of provincial government buildings and installations. Some consideration also was given to seizing the Pfenningberg heights overlooking the working class districts, lest the army use the position to bombard Linz as Windischgrätz had done at Prague in 1848. Aside from a fantastic scheme on the part of a Socialist flying club enthusiast to secure the position by air, the problem seems to have been left unresolved.[73]

While it is not known whether Bernaschek intended to implement this particular operational plan on 12 February, there can be no doubt that he and his men shared Eifler's defensive cast of mind. In contrast to 1927, few contingents were to advance beyond the Socialist strongholds of Linz, Steyr, or the mining districts of Upper Austria. The railroad remained in government hands, and the general strike was a general failure. It is of course possible that the *Schutzbund* would have fought more aggressively had Bernaschek not been captured by the police. Although unlikely, that is a factor which cannot be ignored, especially since three other company commanders, including Otto Huschka, were also taken into custody at the Hotel Schiff. Unled, confused, and lacking a common purpose, the Linz *Schutzbund* went into action under the worst possible circumstances.

Although widespread, the fighting in Linz lasted only one day, with major clashes occurring at the Hotel Schiff, the Jägermayerhof inn adjoining the radio transmitter, the docks and bridges on the Danube, the municipal steam baths, and the working-class district in the eastern part of town.[74] At the Schiff, it will be recalled, the police requested reinforcements the moment they were pinned down by *Schutzbund* machine gunners. Since the entire 4th Brigade of the Linz garrison was already on full alert, help was not long in coming. At 8:45 Major Adolar Schusta arrived with a full company of the 7th Alpine *Jäger* regiment. An experienced combat officer, Schusta realized immediately he was outgunned and called on a machine gun company. Rather than take the Schiff by storm, he deployed his machine guns in the neighboring Commercial Academy and in the baroque steeple of the Carmelite Church across the Landstrasse. Under cover of that fire he led a platoon into the Schiff. The soldiers carefully worked their way into the hotel's kitchen and dining hall. Before they got to the central cinema, however, an army sharpshooter put a bullet through the head of the *Schutzbund*'s key machine gunner, Rudolf Kunst. Thereafter, Socialist morale deteriorated rapidly, and shortly before 11:00 the hapless workers surrendered.[75]

Word of the fighting at the Hotel Schiff spread rapidly, if somewhat unevenly, through Linz. As early as 7:45 A.M., workers were under arms in the Poschauer brewery, the essential services institute, and the general hospital. A group at the hospital, in fact, put up such heavy fire that an army relief column was prevented from reaching the Schiff. By 8:30 Kleinmünchen was also on alert, although very few workers in that industrial suburb seem to have left their jobs. At the steam baths some fifty *Schutzbündler* stood in position before dawn. Smuggling their weapons through a police cordon on a manure wagon, they managed to arm themselves by 9:00 A.M. It was not until two hours later, however, that the siren signaling the general strike was sounded. The man charged with that task worked until 10:00 A.M. at the railway heating plant. Hearing rumours of trouble, he walked to the Chamber of Labor for confirmation. Still hesitant, he did not return to his post and sound the alarm until 11:15.[76]

By way of contrast, the army moved with resolve and dispatch. Even before the incident at the Hotel Schiff, Brigade Commander Wilhelm Zehner had placed his troops on full alert. Notifying the garrisons in Steyr, Wels, Enns, and other towns in Upper Austria, he quickly ascertained that Linz was the main center of hostilities. Even before the situation was entirely clear, he ordered reinforcements from Wels and Enns to converge on the capital.[77]

By noon, fighting was raging through much of Linz. The workers controlled the working-class district between the Landstrasse and the Danube, the dockyards and bridges on the river, some isolated pockets on the edge of town, and virtually all of Urfahr. Had they planned or coordinated their efforts, they might possibly have taken control of the entire city. Lacking an aggressive operational plan with their leaders under arrest, that was, however, impossible. As a matter of fact, no effort was made to block main roads leading out of town or to destroy the railroad tracks. The government forces thus moved supplies from one combat zone to another without serious impediment. Using trench mortars and artillery, they systematically reduced all pockets of resistance within twenty-four hours.[78]

One strategic objective the *Schutzbund* came close to seizing was the radio transmitter near the Jägermayerhof inn on the Freinberg heights. Nearly one hundred workers barricaded themselves in the Jägermayerhof or hid in the nearby woods. The army was able to prevent them from capturing the radio station, but was unable to dislodge them from the inn. With a broad field of fire, the workers beat off several assaults, killing two soldiers and wounding three others. At 1:45 P.M. the army brought up trench mortars, but had a difficult time positioning the weapons in the hilly terrain. Not until 3:30 was the assault resumed. After three more hours of combat, the *Schutzbund* surrendered, although only twenty-six workers actually emerged to stack arms. The rest disappeared in the woods under the cover of night.[79]

Below on the Danube, the *Schutzbund* fortified the dockyards, the steam baths, and the railroad bridge to Urfahr. This was a strong defensive position, but once the army brought up its mortars, the workers were unable to break out of their perimeter or to summon reinforcements from Urfahr. At one point 150 men nearly made it across the bridge, but they were driven back by the military. Toward dusk an artillery barrage brought an end to resistance at the dockyards, while a machine gun assault secured control of both bridgeheads. The steam baths also were captured at this time, although most of the defenders escaped into the darkness, as they had at the Jägermayerhof.[80]

In the eastern part of Linz the *Schutzbund* occupied a complex of buildings that included the general hospital, the Spaten bakery, and the vast Institute of Essential Services. With access to communal trucks and vehicles, the workers were able to transport weapons and supplies to the Dorfhalle on the Franckstrasse and to isolated strongholds in Klein-münchen. In front of this complex, at the intersection of six streets called Zur Eisernen Hand, and at the nearby Diesterweg school they positioned machine gunners and riflemen. So impregnable was the Eiserne Hand position, that it was deliberately bypassed by Major Erich Riva, the soldier charged with "cleansing" Linz. A highly decorated officer with experience in street fighting, Riva avoided exposing his men to fire until two mountain howitzers were rolled into place before the Institute of Essential Services. After a barrage of only fifteen minutes, his *Jäger* broke into the building at 4:00 P.M. They encountered almost no resistance and within a hour secured the complex.[81]

Meanwhile, at the Eiserne Hand strong point, the *Schutzbund* fought more effectively than anywhere else in Linz. Under command of Ferdinand Hüttner, one of Bernaschek's chief associates, the workers for once pursued the sort of tactics that might have led to a favorable outcome. Having served in World War I as an officer, Hüttner appears to have given considerable thought to urban guerilla tactics. Instead of barricading his men behind ramparts or closed doors, he deployed snipers at key intersections and sent patrols along side streets to harass the enemy. Capturing the Wilmhölzestrasse police station just before noon, his men fanned out through the working-class district of town, beseiged a company of *Heimwehr* in the abandoned South Railway Station, and fought a contingent of constable cadets to a standstill. Not until 6:30 P.M. could government forces marshal enough men to mount a counterattack. For another one and one half hours the *Schutzbund* held them off, but as Riva brought his howitzers into action, the workers gradually slipped into the night. When the army captured the Diesterweg school at 10:30, the building was virtually empty.[82]

The fall of the Diesterweg school brought the fighting in Linz to an end, although sporadic firing persisted on the outskirts of town for several days. In other parts of Upper Austria, especially in the mining districts southeast

Arrest of a Socialist worker in Linz during the civil war of
12 February 1934. DÖW.

of Wels, hostilities continued for a week. At Steyr the *Schutzbund* was not able to mobilize until the afternoon of 12 February. By then many Socialist weapons were already in the hands of the police, but the workers were able to take control of the Steyr motor works, blow up a railroad viaduct, and fortify the suburb of Ennsleithen astride a bluff on the other side of the Enns river. The defenders of this mini-Montsegur successfully repelled an attack by the army in late afternoon but failed to maintain contact with *Schutzbund* contingents operating in Steyr itself. Once the army encircled Ennsleithen with artillery, the position was doomed. After nearly four hours of ferocious fighting and the destruction of many buildings the next day, Ennsleithen fell to the government forces at 5:45 P.M.[83]

Ironically, it was in small industrial localities, mining towns, and even rural villages in Upper Austria that *Schutzbund* units fought most effectively. Given the advantages of forested, mountainous terrain, the workers were able to use the sort of hit-and-run tactics that alone assure success in a guerilla conflict. Near Steyrmühl they ripped up the railroad tracks; at Ebensee they took control of the local constabulary; and at Stadl-Paura they occupied the entire town. Again, the lack of a coherent command structure ultimately played into the hands of the government forces, enabling the army to reduce these *Schutzbund* positions one by one. Nevertheless, for nearly a week the workers successfully used their bases to harry military supply lines and to demoralize their opponents.[84] At Holzleithen near Vöcklabruck, moreover, they mounted some of the most ferocious resistance in the entire province. Under Ferdinand Fageth, a close associate of Bernaschek, they seized the Hausruck railroad tunnel and successfully held off wave after wave of elite mountain troops. When the 9th Alpine *Jäger* finally captured Holzleithen using prisoners as hostages, they selected six workers at random and shot them on the spot.[85]

AFTERMATH AND CONCLUSION

The defeat of organized labor in the Austrian Civil War put an end to the moderate political culture of Upper Austria. On the urging of Starhemberg, the Dollfuss regime accused Schlegel of colluding with the Social Democrats and dismissed him from office. The central government then dissolved the Linz city council, prorogued the Upper Austrian diet, and, as elsewhere in Austria, outlawed the Social Democratic party. Since Upper Austria had been the scene of widespread fighting in which twenty-nine people were killed and sixty-four others wounded, the Ministry of Justice convened special courts at Linz to try the defeated workers. In keeping with the uneven quality of justice under the Dollfuss-Schuschnigg regime, the sentences meted out were far from consistent with the charges: two simple workers were hanged; three members of the "Red General Staff," including

Ferdinand Hüttner were sentenced to long prison terms, and roughly one hundred other participants were dispatched to the Wöllersdorf detention camp. In a number of proceedings the *Schutzbündler* were represented by attorneys with close ties to the underground Nazi party. Of those workers not actually placed on trial, many, including 180 Linz railwaymen, were summarily dismissed from their jobs. In the depths of the depression that was a fate only slightly more desirable than imprisonment.[86]

It is perhaps significant that judicial authorities generally ignored the members of the Social Democratic leadership cadre in Upper Austria. Since party chairman Gruber was confined to a hospital bed in Vienna, charges of conspiracy in his case could not have held water. More remarkable was the fact that Richard Bernaschek also avoided trial and punishment. On the night of 2 April 1934, he, Otto Huschka, and Franz Schlagin, commander of the *Schutzbund* forces at the Jägermayerhof, made a spectacular prison escape to Munich. While Bernaschek moved on to the Soviet Union, Huschka and Schlagin remained in the Third Reich. Four years later, clad in the black gabardine of Hitler's dreaded SS, they would return to Linz to settle accounts.[87]

The outbreak of the Austrian Civil War in Linz on 12 February 1934 represented more than a last-ditch act of defiance by Socialist workers. Through armed force Bernaschek and his followers hoped to goad the Social Democratic Party Executive into action and to mobilize widespread popular support against the Dollfuss regime. In this sense, they acted to preserve a system in which they had a very real stake. To what extent their motives reflected purely local conditions cannot be said, but there is no doubt that they considered the democratic achievements of the past quarter century worth defending. To them Hauser's moderate political order gave strength and vitality to the otherwise weak and fragile First Republic.

What transpired in Linz between 1918 and 1934 both reflected and refracted major trends in interwar Austria. As in Vienna and Styria the culture of Upper Austria was highly polarized. The two mass-based parties incessantly engaged in political mobilization and tried to furnish patronage as well. Their leaders took the profession of politics seriously, and like Lueger, Seipel, and Bauer, they rarely refrained from radical rhetoric as a means of galvanizing or disciplining support. In keeping with the Austrian blend of traditional and modern, Christian Social and Social Democratic elites relished the vision of a final confrontation while presiding over movements that were increasingly bureaucratic in nature; despite divergent socioeconomic interests, they clashed more frequently over religion than over the allocation of scarce economic resources. As for the German Nationalists, they persisted as a traditional *Honoratiorenpartei*, and for that reason they fell prey to racialism and eventually to absorption by the National Socialists.

Economically, developments in Linz paralleled those elsewhere in Austria. Despite initial optimism, the town's economy stagnated, remaining dependent on traditional forms of manufacturing and farming. The protectionist legacy of the imperial era then combined with federal policies favoring agriculture to arrest industrial development and modernization. Lacking both a solid economic base and a network of municipal enterprises, the Social Democrats gradually lost influence in an environment that favored the older *Mittelstand* and the wealthy. In the depression, however, the status of the traditional producers also became precarious. Seeing little opportunity of defending their proprietary interests democratically, they accepted the authoritarianism of the Dollfuss regime as a means of disciplining labor and of protecting their position. Significantly, neither the traditional establishment nor the Social Democrats offered accomodation to the rising new *Mittelstand* of private and public employees.

Despite cleavage and polarization, the political culture of Linz and Upper Austria was distinctly less divided and more moderate than that of Vienna and Styria. As in the Second Republic a generation later, elite collusion exerted a soothing effect that limited conflict and created an atmosphere of détente. The relatively low level of regional violence coupled with the general failure of paramilitary politics in the province attests to the success of the system. In this regard, it is ironic that the most modernized of the political parties, the Social Democrats, was also the most militarized. That consociational procedures persisted in Linz until 1933 may be attributed in the final analysis to the sufferance of the Catholic People's Association. While the Catholic party contained many of the same petty bourgeois elements comprising the Christian Social movement in Vienna, the local organization remained firmly in the hands of the lower clergy and the peasants, two groups less hostile to organized labor than the urban *Mittelstand*. What happened in Linz admittedly could not determine the course of events in Vienna, Rome, or Berlin, but the fact that self-government in Upper Austria resided on a religious and agricultural base helps to explain why the provincial order ultimately failed to adjust to the demands of a modern capitalist economy and why in 1934 it collapsed under pressure from the Dollfuss regime.

SIX

Christian Corporative Interlude 1934–1938

On Tuesday, 27 February 1934, thirty-one deputies of the Upper Austrian diet took their seats in the Renaissance state house in which three centuries before the mathematician Johannes Kepler had written his *De Harmonice Mundi*. Where Kepler mistakenly believed he had found escape from the thought control of the Counter-Reformation, the once sanguine deputies sat impassively awaiting the arrival of a new age of intolerance. The day before they had learned of Governor Schlegel's dismissal. Now, in the absence of their Social Democratic colleagues, they solemnly renounced their legislative powers, transferring them to a new provincial government headed by a close associate of Dollfuss. In league with the federal government the new regime hammered out a constitution for Upper Austria based on the principles of *Quadragesimo Anno* and the rule of estates. What emerged was an authoritarian order supported by elements of the Christian Social party, the Roman Catholic hierarchy, and, above all, the old *Mittelstand* of landowners, peasants, and small producers.[1]

In this respect Upper Austria was hardly unique. Between 1934 and 1938 there was an especially close parallel between developments in the province and those on the larger Austrian stage. Investigation of political life in Linz may, therefore, cast light on the Dollfuss-Schuschnigg dictatorship, a regime whose contours in the endless debate on the nature of fascism continue to defy precise determination. Increasingly characterized as "authoritarian" or "bureaucratic-oligarchic," the Christian Corporative order clearly lacked the mass base, pseudorevolutionary elite, and aggressive style normally associated with the fascist systems of interwar Europe. At the same time, the regime was ruthlessly anti-Marxist and openly sought to imitate Mussolini's Italy, especially in the suppression of democratic freedoms and in the establishment of detention camps for political opponents. Delineating the exact boundary lines between authoritarian-bourgeois, fascist, and totalitarian, as Martin Kitchen has recently emphasized, thus remains a formidable task.[2] For this reason examination of the economic and social relations of those wielding power on all levels in Austria is the necessary prerequisite for determining how the system functioned and where it belongs on the political spectrum.[3]

THE POLITICAL INSTITUTIONS IN UPPER AUSTRIA

Generally speaking, the political institutions of Linz and Upper Austria under Christian Corporatism constituted a throwback to the bureaucratic absolutism of the mid-nineteenth century. As in Vienna, government was sustained almost exclusively by the Church, the bureaucracy, and the police. Supported by the remnants of the Christian Social movement, the regime operated on an ad hoc basis with little regard to long-range goals. It depended primarily on the force of tradition without, however, providing a father figure to attract the masses or to resolve their conflicts. Lacking the brutal instincts of contemporary fascist regimes, the Dollfuss-Schuschnigg dictatorship drove its opponents underground without destroying them or winning their loyalty. As a consequence, it stumbled from crisis to crisis until Austria itself was devoured by Hitler's Reich.[4]

Just as regional autonomy had been weakened by the failure of the revolutions of 1848, so was local self-government virtually eradicated in the aftermath of 12 February 1934. According to the Upper Austrian constitution of 9 July 1935 the provincial governor received his appointment from the federal president. The provincial chief executive then named a cabinet from outside the *Landtag* with the approval of the federal chancellor's office. The post of lieutenant governor, so important under Hauser, ceased to exist, reappearing only later in the hands of a *Heimwehr* chieftain as the office of *Landesstatthalter*. In theory, the provincial government was henceforth to work in harmony with the provincial diet, a rather easy matter in light of the severely circumscribed powers of that assembly. Without parliamentary immunity, dietal deputies were to be elected by formal cultural and occupational estates. They could approve or reject legislation but not initiate or amend it. As in the days of neoabsolutism, their acts were subject to veto by the *Ballhausplatz*.[5]

Even more restricted were the rights and privileges of the city of Linz. Administered throughout most of 1934 by a commissioner appointed by federal authorities, the Upper Austrian capital obtained a corporate charter on 9 July 1935. The work of a group of Christian Social and *Heimwehr* dietal deputies, the charter abrogated municipal rights granted in 1862. Unlike the provincial governor, the lord mayor was actually elected by a representative assembly or communal diet (*Gemeindetag*). With an executive committee consisting of a vice-mayor and four elected city councillors, the chief magistrate administered the city—but only at the sufferance of the provincial governor. The governor had the right to veto the election of the mayor and his municipal colleagues as well as to remove them from office. The communal diet (city council), whose deliberations were henceforth closed to the public, was to be composed of members nominated by the cultural and occupational estates of industry, commerce, agriculture, public service, and the free professions. Also without parliamentary immunity, its members—and all municipal officials and employees—were subject to dismissal by the mayor for subversive activities. In addition, individuals imprisoned or confined on political grounds were barred from public office for three years from the time of their release. In keeping with this slap in the face of the defeated Socialists, the poor and the indigent also were barred from political participation.[6]

THE POLITICAL ELITE

It hardly needs to be emphasized that real power in Linz and Upper Austria after February 1934 lay in the hands of the federal chancellor's *missi dominici*. As a rule, these officials were rural conservatives with little understanding of urban industrial society. They were "agrarian technocrats" who, like Dollfuss, had carved out careers in the bureaucratic network spawned by modern commercial farming.[7] The provincial governor, Heinrich Gleissner, had been a minor official in the Upper Austrian Chamber of Agriculture. A member of the conservative wing of the Catholic People's Association, he had served as a combat officer with Dollfuss in World War I. Solely on the basis of his friendship with the chancellor, Gleissner in 1933 became provincial director of the Patriotic Front, the government's organization designed to rally the masses to its cause. After a mere seven weeks in that capacity, he advanced to federal undersecretary of agriculture. At the time of his appointment as Upper Austrian governor in February 1934, Gleissner could fall back on some political experience but was otherwise ill prepared to cope with problems beyond the world of agricultural management and rural banking. His chief lieutenants were equally narrow: Franz Heissler, a retired president of the provincial Chamber of Commerce, Count Peter Revertera, an estate owner and pro-Nazi *Heimwehr* chieftain, and Heinrich Wenninger, a businessman and *Heimwehr* official. Three other members of the provincial cabinet, Anton Gasperschitz, Franz Lorenzi, and Felix Kern, had long been in Christian Social politics, but they too were concerned primarily with agriculture.[8]

As rural conservatives, Gleissner and his associates could hardly be expected to acknowledge the problems of semi-industrial Linz (or Steyr) or to cope with them effectively. That this was also true of the provincial capital's new lord mayor, Wilhelm Bock, was even more lamentable. Bock was a onetime Christian Social youth leader and deputy director of the Upper Austrian Fire Insurance Institute. A man of limited intelligence, he blamed the Jews for Austria's economic, social, and political woes, proposing, for example, the introduction of a numerus clausus in the schools and free professions as a remedy for the ills of the depression. Like other officials of

Christian Corporatism in Upper Austria, 1934–1938. Seated second from left is Governor Heinrich Gleissner. Next to him are Bishop Johannes Maria Gföllner and Lord Mayor Wilhelm Bock. Stadtmuseum Linz.

the Dollfuss-Schuschnigg regime, he was genuinely disliked by a broad strata of the population.[9]

This was hardly unusual. As on the federal level, the laboring population was excluded from nearly all vestiges of power in Linz and its hinterland. Despite the events of 12 February 1934, this group should not theoretically have been since all segments of society were to find representation in the existing Christian Corporative state. Without exception, however, the corporative bodies that came into being in Upper Austria were either controlled by wealthy interest groups or organized from associations that already represented the upper and middle strata of society. The occupational estate of "agriculture and forestry," for example, was the domain of aristocratic estate owners and farmers; that of the "free professions" of local notaries, engineers, pharmacists, physicians, dentists, and underwriters. By the same token, the occupational estate of "industry and mining" was formed from the provincial branch of the Association of Austrian Industrialists; "trade and transportation" from the Association of Merchants and from the Transportation League; "banking, credit, and insurance" from the Association of Finance; and "civil servants" from the provincial Chamber of Civil Servants. An additional body representing labor was never established, although this was required by the federal and provincial constitutions of 1934.[10]

That labor should have been so thoroughly removed from influence in a province where it normally enjoyed the support of one-third of the population was bad enough. That this was the case in Linz, long dominated by Social Democrats, was far worse. Here the new city council represented the venerable middle strata of society. Born into lower-middle-class families long involved in the traditional economic life of the town, most of the councillors were civil servants, teachers, clerks, retailers, merchants, skilled craftsmen, or small producers (table 21).[11] Only three of the group (5.7 percent) belonged to the professions, and only two could be considered proper entrepreneurs. Of some significance was the fact that only one was engaged in industrial manufacturing. The social profile of the Linz city council between 1934 and 1938, in other words, rather resembled that of the Christian Social *Lager* with its disproportionate share of small producers and self-employed and its insignificant numbers of professionals and private employees. Sociologically speaking, therefore, over 90 percent of the city council was distinctly *kleinbürgerlich* with at least 45 percent belonging to the old *Mittelstand*. While it is true that the other half might be considered new *Mittelstand*, it should be emphasized that few were involved in industrial manufacturing or its service sectors. The Dollfuss-Schuschnigg regime in Linz thus enabled small-scale and preindustrial manufacturers (*Gewerbe*) to reassert local political control and to hold sway over the economy largely at the expense of industry.[12]

That agricultural interests and small producers would be given special preference over industrial manufacturers in the Christian Corporative state was at first not all that evident in Upper Austria. Nearly all Linz merchants, financiers, and entrepreneurs initially welcomed the government's orthodox fiscal policies and brutal treatment of organized labor. Even the pro-Nazi yellow unions (DHV and VdwA) expressed approval, naively arguing that white-collar employees would at last enjoy an officially sanctioned status worthy of their own high self-esteem.[13] By June 1934, however, members of the provincial Association of Austrian Industrialists, as well as the DHV, were having second thoughts. While continuing to support the regime's authoritarian course, the industrialists protested its reluctance to make funds available to industry and its persistent hostility to Nazi Germany. As a consequence, a number of local industrialists such as the influential Oskar Hinterleitner, manufacturer of wood-burning stoves, gradually broke their ties with the government and drifted into the underground Nazi movement.[14] Considering the benefits bestowed on traditional producers at the expense of more technologically advanced enterprises, the fears of Upper

Austrian industrialists were well founded. It was hardly accidental, in other words, that on the eve of the Anschluss nearly 80 percent of Linz's firms were still family owned.[15]

Without doubt, the one group from which the Dollfuss-Schuschnigg regime derived its greatest local support was the Roman Catholic hierarchy. Granted wider latitude in the naming of bishops and the general conduct of affairs than under the monarchy, the Catholic Church steadfastly supported the new order.[16] In Linz Bishop Gföllner, who had helped dismantle Hauser's democratic Catholic People's Association, played an especially active role in politics. In numerous pastoral letters the bishop lauded the achievements of Christian Corporatism, denounced the evils of democracy, and demanded the "removal of all smut and trash from the theater, cinema, and film," as well as "strong measures . . . against nudity and physical culture." The bishop was instrumental in reinstituting compulsory mass in the schools and actively participated in the purging of "unhealthy" books— including the *Travels of Baron von Münchhausen*—from the curriculum and in the dismissal of "subversive" teachers from the classroom. An eager sponsor of the renascent monarchist movement, Gföllner on one occasion served as an emissary between Chancellor Kurt Schuschnigg and the Habsburg heir, Archduke Otto, in Belgium.[17]

THE PATRIOTIC FRONT

Backed by a coalition of traditional producers, the bureaucracy, the police and the army, and the Roman Catholic hierarchy, the government of authoritarian Austria deliberately relied on those forces that had sustained the Habsburg monarchy. In this respect, it rather resembled a nineteenth-century *Polizeistaat* based on agriculture and the rule of traditional elites. At the same time, the regime displayed certain transitional or fascistic features, such as an agrarian-technocratic leadership corps and an umbrella party designed to win mass support. Called the Patriotic Front, this all-encompassing organization was established in March 1933. It was founded according to the fascist leadership principle and was to enroll hundreds of thousands of uniformed participants to stage mass rallies vaguely reminiscent of those at Nuremberg or the Palazzo Venezia.[18] On 29 April 1934, for example, over 55,000 men, women and children were brought out in Linz to hear Dollfuss speak on the public square by the Danube.[19] These mass demonstrations were generally all that the Patriotic Front was able to accomplish. Lacking a dynamic ideology and common purpose, dominated by proclerical conservatives, and enjoying little grass-roots support, the front was a poor imitation of a fascist organization. Only with reluctance were common citizens inclined to join it, usually out of fear of losing their jobs. Designed to attract all social classes, the Patriotic Front achieved the opposite. It was hated by the workers as the agency of a repressive government, by the urban middle class as a bulwark of reactionary clericalism, and even by the peasants as an unnecessary association whose dues they could ill afford to pay. Most of all, the Patriotic Front was opposed by *Heimwehr* leaders who correctly viewed it as a competitor and hence an obstacle to the establishment of what they regarded as true Austrofascism.[20]

In Linz and Upper Austria the Patriotic Front won few adherents before February 1934. Thereafter, as a result of pressure and coercion, it grew so rapidly that within a year nearly a third of the total provincial population belonged to it. In Linz as of March 1935 there were 10,269 registered members; by autumn, according to the police, between 40 and 50 percent of the adult population had signed up.[21] With the exception of a handful of legitimists and Jewish war veterans, however, hardly anyone seems to have joined the Patriotic Front from any sense of conviction. Numerous individuals, in fact, resented the front's approval of government commissioners in their towns as well as its constant anti-German propaganda.[22] Egged on by the *Heimwehr* and the underground Nazi party, young people were especially put off by what they perceived as increased clerical supervision of their lives.[23] In almost all cases, membership in the Patriotic Front was sought for social or economic reasons rather than political ones. In Freistadt, Eferding, Linz, and presumably elsewhere in Upper Austria, job preference was routinely given to front members, while social services such as maternity benefits and free food parcels were made available. The Patriotic Front was in the words of one authority "a kind of social insurance scheme" rather than a genuine fascist organ.[24]

Nor was the front's leadership cadre fascistic. Like the oligarchic-bureaucratic dictatorships of interwar Hungary, Yugoslavia, Rumania, Spain, and Portugal, most front officials were recruited from existing parties and pressure groups. Rather than constituting a self-appointed pseudo-revolutionary elite, they were normally appointed to their posts. For that reason the social structure of the Linz Patriotic Front tended to represent a fairly wide spectrum of the community. Some 9.4 percent of the officials were self-employed, 15.3 percent were private employees, and some 37.7 percent came from the working classes. In this respect the Patriotic Front came closer to mirroring the occupational structure of the municipal population as a whole than any other political movement during the interwar period except the Social Democrats (Cf. tables 3, 4, and 22).

In two distinct ways, however, the identity of the leaders of the Patriotic Front reflected the interests of those actually wielding power in Linz. First, very few were academically trained professionals. As on the city council and in the *Landtag*, the bourgeois members tended to be independent producers or middle-level bureaucrats. Secondly, although nearly 40 percent of the officials could be labeled working-class, a substantial number appear to have had craft occupations such as tailoring, upholstering, woodworking, typesetting, masonry, and so forth.[25] In contrast to fascist elites in Germany and Italy as well as to homegrown Nazis and *Heimwehr*, the Linz Patriotic Front was notable for its striking absence of intellectual bourgeoisie, industrialists, and, above all, white-collar employees. The sociological ingredients for a real fascist brew simply were not present in the organization (cf. Tables 21 and 22).

A RIGHT-AUTHORITARIAN REGIME

At this juncture it should be emphasized that our microanalysis cannot explain decisions made by the Dollfuss-Schuschnigg dictatorship involving Austria's precarious international position, or, with some exceptions, its severely depressed economy. An examination of local institutions, constitutional forms, and interest groups should, however, cast light on the nature of the regime itself. Based on agricultural and traditional forms of manufacturing, Christian Corporatism in Linz approximated the system of government practiced in the underdeveloped states of Eastern Europe after World War I. With a single party enjoying a monopoly of power, the ruling classes of those states assumed the privileges of their former imperial masters. Far from seeking to modernize society, they were committed to a status quo based on agriculture and authoritarian rule. As in many underdeveloped states today, the leaders tried to forge a sense of cohesion by engaging the masses in a special form of nation building. Between 1934 and 1938 Dollfuss, Schuschnigg, Gleissner, Bock, and their right-wing Christian Social compatriots might be said to have stepped into the shoes of the Habsburgs. Like their counterparts in other successor states, they pursued deflationary policies favoring traditional urban and rural producers in a depressed agricultural market. The result of their policies was persistent economic stagnation. Having used force to contain their opponents, the officials of the Christian Corporative state also sought to rally the masses by emphasizing a distinct Austrian mission. In the state nobody wanted, however, their words appeared self-serving or ludicrous.[26]

That the Dollfuss-Schuschnigg dictatorship was clearly not fascist has been emphasized by apologists and neutral observers alike.[27] Compared to the ruthless brutality of National Socialism with its contempt for human life and Christian values, the Austrian regime was indeed moderate. To dismiss the matter at that, however, tends to obscure or trivialize the severely repressive nature of an intensely hated government. Like other right-authoritarian regimes, Christian Corporative Austria fostered an order that was hierarchial, parochial, and selfish. On the purely local level the system combined favoritism and ineptitude as well. So shortsighted and incompe-

TABLE 21   Principal Occupations of Linz City Councillors, 1934–1938 (percentages)

Self-employed	26.8
Professional	3.8
Public Service (*Beamte*, employees)	34.5
Public Service (workers)	1.9
Private Employees	21.2
Workers	5.8
Other	6.0
(Sample Size)	(41)

Computed from Bart and Puffer, *Die Gemeindevertretung der Stadt Linz.*

TABLE 22   Occupational Leadership of the Municipal Leadership of the Patriotic Front in Linz, 1935 (percentages)

Nobility	—
Clergy	—
Farmer/Peasant	2.4
Civil Servant/Public Employee	29.4
Professional	2.4
Self-Employed	9.4
Private Employee	15.3
Workers:	
Skilled	18.8
Unskilled	16.5
Apprentice	2.4
Military	—
Other	3.5
(Sample Size)	(85)

SOURCE: OÖLA, Politische Akten, box 77.

tent were the policies of the Dollfuss-Schuschnigg regime in dealing with political adversaries that within only four years substantial numbers of the population of Linz, including many downtrodden wage earners, were driven into the arms of the National Socialists.

Toward its opponents the Christian Corporative dictatorship tried to maintain its position of dominance by means of a two-pronged approach. Having defeated the Social Democrats in February 1934, the government applied just enough repression to keep organized labor from the political battlefield while seeking to use the Patriotic Front "to make reaction and conservatism popular and plebeian."[28] Toward the National Socialists the regime took a different tack. Despite a distaste for Nazi methods and goals, both Dollfuss and Schuschnigg sought to negotiate a preemptive alliance with Hitler's movement. Even after Dollfuss's assassination by SS troopers in July 1934, Schuschnigg considered an accommodation with the National Socialists preferable to an understanding with the Social Democrats. The result of this shortsighted policy was the alienation of a majority of the population, a narrowing of the government's power base, and a strengthening of the Nazi movement.[29]

THE PLIGHT OF LABOR

The Upper Austrian labor movement was severely demoralized by its defeat on 12 February 1934. With over a hundred dead and wounded, at least a thousand under arrest or detention, and numerous others subject to dismissal from their jobs, local workers held little hope for the future. According to a letter intercepted by the police in April 1934, the February fighters were also dismayed by Bernaschek's flight to Munich.[30] Feeling betrayed by Social Democratic bosses in Vienna and deserted by trusted militants at home, Linz workers fell into a state of despair from which they did not recover. While elsewhere in Austria an illegal party called the Revolutionary Socialists came into being that was able to infiltrate the Patriotic Front and counter its propaganda, little interest was evinced at first in such a movement in Linz. Not until June 1935 was a marginally effective provincial branch established, and that was only after considerable prodding by underground leaders in Vienna.[31]

Having suffered total defeat in February 1934, Upper Austrian workers could hardly be expected to have much stomach for renewed struggle against the Dollfuss regime. Isolated in a rural province with little chance of outside aid, they were all too aware of the odds against them. Because those still fortunate enough to have jobs were employed primarily in family-owned, small-scale firms, opportunities for sabotage or organized underground resistance here were, in contrast to Vienna, severely limited. Embittered, frustrated, and angry, many Linz workers gave up hope or expressed vague interest in Nazi appeals for common revenge.[32] Only among railroad workers with their links to Otto Bauer and Julius Deutsch in Czechoslovakia was their any kind of cohesion or sense of continued party loyalty.[33] In June 1934, moreover, when former city councillor Edmund Aigner halfheartedly tried to organize a municipal branch of Revolutionary Socialists, he aroused the interest of only a few of the party faithful. His tiny group thus devoted most of its attention to helping the families of imprisoned Socialists, rather than to distributing illegal literature or to sponsoring subversive agitation.[34]

In the months immediately following the fighting of February 1934, it was the Communists who seem to have mounted the most effective resistance in Linz and Upper Austria, at least in terms of organization and propaganda. While the party remained small and faction-ridden, it attracted a number of working-class militants in the dockyards, the state tobacco plant, and the Kleinmünchen textile mills. No doubt many of the new activists were little more than self-proclaimed Bolsheviks,[35] but they took an active part in circulating leaflets demanding freedom for imprisoned February fighters, jobs for the unemployed, and solidarity with the Revolutionary Socialists.[36] On a number of occasions the Communists managed to post large placards at crossroads or on walls in the city's residential districts.[37] Under the aegis of a former Socialist trustee, Josef Teufl, they also set up an underground printing press and established a courier service with the Austrian Communist central committee in Czechoslovakia. When finally infiltrated by the police in September 1934, the Linz KP was found to have spawned an extensive network of cells that reached into some of the smallest hamlets of Upper Austria.[38]

Despite the efforts of local Communists and the increasing availability of illegal Socialist literature in Linz, most provincial wage earners adopted a wait-and-see attitude toward the government. Given the town's fragmented, small-scale workplaces as well as constant surveillance by the police, communications among workers were unwieldy and opportunities for common action therefore remote. In June 1935 when Josef Podlipnig, a member of the Central Committee of the Austrian Revolutionary Socialists, paid a visit to Linz, he found the labor movement there in complete disarray. With underground groups such as Aigner's barely operative or, in the case of the Communists, broken up by the police, illegal activity was at a standstill. Bypassing Aigner, Podlipnig appointed a veteran trade unionist as provincial chairman. This man, Karl Schachinger, in league with a onetime Schutzbund functionary, Josef Buchner, managed to recruit a small group of activists from union comrades and former Defense Corps men.[39] Although the Upper Austrian Revolutionary Socialists subsequently acquired a reputation as one of the more effective underground organizations in Austria, their activities seem to have been confined to leaving Socialist fliers and leaflets in public toilets or to distributing copies of the illegal Arbeiter Zeitung in the depots, shops, and switchyards of the federal railways. However such efforts may have irritated the authorities, they cannot be regarded as more than pinpricks in the skin of the regime. Just how weak the Revolutionary Socialists actually were in Upper Austria is revealed by the fact that they failed to set foot in Steyr, the former Montsegur of provincial labor.[40]

OFFICIAL ATTITUDES TOWARD LABOR

That Socialist resistance to the Dollfuss-Schuschnigg regime did not revive in Linz after February 1934 may also be attributed to the behavior of certain municipal and provincial officials. While Lord Mayor Bock, Bishop Gföllner and various *Heimwehr* chieftains such as Revertera and Wenninger had little sympathy for labor, a number of Christian Socials, including Governor Gleissner tried to show a modicum of concern. In accordance with Dollfuss's scheme of pacifying the workers by offering them a token role in the corporative state, Gleissner authorized a youthful Linz barrister, Dr. Alfred Maleta, to negotiate with the defeated socialists. Like his superior at Vienna, Dr. Karl Ernst Winter, Maleta sought cooperation with moderate Social Democrats, and proposed government grants of institutional privileges such as the right of codetermination in shops.[41] Such suggestions aroused the full fury of the *Heimwehr* as "confusing to the working masses,"[42] but they did not cost Maleta his job as they did Winter. Instead, the young attorney remained at his post as first secretary of the Upper Austrian Chamber of Labor and, after May 1935, head of the provincial *Soziale Arbeitsgemein- schaft* (SAG), a suborganization of the Patriotic Front designed to "convert" the workers to Christian Corporatism.[43] Working with Maleta, as well as other provincial authorities, moreover, was a former Linz city councillor and Chamber of Labor official, Dr. Ludwig Hiermann. The only Socialist appointed to Upper Austria's corporative diet, Hiermann advised Gleissner on labor matters. Enjoying the confidence of the governor, he also had the authority to defend the rights of workingmen in public.[44] In light of the federal government's uncompromising hostility to organized labor, especially after the death of Dollfuss, Hiermann's presence and Maleta's behavior suggest that in Upper Austria a faint shadow of tolerance may have lingered after February 1934.

Although local working-class attitudes and behavior under Christian Corporatism are hard to detect, it does seem that by 1936 substantial numbers of Linz wage earners were joining government-sponsored unions and works councils in hopes of capturing them from within. Provincial membership in the puppet Trade Union Federation, for example, rose from 31,000 in 1934 to 46,691 in May 1937. By the same token, electoral participation in state-controlled works councils (*Werksgemeinschaften*) at the end of 1936 was actually higher than it had been in the independent works councils of 1919.[45]

Since opportunities for securing a stronger position for organized labor through infiltration of government front organizations remained limited, most workers in Linz focused their major political attention on the semiautonomous consumers' cooperatives. Under pressure from small businessmen and producers, the cooperatives had been subjected to government control in 1933 and after February 1934 were used to provide jobs for unemployed *Heimwehr* men. The workers retaliated with a boycott that in Linz reduced the output of the municipal Spaten bakery by 50 to 70 percent. Rather than alienate Austria's farmers and peasants, whose best customers were the cooperatives, the government for once had to back down. In 1935, much to the anger of provincial Security Director Revertera and his cock-feather followers, the cooperatives regained their autonomy. Permitted the right to debate and to elect officers, they evolved into a legally sanctioned forum for Social Democratic politicians and their followers.[46]

ECONOMIC TRENDS

Although politically hostile, the Austrian working classes might have been reconciled to the Dollfuss-Schuschnigg system by means of economic recovery and sustained industrial growth. This, after all, had occurred in Imperial Germany (as it would in Singapore, Taiwan, and South Korea after World War II). So long as Vienna pursued deflationary policies favoring cottage producers and rural interests, however, economic conditions could not improve. Between 1929 and 1937, in fact, Austria's share of world trade declined substantially while industrial production remained 23 percent below 1913 levels. On the eve of the Anschluss, the standard of living in Austria was among the lowest in Europe.[47] In Upper Austria, it is true, economic conditions were not quite as bleak as elsewhere. As a region relatively self-sufficient in foodstuffs and not particularly dependent on foreign trade, the province experienced lower unemployment than other parts of the country (in 1937, 7.13 percent vs. 20.3 percent federally). In summer months, moreover, this rate declined even further as seasonal jobs opened up in fields and forests.[48]

Yet these impressive advantages made little impact on the local population. In Linz unemployment was high and persistent. While some 19,634 persons had been employed in firms having more than five employees each in 1930, only 14,254 held similar jobs in 1937.[49] With 11,521 unemployed in January 1936, moreover, more urban dwellers depended on public assistance than at the depths of the depression three years before.[50] As for those still holding jobs, fear of dismissal, wage cuts, increased hours, and a decline of real income reinforced a general sense of despair and hopelessness. In 1937 provincial unemployment finally started to recede as an indirect result of German rearmament, but the decline was modest and scarcely perceptible to the bitterly alienated working classes. By that time, few in Linz and Upper Austria, regardless of their social rank, viewed their economic problems in purely Austrian terms. They looked instead to neighboring Bavaria, where prosperity was returning and unemployment rapidly disappearing. Little imagination is required to understand the psychological impact in Linz of a German drive in 1937 to recruit agricultural workers in Upper Austria.[51]

In all fairness, provincial and municipal officials had few options in dealing with the ravages of the depression. Austria was a country living on foreign credit, dedicated to maintaining the integrity of its currency, and rapidly falling under German economic control. In Linz itself obsolescent machinery, particularly in government-pampered textiles, made recovery difficult and unlikely. Compounding the economic malaise were the protectionist policies of the Christian Corporative regime. The federal government raised tariffs and subsidies to agriculture in such a way as to keep food prices high and to stifle demand. The results were continued high unemployment and declining production.[52]

On the purely local level, Gleissner and his associates in Upper Austria genuinely wanted to alleviate the hardships of the depression. Nevertheless, they took a narrow and dogmatic approach to economic problems. As if wanting to emulate former German Chancellor Brüning, Gleissner appealed to self-help and proclaimed a policy of "rigorous austerity." His administration cut provincial expenditures by eliminating relief payments to the elderly, by reducing the salaries of public officials and teachers, and in a number of cases by simply dismissing teachers, especially women, from their posts.[53] These measures quickly succeeded in balancing the budget, but they did not solve the problem of unemployment, which remained intractable.[54] To provide jobs Gleissner and his Christian Social supporters were unwilling to underwrite a program of industrial development for fear of strengthening organized labor. In 1937 they did, however, sponsor a series of public works projects in Linz that included construction of a scenic road through the Freinberg residential district, the improvement of municipal harbor facilities, the renovation of the square before the Linz cathedral, and initial work on a new Chamber of Commerce building.[55] While these projects may have reduced unemployment somewhat, they could hardly have mollified many workers. Modest in scope, the program clearly benefitted the rich and the clergy more than the common good.

Between 1934 and 1938, then, the Christian Corporative system offered the depressed workers in Linz and Upper Austria little more than promises and sanctimonious cant. Excluding the labor movement from meaningful political participation, the regime also made threats of dismissal or arrest. For their part, local wage earners remained politically disengaged or vaguely loyal to Social Democratic traditions. By 1937, however, some segments of the laboring population were clearly drifting toward the illegal Nazis. While there is no way of determining how many local blue-collar workers now took up the swastika banner, a Gestapo report from 1940 states that during the Anschluss in Linz "an enthusiasm existed among workers for National Socialism such as no other government before had been able to sustain in this layer of the population."[56] Whatever their numbers, it would seem Hitler's proletarian supporters were drawn to Nazism by despair, by frustration, and, above all, by contempt for Schuschnigg's dictatorship—a regime which excluded them from power, denied them jobs, and yet demanded emotional loyalty to a value system they despised. If they could find no other area of agreement with their onetime National Socialist adversaries, they could at least pool their pent-up hatred to seek revenge.

DOLLFUSS AND THE NAZIS

That National Socialism ever became a viable alternative in the eyes of Linz's distressed masses was a striking consequence of the misplaced priorities and shortsighted policies of the Christian Corporative regime. As late as 1933, it will be recalled, the Nazis had failed to win much of a following in Upper Austria although they had disengaged the German Nationalist bourgeoisie and clearly stood on the verge of an electoral breakthrough in Vienna, Styria, and other parts of the Alpine state. Late in the evening of 12 June 1933, however, federal party headquarters in Linz had been surrounded by the police and Inspector General Theo Habicht was placed under arrest. After a brief interrogation, the inspector general and three other German Nazis were driven to the Bavarian frontier and expelled from Austria. The next day prominent Austrian Nazis were detained, and on 19 June the NSDAP was outlawed altogether by the government.[57]

Despite its suppression of the Nazi party, the Dollfuss regime had no intention of abandoning the search for a modus vivendi with Hitler's followers. Dollfuss admired the idealism and energy of National Socialism. Like Papen and Schleicher in Germany, he sought to subdue the radicals of the movement while enlisting the support of those he considered moderates. This was a goal that appeared within reach once the respectable German Nationalists assumed the role of keepers of the Nazi grail, as they did in the summer of 1933.[58] Acting on their own authority, Hermann Foppa and Franz Langoth, in fact, proposed a series of conferences with the government to discuss the pacification of the entire German Nationalist-Nazi camp.

Although Dollfuss preferred to deal with Hitler or a representative of the German foreign office, he readily agreed to recognize the two Upper Austrians as intermediaries. Meeting with them on 13 October 1933, the diminutive chancellor expressed a willingness to grant portfolios to an unspecified number of German Nationalists and Nazis from the "national battle alliance" as part of a general settlement with Germany. Foppa and Langoth then hastened to Munich, where the exiled Habicht accepted Dollfuss's proposals but demanded one half of the cabinet posts for the Nazis and the vice-chancellorship for himself. To emphasize his case the inspector general threatened to resume his springtime campaign of terror should his demands be rejected. Refusing to be intimidated, Dollfuss ended the negotiations with Habicht but retained Foppa and Langoth as trusted contact men within the illegal Nazi movement.[59]

If Dollfuss believed that the German Nationalists really represented the outlawed NSDAP in Austria, he was sorely mistaken. For some time the underground rank and file looked to Germany for guidance. In nearby Munich, Habicht had established an exile party headquarters, a party hierarchy, and a paramilitary organization of refugees called the Austrian Legion. With Upper Austrian *Gauleiter* Andreas Bolek ensconced in Passau only sixty kilometers from Linz, it was not surprising that Upper Austrian Nazis, in particular, remained more directly under the control of old leaders than did their party comrades elsewhere in Austria.

Throughout 1933 the outlawed Nazis carried on an intensive campaign of propaganda and low-level terror. In Upper Austria they flooded the airwaves with countless radio speeches from Munich and littered the fields and forests with leaflets dropped from German airplanes.[60] In cars belonging to provincial SS men or owned by the manager of a Linz taxi and trucking firm they smuggled stocks of dynamite, hand grenades, and guns into the city. Because the provincial capital was tightly controlled by municipal and federal authorities, the police intercepted many of the explosives, forcing Hitler's followers to confine their activities to word-of-mouth propaganda, to the distribution of circulars, or occasionally to the dynamiting of plate glass windows.[61] In January 1934, for example, Nazi explosives shattered hundreds of windows in public buildings at the center of town.[62]

During the Austrian Civil War of February 1934 the Nazis looked on in silence, savoring the defeat of the "Jewish Marxists" but hoping to pick up the pieces once hostilities ceased. That the defeated Social Democrats were eagerly defended by Nazi attorneys in the courts and that Richard Bernaschek was spirited to Germany by brownshirted activists was more than a coincidence. At the same time, thousands of leaflets appeared in the streets addressed to the workers:

> Socialists do not despair! Criminal leaders harried you to the barricades; Marxist Jews betrayed your Socialism; and cowards have left you in the lurch. Hard fate has opened your eyes and forever separated you from Jewish Marxism. . . . But you are not alone. Year after year we National Socialists have fought for your hearts. We knew that someday the voice of your blood would lead you to our ranks. Now that has occurred. From the tragedy of Marxism the dawn of German Socialism is breaking. Socialists to the front! Hitler alone will lead us to light.[63]

Although underground Nazi propaganda initially had little impact on the demoralized workers in Linz or Steyr, it seems to have had some effect on the rural inhabitants of small towns and villages in the western districts of

Upper Austria. In March 1934 the provincial security director suggested that perhaps as much as 80 percent of the population of towns like Braunau, Ried, and Mettmach sympathized with Hitler's cause. Far from lending their support to the Dollfuss government for having crushed the Social Democrats, these town dwellers along with a substantial number of peasants near the Bavarian frontier were willing to give the Nazis a chance.[64]

THE NAZI REVOLT AGAINST DOLLFUSS

Meanwhile in Munich, Habicht was becoming increasingly frustrated by the failure of his party comrades to come to power in Austria. Even before the breakdown of indirect negotiations with Dollfuss in late May 1934, the exiled inspector general feared that the Austrian Nazi party was fragmenting and spinning out of control. Sometime in the spring of that year he authorized the Viennese SS to plan an armed insurrection for the coming summer. Counting on help from Nazi sympathizers in the armed forces, Habicht hoped to overcome the rivalries within the Austrian Nazi movement, to reestablish his own control of the party apparatus, and, almost as an afterthought, to overthrow Dollfuss. As the American historian Bruce F. Pauley recently put it: Habicht, like Hitler in the Beer Hall putsch, acted from weakness, not strength.[65]

In Linz and throughout Upper Austria the Nazis had no knowledge of Habicht's plans. In September 1933 a village schoolteacher, Benedikt Klaushofer, had become provincial *Gauleiter* with the task of reorganizing the underground party and coordinating its activities with Bolek in Passau. A skilled propagandist, Klaushofer considered Habicht's terror tactics self-defeating, and in May 1934 he wrote Bolek threatening to break with Munich. According to Klaushofer, a shakeup then ensued at exile party headquarters in the Bavarian capital which resulted in a break with the Upper Austrian organization.[66]

On 25 July 1934 news of the abortive uprising of SS Standard 89 in Vienna and the assassination of Englebert Dollfuss came as a total surprise to Hitler's followers in Linz. No prior warning had been given to the German Nationalists around Langoth nor to the Klaushofer group.[67] Although arms and explosives had been hidden and stored, virtually no operational plans had been drawn up by the SA or the SS. By comparison, Richard Bernaschek's muddled schemes for defending Linz five months before must be judged a masterpiece of military planning.

At the time of the coup, the commander of the Upper Austrian SS Standard 76 was on vacation in Czechoslovakia. One of his men, Karl Eberhardt, learned of the uprising over the radio and on his own initiative drove to Salzburg for instructions. There a German contact told Eberhardt to mobilize the SS in Upper Austria only in case of a change of government in Vienna. The next day, Heinrich Weithner-Weithenthurn, an official of the Linz branch of the Steyr works, assumed command of the SS in Linz. Establishing contact with SA units in the city, Weithner prepared for action in the Linz suburbs. That evening (26 July) he met with four other municipal SS leaders and decided to dispatch twenty SS men to federal police headquarters. There, Weithner argued, they would be equipped with arms by sympathetic police authorities. An additional twenty men were to seize the administrative offices of the provincial security forces.[68]

These plans were never carried out. Weithner suspected that SA reports of an invasion by the Austrian Legion were exaggerated and drove to Salzburg to observe the situation for himself. There, as throughout the countryside, he found only tranquility. Returning to Linz, Weithner learned that his men possessed only a limited supply of explosives and that some of them had reservations about the planned coup. For several days the municipal SS remained on alert but undertook no operations. Early in August Weithner, Eberhardt, and most of their compatriots were arrested by the authorities.[69]

In contrast to the municipal SS, the leaders of Linz SA Standard 14 actually managed to mobilize several hundred youngsters to execute a predetermined contingency plan. Although just as ill-informed as the SS, the stormtroopers sought to disrupt communications on the outskirts of Linz and to block the roads leading to Ottensheim and Eferding on either side of the Danube. According to a subsequent police investigation,[70] the uniformed brownshirts never dreamed of seizing control of the Upper Austrian capital by themselves but hoped to ease the way for an invasion from Bavaria by the Austrian Legion. Whatever their intentions, several hundred of them surrendered without firing a shot to the security forces north of Urfahr just after midnight on 26–27 July. To the south, near Wilhering, eighty-seven others gave up after a brief firefight at approximately the same time. Elsewhere in the province the police were able to contain SA disturbances in Gmunden, Laakirchen, Goisern, Gaspoltshosen, and Grünau.[71]

The vain attempt of the Upper Austrian Nazis to support the SS uprising in Vienna was the result of a variety of factors, including ignorance of the coup beforehand, an insufficient supply of arms,[72] and wretched timing. Most of all, the failure of the putsch in Linz, as in Vienna, can be attributed to rivalries within the Nazi movement, particularly between the SS and the SA. So great was the friction between these two formations following the Röhm purge in Germany that it was impossible to coordinate operations once news of Dollfuss's assassination became known. In an incredible display of poor planning and confusion, *Gauleiter* Klaushofer rushed off to Vienna in search of advice, SS commander Weithner halfheartedly formulated plans to storm Linz police headquarters, and various SA leaders mobilized their men in hopes of securing the Danube for the Austrian Legion. Ironically, no one had knowledge of the heavy fighting to the south at the Pyhrn pass or to the north on the Bavarian frontier. Thanks largely to the incompetence of the underground NSDAP in Upper Austria, the federal army was able to deploy its considerable forces in those combat zones without fear of losing control in the province.[73]

The disastrous outcome of the July putsch with its subsequent arrests and renewed flights to Germany virtually ended the Nazi movement in Upper Austria. Equally damaging were a series of face-saving actions taken by Hitler himself. Recalling Habicht, the Führer dissolved the exile organization in Munich, forbade German Nazis from interferring in Austrian affairs, and appointed the conservative Franz von Papen ambassador to Vienna. Hitler also eliminated financial subsidies to the Austrian party and ordered an end to illegal activities. Suppressed by the federal government and cut off from German aid, the remnants of the NSDAP in Linz and its hinterland had no choice but to cease all agitation.[74]

Under these circumstances, the respectable German Nationalists once again stepped forward as spokesmen for the Nazi cause. For over a year, Langoth and Foppa had been negotiating on an on-again, off-again basis with federal and provincial authorities. Now with the disreputable elements of the Nazi movement finally exposed and pushed aside, it seemed possible for the German Nationalists at long last to negotiate a settlement with Austria's traditional conservatives. In the eyes of Schuschnigg, Gleissner, Revertera, and the supporters of the Christian Corporative system, this was a golden opportunity not to be missed. By effecting a reconciliation with the German Nationalist-Nazi camp it would be possible to broaden the government's base and to improve relations with Germany, both key ingredients, it was believed, in reviving Austria's economy. As the Austrian historian Wolfgang Rosar has noted, what Dollfuss had always wanted became ironically possible as a result of his own assassination—or at least so it seemed.[75]

SCHUSCHNIGG AND THE NAZIS

Within less than a month of the July putsch, Kurt von Schuschnigg responded favorably to what he hoped was an olive branch from the Nazis. To a greater degree than Dollfuss, Schuschnigg regarded German identity as an essential component of the Christian Corporative order. For that reason he was prepared to go much further than his unfortunate predecessor in appeasing Hitler and the Austrian Nazis. Stubbornly refusing to negotiate with the Social Democrats, the new chancellor considered an agreement with the National Opposition—as the coalition of German Nationalists and National Socialists was now known—to be the best means of strengthening his own position. It was thus with some enthusiasm that in late summer 1934 he welcomed the proposal of former regimental comrade, Anton Reinthaller, to begin discussions aimed at reaching an accommodation.[76]

Reinthaller was an Upper Austrian agricultural engineer who had belonged to the DSNAP, later to the *Landbund,* and since 1930 to the Hitler movement. Having broken with Habicht over the use of terror, he was a moderate who still enjoyed the confidence of more radical Upper Austrian Nazis, such as SS chief Ernst Kaltenbrunner, and who maintained contact with the superradical Carinthian branch of the NSDAP under Hubert Klausner, Friedrich Rainer, and Odilo Globocnik. Backed by Langoth, Foppa, and the German Nationalist establishment and encouraged by Gleissner as well, Reinthaller agreed to have the National Opposition join the Patriotic Front. In return he insisted on a share of federal, provincial, and municipal cabinet posts and on full government recognition of the national government. Schuschnigg was willing to appoint *individual* German Nationalists or Nazis to positions of power, but he could not accept such open-ended conditions. In October 1934 he ended his negotiations with Reinthaller without, however, closing the door to future discussions.[77]

Another way in which Schuschnigg demonstrated his interest in reaching an understanding with the National Opposition was in tolerating the activities of the Austrian Refugee's Relief Society (*Österreichisch Flüchtlingshilfswerk*). Founded soon after the abortive July putsch by Franz Langoth, the Relief Society aided those families with Nazi relatives in prison or detention centers. Thanks to the cooperation of the Austrian government as well as to renewed financial subsidies from Germany, the organization was able to funnel money to Nazi families, to sympathetic peasants and farmers, and even to businessmen who faced harassment from the authorities. That Schuschnigg and Gleissner tolerated or at times encouraged the Relief Society, even when it spread from Upper Austria to other provinces, was yet another manifestation of the Christian Corporative regime's desire to come to terms with its national opponents so long as unsavory, radical Nazis were not calling the shots.[78]

By early 1935 Schuschnigg seems to have concluded that the respectable German Nationalists were sufficiently in control of the National Opposition for him to tolerate the formal establishment of a political organization. With headquarters in Linz the so-called National Front was founded on 5 March 1935. It was made up primarily of Upper Austrian German Nationalist politicians long affiliated with the Nazi movement. Besides Langoth, Foppa, and Reinthaller, these included Rudolf Lengauer, a former editor of the *Volksstimme;* Dr. Franz Hueber, brother-in-law of Herman Göring; and Dr. Ernst Kaltenbrunner, Linz attorney and provincial SS chief.[79] The National Front agreed to cooperate on a limited basis with the Patriotic Front in guaranteeing the independence of Austria; in return it demanded either the dissolution of the *Heimwehr* or the right of the SS and the SA to reorganize.

The program appeared to recognize the divergent interests of the German Nationalists, the Nazis, the Austrian government, and Berlin in the sense that all parties agreed to an indefinite postponement of the Anschluss. It was consequently endorsed informally by Schuschnigg, by Papen, and on 21 May 1935 by Hitler himself.[80]

THE UNDERGROUND NAZI MOVEMENT

Schuschnigg's cautious search for a settlement with the National Opposition provoked great resentment among the underground Nazi rank and file, especially in Upper Austria. Initially supporting the Reinthaller negotiations, the remnants of the provincial party were stunned by mass arrests of SA leaders at Linz, Wels, Steyr, Braunau, Bad Ischl, and Mühlkreis in January 1935. Even more shocking was the discovery that *Gauleiter* Klaushofer had agreed to the dissolution of the entire underground apparatus in Upper Austria in return for the stormtroopers' freedom.[81] The unveiling of the National Front at Linz barely six weeks later, therefore, struck the "old fighters" as a cruel betrayal to the hated "system." While Reinthaller or Langoth sat secure in their jobs, common party members faced the threat of unemployment or detention. On the strictly local level they especially resented Security Director Revertera's policy of cooperating with "moderate" bourgeois Nazis while simultaneously sending "extremist," plebeian ones to jail. That these ordinary National Socialists more than ever viewed terror and armed rebellion as the best means of achieving their goals was altogether understandable.[82]

The dissatisfaction of the radicals spurred the formation of a more conspiratorial Austrian party under the *Gauleiter* of Lower Austria, Josef Leopold, in the spring and summer of 1935. Opposed to intellectuals and gradualists, this organization considered itself independent of other Nazi factions and was composed primarily of youthful activists.[83] In Linz the leadership of the new provincial and municipal party was young and strikingly plebeian. The *Gauleiter,* August Eigruber, though a member of the Hitler movement for over a decade, was only twenty-eight at the time of his appointment. The son of poor parents, he received little more than an elementary education and until 1934 had worked first in a calculating machine factory and then in the automobile works in Steyr. Eigruber's deputy, Hans Eisenkolb, was two years older, a party member since 1922, and a goldsmith by trade. Other members of the local illegal party came from similar backgrounds: business manager Franz Fehrer, age twenty-four, soldier and factory worker; press secretary Franz Steiner, age thirty-two, barber; *Kreisleiter* (later mayor) Sepp Wolkerstorfer, age thirty, haberdasher; *Bezirksleiter* Walter Gasthuber, age thirty, soldier (until 1933), engine fitter, and then warehouseman in a plumbing firm. Only two members of the provincial *Gauleitung*, Wolkerstorfer and press director Anton Fellner, who held a law degree, were definitely bourgeois.[84]

Despite the plebeian nature of the new *Gauleitung* and despite certain changes in social composition, the illegal Nazi movement remained very much a youthful, middle-class organization. Judging from police files and other data, the number of white-collar employees, civil servants, and public employees declined by some 28 percent from the previous decade, but the number of self-employed and professionals increased substantially. Similarly, although well over a quarter of Linz underground militants might be considered wage earners, most of them were artisans or skilled workers; few—with the notable exception of Eigruber—had ever worked in a factory. The difference seems to be that whereas the municipal Nazi party of the 1920s was composed of accountants, clerks, teachers, servicemen, postal employees, railwaymen, and artisans, the party of a decade later consisted of professionals—especially attorneys, engineers, and pharmacists—public and private employees, shopkeepers, and skilled workers such as electricians, master mechanics, barbers, and truck drivers. By way of contrast to the German NSDAP of 1933, the underground Nazi movement in Linz appears to have had a larger civil servant–public employee component and to have appealed to fewer white-collar workers. On the other hand, the Linz party seems to have had a social profile rather similar to the famous Abel sample of Nazi activists from 1934 (table 23).[85]

Just how long the various German Nationalist and Nazi factions remained at odds in Linz and Upper Austria, is unclear. After an undetermined period of turmoil, the plebeian underground party organization realized that it needed the political skills of the German Nationalists—not to mention the financial resources of Langoth's Relief Society—and expressed a willingness to bury the hatchet.[86] Since both groups wanted to avoid the meddling of exiled Austrian Nazis, internal conflicts were resolved and a division of labor agreed upon. *Gauleiter* Eigruber testified after World War II that although he had almost no personal contact with members of the bourgeois National Front, he did maintain friendly relations with SS chief Ernst Kaltenbrunner, whom he described as "well-liked."[87] Since the youthful Kaltenbrunner received orders directly from Heinrich Himmler and Reinhard Heydrich, it is possible that he convinced Eigruber of the necessity of maintaining discipline and of following the line laid down by Hitler. Whatever the reason, *Kreisleiter* Wolkerstorfer, who distributed funds from the Relief Society to local stormtroopers, also accepted this approach, and willingly took his cues from Langoth and German Nationalist attorney, Dr. Heinrich Steinsky.[88]

The underground Nazi movement in Linz seems to have made little headway in 1935–36, but it apparently did achieve a greater measure of internal cohesion than other Nazi groups in Austria at that time. This was made clear in the weeks after publication of the Austro-German

TABLE 23   Occupational Composition of the NSDAP (in percentages)

	Linz Activists 1933–38	Reich 1933	Abel Activists 1934
Farmer/Peasant	1.4	10.7	8.2
Civil Servant/Public Employee	18.9	13.0	19.9
Professional	16.2		
Self-employed	13.5	20.2	13.6
Private Employee	13.5	20.6	18.7
Workers:		32.1	27.1
Skilled	16.2		
Unskilled	4		
Apprentice	8		
Students	2.7		
Military	4.0		
Other	1.3	3.4	12.5
(Sample Size)	(74)		(581)

SOURCE: Computed from BDC Berlin; Bart and Puffer, *Die Gemeinde-vertretung der Stadt Linz*; and Merkl, *Political Violence Under the Swastika*, p.14

Gentlemen's Agreement of 11 July 1936. An indirect consequence of Mussolini's involvement in Ethiopia and Spain, this pact was negotiated by Schuschnigg in a desperate attempt to shore up Austria's international position and his own power by coming to terms with the National Opposition. The only alternative would have been to deal with the Social Democrats.[89] According to the agreement, Germany lifted all economic sanctions and recognized Austria's independence in exchange for a general amnesty for all Austrian National Socialists and the appointment to the federal cabinet of members of the National Opposition. Although suddenly given the chance to pursue their goals without fear of police harassment, many Austrian Nazis felt betrayed by Berlin and vowed to continue the struggle by radical means.[90] In Linz and Upper Austria, however, the Gentlemen's Agreement was welcomed by local Nazis as a golden opportunity for action. While Langoth, Reinthaller, and the "moderates" continued talks with federal and provincial authorities, Eigruber and the "radicals" prepared the ground for seizing power through sabotage and force. With Kaltenbrunner and the SS acting as intermediaries and directing the infiltration of public institutions, the factions avoided friction and coordinated their activities.

The Gentlemen's Agreement of 11 July 1936, then, gave respectability to a terrorist movement that the Austrian government had kept under control only with great difficulty.[91] As in Germany during Papen's chancellorship, Schuschnigg granted the National Socialists a quasi-official status that enabled them to conduct both legal and illegal activities simultaneously. The police were thereby thrown into confusion and effectively enjoined from determined action against the Nazis lest they incur the wrath of the German embassy or the National Opposition. In Linz the authorities were also confronted with the problem of dealing with German Nazis who began streaming into the city to pay their respects to the boyhood home of their Führer. On 6 September 1936, for example, some 302 tourists arrived by riverboat from Passau to be received by at least 5,000 enthusiastic Austrian Nazis. For two days the Germans toured the city, laid wreaths at the grave of Hitler's parents in Leonding, and sponsored rallies and meetings in local inns and hotels. Although most of the participants were themselves Austrian, the police felt powerless to intervene.[92]

Compounding the growing paralysis of the police forces in Upper Austria after July 1936 was the open sympathy of the provincial director of security for the Nazi cause. A former *Heimwehr* chieftain, Count Peter Revertera had maintained amicable relations with "moderate" National Socialists for years, only now and then wringing his hands at acts of sabotage or decrying what he considered stupid, illegal propaganda.[93] Like so many traditional conservatives in Central Europe, the count relished playing a cat-and-mouse game with the Nazis. He prided himself on his ability to track down illegal groups on the one hand, while simultaneously maintaining cordial relations with German Nationalist dignitaries on the other. Officially admonishing the brownshirts for their "pranks" and occasionally sending them to jail, Revertera normally went out of his way to be conciliatory. After a noisy horn-blowing caravan of Nazi-driven automobiles completely disrupted Linz traffic one day in 1937, for example, the count saw to it that the ringleaders were released from police custody with a smile and a handshake. Looking back over forty years later, *Kreisleiter* Wolkerstorfer recalled, "Revertera was really first rate."[94] Or as a Gmunden stormtroop commander put it at the time, "Count Revertera is a man one can deal with."[95]

ON THE EVE OF ANSCHLUSS

The Christian Corporative interlude in Linz was a right-authoritarian throwback to an earlier era. It represented an attempt to settle the social and economic dislocations of the interwar period by abandoning a corporative-pluralist order of constant brokerage in favor of a corporative-closed system of authoritarian rule.[96] Designed to preserve late nineteenth-century society in the face of rapid change, it altered institutions to buttress the declining position of agriculture and, above all, nonmechanized manufacturing. The regime saw its principal opponents on the left and for that reason attracted the initial support of industrial businessmen and anti-Socialist employees. Because the system eschewed technocratic development, however, it stood little chance of retaining the continued loyalty of the new *Mittelstand*. In the place of economic concessions the government resorted to fascistic trappings, such as the Patriotic Front, and to ongoing negotiations with the German Nationalist-Nazi camp. In the July Agreement of 1936 the Schuschnigg cabinet had reason to believe that it had cemented an alliance with the National Opposition, but it had in fact signed its own death warrant. The agreement provided an opportunity for Hitler's followers to mobilize the new *Mittelstand* against the Christian Corporative regime and in the case of Linz to lay the groundwork for even wider popular support of a genuine fascist order.

SEVEN

Anschluss in Linz
1938–1939

Early in the morning of 12 March 1938, five German divisions marched into Upper Austria and by noon had reached Linz. Advancing through the city toward Vienna, the gray-green columns were met with garlands of flowers and hysterical applause. As wave after wave of the Luftwaffe passed overhead, Nazi officials added to the popular enthusiasm by proclaiming the imminent arrival of Hitler himself. It was not until 7:30 P.M. that the Führer's three-axle Mercedes actually drove through the Schmidt Gate onto the town square, but once Linz's prodigal son stepped onto the Rathaus balcony, between 60,000 and 80,000 Austrians roared their approval.[1]

While the dramatic events surrounding Hitler's annexation of Austria are generally well known, it should not be forgotten that the quasi-legal change of government in Vienna and the subsequent German invasion were preceded by pseudorevolutionary uprisings in the provincial capitals, most notably in Graz. In the case of Linz, the "brown revolution" came relatively late in the day, but, as Hitler himself discovered, it clearly enjoyed extensive mass support. The local uprising lent an air of revolutionary dynamism to the new regime. It also brought to power a group of energetic and brutal Nazis who sought to lay the groundwork for a radical restoration of German Nationalist rule.

NAZI PENETRATION OF THE CHRISTIAN CORPORATIVE STATE

In the eighteen months after the July Agreement of 1936, the Christian Corporative regime in Austria appeared to make some headway in strengthening its internal position. With Hitler's attention focused on domestic matters and the Spanish Civil War, Schuschnigg managed to contend with the divided Nazi movement by co-opting the support of several respectable members of the National Opposition including the Viennese lawyer Arthur Seyss-Inquart. The Austrian chancellor also presided over a slight upswing in the economy that offered the tantalizing prospect of broadening the base of the government without making concessions to organized labor. On 5 November 1937, however, Hitler decided to step up pressure on Vienna and bring Austria into the German orbit as soon as possible.

Without resorting to military occupation, the Nazi dictator proposed to "coordinate" Austrian institutions with those of the Third Reich and to reduce the country to the status of a satellite. On 12 February 1938 he met Schuschnigg at Berchtesgaden and, after a stormy session, compelled the Austrian chancellor to agree to his terms. Two weeks later, in a moment of desperation, Schuschnigg tried to pull his chestnuts out of the fire by calling a plebiscite on the question of Austrian independence. Provoked by such a dramatic reversal of policy, Hitler gave Austrian Nazis the green light for a domestic uprising and, after some additional confusion, on 11 March 1938 ordered the Wehrmacht to invade Austria at dawn the next day.[2]

In Linz and Upper Austria, as we have seen, the underground Nazi movement had responded vigorously to the July Agreement of 1936 by conducting legal and illegal activities simultaneously. The "illegal" *Gauleitung* regarded its role as similar to that of the German NSDAP in the years before Hitler's rise to power. In Linz that meant recruiting collaborators from the staffs of the police, prison, post, and telegraph services. The collaborators were not required to become party members or even to subordinate themselves to the rigid discipline of the movement, but they were to provide the underground organization with information and to accept orders in case of a coup. As for the Nazi party itself, it made little attempt between 1936 and 1938 to expand the party's rolls as one might have expected.[3] Without the tolerance of Revertera's police forces or the intervention of the German Wehrmacht, it is still difficult to see how the illegal Nazi movement in Upper Austria could have won power on its own.

Two days after the July Agreement, the underground party in Linz did, however, launch a determined and at least partially successful drive to attract the hard-pressed workers of the city. Under the aegis of Dr. Anton Fellner, an experienced German Nationalist newspaper columnist, the *Gauleitung* began publication of the *Österreichischer Beobachter* (OB), a virulently anti-Semitic sheet with a working-class orientation. The paper was printed initially in Urfahr and dispersed throughout Upper Austria by a retired railwayman who could ride the trains for a nominal fee. Many issues of the OB were intercepted by the police, but provincial circulation in the estimate of the authorities rose steadily from 3,000 in 1936 to 30,000 copies per month at the time of the Anschluss.[4] In 1937 Fellner, with the aid of the German Press Bureau in Berlin and two local industrialists, Oskar Hinterleitner and Stephan Berghammer, managed to get control of the former Social Democratic publishing house in Linz. Although formally owned by *Heimwehr* interests and the federal government, the onetime Socialist newspapers, *Tagblatt* and *Neue Zeit*, increasingly purveyed the

Nazi line. While there is no way of determining how successful Fellner's publications were in winning the municipal working population to Hitler's cause, some evidence suggests that readers tended to place a certain amount of credence in Nazi propaganda simply in reaction to the government's policy of censorship.[5]

This of course raises the issue of the public mood, which by 1937 was clearly shifting in favor of the Nazis. Although no real measurement of public sentiment exists for the period, the works of foreign journalists and later historians indicate that Linz was known as a "brown city" long before the Anschluss. In the months after the July Agreement substantial numbers of Upper Austrians appear to have moved from an attitude of sullen indifference to acceptance of National Socialism as an alternative to the existing order; many also perceived Hitler's movement as a powerful agent of change.[6]

Besides the German Nationalists and some segments of the outlawed Social Democrats, the Nazis seem to have attracted the young of all classes, but especially those of bourgeois background such as the fanatical sons of Franz Langoth and the students of Linz's Commercial Academy. It has been estimated that on the eve of the Anschluss at least three-quarters of the active Nazis in Austria were youngsters. Untroubled by thoughts of responsibility, the youth were especially prone to accept violent, reckless solutions to complex problems. In Linz only the absence of a university may have kept the level of youthful Nazi activity somewhat lower than in Vienna, Graz, and Innsbruck.[7]

Another group notably susceptible to Nazi blandishments were teachers and educators. The teachers had long been known for their radical German Nationalist views and might rightfully claim to have inspired Hitler himself during his school years in Linz. Under the Christian Corporative system, government officials fanned their anticlericalism to a frenzy by removing them from their posts while insisting on membership in the hated Patriotic Front as a condition of employment. Hundreds of provincial school teachers remained unemployed throughout the depression. That so many of them eagerly turned to Nationalist Socialism was not surprising.[8]

In addition to mobilizing the municipal population through propaganda and promises of revenge, the Nazis also resumed their campaign of confrontation and violence. In February 1937 local stormtroopers etched swastikas in the display windows of Jewish-owned shops; several weeks later, dressed in Alpine shorts, they staged a so-called *Dirndlabend*, turning a dance at a local restaurant into a noisy rally punctuated by cheers of "Sieg Heil" and the playing of the Horst Wessel song.[9] Continuing this musical motif into July, Upper Austrian brownshirts infiltrated a large meeting of German and Austrian war veterans at Wels. In the presence of Governor Gleissner and German ambassador Papen, they threw a solemn meeting into turmoil by singing "Deutschland über Alles" in place of the Austrian hymn. When federal police responded with force, the Nazis won a double victory by arousing public sympathy and exposing the growing weakness of the Schuschnigg regime. Similarly, in November of the same year stormtroopers took to the pavements of Linz in large numbers for the first time since 1933. Wielding knives and throwing beer steins, they waded into a meeting of legitimists at the municipal auditorium, sending ten of them to the hospital before the arrival of the police.[10]

THE NAZI SEIZURE OF POWER

After Hitler's meeting with Schuschnigg at Berchtesgaden on 12 February 1938, Nazi marches and demonstrations became common occurrences in Linz. Connected by courier to all parts of Upper Austria and receiving orders from Kaltenbrunner's SS, local party leaders were able to coordinate their activities with other areas of the doomed Alpine state. With Security Director Revertera fatuously believing himself in control of the situation, the Nazis held more and more rallies in order to keep pressure on the Schuschnigg government and to prevent a relaxation of tensions. On the night of 10 March, just after the announcement of Schuschnigg's proposed plebiscite for the 13th, thousands of Nazis and their sympathizers marched shouting and singing across the square before City Hall. Some climbed onto the balcony and raised the swastika banner. In Urfahr, on the other side of the Danube, SA men exchanged shots with paramilitary troops of the Patriotic Front.[11]

Although the Upper Austrian National Socialists acted with growing self-confidence in early 1938, the leaders of the provincial movement hesitated to break with the 'legal and evolutionary way' to power worked out by Hitler. In contrast to party comrades in Styria and elsewhere, *Gauleiter* Eigruber refused to take direct action on his own. On the morning of 11 March 1938, however, he met with his provincial staff at a tavern in the south of Linz. He told those present that German troops were deployed on the border and that he had received orders both from Austrian and German Nazis to take power. Until further word, the municipal leadership was to devote its energies to whipping up mass enthusiasm. After scheduling a torchlight procession for that evening, Eigruber returned to his command post in Langoth's apartment.

In Linz itself that afternoon most work came to a virtual standstill. The streets filled with thousands of tense, nervous people who sensed that political decisions were being made affecting their own personal lives. In public buildings officials of the Patriotic Front left their posts and went home, though some, including Gleissner, stayed on the job. Everywhere armed police stood nervously watching the growing crowds. Toward evening, thousands of Nazis assembled in the Goethestrasse. Carrying flaming torches, they marched over the Landstrasse toward the huge public square on the banks of the Danube. As the brown column streamed past the Chamber of Commerce building, Eigruber left the line of march and proceeded to the *Landhaus*, where he confronted Security Director Revertera. The count, who had so often cooperated with Nazis in the past, managed to stall Eigruber by insisting on written authorization from Vienna. Below in the courtyard, municipal SS leaders Anton Fellner and Josef Plakolm, both well-known Linz attorneys, requisitioned an auto and drove to the federal police headquarters in the Mozartstrasse. Dressed in the black trousers and white shirts of the illegal SS, they found the building already occupied by their followers. The police, although still armed, stood by in small groups. Out of a total force of five hundred no more than twenty turned out to be active Nazis, but the majority was too stunned to offer any resistance. Presently, police president Dr. Victor Bentz stalked out of his office to denounce Fellner and Plakolm to their face. In a rage he left Linz for his home in the country, where three days later he was shot to death.[12]

In the meantime, Fellner and Plakolm returned to the *Landhaus* where Eigruber was patiently waiting for Governor Gleissner to finish his last cabinet session. Although the governor was actually burning documents, the *Gauleiter* refused to intervene until Gleissner formally adjourned the meeting. Across town in the *Rathaus* similar courtesies were shown to the outgoing municipal government. Sepp Wolkerstorfer refused to force open Mayor Bock's locked desk. Instead, he summoned the mayor, handed him a briefcase, and asked him to unlock the drawer. Instructing Bock to remove his personal possessions, Wolkerstorfer left the room to ensure privacy. Within a few months both Gleissner and Bock were sent to Dachau.

Throughout the remainder of Friday evening, 11 March, other important buildings and installations were rapidly occupied by the Nazis. These included: the state radio on Freinberg heights, the provincial mortgage office, the Chamber of Labor, both newspapers, the train stations, the excise and customs offices, and all offices of the Patriotic Front. By 11:30 P.M. every police station, every municipal building, and all public offices in Upper Austria were in the hands of the Nazis. The internal "seizure of power" was complete.[13]

HITLER'S HOMECOMING

For the next two days the eyes of the world were riveted on Linz. Early Saturday morning word arrived that German troops were crossing the frontier and would soon pass through the Upper Austrian capital on their way to Vienna. Most local Nazis reacted to the news with dismay, for they believed that victory belonged to them alone. Indeed, when the first

Anschluss in Linz. German reconnaissance vehicles enter
the city at noon on 12 March 1938. DÖW.

German reconaissance vehicles entered the city at noon, Sepp Wolkerstorfer
was so distraught that he telephoned Eigruber to ask that the vehicles'
hatches be opened so as not to alarm the population.[14] But whatever
Wolkerstorfer's reservations, they rapidly melted away as General Guderian's soldiers were acclaimed by cheering throngs and pealing bells. When
Hitler himself arrived in Linz, he was so touched by the wild jubilation that
he impulsively decided to abandon an earlier plan for a "personal union" of
Austria and Germany and to incorporate his homeland into the Reich.[15] In
his speech he proclaimed, "If it was Providence that once called me forth
from this city to the leadership of the Reich, then it must also have given me
the mission—and it can only have been a mission—to restore my homeland
to the German Reich."[16]

    Early next morning Hitler met with his military chiefs, Keitel and
Brauchitsch, as well as with several party officials to announce that forthwith
Austria would become a province of the Reich. Later that day after a visit to

The Prodigal's Return. Hitler on the balcony of the Linz
Rathaus, 12 March 1938. DÖW.

his parents' grave in Leonding, he invited ten leading Upper Austrian Nazis to dinner at the Hotel Weinzinger. There, over pea soup and rice, he signed the so-called Anschluss Act, and in a rambling monologue he discussed foreign affairs, the construction of a new Autobahn, and his intentions of transforming Linz into a cultural metropolis. In explaining his construction plans, Hitler became so enraptured that in Upper Austrian dialect he blurted out, "the cares and troubles of this city are over because I have assumed its personal protection."[17]

The Nazi seizure of power in Linz was thus the direct result of German pressure and intervention. It did not occur as a consequence of a deal with traditional elites nor in the wake of a mass upheaval. While sometimes tolerant of Nazi activities, local authorities and police forces remained loyal to the Christian Corporative regime until the end. As for popular sentiment, it was clearly more sympathetic to the Nazi cause than in the past though more in a passive than a participatory sense. In the surrounding Upper Austrian countryside the Catholic peasants continued aloof and suspicious of the Third Reich.[18] Still, when the Anschluss occurred, it unleashed a torrent of enthusiasm for Hitler that may never be adequately explained. To what extent decades of German Nationalist propaganda, the release of pent-up emotions, or hopes for economic betterment contributed to the psychological hysteria must remain matters of conjecture. In the excitement of the moment what was indisputable was that the Christian Corporative system was dead. It had failed not only to win the loyalty of the Austrian people but to protect their basic security. At the very least, it was a form of government that in the twentieth century had become outmoded and ineffective.

THE NEW ELITE

At 10:30 A.M. on Monday, 14 March 1938, Hitler emerged from the Hotel Weinzinger, climbed into his open Mercedes, and resumed his triumphal tour to Vienna. Although he left behind token German military and police units as symbols of the Anschluss, he had resolved to strengthen Austria's provinces at the expense of Vienna and thus permitted local Nazis to retain the power they had so recently won. Without prodding, these municipal and provincial party members moved swiftly to consolidate their control.[19] In Linz and Upper Austria this was a task made easier by the compact, cohesive nature of the provincial NSDAP. With only 2,128 officially registered members at the time of the Anschluss,[20] the regional organization retained the character of a tight-knit cadre able to expand its membership with discretion. Lacking a Catholic Conservative component, the Upper Austrian movement was also spared the internal dissension that at times plagued the larger organizations of Vienna, Lower Austria, Styria, and Carinthia. In the halcyon days following the Anschluss this gave *Gauleiter* Eigruber a distinct advantage in shaping the party as well as in retaining and expanding his own personal power.

Eigruber was the sort of brutal political infighter most admired by Hitler. The illegitimate son of a Steyr handicraftsman, he had joined the Austrian NSDAP as a teenager and become *Bezirksleiter* of Steyr at age twenty-one. During the period of unlawful activity he was appointed provincial *Gauleiter* by Leopold, possibly because of his working-class background. Although unemployed for months on end and imprisoned off and on for over a year, Eigruber strengthened his hold on the underground Upper Austrian party, partly by conciliating German Nationalist hangers-on and partly by bullying more plebeian members. Hitler's tumultuous homecoming celebration gave Eigruber the opportunity to make a favorable impression on the Führer and to establish cordial relations with Martin Bormann. Not by chance was he the only "illegal" Austrian *Gauleiter* to retain his post.[21]

Short, stocky, and muscular, Eigruber always regarded himself as a worker.[22] He customarily addressed crowds in his shirt sleeves and argued that the founding of state industries, such as the famous Hermann Göring Steel Works, freed wage earners from dependence on capitalist plutocrats.[23] With a genuine concern for the common man and a domineering personality, he was able to hold his own with Reich officials like Minister of the Interior Frick and even SS chief Heinrich Himmler. Eigruber considered the "Home District of the Führer" a special trust and refused to brook interference in that bailiwick. Totally dedicated to Hitler, the *Gauleiter* endorsed the dissolution of Austria into its constituent parts, was an active planner in the transformation of Linz into a cultural metropolis, and worked closely with the commandant of the nearby Mauthausen concentration camp.[24]

Eigruber's protégé in the city of Linz was Josef Wolkerstorfer. Also of plebeian background (his father had been a laborer at the Institute of Essential Services), Wolkerstorfer was a hatmaker who owned an elegant men's clothing store on the Landstrasse. Outgoing, athletic, and ambitious, he had joined the Nazi party in 1933 with his friends in a *völkisch* sporting club. Thereafter, in the dark days of the Schuschnigg regime he played an important role in mobilizing urban workers for Hitler's cause and in disbursing funds from Langoth's Relief Society. On 12 March 1938 he found himself lord mayor of Linz. Neither as intelligent nor as ruthless as Eigruber, Wolkerstorfer did not succeed in his job. With little knowledge of municipal administration, he presided over a scandal at City Hall involving the sale of ration stamps on the black market. In 1940 under pressure from Kaltenbrunner, he was eased out of his position.[25]

Although the NSDAP in Linz appeared dominated by men of proletarian origin, an analysis of the town's new elite reveals that Nazi rule was simply another form of petty bourgeois dominance. Whether in the *Gauleitung*,

the *Kreisleitung*, or the city council, middle-class personnel controlled the
major posts. It is true that Eigruber, Wolkerstorfer, and other members of
the "Leopold faction" came originally from the working classes, but as tough
infighters their careers were illustrative of those persons, much admired in
middle-class ideology, who now and then rise to the top in a competitive
environment. Certainly Eigruber, much as he emphasized his own background, never questioned the existing social order or, for that matter, made
way for other workers in the Nazi elite.

A close examination of the Nazi leadership structure in 1939 does reveal
some differences in the *Gau*, *Kreis*, and city council levels.[26] The
Gauleitung, for example, apparently had the widest age distribution with
two key members over sixty years of age, at least one still in his twenties, and
fully half between thirty and fifty. On the city council and in the *Kreisleitung*
the age configuration was somewhat lower, with 75 percent of the elites in
both structures under the age of fifty and in the *Kreisleitung* about 58
percent under forty (table 24).[27]

Educationally, the *Gau* also had the widest distribution with some leaders
who had completed only primary school and about 45 percent with some
university training. All members of the city council and apparently of the
Kreisleitung had completed secondary school with one-third of the councillors holding university degrees. Only 17 percent of the *Kreisleitung*
appeared to have attended institutions of higher learning (table 25).

Not surprisingly, the distribution of elite occupations mirrored education.
Nearly half of the *Gauleitung* belonged to the free professions, as did
one-quarter of the city council though only 8 percent of the *Kreisleitung*.
Similarly, one-third of the *Kreisleitung* were self-employed businessmen for
whom a secondary education usually sufficed (table 26).

These differences aside, most Nazi elites had a good deal in common. To

TABLE 24   NSDAP Elite in Linz, 1939 Age Distribution

Class	Age	Gauleitung	Kreisleitung	City Council
1870–9	60–69	10	—	4.2
1880–9	50–59	10	16.6	18.8
1890–9	40–49	15	25.0	37.5
1900–9	30–39	35	50.0	39.5
1910–9	20–29	5	8.3	—
Not ascertained		25	—	—
(Sample Size)		(20)	(12)	(48)

Computed from BDC Berlin and Bart and Puffer, *Die Gemeindevertretung der Stadt Linz*.

TABLE 25   NSDAP Elite in Linz, 1939 Highest Level of Education
Obtained (percentages)

	Gauleitung	Kreisleitung	City Council
Primary	10	—	—
Secondary	15	50.0	64.0
Higher	45	16.6	33.3
Not ascertained	30	33.3	2.1
(Sample Size)	(20)	(12)	(48)

Computed from BDC Berlin and Bart and Puffer, *Die Gemeindevertretung der Stadt Linz.*

TABLE 26   NSDAP Elite in Linz, 1939 Occupational Composition
(percentages)

	Gauleitung	Kreisleitung	City Council
Private Employees	—	16.6	18.8
Civil Servant/Public Employees	17.6	8.3	14.7
Teachers	11.8	8.3	10.5
Professionals	47.1	8.3	23.0
Self Employed Business	11.8	33.3	10.7
Workers:			
Skilled	5.8	25.0	18.8
Unskilled	5.8	—	—
Other	—	—	4.2
(Sample Size)	(20)	(12)	(48)

Computed from BDC Berlin and Bart and Puffer, *Die Gemeindevertretung der Stadt Linz.*

begin, nearly all were native Austrians and at least three-quarters were from
Upper Austria. Very few Reich Germans, in other words, wielded *political*
power in the Danubian city after 1938 (Table 27). Secondly, most elites had
been active in the Nazi party before the Anschluss, primarily in the "illegal"
movement (only about a fourth seem to have belonged to Hitler's movement
before 1932). Most were under fifty, nearly all had at least a secondary
education, and the overwhelming majority, to repeat, came from the middle
strata of society. National Socialism, in other words, constituted an authoritarian form of middle-class dominance dependent on full employment,
manipulative propaganda, and terror.

TABLE 27   NSDAP Elite in Linz, 1939 Geographical Origin (percentages)

	Gauleitung	Kreisleitung	City Council
Linz	22.2	41.6	27.1
Environs	—	8.3	12.5
Upper Austria	72.2	25.0	29.2
Austria	5.6	8.3	18.8
Bohemia/Moravia	—	—	6.3
Other	—	16.3	6.3
(Sample) Size)	(20)	(12)	(48)

Computed from BDC Berlin and Bart and Puffer, *Die Gemeindevertretung der Stadt Linz.*

TABLE 28   NSDAP Elite in Linz, Occupation of Father (percentages)

	Linz City Council 1939	Lerner (administrator)	Lerner (random)
Landowner	10.4	2.0	1.9
Military	4.2	5.3	1.3
Ecclesiastical	—	1.3	1.3
Professional	4.2	11.9	18.9
Civil Service	25.2	7.9	14.5
Business	27.1	9.9	19.5
Artisan	8.3	6.0	2.5
Peasants	—	7.3	3.1
Other	—	5.3	1.9
Not ascertained	8.3	43.0	34.0
(Sample Size)	(48)	(151)	(159)

Computed from BDC Berlin; Bart and Puffer, *Die Gemeindevertretung der Stadt Linz;* and Lerner, "The Nazi Elite."

An intensive analysis of the 1939 city council in Linz, for which more complete data are available, provides an even more revealing picture. Of forty-eight members, thirteen (27 percent) were the sons of hoteliers, retailers, merchants, or entrepreneurs; four (8 percent) of craftsmen; and two (4 percent) of public officials or employees. Of the total group approximately 65 percent hailed from the old *Mittelstand*, and, at most, only five (10 percent) from the proletariat or lower classes (table 28).

Nevertheless, the Nazi city councillors were socially quite different from

TABLE 29   NSDAP Elite in Linz, Highest Level of Education Achieved (percentages)

	Linz City Council 1939	Lerner (administrator)	Lerner (random)
University	18.8	25.2	60.4
Technische Hochschule	12.5	6.6	7.6
Other higher schools	2.1	11.3	3.0
Trade schools	6.3	25.2	11.3
High school	58.3	27.8	12.6
Grade school	—	3.3	5.0
Unknown	2.0	0.7	0.0
(Sample Size)	(48)	(151)	(159)

Computed from BDC Berlin; Bart and Puffer, *Die Gemeindevertretung der Stadt Linz;* and Lerner, "The Nazi Elite."

their fathers, for they had moved from the old into the new *Mittelstand*.[28] In terms of education, for example, one-third of the group held university-level degrees and another quarter had graduated from higher secondary schools. A solid majority (56.2 percent) might therefore be considered the equivalent of American college graduates, though it should be emphasized that 70 percent of those with higher secondary educations had attended commercial academies, normal schools, technical institutes, or *Realschulen*, which in Central Europe had decidedly lower prestige than classical gymnasia.[29]

Occupationally (table 26), eleven of the councillors belonged to the free professions; five were farmers, craftsmen, or entrepreneurs; nine were white collar employees; and twelve were teachers, soldiers, policemen, public servants and employees, or university professors. At least thirty-three (68.8 percent) of the total, belonged to the new *Mittelstand*, indicating that for many National Socialism was a means of maintaining or, after a period of dislocation, *reachieving* social, economic, and political dominance in Linz. It is interesting to note, incidentally, that after World War II only two of the councillors were forced into long-term menial work and that sixteen (33.6 percent) rather quickly reassumed positions of importance. Indeed, two were reelected to the city council in 1955, and shortly thereafter seven received high awards (such as the *Ehrenring*) for public service.

The National Socialist elite in Linz, then, was strikingly similar to the Nazi elite in Germany, particularly as analyzed in Lerner's famous study of the *Führerlexikon*.[30] As in the *Altreich*, most Linz elite elements were under fifty years of age, many had attended institutions of higher learning, and nearly all were middle-class. The principal leaders, moreover, such as

Eigruber and Wolkerstorfer virtually epitomized Lerner's administrative elites, rising from plebeian origins to top positions. That Linz elites might also be considered "marginal men," however, is open to some doubt.[31] Before 1931 most important local Nazis such as Alfred Proksch did admittedly fit this pattern, as did most of their followers. But, as we have seen, once the German Nationalists went over to the Nazis, National Socialism seems to have become a means of reestablishing urban middle-class power. It was no coincidence, in other words, that the wartime mayor of Hitler's favorite city was Franz Langoth, the German Nationalist politician whom Hitler had known and admired since his youth.[32]

Significantly underrepresented in the Nazi elite was the Linz business community, at least initially. As examination of lists of party activists for the interwar period makes clear, few producers, merchants, or financiers—with some notable exceptions—expressed much of an interest in Nazism or before 1938 gave it much support. As we have seen, in fact, most municipal businessmen cast their lot with the more reactionary Christian Corporative system whose orthodox fiscal policies and brutal treatment of organized labor were more to their liking.

In sum, those people and groups who dominated the Nazi movement in Linz throughout the entire interwar period and who after 1938 shared the spoils of victory, came primarily from the professional and bureaucratic strata of society. They were not the "losers of the industrial revolution,"[33] but they were the local losers of the collapse of the Habsburg monarchy. Denied entrance to what had once been a vast imperial civil service or to upwardly mobile careers in the Austro-Hungarian railways, post, or telegraph services, these men, many of them the sons of the anticlerical old *Mittelstand* that had supported German Nationalist rule before 1918, found themselves "stifled" in the First Austrian Republic. Unable to find alternate careers in Linz or Upper Austria, they joined white-collar employees in flocking to Hitler's banner. Together they constituted a microcosm not just of the Nazi elite in Austria or Germany, but rather of the upwardly mobile elements of modern industrial society in general.[34]

Once in power, the Nazis proceeded to reorganize and to expand the Austrian NSDAP in their own image. On orders from Hitler, they were not to enroll more than 10 percent of the population so that party membership would retain its elite character. Between 1938 and 1945 they registered over half a million Austrians, a proportion of 8.2 percent of the inhabitants of the Ostmark. In Tyrol, Salzburg, Voralberg, and Upper Danube (Upper Austria) they succeeded in expanding membership enormously, at least in part as a consequence of increasing prosperity and a shift of the economy to the industrializing west. The Upper Austrian party thus grew from 2,128 registered members at the time of the Anschluss to 87,588 in 1942; through war losses the number declined to 74,128 in 1946, a proportion of 8.1 percent of the population.[35]

In the absence of available party membership lists, it is difficult to draw conclusions on the social composition of the post-Anschluss NSDAP in Linz. On the basis of exiguous data, it seems that the proportion of registered blue collar workers declined after 1938. The number of working class party members in the municipal administration as of 1 May 1945, for example, was very small: out of 2,369 manual workers only 46 (1.9 percent) belonged to the party. It may be that overall urban membership was much higher, but a postwar survey of Nazi registration in the American zone of Upper Austria and Salzburg (province) reveals a total blue-collar membership of only 17 percent for the region. The same survey suggests an increase in the proportion of self-employed, with just under 40 percent belonging to this class. Other middle-class elements also seem to have predominated (table 30). Of 139 university-trained officials in the Linz municipal administration at the end of the war, no less than 77 (55 percent) were party members; among middle-level administrators and employees the percentage was 27. All told, the NSDAP in Linz remained primarily a movement of the new *Mittelstand*, though after 1938 it opened its rolls to the broadest possible spectrum of the nonagrarian middle strata, largely at the expense of the industrial proletariat and the peasantry.[36]

THE APRIL PLEBISCITE

Within days of the Anschluss, Nazi authorities turned their full attention to organizing the plebiscite ordered by Hitler for 10 April 1938. The referendum was designed to conceal the harsh reality of German annexation by demonstrating to the world that the Austrian people stood behind the Führer and the newly created Greater German Reich.[37] In order to ensure a positive response *Gauleiter* Josef Bürckel of the Saar was posted to Vienna with 17.1 million marks placed at his disposal both by the Ministry of the Interior and the Nazi party. As director of the April plebiscite, Bürckel established a tight-knit apparatus that gave him effective control not only of the electoral process but of Austria itself. As a consequence, many prominent Austrian Nazis were pushed aside, provoking considerable resentment especially in Vienna. This was not, however, the case in Linz where Eigruber and his subordinates held their own throughout the electoral campaign.[38]

In the month before the plebiscite an endless parade of German Nazi dignitaries descended upon Upper Austria. Among those campaigning at Linz in those hectic days were National Women's leader Gertrud Scholz-Klink, SA chief Viktor Lutze, Hitler Youth leader Baldur von Schirach, SS chief Heinrich Himmler, Reich Marshal Hermann Göring, and Hitler

TABLE 30   Occupation of Austrian Nazi Party Members in 1946

| | In the U.S. Zone of Upper Austria and Salzburg | | In Austria | |
	Absolute Figures	Percentages	Absolute Figures	Percentages
Self-employed (and assisting family members)	41,418	37.0	212,764	39.3
Of these in:				
agriculture & forestry	12,969	11.6	69,100	12.8
industry & crafts	14,084	12.6	70,369	13.0
commerce & transport	6,395	5.7	32,534	6.0
free professions	5,165	4.6	22,699	4.2
other trades	2,805	2.5	18,062	3.3
Public Servants	15,729	14.1	97,562	18.0
Of these:				
employees	13,135	11.8	84,576	15.6
workers	2,594	2.3	12,986	2.4
Employees in private enterprises	13,058	11.7	58,560	10.8
Workers in private enterprises	16,157	14.5	62,551	11.5
Others	25,373	22.7	110,286	20.4
Of these:				
pensioners	3,342	3.0	20,223	3.7
students	1,412	1.3	6,856	1.3
housewives	18,134	16.2	68,331	12.6
not ascertained	2,485		14,876	
Total	111,735	100.0	541,723	100.0

SOURCE: Botz, "The Changing Pattern of Support for Austrian National Socialism," p. 219 and Luža, *Austro-German Relations*, p. 381.

himself. In their speeches the Nazi leaders promised the fulfillment of national destiny, the establishment of social harmony, and the rapid elimination of unemployment.[39] Addressing 10,000 fellow Linzers at the former Krauss locomotive works on 7 April, Hitler reminded his audience of the misery Germany had experienced before his rise to power and of the wonders accomplished since by National Socialism. "As of 13 March," he declared, "the city of Linz has been insoluably linked to Greater German history."[40]

Besides making reassuring promises of economic well-being and impressing the population with the might and power of the Third Reich, the Nazis made specific appeals to the Roman Catholic hierarchy and to the remnants of organized labor. As he had done in Germany five years before, Hitler deftly threw the Austrian clergy off balance by suggesting that once conditions returned to normal, the Church would enjoy the sort of autonomy it normally enjoyed in state and society. The Viennese cardinal, Theodor Innitzer responded eagerly, without pausing to insist on specific guarantees for his flock, by giving thanks for the "bloodless revolution" and by persuading his bishops to sign a pastoral letter endorsing the Anschluss: "On the day of the plebiscite it will be for us bishops a national duty to declare ourselves as Germans for the German Reich. We expect from all faithful Christians an awareness of their debt to the nation."[41]

In Linz and Upper Austria these words were hard to swallow. As we have seen, Bishop Gföllner despised National Socialism; after 1933 he had, in fact, reproached the German bishops for their accommodations with the Nazi state. During Hitler's homecoming celebration the bishop refused to greet the Führer at the Linz cathedral and sought to dissuade Innitzer from supporting the new order. It was only with great reluctance and under considerable duress that Gföllner was compelled to sign the declaration of his fellow bishops.[42]

But while Gföllner abominated the Nazi regime, a number of other Upper Austrian churchmen did not. The canon of St. Florian, Dr. Alois Nikolussi, published an appeal for priests to campaign actively for the plebiscite:

> National Socialism is against abuse of religion. With all its strength it protects the true faith and demands from all ethnic-comrades Christianity of action and committed belief in God. Already, in dozens of cases, priests have pledged their loyalty to their people. Priests are invited to contribute actively to the Greater German movement. If we do not recognize the great hour, we shall once again be without a nation.[43]

Endorsing Nikolussi's testimonial, Eigruber added:

> Many priests have already turned to us in order to contribute with all their might in explaining to our people the great events of our times. . . . I welcome this demonstration of national solidarity from which only good can emerge for folk and home and all positive forces which should serve them.[44]

Turning to the Social Democratic working classes in Linz, the Nazis encountered an unexpected degree of support. Many blue-collar workers were so bitterly alienated by the Christian Corporative system that they were willing to collaborate with the new regime out of spite for the old.[45] For their part, the Nazis emphasized their common suffering under the Dollfuss-Schuschnigg dictatorship and professed a concern for labor within the folk community. They admitted that economic conditions could scarcely improve in only four weeks, but they took dramatic steps to arouse realistic hopes for the future.[46]

On 26 March, Göring announced in Vienna the immediate transfer of 60 million marks for industrial development and agricultural modernization.[47] Simultaneously, German social security benefits were extended to Austria. Within just days of the Anschluss, representatives of the Strength Through Joy (KdF) agency of the German Labor Front arrived in Linz with ambitious plans for the city's workers. About a thousand of them were selected to join other Austrians on a free vacation in North Germany. Special trains took them to Hamburg where they embarked on the *Wilhelm Gustloff* for a North Sea cruise. The KdF also arranged for weekend cruises on the Danube and short-term excursions (such as to Obersalzberg) on a more-or-less regular basis. The KdF's recreational projects found popular support in Linz, but they comprised only one part of an extensive welfare program. Beginning on 29 March, relief payments to the unemployed were assumed by the Four Year Plan, while free meals and emergency housing were made available by the National Socialist People's Welfare organization (NSV).[48] Under these circumstances, it was hardly surprising that important labor leaders were persuaded to endorse the April referendum. On 5 April, Ludwig Bernaschek addressed 5,000 railway men—many of them his brother's former *Schutzbündler*—urging them to cast their ballots for Greater Germany.[49]

In generating popular enthusiasm for the new order by means of persuasion, censorship, and promises of economic revitalization, the Nazis did not ignore their opponents. Over the weekend of 12–14 March local SS troopers strangled police detective Josef Schmirl at police headquarters, shot his colleague Josef Feldmann, and gunned down police president Bentz at his home outside Linz. On Monday the blackshirts dragged police inspector Ludwig Bernegger from his home, interrogated him, forced him to urinate on himself, took him out into the street, and killed him. In the meantime, stormtroopers occupied the Kraus and Schober department store, dismissed its Jewish employees, and arrested the firm's managers. Within just a matter of days the city's Jewish shops were "Aryanized," Jewish attorneys were forbidden to practice, and the head of the Jewish religious community, Dr. Karl Schwager, was taken into custody.[50]

As in many parts of Austria, indiscriminate Nazi terror produced near anarchy in Linz. By Tuesday, 15 March, conditions had become so chaotic that Eigruber issued a proclamation demanding "unconditional discipline" from all party members.[51] Thereafter, procedures became more orderly and systematic, although arrests to settle personal grudges were still taking place as late as 20 May.[52] Among those detained were prominent local Jews and important officials of the old regime such as Gleissner, Bock, Felix Kern, police inspector Josef Seber, provincial school superintendent Hubert Messenbock, and the legitimist General Oskar Englisch-Popparich.[53] Significantly, most municipal Social Democrats at this early period were left in peace. Not until much later would they suffer grievously at the hands of the Nazis.[54]

In the meantime, some 40,000 German security police were streaming into Austria to orchestrate and coordinate the arrest of Hitler's political opponents. Under Himmler and Heydrich the security forces operated independently of both German and Austrian political authorities; at times they even interfered with the campaign for the April referendum.[55] In Linz, however, there was little friction with local officials as Gestapo headquarters remained largely in the hands of the Upper Austrian Nazi, Dr. Josef Plakolm, assisted by Dr. Rudolf Mildner, a Reich German born in the Sudetenland who had grown up in Salzburg. After an initial period of arbitrary arrests, the police placed under surveillance or took into custody those persons and groups—"Communists, Revolutionary Socialists, etc."— who might be expected to exert a negative influence on the upcoming plebiscite. Most of those actually detained, however, seem to have been affiliated with the Christian Corporative regime.[56]

As a rule, the Linz Gestapo proceeded with caution so as not to alarm the local population. On 27 March, Deputy Security Director Mildner ordered the immediate release of "lower- and middle-level functionaries of the Communist and Marxist parties respectively and of the Patriotic Front." In addition, he insisted on common sense in dealing with the "Jewish question." While Jews were proscribed from voting, it was not necessary, he directed, to examine the racial origins of all registered voters.[57]

On 10 April Upper Austrian voters went to the polls to ratify the Anschluss and to vow fealty to Hitler. Buoyed by mass rallies, martial music, and a carnival-like atmosphere, most of them had every intention of registering their approval. At the polling place they had little choice. As in Berlin five years before, when the Reichstag convened to pass the Enabling Act, the polls in Linz were surrounded by uniformed stormtroopers. In some locations voters had the option of entering a voting booth, but usually they were required to mark their ballot in the presence of a Nazi magistrate. At the tavern Zum Zeppelin on Linz's Franckstrasse—a working class district— premarked ballots were distributed by SA men. Under such conditions, it was virtually impossible to vote against the Anschluss. According to the results, 99.87 percent of Linz's voters concurred with Austria's "reunion" with the German Reich. This affirmative vote was higher than in Upper Austria (99.82 percent), Austria (99.73 percent), and Germany (99.08 percent).[58]

To what extent the April plebiscite reflected the actual desires and wishes of the Austrian people must remain an open question.[59] In endorsing Nazi rule the masses lent their support to a regime promising dramatic if ambiguous change. In Linz the referendum legitimized the administration of a new generation of German Nationalists who shared little sentimental attachment to the preindustrial world of their fathers. Although interested more in political power than in economic rationalization, the indigenous Nazis showed little hesitation in subscribing to a program of secularization and industrialization laid down in Berlin. Under Hitler's tutelage, they inaugurated a process that would ruthlessly alter the structure of local production and transform Linz into a modern industrial city.

EIGHT

Hitler's Hometown 1939–1945

Less than fifteen months after the April plebiscite, Hitler plunged Europe into war. At last freed from the constraints of peacetime legality, he moved ruthlessly to consolidate and expand his control of the home front. Already in the newly incorporated *Ostmark* he was largely unencumbered by compromises with traditional structures and institutions. Focusing his attention on Linz, he proceeded to fashion in his homeland the kind of society he envisaged with greater freedom than in the Old Reich. What happened in the Upper Austrian capital thus foreshadowed something of Hitler's intentions, not simply for Austria but for much of the Greater German Reich. For our purposes the experience of Nazi rule should provide a key to understanding the confusing problem of coercion and consent under the German occupation.[1] It should also illuminate such issues as the role of the Roman Catholic Church, the extent of German penetration of Austrian institutions after 1938, and the impact of fascist industrialization in transforming and modernizing Austrian society.

A NATIVE-BORN ELITE

Although Hitler occupied Austria with German troops, he entrusted the administration of the provinces outside Vienna to indigenous Nazis. His aim was to hasten the dissolution of the country as an entity by strengthening the forces of regionalism.[2] As a consequence, at least two-thirds of the political posts in the new *Reichsgau* of Upper Danube were controlled by Upper Austrians and the rest by native-born Austrians. With regard to the police and security sector, the picture is less clear. Hitler ordered some 40,000 German regular and security police into Austria during the Anschluss, but just how many of them wound up in Linz is unknown.[3] Evidence available does suggest, however, that important positions in the SD and the Gestapo were largely in the hands of local men. The police president, Dr. Josef Plakolm, for example, was a well-known Linz attorney with close personal ties to Austrian SS chief Ernst Kaltenbrunner, also from Linz. At Gestapo headquarters other local functionaries such as Franz Stangl, the future commandant of Treblinka, held key posts as well. It is true, of course, that Reich Germans, such as Gestapo chief Georg Prohaska, served at Linz as police officers and security men after 1938. Nevertheless, by 1945 at least five of the most prominent municipal Gestapo officials were Austrian.[4] In other areas of Upper Danube police personnel remained largely provincials. In the village of Perg near Mauthausen, for example, the police forces did not change at all between 1937 and 1945.[5] Judging from the files of one SS officer, it also appears that local SS men were frequently reassigned to their hometowns after service in a concentration camp or at the front.[6]

This is not to say that German penetration of Linz, Upper Austria, or Austria did not take place after the Anschluss. In the military sphere Reich Germans were regularly assigned most of the command positions in the integrated armed forces after 1938, although once again in Upper Danube an Austrian general staff officer (Major General Friedrich Materna) assumed command of the Wehrmacht's 45th (Linz) Infantry Division.[7] Within the *administrative* bureaucracy of the *Reichsgau* the situation was somewhat reversed in that most of the key political posts were held by Austrians, while the office of chief administrative assistant (*Regierungspräsident*) was usually reserved for a German. At Linz, for example, the *Gauleiter's* Austrian deputy (Hans Eisenkolb) was replaced by a Reich German (Christian Opdenhoff) in 1940. Whether the appointment was the consequence of the appointee's considerable experience in Prusso-German-Nazi administration or part of a deliberate "personal-political" policy of infiltration is not clear. In all likelihood, as the Austrian historian Gerhard Botz has suggested, the increasing assignment of German personnel to bureaucratic posts in Austria was primarily "the outcome of administrative unification and the adoption of Prussian-German rules."[8] Whatever the cause, by 1 January 1945 some 45 percent of the executive officials of the Linz revenue office were Reich Germans as were 46 percent of those in middle-level positions and 20 percent in subordinate posts. In the post, telegraph, and railways the situation was similar.[9]

While substantial numbers of local personnel occupied positions of authority in Hitler's hometown after 1938, it is still not altogether clear who gave orders to whom. Control of the SS-SD-Gestapo apparatus resided indisputably in Berlin, but, despite an influx of Reich German administrators, the lines of authority within the state bureaucracy remained tangled throughout the entire period of Nazi rule.[10] As in neighboring Salzburg, however, the indigenous NSDAP clearly exercised something approaching a hegemonic role. According to the *Ostmark* Law of 14 April 1939, the party organization in each *Gau* of the *Ostmark* was given a virtual monopoly of power on the provincial level. Unconstrained by semiautonomous, traditional structures such as the army, the bureaucracy, and the Church, the

Nazi party had the potential of wielding greater local power in Austria than in Germany.[11] In the case of Linz, the native-born party organization through its network of parasitic associations extended its influence over virtually all aspects of public life in Upper Danube. Under Eigruber's able leadership, the party also held its own against competing authorities from outside the *Reichsgau*: the *Gauleiter* regularly ignored orders from Frick, clashed occasionally with Himmler, and even wrested some control of foreign labor in Upper Danube from the SS.[12] It would be misleading to suggest that the homegrown party organization called all the shots in Linz, but even with the presence of substantial numbers of Reich German administrators and industrialists, there can be no doubt that Upper Austrian functionaries constituted the core of the town's ruling elite.

THE NAZI CONSENSUS

At this point, the question can be posed To what extent did the Nazi regime rest on popular consent? Despite the best efforts of postwar historians in arguing the contrary,[13] the truth seems to be that in Linz National Socialism enjoyed the warm endorsement of the town's inhabitants. From the moment of Hitler's triumphal homecoming in March 1938 until well into the Second World War strong grass-roots support extending down into the working classes was revealed not only by foreign journalists and secret Gestapo surveys but also by indirect social indicators such as a skyrocketing birth rate twice that of the national average.[14] The rapid introduction of measures relieving social distress, especially by the Strength Through Joy organization, the revitalization of the Linz economy, and, above all, the elimination of local unemployment within six months of the Anschluss all created a psychological euphoria affecting every class of society including the workers. As two Austrian historians have recently written, "for many employment became the measure of all things; lost rights were tolerated and compensated by the feeling of having at last found work again."[15]

Generally speaking, the Nazis tackled the unemployment problem in Linz through a combination of labor conscription and exchanges, compulsory military service, and urban renewal projects. Immediately after the Anschluss, they commenced organizing the young and the youthful unemployed into the Reich Labor Service (RAD). By summer, the first labor battalions were at work in the city and in the surrounding countryside while a number of skilled workers were sent to Braunschweig to take jobs in plants there. In the meantime, Hitler's elaborate construction schemes for Linz were already providing money and jobs. The Führer intended to transform his hometown into a cultural metropolis by erecting monumental buildings on both banks of the Danube, including a city hall, a stadium, theaters, cultural and military museums, several party buildings, and an impressive bell tower to hold his own crypt. During his stay in the Hotel Weinzinger on 13 March 1938 he announced the immediate construction of a new bridge, and within days the first engineers arrived to begin the task. By 1 April 1939, the bridge heads of the Nibelungen bridge (designed years before by Hitler himself) were well under way. In addition, substantial credits were made available for slum clearance and housing construction.[16]

The most important factor in the economic revitalization of Linz—and Austria—was to be the restructuring of its industrial base. On a Danubian cruise on 25 March 1938, Hermann Göring, as director of the Four Year Plan, met with Austrian and German planners to coordinate schemes for the economic development of Austria. Under strong pressure from the armed forces and the German business community, Göring advocated a seventeen-point program for the increased exploitation of raw materials, the expansion of energy production, and the development of heavy industry.[17] "The Austrians must rely on themselves to develop their own country,"[18] Göring said, but he provided 60 million marks to ensure success. When adopted and implemented, as we shall see, his program was of enormous benefit to Austria's western provinces and particularly to Linz.

The immediate results of these efforts were dramatic. At the time of the Anschluss some 37,120 people were out of work in Upper Danube, of whom nearly 12,000 resided in Linz. By October 1938 the provincial figure had dropped to 3,195 and that in the Danubian city to 1,098. Seasonal demand accounted for some of this breathtaking decline as it had in the past; by the first of the year, in fact, provincial employment had climbed again to 8,721. Within six months, however, the development of a labor shortage revealed that the ravages of the depression were at last over. Less than two years after the Anschluss, 13,900 jobs were going unfilled in Upper Danube.[19] The extension of German social benefits and the creation of jobs were not the only means used by Hitler's regime to generate support in Linz and its hinterland. The Nazis also took steps to improve working conditions and sanitary facilities. Of 763 workplaces in Upper Danube at the time of the Anschluss, 65 percent were without toilets, 84 percent without washrooms, and 86 percent without a commons room or canteen. Within just one year, however, the DAF installed 80 indoor toilet facilities, built 149 washrooms and 110 locker rooms, and set up 75 canteens and 27 clubs.[20]

Finally, as part of their attempt to sustain popular consent the Nazis sought to regulate inflationary pressure, especially that affecting urban consumers. Between April 1938 and April 1939 the Reich Office of Price Control kept the cost of housing in Linz at its pre-Anschluss level while reducing the costs of heating and electricity 9.1 percent; at the same time, food prices rose 4.3 percent and clothing, 1.4 percent. The cost of luxury goods, on the other hand, increased 50.2 percent. With the outbreak of World War II, the Nazis tightened wage and price controls and applied draconian measures for hoarding and other black market activities. Until the last year of the war they managed to keep prices fairly constant, so that between April 1939 and April 1944 the cost of housing did not change at all while the cost of heating and electricity declined another 6.1 percent. The price of food did increase 5.3 percent and that of clothing, a substantial 19.8 percent. Luxury goods, such as they were, rose only 1.5 percent from their 1939 level.[21]

Although the Nazi consensus was maintained in Linz through concrete benefits, that was not its only appeal. Fear and loathing were important factors too. As we have seen, many Socialist wage earners were so embittered by the Dollfuss-Schuschnigg dictatorship that they cast their lot with the German Nationalist *Mittelstand* in endorsing Hitler's regime. According to surviving SD and Gestapo records, approval of National Socialism was especially strong among workers in Linz and Steyr as well as among those in remote towns like Kleinraming, Gleink, and Reichraming.[22] In some parts of Austria, particularly Vienna, proletarian consent did not last very long as working hours increased, totalitarian controls intensified, and—after 1939—casualty lists mounted. In Upper Danube working-class disillusionment eventually spread to Steyr, where the once highly organized workers had access to Communist counterpropaganda, and to the mining districts of the Salzkammergut. In Linz, however, the town's work force remained acquiescent or at least nonhostile. Here deep-rooted German Nationalist sentiment combined with an enormous industrial boom, the successful regulation of inflationary pressure, and longtime immunity to Allied air attacks to instill in many workers a sense of identity with the Nazi people's community. Until late 1943, in fact, Linz remained the only major city in Austria without a significant underground Socialist organization.[23]

Outside the socioeconomic sphere, popular support also existed for Hitler's persecution of the Jews. In contrast to most cities and regions of the Old Reich where anti-Semitic restrictions were not infrequently met with popular disgust or apathy,[24] the Nazi program of intimidation was widely applauded in Linz and its environs. Inhabited by less than a thousand Jews,[25] the city was well known for its stifling anti-Semitic atmosphere, especially since the turn of the century, when its German Nationalist elite had embraced the poisonous doctrines of Georg Ritter von Schönerer. That placards banning Jews sprang up in innumerable hotels, restaurants, and parks of Upper Austria immediately after World War I was hardly unusual.[26] Furthermore, Judeophobia was encouraged by the Church. In 1933 when Bishop Gföllner published his blistering attack on National Socialism, he also assailed the Jewish religion, holding it responsible for such secular evils as capitalism, socialism, bolshevism, and atheism.[27] Even the Social Democrats were not immune to anti-Semitism. Throughout the 1920s grumbling about Jewish party leaders could be heard regularly among the rank and file

of organized labor, especially on the part of militants like Richard
Bernaschek and Otto Huschka. While anti-Semitism was officially condemned by provincial elites of both Social Democratic (Gruber and Koref)
and Christian Social (Hauser and Schlegel) camps, it remained a prejudice
deeply ingrained in the local psyche.[28]

As for the Jews themselves, few could have succumbed to illusions of
assimilation in the municipal community. From an early age Jewish school
children were tormented as Christ-killers or shunned as aliens, especially in
the German Nationalist-dominated secondary schools and commercial academies. Such discrimination reinforced exclusivist tendencies among Linz
Jews and prompted them to organize their own athletic societies, political
associations, and social clubs. According to one survivor, a boys' hiking club
(founded in 1911) began propagating Zionist ideas before World War I.
While the older generation with its links to Vienna and Bohemia rejected
Herzl's ideology out of hand, increasing numbers of young people seem to
have subscribed to it.[29] How many of them actually emigrated to Palestine
before the Anschluss, however, is not known. By 1934 the Upper Austrian
Jewish community had shrunk to 966 individuals, or about three hundred
families. Also living in the province were several hundred baptized or "half"
Jews.[30]

Quite appropriately, the Nazi seizure of power in Hitler's hometown
began with a savage pogrom. On the evening of 12 March 1938 stormtroopers broke into Jewish shops on the Landstrasse, beat up their owners, and
expropriated their property. By the time of the Führer's entry into the city
the next evening, the "cleansing" of Linz was established as a top priority.[31]
Five days later, an order was issued by the Gestapo for the immediate
confiscation of all "ski lodges, mountain huts, athletic fields, and rest homes"
as well as "all sail and paddle boats with outboard motors in the possession
of Jews or enemies of the state."[32] These and other anti-Semitic measures
did not apply, incidentally, to Hitler's boyhood physician, Dr. Eduard
Bloch; under orders from Kaltenbrunner, the doctor and his family were
placed under the protection of the regime.[33]

Throughout the spring and summer of 1938, the Nazi party organization in
Linz proceeded ruthlessly against the Jews. Eigruber was so bent on ridding
Hitler's "home district" of Jews that he did not hesitate to ignore procedural
guidelines laid down in Vienna, first by Göring and later by Eichmann. As
early as 31 March 1938 the *Gauleiter* ordered the names of all Jews living in
Upper Danube sent to the Linz Gestapo. Thereafter, local authorities closed
the municipal branch of B'nai Brith, seized Jewish communal property, and
told the Jews to pack their bags. Until 21 June they could simply leave the
Reichsgau, but thereafter they were required to indicate a destination.
Three days later, the Gestapo "suggested" that they proceed to Vienna.[34]

Within the Jewish community the merciless wave of terror provoked great suffering and confusion. In the early March days local notables such as Karl Schwager and the Mostny brothers—wealthy owners of an Urfahr distillery—were packed off to Dachau. Others were murdered or committed suicide. Since Max Hirschfeld, head of the Chevra-Kedushah burial society, acquired a grim prominence in those days, local Nazis cynically appointed him director of an ad hoc Jewish Council. For the next year it was his thankless task to facilitate the deportation of his fellow Jewish citizens by raising funds for exit visas and by assisting SS emigration authorities. Although exact numbers are not available, approximately one-third of Linz's Jews managed to leave their homeland during the summer. Of those who remained, most were older or poorer. A Jewish school, established with much fanfare on 19 May, for example, closed its doors six months later for lack of pupils. In the autumn Eichmann's Central Office for Jewish Emigration in Vienna exerted additional pressure. So successful were anti-Semitic restrictions in Upper Austria that on "Crystal Night"—10 November 1938—local stormtroopers found no Jewish property left to plunder or to expropriate. The synagogue was burned the next morning almost as a routine matter, and ninety-six of the remaining Jews were rounded up by the Gestapo. They were given three days to leave so that the Führer's hometown might at last be "cleansed of Jews."[35]

Despite intense persecution, roughly three hundred Jews continued to cling to life in Upper Danube. Forbidden to work or to practice a profession, denied the right to travel, and compelled to wear a yellow Star of David, they suffered daily humiliation and harassment. Some may have been helped by friends or neighbors, but most were ignored, shunned, or despised.[36] Finally, in mid-summer 1942 the surviving Jews were deported to Poland where they perished in the "final solution," many at the hands of the former Linz patrolman, Franz Stangl.[37]

According to surviving Gestapo records, Hitler's anti-Semitic barbarities elicited widespread support in Upper Danube. From Hörsching near Linz the police wrote on 30 April 1938, "the measures against the Jews are especially welcome."[38] Similarly, in reporting the burning of the Linz synagogue seven months later, the SD emphasized that the municipal population "welcomed the protest action . . . as absolutely necessary."[39] From neighboring Steyr came word that "the entire population approves the measures of the government against Jewry without exception and without reservations."[40] Nor did anti-Semitic fervor abate with time. As late as 1942, according to the SD, the provincial population continued to endorse such measures as the mandatory wearing of the Star of David and the deportation of Jews to the east.[41]

Outside of Linz in the rural areas of Upper Danube, support for the Nazis (though not for their anti-Semitic actions) was lukewarm from the beginning. As beneficiaries of the pre-Anschluss Christian Corporative regime,

provincial farmers and peasants did not welcome the annexation of Austria
by Germany with the same enthusiasm as town dwellers. At Gleinck near
Steyr, for example, farm owners anticipated "no improvement in their
existence."[42] For many peasants Nazi agricultural policies were already
known to be disadvantageous. The introduction of the Entailed Farm Law
establishing 32,000 peasant entails of between 7.5 and 125 hectares confirmed their fears. As in neighboring Bavaria, local farmers found it hard to
obtain credit and cash loans. The Reich Food Estate (Reichsnährstand) then
intervened to maintain production by providing compensation for indebt-
edness and credits for fertilizers. After the outbreak of war, however, these
and other price supports were reduced in favor of rigid controls. The
introduction of military conscription, compounded by a general flight to the
cities, aggravated the situation further. Compelled to deliver specified
amounts of fruits, vegetables, grain, meat, eggs, and dairy products at fixed
prices or to shift to the cultivation of rapeseed, turnips, and poppies, Upper
Austrian farmers were hard put to meet expenses. Since they could not
balance their own rising costs with prices fixed by the regime, they became
ensnarled in a de facto inflationary spiral in which expenses rose as high as
300 percent.[43]

The Nazis were aware of the price squeeze caused by their policies, but
they did little to alleviate it. As members of an urban movement, Hitler's
hometown followers supported government measures regulating prices in
the cities at the expense of the countryside. They no doubt recalled the food
shortages and black-marketeering of the First World War which had caused
so much suffering in Linz, Steyr, and the other cities of Cisleithania. For
that reason it was hardly by chance that the party prohibited the making of
cheese and butter outside the cities of Upper Danube.[44]

Coercive economic measures alone do not account for the failure of the
Nazi consensus to spread to the countryside. With the outbreak of World
War II, the conscription of 200,000 Upper Austrians created a manpower
shortage that was only filled by prisoners of war, foreign laborers, and,
toward the end of the war, concentration camp inmates. The farmers
resented being called to fight in a war they scarcely comprehended, while
leaving their parents, wives, and children to manage by themselves or with
foreign help. They also objected to Nazi regulations prohibiting fraternization with foreign workers, especially Poles. Many peasants regarded the
Catholic Poles as welcome farmhands and saw to it that they received extra
provisions of food and clothing. Much to the irritation of the Nazi authorities, relations between Upper Austrian farmers and Polish laborers were by
no means disharmonious. Furthermore, despite threats of punitive action by
Eigruber or the SS, peasant acts of solicitude and charity were encouraged
by the Church.[45]

Ultimately, National Socialism failed to appeal to the Catholic peasants of

Upper Austria for ideological reasons. Before the plebiscite of 10 April 1938, some farmers were reassured by the sanguine pronouncements of the Roman Catholic episcopate, but others feared quite rightly that "in the religious domain they will be subjected to restrictions."[46] With the extension of economic controls to the countryside and the inauguration of an anticlerical campaign in the summer of 1938, rural antipathy began to grow.[47] To what extent increasing anger and bitter complaints were translated into an oppositional mood is impossible to say. In the judgement of the Nazis themselves the hostile elements in the villages and hamlets of Upper Danube were never the peasants. As a Gestapo report put it in 1941, "the Catholic Church now as before has contributed the main contingent of enemy subversion."[48]

That Hitler's regime encountered enthusiastic support in his hometown coupled with apprehension in the surrounding countryside, especially among the Roman Catholic clergy, suggests that the record of National Socialism in Linz was one of a powerful secularizing and industrializing force. In Austria the Nazis were less inhibited by compromises with traditional structures and institutions than in Germany, so that Hitler could shape his plans with considerable leeway. To achieve his goals he assigned to the autochthonous Nazi party, rather than to state organs, the task of cutting the Roman Catholic Church down to size, while to German industrialists he awarded the job of gearing the Austrian economy to the war machine of the Reich.

THE NAZI ATTACK ON THE CHURCH

Long before the Anschluss, as we have seen, the Nazis in Austria had succeeded in appealing to the anticlericalism of the German Nationalist *Mittelstand* and, to a lesser extent, to that of the Austromarxist working classes. The urban and small-town middle strata, in particular, despised the Roman Church as the bulwark of the nobilitarian Habsburg Empire and of the more recent Dollfuss-Schuschnigg dictatorship whose policies had favored the interests of agriculture over those of trade, commerce, and industry. In Linz, where anti-Catholic sentiment dated from the days of the Counter-Reformation, the Nazis proceeded eagerly against the Church with little prodding from Berlin. By June 1938, they had deported a good many priests to Dachau, purged the provincial school board of clergymen, placed restrictions on religious announcements in newspapers, and forced sixteen Catholic associations—including the Boy Scouts—to dissolve. On 12 July Hitler announced the abrogation of the Austrian concordat of 1933, depriving the Church of its international status. In the months that followed, the NSDAP closed or secularized 291 parochial schools in Upper Danube, turned St. Peter's seminary into a military barracks, and drove the bishop of

Linz from his canonical court. When the Reich government introduced compulsory civil marriage and legalized divorce in Austria on 1 August 1938, Hitler's hometown retainers took great pains to publicize the two measures by staging a number of elaborate wedding ceremonies in the Linz Rathaus. There under flaming torches and blood-red swastika banners *Kreisleiter* Walter Gasthuber, *Gau* Inspector Franz Peterseil, and Lord Mayor Sepp Wolkerstorfer all took their vows.[49]

The bishop of Linz reacted to these restrictions with considerable personal dismay and public caution. Unlike Vienna's Cardinal Innitzer, who eagerly sought to make his peace with Hitler, Johannes Maria Gföllner may have been the only bishop in Germany or Austria to have opposed National Socialism for nearly two decades.[50] Gföllner had reluctantly signed the bishop's declaration of support for the Anschluss, but thereafter he ordered a strict separation of church and state, forbidding the display of Nazi banners or regalia in church buildings and the holding of political meetings on church property. The bishop reminded his flock that they were still liable to ecclesiastical marriage laws and urged them to continue the religious education of their children. In dealing with the Nazis he followed his own motto "Keep silent, be patient, pray and hope."[51]

Commendable and almost unique as Gföllner's passive resistance was, it did not in practice prove very effective. The bishop's neutrality hardly seemed convincing in view of a long record of antidemocratic behavior and support of the Dollfuss-Schuschnigg dictatorship. In caring solely for believing Catholics, moreover, he took an extremely narrow stance which circumscribed his own moral authority and limited his appeal. The plight of nonbaptized Jews or "atheistic" Social Democrats did not concern him. Most of all, in keeping silent except in the most narrow ecclesiastical matters, the bishop played into the hands of the Nazis and permitted them to define the boundaries of church-state relations. As Eigruber could proclaim after conferring with Gföllner in October 1938:

> We agree with the words once uttered by Jesus: "My kingdom is not of this earth." The NSDAP is the leader of the German people in this world. The local group leader is the dignitary of the NSDAP. His task is to see to it that things go well for party comrades here on earth. The task of the clergy is to make sure that we some day get to the world beyond. Everything is therefore quite clear . . . and woe to the priest who meddles in politics. The priest is to concern himself exclusively with spiritual matters and not with other things. . . . A few days ago I had a thoroughly satisfactory conversation with the Linz bishop. From now on, priests who talk politics will be removed.[52]

Eigruber maintained his church contributions throughout the course of the Third Reich and may have been as sincere in his definition of church-state separation as Gföllner was in his.[53] Nevertheless, the Linz diocese suffered continued abuse from the Hitler regime. With seventeen local priests already languishing in Gestapo prisons at the end of 1938, the Nazis placed new restrictions on the Church. During the following nine months they curtailed or eliminated religious holidays, placed missions under surveillance, and severely circumscribed religious instruction in the schools. On 28 April 1939 a Führer decree terminated all state financial assistance, compelling the Church to depend on voluntary contributions. Not surprisingly, 16,026 Upper Austrians formally renounced their church membership before the end of the year.[54] On one occasion, Gföllner tried to stem the antichurch drive by protesting the pagan pronouncements of the National Socialist Women's Organization to the provincial school board. In response Eigruber brutally wrote, "will you for once and for all take notice that in writing to authorities of the province you can neither request nor demand anything."[55]

With the outbreak of World War II, anticlerical measures intensified in Upper Danube despite Hitler's wish to call a truce for the duration of hostilities. Spurred on by *Gau* Inspector Peterseil, local functionaries expropriated numerous abbeys, monasteries, seminaries, and churches and put them to secular use: the Catholic Youth Club at Kleinmünchen was turned into an SS canteen, the Linz seminary was handed over to the NSV, both churches of the Brothers of Charity were seized, and the ancient monastery of Wilhering was converted in 1943 on Hitler's direct orders into a college of engineering. The most frightful use of church property occurred at Schloss Hartheim, a school for retarded children a few kilometers outside the city. There under the aegis of a Linz physician, Dr. Rudolf Lonauer, a euthanasia sanatorium was established in which 12,000 mentally ill were gassed and cremated. The war also gave the Gestapo wider latitude to arrest and imprison churchmen for sedition or treason with the result that the Linz diocese contributed its share of Christian martyrs. Among them was Carmelite Father Paulus Wörndl, beheaded in 1944 for simply corresponding with an anti-Nazi soldier serving in Norway. All told, between 1938 and 1945 over 150 local churchmen suffered severe persecution: thirty-two priests were sent to concentration camps, ninety-nine were imprisoned for terms ranging from one month to five years, and sixteen were tortured to death, executed, or died in captivity.[56]

So long as Bishop Gföllner lived, opposition to the Nazi persecution of the Church in the Linz diocese was sporadic and localized. A number of parish priests took issue with the bishop's policy of passivity, suggesting that the Church should resume its active ministry.[57] At Wels, for example, a youth movement was organized that attracted the attention of boys and girls from throughout the diocese. On Ascension Day 1939 nearly a thousand youngsters pedaled to Maria Scharten to celebrate mass as a demonstration of support of Christian values. Such large celebrations were, however, rare and virtually ceased with the outbreak of the war.[58] Confounded by a long tradition of support for the state in wartime and effectively removed from the spheres of social and educational action, churchmen increasingly emphasized individual faith and belief in a God whose justice would be revealed in the fullness of time. They were, therefore, in no position to resist a new onslaught in early 1941 that resulted in the expropriation of the Upper Austrian monasteries of St. Florian, Schlägel, Hohenfürth, Wilhering, and Kremsmünster. The unrest provoked throughout Austria and Germany by that latest wave of persecution and by increasing awareness of the euthanasia program, however, led to a strong protest in June 1941 by the German Bishops' Conference at Fulda. The protest was accompanied within weeks by pastoral letters from the bishops of Münster and Trier condemning mercy killings. Faced with what threatened to become massive resistance in wartime, Hitler abruptly backed down and called a halt to his anticlerical campaign.[59]

In the Linz diocese Hitler's decision to temporize coincided with the death of Bishop Gföllner on 3 June 1941. The new shepherd of Linz, Josef Calasanctius Fliesser, was unaware of the regime's reversal of policy, but he was determined to safeguard the institutional integrity of the Church. By modifying the diocese's policy of passive resistance to one of limited cooperation, he hoped to persuade the Nazis to spare seminarians from conscription and to suspend the confiscation of church property. In contrast to Gföllner, Fliesser met Eigruber frequently. According to subsequent testimony of the bishop, they hammered out a rough working relationship in which the Gauleiter refused to discuss the "confiscation of cloisters and the arrest of clergy suspected of listening to illegal broadcasts or of participation in political resistance movements,"[60] but left open all other matters of church-state relations. Apparently flattered by Fliesser's cooperative attitude, Eigruber provided additional supplies of gasoline to the diocese for official use. He also responded favorably to a number of Fliesser's requests. In July 1942 when Gau Inspector Peterseil announced the sequestration of more cloisters and abbeys for secular schooling, Eigruber reversed the order and in October suspended the confiscations indefinitely. With regard to the call up of seminarians, Fliesser was less successful. Nevertheless, by demonstrating his support of the war in countless sermons, he did manage to have a number of clergymen in the armed forces transferred to less hazardous duties.[61]

To what extent Fliesser succeeded in moderating the Nazi assault on the Linz diocese must remain an open question. While some property was returned or leased to the diocese, many buildings remained in the hands of the Reichsgau as Nazi secondary schools (Lambach), colleges (Wilhering), museums (Marsbach), or cultural institutes (St. Florian). By the same token, although Fliesser frequently arranged for the transfer of priests in danger of

The old bridge over the Danube, 1935. Stadtmuseum Linz.

induction or arrest to the relative safety of remote mountain villages, he never utilized the diocesan newsletter to protest the cases of those actually conscripted or imprisoned. By 1944, in fact, more Linz churchmen were in the hands of the Gestapo or the SS than at any time since the Anschluss. More seriously, although the diocese offered aid and comfort to the thousands of Roman Catholic Poles, Italians, and French at work in Upper Danube, the plight of deeply religious baptized Jews was blithely ignored.[62] On balance, although the Roman Catholic Church suffered greater abuse from the Nazis in Linz—and Austria—than in the Old Reich, the experience of the diocese closely paralleled that of the German episcopate: in the face of Neronian persecution clerical authorities were reluctant to offer resistance beyond the most limited or narrow kind.[63] In the case of Gföllner, a man who harbored no illusions about the Nazis, a policy of resignation was followed with virtually no success. Under his successor, Fliesser, some property was saved from expropriation but only through a program of accommodation whose consequences were, in a larger sense, counterproductive. That program not only made it easier for the Nazis to achieve their goals, it also helped to ensure the continued support or acceptance by the faithful in Upper Danube of Hitler's regime. What Fliesser never grasped was a simple truth understood by some of his more humble flock and perhaps even by Gföllner. The truth was that to be critical of the Nazis and loyal to the Greater German Reich was impossible.[64]

HITLER'S PLANS FOR LINZ

Although Hitler took a keen personal interest in the antichurch drive in Upper Danube—and the *Ostmark*—he was perfectly willing to allow local Nazis to tackle the job without much interference. When it came to Linz, he played a more active role, dabbling in municipal politics and taking dramatic steps to alter the entire life of the city. Obsessed with making his hometown into a "Second Budapest," he entrusted German architects with the task of redesigning Linz and establishing an industrial base to support the Parnassus he envisaged. The Führer's patronage did not result in the transformation of the city into a cultural metropolis, but it did contribute to its development as a major manufacturing center with substantial benefits to the population.

As an adolescent Hitler had spent hours sketching and resketching plans for rebuilding Linz on a monumental scale. The iron bridge across the Danube especially annoyed him, since it was architecturally out of proportion and too narrow for traffic. According to his boyhood friend, August Kubizek, Hitler planned to build a broader bridge that would conform to the contours of the Danube and to the surrounding landscape. The main square in Linz would be retained, but several buildings demolished for an unobstructed view of the hills beyond. Hitler admired the ornamental provincial museum on the Museumstrasse, which had been completed in 1887 by the German architect Bruno Schmitz. Nevertheless, the structure had to be expanded so that its marble frieze would be the longest in Europe. Also slated for renovation were the dilapidated Renaissance castle, the provincial theater, the municipal auditorium, and the city hall. In the latter instance an entirely new structure was to be constructed in its place.[65]

Hitler's proposals were not entirely fanciful or impractical. As the fifteen-year-old city planner had shrewdly observed, Linz was paradoxically imperiled by the railroad line running near the center of town. To his mind the tracks were not only ugly, but, above all, an impediment to the development of commerce. The central depot should therefore be moved to the south and the tracks placed underground. In addition, parks and recreation areas should be established for the public at large. These essentially sensible ideas were balanced by a number of purely utopian schemes. Without regard to cost or function, Hitler also planned to construct

Architect's drawing of Hitler's design for the renovation of
the Schmidttor, 1943. The view is from the Landstrasse.
Stadtmuseum Linz.

a cog railway on the other side of the Danube, several lavish hotels, and a
gigantic statue of Siegfried high atop the Freinberg heights.[66]

When Hitler returned to Linz as dictator of the German Reich, he
received Kubizek in the Hotel Weinzinger. Gesturing out a window to the
iron bridge across the Danube, he exclaimed: "That ugly thing still there!
But not much longer. You can be sure of that Kubizek!"[67] The Führer
repeated long-forgotten plans for the renovation of his hometown to be
realized at last, he explained, with the construction of a new bridge, an opera
house, and a concert hall named for Anton Bruckner. Kubizek was astonished.
As he later wrote, "The plans which that unknown boy had drawn up
for the rebuilding of his hometown Linz are identical with the town planning
scheme which was inaugurated after 1938."[68]

In point of fact, Hitler's plans were much more grandiose than his onetime
roommate could ever imagine. It is true that the core of the Führer's

adolescent dreams remained intact and that in the case of the Nibelungen bridge an early design was actually executed. Yet these early schemes constituted only a small part of the whole. Linz was to take its place beside Hamburg, Nuremberg, Berlin, and Munich as one of five "Führer cities."[69] It was to be expanded in two stages from a population of 100,000 to nearly half a million. Between 1938 and 1942, for example, 12,900 living units were to be constructed, of which 8,600 were actually completed.[70] On both sides of the Danube magnificent buildings were to be constructed so as to make the river an integral part of the city. "Budapest is by far the most beautiful city on the Danube," Hitler remarked in 1942. "But I am determined to make Linz a German town on the Danube which surpasses it, and by so doing to prove that the artistic sense of the Germans is superior to that of the Magyars." Almost as a second thought he added, "also I intend to build a number of dwelling houses which will be models of their kind."[71]

The design and development of the Linz riverfront complex was entrusted to the architect Hermann Giesler.[72] It was, in a sense, to stand apart from the old city and form a new cultural center which would be built several kilometers to the south. Along the shores "the individual structures should not arise schematically or in accordance with the old baroque city," explained Hitler to his architect, "but independently as monumental buildings, richly arranged and various."[73] As Giesler's plans took shape, first as a blueprint and then as a wooden model, the Danubian riverfront was to be framed by heavy neoclassical colonnades, massive rectilinear facades, and severe, starkly set porticoes and windows. Between the river and the buildings were to be laid out terraces of rose gardens, a broad avenue, and several public squares.

Proceeding downstream from the Nibelungen bridge, the principal buildings were to be a new city hall (*Stadthaus*), a fourteen-story county seat, a *Gau* house (district headquarters for the Nazi party), and a large meeting hall for 30,000 to 35,000 people. Of these structures, Hitler was most concerned with the design and construction of the city hall. He personally drew and redrew sketches of the edifice, which syncretically combined features of an Upper Austrian rural manor, a Roman villa, and the Stockholm city hall designed by Ragner Ostberg. The rectilinear *Stadthaus* was to be 6,400 square meters in size with a facade of eighty meters. It was to enclose an elevated court, connected to the ground floor by a staircase similar to that in the baroque monastery of St. Florian. From the city hall Hitler's hometown would be administered by a senate of notables and party members.[74]

Also in Urfahr Hitler proposed to build a monument to Bismarck—as the German Nationalists had dreamed at the turn of the century—and a "Tower on the Danube." The tower was to stand 160 meters high and be so situated as to reflect the first rays of the sun in the morning and the last ones at dusk.

Wooden model of Hitler's retirement home on the
Freinberg. Stadtmuseum Linz.

It was to contain a vaulted crypt for the remains of Hitler's parents and a
carillon to play passages from Bruckner's fourth (*Romantic*) Symphony.[75]
According to Albert Speer, the Führer himself also intended to be buried in
the bell tower.[76] Behind the Danubian complex on the Pöstlingberg heights
overlooking Linz, an observatory worthy of the memory of Johannes Kepler
was to be erected. It was to contain a telescope and a planetarium under a
vast cupola. "Thus in the future," mused Hitler, "thousands of excursionists
will make a pilgrimage there every Sunday. They'll thus have access to the
greatness of our universe. The pediment will bear this motto: 'The heavens
proclaim the glory of the everlasting.' It will be our way of giving men a
religious spirit, of teaching them humility—but without priests."[77]
     On the south bank of the Danube the baroque core of Linz was to be left
intact and renovated. To the east, along the shore, a massive complex was to
complement the structures on the Urfahr side. The chief buildings were to
be a European banking center, a twenty-story KdF luxury hotel, and a vast
Adolf Hitler Technical University. Both shores were to be united by a
network of bridges including the Nibelungen bridge, a suspension bridge,

and a granite viaduct running from the Bismarck monument to the Göring Works.[78] From Giesler's riparian quarter and the old city—which was also to contain Hitler's retirement home—the Landstrasse was to be widened into a boulevard. While retaining its character as a shopping area, the avenue was to embrace police headquarters, a weapons museum, and the provincial offices of the SS and SA. At the end of the Landstrasse (by the Blumau intersection) a huge square was to be laid out that would make Linz the Paris of Central Europe. The square was to be flanked by an opera house, a theater, the Anton Brucker Concert Hall, an operetta theater, a cinema, an art gallery, a museum, and a library;[79] on the dictator's orders the cultural center was to include a good many pastry shops and (glass-covered) coffee houses.[80]

In keeping with his adolescent dreams and megalomanic edifice complex, Hitler insisted on moving the central depot, repair shops, and switch yards of the railroad approximately a kilometer to the south. In their place a three-hectare park was to be laid out with an orange grove and an open portico reminiscent of the Gloriette at Schönbrunn in Vienna. Between the opera square and the new train station a huge ceremonial avenue (*Prachtstrasse*) was to run that would be sixty meters wide and 800 meters long. Named *Zu den Lauben* by the Führer, it was to be lined by trees and a horizontal row of buildings to include a vocational school, a concert hall, a theater, a music hall, an elegant theater-restaurant, and a cafe.[81] The avenue was designed to impress, but it was also meant to provide an atmosphere of well-being and relaxation. As Hitler mused to his architects, "the best stroll in the world will be in Linz."[82]

Apart from the Nibelungen bridge and one or two minor buildings, Hitler's vast urban renewal project remained in the planning stage in 1945. The director of the renovation of Linz, Roderick Fick, was never able to establish his authority over rival prima donnas like Giesler and Speer, who in turn refused to coordinate their efforts with each other. When agreements were occasionally hammered out or blueprints actually drawn up, emendations could be expected from the master builder in Berlin. So many changes were made over an illuminated model at the Reich Chancellery that, as a practical matter, construction in Linz could not get under way.[83]

In assembling thousands of paintings and objects of art in Upper Danube, tangible progress was made toward the realization of at least one of Hitler's cultural dreams. The proposed art gallery on the opera square was probably his fondest project. In obvious imitation of the Kunsthistorisches Museum in Vienna, it was to contain collections of weapons, coins, rare books, and the greatest German paintings of the nineteenth and twentieth centuries as well as examples of Flemish and Italian masters.[84] On 26 June 1939 the director of the Dresden Gallery, Dr. Hans Posse, was commissioned to begin scouring Europe for the Linz museum. Objective and professional, he

Hermann Giesler's model of Hitler's Linz, 1945. The view
is from the southwest toward Urfahr. Druffel Verlag.

rejected a great many treasures already selected by Hitler as "scarcely
useful" or "not in keeping with the stature of the gallery as I conceive it."[85]
Posse managed to buy, borrow, or confiscate hundreds of paintings for the
Linz collection. The pictures were photographed and catalogued in brown
leather volumes for Hitler's perusal. After Posse's death in 1942, the
collection of treasures for the Linz gallery became less systematic. Posse's
successor, Dr. Hermann Voss, purchased over 3,000 paintings for Hitler,
but how many of these were intended specifically for the Upper Austrian
capital is difficult to determine. All told, at least 5,350 paintings, drawings,
and prints were officially designated for Linz. Together with tapestries,
sculptures, and pieces of antique furniture, they were initially assembled
and stored in Munich. Toward the end of the war, the entire trove, including
works slated for other museums, was shipped to the fourteenth-century salt
mine of Alt Aussee, some eighty kilometers to the south of Linz.[86]

HITLER AND THE
INDUSTRIALIZATION OF LINZ

Hitler's art collection never went on display in his hometown. The gallery to
exhibit it remained unbuilt, and Linz did not become the Parnassus of the
Danube. Nevertheless, in the space of only seven years the Upper Austrian

capital developed into one of Europe's major industrial centers. Long before the Anschluss, Austrian economists and entrepreneurs had wanted to construct an iron, steel, and coking complex on the Danube, but they had been inhibited by both a shortage of capital and the opposition of the country's traditional manufacturers. After the annexation of Austria by Germany, the situation changed dramatically. Suddenly, the revaluation of the Austrian schilling, the shortage of available labor in the Old Reich, and the demands of the German war machine combined to dictate a policy of rapid economic mobilization.[87]

That Linz stood to gain from the Nazi program of modernization was not obvious initially. In the course of a Danubian cruise on 25 March 1938, Austrian and German economic experts advised Göring to underwrite the construction of an iron and steel complex somewhere between Linz and Vienna. After further discussion, they proposed as the site Asten-St. Florian at the mouth of the Enns River. The estimated costs of a new town to support the plant there, however, turned out to be prohibitive. In addition, (Austrian) Nazi agricultural secretary Anton Reinthaller raised ideological objections that industrialization of the region would displace over forty peasant entails.[88] At this point Hitler himself became involved in the decision-making process. In order to bear the costs of his grandiose plans for Linz, the Führer argued that the industrial plant should be constructed immediately adjacent to the Danubian city where it would generate municipal tax revenue.[89] As a consequence, St. Peter-Ebelsberg on the outskirts of Linz was chosen as the location. Given the Upper Austrian capital's ability to produce goods and services, its position on the Danube, and its proximity to German markets, Hitler's hometown became a center of heavy industrial development that included the massive Hermann Göring Steel Works, a nitrogen plant, a chemical works, and other large-scale enterprises manufacturing aluminium, artificial fibers, and armaments.[90]

The Hermann Göring Incorporated State Works for Iron Mining and Smelting was officially founded on 4 May 1938 with an initial capital outlay of 5 million marks. That amount, soon raised to 400 million marks, was provided by the Göring consortium of state enterprises and the privately owned but German-dominated Alpine Montan Company in Styria. Although the Rhenish Vereinigte Stahl A.G.—principal stockholders of the Alpine Montan—attempted to put up 50 percent of the investment capital, Göring insisted on state control. Through an intermediary he instructed the Dresdner Bank to purchase a 13 percent interest in the Styrian firm. Bowing to the inevitable, Vereinigte Stahl sold its controlling shares in Alpine Montan, in effect leaving large-scale industrial development in Austria to the state. By the spring of 1939, some eighty-four Austrian firms were affiliated with the Göring organization at Linz. On the whole, most of the leading positions of the new enterprise were occupied by Germans. With the exception of *Gauleiters* Eigruber and Uiberreithner (Styria), in fact, all but one of the members of the board of directors were Berliners.[91]

Construction of the Göring Steel Works got under way within weeks of the organization's incorporation. Originally located on 700 hectares, the concern rapidly grew to cover over a thousand hectares so that by 1943 it was about three times the size of the Krupp Works at Essen. The Upper Austrian complex included a coking plant processing 491,000 tons of coke (in 1944) as well as gas for the city of Linz, four blast furnaces (with two others under construction), an integrated iron and steel mill producing 541,000 tons of steel (in 1943), a 175-megawatt thermal power station, nearly ninety kilometers of railway track, and extensive dock facilities on the Danube. The plant was built by 8,000 workers, many of whom were slave laborers and concentration camp inmates. The adjoining nitrogen plant was founded in 1939 by a syndicate of German chemical firms including I.G. Farben and eleven other concerns. With an initial outlay of 20 million marks, the nitrogen plant was run exclusively by Germans. After three years, it was producing 50,000 tons of lime, ammonia, and fertilizers.[92]

The developing heavy industry of Linz was designed to meet German needs, but it was not at first geared directly to defense or military production. Before the outbreak of World War II only the Linz dockyards, the Steyr Works, and a handful of smaller firms were officially designated defense plants. Military contracts were awarded, of course, to a number of local manufacturers after the outbreak of hostilities, but the number still remained small. Only with the deepening of the war and the intensified allied bombing of the Ruhr, was local industry converted to full wartime production.[93]

As a rule, the manufacture of weapons in Upper Danube was concentrated in the so-called armaments triangle of Steyr, Linz, and St. Valentin (in Lower Austria), although a number of plants were also set up in remote Alpine valleys, especially toward the end of the war. At Steyr a wide variety of military trucks and vehicles, including caterpillar-tread tractors, were produced as well as ball bearings, airplane engines, cockpits, and landing gear. As the onetime "armorers of the Habsburgs" the Steyr Works also manufactured millions of rifles (the K 98 and the Polish C 29/40), carbines, machine pistols, machine guns (the MG 34 and the MG 42), and assault guns. All in all, approximately 10 percent of all German small arms during World War II came off the assembly lines at Steyr. In Linz military production was of a heavier sort. Under the efficient management of the German navy, the dockyards gradually evolved into a major inland manufacturing and repair facility. Between 1939 and 1945 a great many barges and tankers were constructed or refitted at the wharves, as were coastal vessels, tugs, S-boats, and even submarines. Several kilometers to the south at the sprawling Göring Works, emphasis was placed on the manufacture of chassis, bodies, housings, turrets, and spare parts for heavy tanks. In the spring of 1943, with the firing of two electric furnaces, component parts for the 45-ton Panther and chassis for the 55-ton Tiger tank destroyer were also brought into production.[94]

Despite promises of safeguarding traditional systems of manufacturing with guarantees for craftsmen and commercial producers, National Socialism radically altered the structure of production in Linz and its hinterland. From May 1939 to December 1943 the number of jobs in Upper Danube expanded from 221,456 to 337,020, while between 1938 and 1942 the *industrial* workforce increased from 30,000 to 65,000 (117 percent). In Linz itself the number of wage earners at the dockyards rose from 500 on 1 April 1938 to 2,000 on 1 October 1942. In the Göring Works, from none to 6,601; in the machine shops, from 70 to 150; at the railway repair works, from 480 to 2,050; in wood finishing, from 100 to 600; and in the city's electrical firms, from about 160 to 500. As of 1 August 1945, with production at a virtual standstill during the early days of the American occupation, no fewer than 94 factories having more than five workers each were employing some 11,134 wage earners, whereas on 1 July 1937 some 79 plants had employed only 5,772. During the same period the city's total wage labor force in firms of more than five workers each rose from 14,254 to 21,240. In the boom years of the war the peak figures were, no doubt, even higher.[95]

While industry flourished under National Socialism, traditional manufacturing and commerce withered on the vine. This was a trend that was not at first apparent, since for some time a high demand existed for handcrafted consumer goods. With the outbreak of war, however, traditional shop and cottage manufacturing fell off sharply. At the outmoded Kleinmünchen cotton mills, for example, production fell from 2,300,000 kilograms in 1938 to 600,000 in the last year of the war. Similarly, in all the city's textile firms the number of workers employed fell from 1,520 in 1938 to 380 at the end of 1942, and in the state tobacco plant, from 1,200 to 850. It is of course true that wartime shortages of raw materials accounted for much of the decline in traditional manufacturing. But so did the lure of higher wages in the industrial sector as well as the death in combat of hundreds of artisans and small producers. Between 1938 and 1942, for example, the number of independent manufacturers in Upper Danube declined some 35 percent from 23,900 to 15,000, while at Linz the number of commercial establishments with more than five employees each fell (between 1937 and 1945) from 148 to 10 and the number of wage earners in those firms from 2,063 to 135.[96] In retrospect, Nazi rule in Linz represented a brutal transition from a semi-industrial mode of production to modern industrial capitalism. In only seven years German economic planners and industrialists were able to sweep aside outmoded structures and interest groups in order to lay the industrial foundation for the transformation of society itself. As one observer has awkwardly generalized, "fascism consisted not only of preserving the established capitalism by force but also transforming it, concentrating it, organizing it, regimenting it, directing it. On the one side, it brought to heel the unions and the leftist parties; on the other, it modernized capitalism by subjecting it to the required changes."[97]

Seen in a wider context, Nazi rule in Linz also contributed to the modernization of the Austrian community. More than in Germany, the Nazis in Hitler's hometown—and in Austria as a whole—were able to push aside or destroy the "quasi-feudal" forces of tradition represented by the region's small-scale economic producers, agricultural interests, and the Church. From this perspective the issue of local collaboration and resistance can be partly, though by no means exclusively, understood as a struggle between the forces of modernization and those of tradition: the Austrians who supported Hitler's rule at Linz tended to benefit from his program of secularization and industrialization; the ones who objected stood to lose from it. With regard to the matter of German penetration of Austria, it was in the economic sphere that Reich Germans played the most conspicuous role since they alone possessed the vision and capital to transform Linz into an industrial city. That local Nazis were only marginally involved in the process was not so much a consequence of deliberate exclusion by alien Germans as a lack of interest and, for that matter, skill on the part of Hitler's hometown followers. As middle class civil servants, professionals, and employees, Linz Nazis were simply more interested in political power than they were in industrial development.

THE NAZI SYSTEM OF LABOR

Essential to the economic development of Linz under National Socialism was the use of foreign and slave labor. Primarily a response to the Reich's chronic manpower shortage, the importation of outside workers created an "industrial reserve army" at minimum cost. In Upper Danube the employment of cheap foreign labor may also have played some role in preempting indigenous working class dissent and in maintaining the Nazi consensus. Even before World War II, some 16,000 Czechs and Slovaks were at work in the *Reichsgau*, primarily at large-scale construction sites. After the fall of Poland, their number was augmented by 5,000 Poles, over half of whom were prisoners of war. By the summer of 1940 over 25,000 foreign workers, including Italians, French, Belgians, Dutch, Bulgarians, and Hungarians, were employed in local fields, forests, factories, and construction sites.[98]

In November 1941 some 115,000 Upper Austrians were called up by the armed forces in a single levy. With 22 percent of the male population removed from the workforce, thousands of additional foreign laborers were imported to take jobs in Upper Danube's thriving industries. By February

1943 nearly a third of the provincial working population was foreign: out of a total of 349,527 employed, 24,721 were prisoners of war and 107,268 were foreign civilian workers. By far, the greatest number of foreign civilian workers were Russian (30 percent), followed by Poles (22 percent) and Czechs (13 percent); the rest were Italians, French, Slovaks, Bulgarians, Croats, Hungarians, Dutch, Serbs, Greeks, Danes, Belgians, Portuguese, Rumanians, Swiss, Turks, Estonians, Latvians, Lithuanians, and Norwegians. While some 41.5 percent of the foreigners worked in agriculture or forestry, most were employed in heavy, often dangerous, industries: 51.6 percent of the *Gau's* metal workers were foreign, as were 46 percent of its chemical workers, 41 percent of its miners, 40.7 percent of its finished metal workers, and 34.7 percent of its railwaymen. At Linz foreign labor was concentrated at the Göring Works (60.7 percent), the nitrogen plant (69.7 percent), and the dockyards (53.1 percent).[99]

As a group, foreign workers in Linz were subjected to harsh and rigorous controls. For their labor they were paid only 55 to 64 pfennig an hour, compelled to live in barracks or makeshift housing (often under guard), and usually denied the right to mingle with native Upper Austrians. The racial and political doctrines of the Nazis forbade normal social or sexual relationships with the indigenous population. Austrian women known to have had sexual intercourse with foreigners were sent to concentration camps, and their lovers were shot.[100] In the judgement of the authorities, fraternization with Austrian industrial workers was to be kept at a minimum as well.[101] Like Marx, the Nazis recognized the potential internationalism of the working classes.

Also integral to the functioning of the Nazi economic system in Upper Austria was the cheap labor made available by nearby concentration camps. In Germany the camps were originally established as institutions of brutalization and terror. By the time of the Anschluss, they were also being touted by ambitious SS leaders as sources of slave labor for Hitler's monumental construction projects. Because of the high quality of granite at the Mauthausen quarries, twenty kilometers southeast of Linz, Himmler established a concentration camp there as a source of building materials. In May some eighty SS guards and three hundred inmates from Dachau were at work building a barbed wire enclosure. When eventually completed, Mauthausen comprised a gigantic granite fortress of 150,000 square meters, with comfortable living quarters for its SS staff. It was surrounded by a tangle of electrified barbed wire and included twenty-four primitive barracks (patterned after Dachau), an infirmary, a brothel for the guards, a prison, a gas chamber, and a crematorium. Outside the complex, at the foot of a steep staircase of 186 steps, lay the quarries. There, between 1938 and 1945, some 113,575 to 122,767 prisoners were slaughtered or worked to death.[102]

Despite its high death rate, Mauthausen was intended primarily as a center of economic exploitation. With the development of full wartime production, especially in Linz, and the expansion of the SS as a big-business enterprise, prisoners were increasingly released to industry. They continued to remain under the jurisdiction of the SS, however, in subcamps, that were little better than Mauthausen. In 1943 and 1944 some thirty subcamps were set up in Upper Danube and nineteen additional ones outside the *Reichsgau*. By the end of the war, Hitler's home district contained more concentration camps than any other *Gau* of the Greater German Reich. The most important of these, after Mauthausen, was Ebensee at the southern end of Lake Traun. There up to 18,500 prisoners were forced to excavate a vast tunnel complex for the eventual manufacture of synthetic fuel, airplane parts, and A9/A10 rocket engines. At Gusen, near Mauthausen, two camps containing crematoria were set up with approximately 11,500 prisoners each, as well as a smaller camp of 250. Other important camps of the Mauthausen system were Grossraming, Gunskirchen near Wels, Lenzing, Redl-Zipf, Steyr Münichholz, St. Valentin (Lower Austria), Ternberg, Vöcklabruck, Wels, and Enns. In Linz itself three subcamps were established housing over 6,000 slave laborers at Hitler's construction projects, in the Göring Works, and at civil defense sites.[103]

Although concentration camp prisoners in industry continued to be beaten, or worked to death, they were treated slightly better than in Mauthausen proper. Nevertheless, they were compelled to work sixty to seventy-two hours per week and provided with only 600 to 1,000 calories of food daily. Occasionally, script amounting to 50 pfennig was issued by the SS, but this was usually spent on cigarettes. As a rule, concentration camp labor was only half as efficient as that of free labor. To the business firms leasing the prisoners from the SS this was a shortcoming made up by the low costs incurred. For a common laborer entrepreneurs were charged only 30 pfennig per day. In 1944 the rate was raised to 1.5 marks for laborers and 2.5 marks for skilled workers; in a few cases the charge was as high as 6 marks. Even so, the costs remained minimal. By the end of the war slave laborers were so well integrated into the Upper Austrian economy that they could be found at work in many local firms as well as those run by the Germans, such as Heinkel, Messerschmitt, Alfa-Vienne, Saurer, and Alpine Montan.[104]

POPULAR OPINION AND POLITICAL DISSENT

The National Socialist consensus in Linz was conceived in the failure of Christian Corporatism, born of the Anschluss, and nurtured by dramatic improvements in the material conditions of everyday life.[105] To a lesser extent, the municipal order also depended on the negative appeal of anticlericalism and anti-Semitism. Underneath the veneer of optimistic

common purpose, however, diversity of opinion and class divisions continued to exist. Beginning in March 1938, the Gestapo sought to gauge the
public mood in Linz and Upper Danube. Information was solicited from
magistrates, police personnel, county lieutenants, rural constables, and
other public officials on the general disposition of the population and its
attitude toward the Nazi regime. Compared to neighboring Bavaria, the
reports that have survived are impressionistic, incomplete, or, in the case of
Linz, exiguous at best. Nevertheless, when added to court records and other
limited evidence, the surveys do reveal certain broad trends of opinion,
especially in the rural areas of the province.[106]

As we have already seen, initial reaction to the Hitler regime appears to
have been especially favorable in Linz and the other towns of Upper Austria.
Since the policies of the Nazis tended to favor cities over the countryside,
this might be expected. That the laboring population of Linz, Steyr, and
towns like Kleinraming, Gleink, and Reichraming actually welcomed the
Anschluss, however, seems to have come as somewhat of a shock to Nazi
officials. Their doctrinaire hostility toward Marxism made it difficult to deal
with the workers in a meaningful, nonrhetorical way. A few Gestapo officials
sensed the hollowness of Hitler's appeal to labor and went so far as to blame
the managers of the Steyr Works for "communist agitation" reported on the
factory floor. At Linz the police expressed concern about the tactless
treatment of wage earners at the hands of high party dignitaries. These
instances notwithstanding, little discontent was reported among the workers
other than constant grumbling over low wages and rising prices. It is of
course impossible to know for sure, but labor unrest at Linz remained
insubstantial until long after the arrival of large numbers of foreign
workers.[107]

In the rural districts of the province, on the other hand, suspicion and
discontent characterized popular opinion from the outset. Farmers and
peasants disapproved Nazi agricultural policies and bristled at the persecution of the Church. What town and country did have in common, even at an
early date, was deep-seated anxiety and fear of war. In the seventeen months
preceding World War II, a substantial majority of Upper Austrians of all
classes appear to have disapproved Hitler's aggressive intentions. After the
signing of the Munich Pact of September 1938, for example, the Gestapo
reported near unanimous relief that the Czech crisis had not led to armed
conflict. In the following spring the SD registered widespread nervousness
at Steyr over renewed rumors of war; during the summer their agents
observed farmers and peasants hoarding food and supplies in anticipation of
hostilities. After Hitler's attack on Poland on 1 September 1939, the mood in
Upper Danube was not at all ebullient. In contrast to 1914, people received
the news with trepidation and despair. From Kremsmünster came word that
"the population was extremely depressed by the outbreak of war"; from

Grünburg, that "the peasants, especially mountain farmers, view the future with fright." In almost all areas of Upper Danube—Linz, Steyr, Kremsmünster, Molln, Steinbach, Spital, Kirchdorf, Micheldorf, Pettenbach—the SD reported public apprehension and concern.[108]

With the conquest of France and western Europe, the mood in Linz and its hinterland improved—but only to a degree. Antiwar sentiment persisted under the surface, even though the war seemed to be won.[109] Since these were the months in which the Nazis proceeded with greatest severity against the Roman Catholic Church, the SD reported considerable unrest in the countryside. The spread of hoof-and-mouth disease from Germany leading to the slaughter of local livestock fanned discontent as well.[110] In Linz a critical housing shortage stoked resentment against Reich Germans believed to enjoy privileged status. Word that the director of the Bruckner Symphony Orchestra, Georg Ludwig Jochum, had moved into a sumptuous ten-room apartment, for example, was greeted with considerable envy and scorn.[111]

After Hitler's invasion of Russia on 22 June 1941 the disposition of the populace became more apprehensive. Hundreds of rallies were staged by the *Gau* propaganda office in the first week of the campaign to whip up public support,[112] but these seem to have met with only limited success. During July and August, on the other hand, tensions apparently relaxed as a consequence of impressive victories in the east. Simultaneously rumors began to circulate of heavy casualties in the ranks of the 45th (Linz) Infantry Division deployed between Brest Litovsk and Kiev.[113]

From the time of the first German setbacks before Moscow in December 1941 to the surrender of the 6th army at Stalingrad fourteen months later, the temper of the Upper Austrian population appears to have become sullen and indifferent. According to Gestapo surveys, dissatisfaction and war-weariness during that period spread rapidly throughout the villages and hamlets of the province.[114] On the other hand, so long as the Roman Catholic Church continued to support Hitler's war against Soviet Russia, the rural population could not be expected to turn against Nazi rule. If nothing else, the lonely struggle of the peasant-pacifist Franz Jägerstätter, who chose death over service in the German armed forces, demonstrated that beyond doubt.[115] Farmers, peasants, and woodcutters were bitterly alienated by the regime, but they and the Roman Catholic clergy still accepted it. In the booming city of Linz morale was apparently higher. As a Swedish journalist traveling in the *Ostmark* reported in 1943, "Linz, Hitler's birthplace [*sic*], is one town that remains faithful to him—or at least it stood firm last February."[116]

After the German defeat at Stalingrad the dimensions of the frightful losses suffered there and elsewhere by Austrian soldiers gradually became known at home. Food and consumer goods became scarcer, and a great many small businesses were forced to close as a consequence of full wartime mobilization. To counter defeatism, hoarding, and black marketeering, the regime added to the growing hardship and despair by resorting to death sentences and executions. In two weeks alone some forty-three individuals were condemned by the People's Court at Graz. By the end of the year, moreover, Vienna and Wiener Neustadt were under aerial bombardment.[117]

It has frequently been pointed out that 1943 was the year in which large numbers of Austrians psychologically turned against what was regarded more and more as an occupation regime.[118] "It was not so much National Socialism they disliked," the Swedish correspondent observed, "as things German in themselves."[119] In the towns and cities of Upper Danube— though not in the countryside—the public mood at first remained less hostile than in Vienna. By the end of the year, however, Linz too began to experience disillusionment and labor unrest. The Upper Austrian 45th Infantry Division, for example, had survived the Stalingrad debacle, but in late summer it was badly mauled northwest of Kursk. Throughout the *Reichsgau*, the Gestapo noted, "our people can no longer imagine a fortunate outcome of this painful struggle. . . . "[120] In the Hermann Göring Works a spontaneous wave of protest greeted the overthrow of Mussolini on 25 July 1943. Brandishing tricolor flags, hundreds of Italian workers walked off the job with "stormy and unrestrained joy" in the company of French compatriots.[121] It is true that no Austrians or Germans were involved in this incident, but by autumn evidence existed of the beginnings of solidarity between Austrian and foreign workers. Before the end of the year, a small underground Socialist resistance group was being organized at the Göring complex.[122]

With regard to the problem of political dissent, it is difficult to discern a pattern of resistance in the local mosaic of overlapping attitudes and opinion. Despite abundant evidence of discontent, especially among the clergy and rural producers, nonconformist behavior in Upper Danube did not generally lead to organized resistance except in a few sporadic and localized cases.[123] As in Bavaria, dissent was usually verbal; it consisted of the sort of complaints heard in most societies in wartime. What the Gestapo regarded as opposition was often little more than partial dissatisfaction with certain aspects of the regime.[124] Examination of the surviving evidence, moreover, reveals a striking absence of middle-class discontent. When added to the many cases of unpolitical informers, it becomes all too apparent that grass-roots support for National Socialism persisted in Linz up to the collapse of the regime.[125]

In the months immediately following the Anschluss, the popularity of the new order was so great in the Danubian city that few discordant notes could be heard anywhere. The police reported sporadic outbursts of opposition by clergymen, ordinary citizens, or Communists. In April 1938, for example, the Gestapo arrested the director of the Institute of the Blind, Father Johann

Gruber, for telling his wards, "the union of tiny Austria with the Reich is an act of cowardice, tyranny, and subjugation. National Socialism is one step removed from Communism. The German military hardly deserves celebration for this rape."[126] By the same token, a salesman received a two-month prison sentence during the summer for speaking out in a tavern against the concentration camp system. Also during the summer the Gestapo arrested some twenty-five workers at Steyr as Communist agitators, although their illegal activities involved little more than muttering against the regime on the floor of the shop.[127]

Aside from a handful of Communists whose members and activities remain obscure in the early days of Nazi rule,[128] the first *organized* underground group to appear in Linz was part of the Greater Austrian Freedom Movement (*Grossösterreichische Freiheitsbewegung*). Founded in Vienna, this illegal organization consisted of clergymen and monarchists who dreamed of restoring the Habsburg Empire or of establishing a Danubian Federation to include an autonomous Bavaria. They realized that the time was not ripe for rebellion, but they planned to gather arms for that purpose. At Linz they met in the Cistercian monastery of Wilhering some six kilometers to the west of the city. In July 1940 the Gestapo arrested the leaders of the conspiracy in Vienna and, shortly thereafter, some fourteen supporters in Linz.[129]

In the face of the Nazi persecution of the Roman Catholic Church, a wide variety of clergy reacted with increasing outrage and anger. Some objected to attacks on religion, some to the euthanasia program, and some to the regime itself. Others protested militarism or the war. Throughout Upper Danube, in fact, large numbers of Catholics, as early as 1940, took to reciting the ditty:

> Wir wollen keinen Krieg
> Wir wollen keinen Sieg
> Wir wollen unser Österreich
> Und eine schöne Führerleich[130]

> We don't want your war
> Victory is such a bore
> For our beloved Austria's sake
> Give us please a Führer's wake

As the attacks on the Church intensified, leaflets appeared in 1943 calling Hitler the "AntiChrist, hated by mankind and cursed by weeping mothers."[131] That nearly 150 churchmen were imprisoned by the Nazis, sixteen losing their lives, is sufficient evidence of Christian protest. Yet so long as the Catholic Church hierarchy remained disposed to an accommodation with Hitler and supported his war, acts of Christian opposition were mostly isolated and, therefore, ineffective. For this reason a Catholic resistance movement as such was never organized in Upper Danube, or for that matter elsewhere in Austria or Germany.

The most important underground group organized in Linz during World War II was founded on the night of 8–9 August 1942. Composed of roughly 350 to 500 individuals from all strata of society, the band adopted the name Countermovement (*Gegenbewegung* or GB). The GB considered it unrealistic to plot the overthrow of the regime and confined its initial activities to gathering intelligence. Information was collected, sifted, and evaluated from a wide range of sources including soldiers on leave, police officials, and foreign radio broadcasts. Under the aegis of Dr. Hans Frenzel, an official in the municipal government, the group established contact with a number of former *Schutzbündler*, such as Ludwig Bernaschek, and with a group of foreign workers at the Göring Works.[132] Gradually, the GB widened its net to recruit such figures as the indomitable Richard Bernaschek, who had returned from exile in 1939, and, in a twist of fate, Dr. Josef Hofer, the onetime police official who had arrested him on the morning of 12 February 1934.[133] How many individuals were actually affiliated with the Countermovement in Linz is difficult to determine in view of the group's deliberately loose and amorphous organization.

In 1944 as the war turned against the Nazis, the scope of the GB's underground activities widened. Acts of passive resistance and sabotage were encouraged, especially at the Göring Works where over a thousand Italians coordinated their activities with Frenzel. In one case, smoke screening devices surrounding the plant were put out of action before an air attack.[134] With an ever realistic eye to the possibilities of opposition, the Countermovement never considered armed action as had occurred in 1934. Even at the end of the war the group refused to take up arms, planning instead to remove tank traps from roads and satchel charges from bridges or to take other measures aiding the Allied advance. In Linz itself GB fighters planned to occupy the gas and water works, the slaughterhouse and the tobacco factory in order to save the buildings from destruction.[135]

As a rule, the other resistance groups that slowly emerged in Upper Danube were scattered and isolated. It is true that the Communists managed to maintain a network of tiny cells in Linz, Wels, and several other cities of the *Reichsgau* and that the Revolutionary Socialists finally organized an underground group of miners and railwaymen in the Salzkammergut.[136] Nevertheless, most resistance bands were largely unpolitical. Like the Countermovement in Linz they were made up of ordinary people of differing outlook. What they had in common was not so much a desire for Austrian independence as a wish to end the war as soon as possible. In this sense they reflected the growing antiwar sentiment of the population in general and might be compared to the spontaneous movements that arose in

Linz and Steyr after January 1918. Given the existence of the Nazi terror apparatus and the continued acceptance of the regime as a whole, their activities were generally muted until the very end of the war. In one remote corner of Upper Danube near Bad Aussee, however, a partisan unit was organized resembling those operating in occupied Yugoslavia or France. Composed of army deserters, foreign laborers, and labor militants, the guerilla band was commanded by an Austrian Communist, Sepp Plieseis. Plieseis had fought on the barricades at Bad Ischl in 1934 and subsequently had seen combat in the Spanish Civil War. After years of confinement, he escaped in 1943 from a subcamp of Dachau near Hallein. Fleeing into the mountains, he managed to organize a partisan group called "Willy"—later "Fred." The band occasionally harassed German units, but until the last days of the war it spent most of its time pilfering arms and eluding capture.[137]

In retrospect, it was only the German army that possessed the resources to check or overthrow the Nazi government from within. The failure of the generals' revolt of 20 July 1944 thus served to tighten the control of the regime as well as that of the dreaded SS. At Linz the NSDAP brought out some 40,000 Upper Austrians the following day to demonstrate their gratitude for the Führer's miraculous escape from Count Stauffenberg's bomb. Four days later, whatever euphoria Hitler's supporters may have generated was shattered by the arrival of 400 American bombers over his hometown. In the attack that followed, the coking plant and the rolling mills of the Göring Works suffered such severe damage that production came to a halt for two weeks. By the end of the war over 800,000 tons of bombs were dropped on Linz, killing 1,679 men, women, and children. Some 602 buildings were reduced to rubble, 795 severely damaged, and 4,719 left in need of repair. No less than 2,940 living units were totally destroyed, 5,264 made scarcely habitable, and 22,617 moderately or lightly damaged.[138]

THE COLLAPSE OF THE NAZI CONSENSUS AND THE END OF THE WAR

Only with defeat looming in World War II did the National Socialist consensus in Linz begin to break apart. As late as September 1944 Ernst Kaltenbrunner reported, after an inspection trip through the *Ostmark*, on the generally positive mood prevailing in Upper Danube, Lower Danube, and Salzburg.[139] Whatever popularity the Nazi regime still possessed, however, soon crumbled under the relentless bombing of the American Air Force. By October a quantum leap in the number of death sentences meted out by the People's Court in Linz revealed a groundswell of local disenchantment. The Nazis also felt it imperative to detain potential opponents. On 7 September the Gestapo dispatched scores of Social Democrats including Richard Bernaschek to Mauthausen. By Christmas the

Allied bombing of Linz, 1945. Stadtmuseum Linz.

local mood had become in the words of one judicial official "extremely depressed."[140]

In the face of collapse, the Nazi establishment in Linz gradually divided between those prepared to follow Hitler into the abyss and those quietly planning for a peaceful transition of power. Of the former Eigruber was by far the most determined; on 1 January 1945 he went on the radio to announce that the "final preconditions for a German victory have at last been met."[141] Already in possession of wide discretionary powers as commissioner for Reich defense in Upper Danube, the *Gauleiter* received additional authorization from Himmler to proclaim martial law and to pass summary sentences of death. While the Upper Austrian population thus hoped for a quick end to hostilities, Eigruber remained convinced that the tide might be turned in his Alpine redoubt.[142] At his initial disposal stood only about 10,000 poorly equipped members of the *Volkssturm* and Hitler Youth, but in the concentration camps of Mauthausen were imprisoned over fifty labor leaders and Social Democratic politicians. Like Hitler, the fanatical *Gauleiter* resolved that there would never be another 1918.[143]

Even after Vienna had fallen to the Red Army, Eigruber remained confident. In mid-April he assumed command of the defense of both Lower and Upper Austria and ordered fleeing Viennese arrested for desertion. Among the first apprehended and shot was Karl Mayerzelt, a member of Vienna's Nazi city council. On 14 April, General Lothar Rendulic lent his support to Eigruber's draconian measures by instituting flying courts martial to try and execute military personnel caught out of uniform or away from their units. With the roads overflowing or clogged by hundreds of thousands of refugees, roving bands of SS and military police proceeded to carry out untold numbers of death sentences. Among those summarily shot were the director of the Upper Danubian labor office and a bookkeeper in the Linz municipal administration. The former was apprehended fleeing Linz with his wife; the latter was overheard remarking after Hitler's suicide that the war would soon be over. Most of all, it was ordinary people who suffered at the hands of the Gestapo. At Freistadt, to cite one example, two women and ten men fell prey to the SS as they tried to lend assistance to starving concentration camp inmates; charged with conspiracy, they were machine-gunned on 1 May—only four days before the arrival of the Americans.[144]

Eigruber's reign of terror should not be regarded as simply self-destructive or gratuitous. From all accounts, the *Gauleiter* believed that his Alpine redoubt might be held so long as the civilian population remained under tight control.[145] To prevent another 1918—that is, a domestic uprising—he ordered the liquidation of those labor politicians and militants imprisoned at Mauthausen. On 18 April Richard Bernaschek was shot in the nape of the neck; eleven days later forty-three of his comrades were sent to the gas chamber. It was hardly by chance that Eigruber's decision to execute the main group of Social Democrats was made the day following Karl Renner's proclamation of the Second Austrian Republic in Vienna.

What the Upper Austrian *Gauleiter* had not reckoned on was the rapid advance of the American Third Army. As late as 24 April, eleven days after the fall of Vienna, General Patton's forces were still operating north of Munich and Regensburg. Then within less than a week, they swept to the Inn River and on 30 April crossed into Austria. At Linz Eigruber ordered a last-ditch defense of the Inn Valley, but, aside from a handful of scattered SS units, he had less than 30,000 militia to offer resistance. The American 65th Infantry and 11th Armored Divisions thus encountered few pockets of resistance as they rolled through the lush Upper Austrian countryside. With the news of Hitler's suicide, moreover, a wave of desertions and uprisings spread through the towns and villages of the province. At Braunau an angry mob seized the *Kreisleiter* and compelled him to surrender the town; at Enns the leading Nazis were placed under arrest by Wehrmacht Major

Franz Peyerl; and in scores of villages like Helfenberg, Perg, Grein, and Treffling, resistance fighters emerged to remove tank traps or road blocks. When the Americans arrived at Grieskirchen, they found the town draped in red-white-red banners under the control of Dr. Josef Hofer. It was to the south, at Alt Aussee, however, that the most dramatic uprising took place. There the entrances to the salt mines holding the art treasures for Hitler's Linz gallery were successfully blocked by a group of partisans. As a result, the priceless collection of Dutch, Flemish, Italian, and German masters were spared destruction by Eigruber, who, in a fit of pique, had ordered their demolition.[146]

Meanwhile, in Linz, it was not resistance fighters but a group of moderate Nazis in the municipal administration of Franz Langoth who unobtrusively succeeded in saving the city from destruction. Langoth had become lord mayor of Hitler's hometown in January 1944 after six years as director of the *Ostmark*'s Nazi Welfare Organization (NSV). If his memoirs are to be believed, the veteran German Nationalist politician took under his protective wing several of his former Social Democratic colleagues including (until his arrest by the Gestapo) Richard Bernaschek, Ernst Koref, and Hans Frenzel.[147] It is not known whether Langoth got wind of Frenzel's activities as head of the Countermovement, but by late April 1945 the two men shared the same immediate goals. As the American 11th Armored Division suddenly descended upon Urfahr, Langoth and *Kreisleiter* Franz Danzer dissuaded Eigruber from proclaiming Linz a fortress to be held to the last man. The fanatical *Gauleiter* still intended to defend the city, however, and ordered the destruction of the Nibelungen bridge. Balking at this directive, Danzer argued that its principal effect would be to cut the electricity to Urfahr. Finally, after two days of furious debate, Eigruber threw up his hands and took his leave, as he put it, "forever."[148]

On the morning of 4 May American incendiary shells began falling on Linz. As soon as possible, Danzer drove to Eigruber's villa on the Guglhof. The *Gauleiter*, who was still packing his bags, authorized Danzer to treat with the Americans, though in the name of the city administration rather than the *Gauleitung*. Coordinating his moves with Mayor Langoth, Danzer then drove his Steyr 50 auto under a flag of truce to Rottenegg behind the American lines. The Americans demanded the unconditional surrender of Linz the following morning at 9:00 A.M. Returning to the provincial capital, Danzer met late in the afternoon with Langoth, Police President Plakolm, and several city councillors. The terms of the surrender were accepted, but not until late that night was the city commandant, Major General Alfred Kuzmany, persuaded to withdraw his troops from the city. Since Danzer was unable to return to Rottenegg as promised, the Americans prepared to storm Linz the next day.[149]

Fortunately, the main elements of the 11th Armored Division were not deployed around Urfahr until 10:00 A.M. By that time Danzer had returned to Rottenegg with word that Linz was an open city. At 11:00 A.M. American tanks entered Urfahr and started across the Nibelungen bridge. Surrounding the Rathaus within seven minutes, the Americans ordered its immediate evacuation. Inside, Lord Mayor Langoth had intended to surrender in SS uniform, but at the last moment wisely changed into civilian clothes. An American general dictated the terms of surrender to him, ordering all civilians off the street within one hour. Langoth was informed that he would remain only three more days in office. In the meantime, the Americans removed some 2,000 pounds of explosives from the Danubian bridges and took a meager 153 German soldiers prisoner. By early afternoon the city was secure.[150]

Toward evening, as troops of the 328th combat team were still moving through the streets of Linz, a delegation of Social Democratic and Christian Social politicians met with American military authorities. Long before the capitulation, representatives of the two parties had agreed that the Socialist Dr. Ernst Koref should become lord mayor of the city on the first day of peace. The Americans asked for forty-eight hours to make inquiries, but on 7 May confirmed the appointment. The following day, as Field Marshal Keitel was signing the German instrument of surrender in Berlin, Langoth, Koref, and other representatives of the political parties, the Church, and the municipal administration gathered in the ceremonial chamber of the Linz Rathaus. With Colonel Russell A. Snook presiding, Langoth was officially dismissed and replaced by Koref. The old German Nationalist was permitted a few words of farewell as well as the privilege of introducing his successor. In response, Koref acknowledged Langoth's services and thanked him for his role in saving the city from destruction.[151] Amidst the carnage, rubble, and ashes of Hitler's hometown, the formal transfer of municipal authority was as civil and urbane as it had been in 1918, 1934, and 1938. This time, however, an era of instability and turmoil had at last come to an end.

The legacy of National Socialism in Linz was one of breathtaking change. In less than a decade the system had permanently transformed the economic life of the city: it had provided jobs and opportunity for Hitler's upwardly mobile supporters; in the shadow of Christian Corporatism it had both disciplined and mobilized the working classes so as to maintain the Nazi consensus until late in the war. The demands of total war accelerated the process of industrialization, though not without ultimately producing unparalleled suffering and devastation. Only in late 1944 did public sentiment in Linz turn against what was gradually perceived as alien domination. Without condemning the Nazi system as such, most town dwellers—including many disillusioned Nazis—became willing to support a constitutional order based on Austrian patriotism and liberal democracy. That the restored democratic system subsequently struck roots and flourished was due in part to the horrible memory of the Nazi past: brutal and capricious as Hitler's rule had been, it also laid the groundwork for a modern pluralistic order in both Austria and Germany. In Hitler's hometown that meant not only the weakening or demolition of traditional structures and institutions, but also the foundation of a modern industrial base upon which economic prosperity and political stability after 1945 would largely come to rest.

NINE

Epilogue

For exactly a decade after World War II Linz was the divided capital of a partitioned province within a disunited country. While the Moscow Declaration of 1943 had called for the reestablishment of an Austrian state, the country remained occupied by the troops of the Great Powers until the signing of a State Treaty in 1955. With the Russians in control of Urfahr and the Americans of Linz itself, the damaged city at first faced a grim and uncertain future. Through the restoration of liberal democracy and the consolidation of the Nazi economic revolution the municipality, however, rapidly overcame its difficulties to emerge as both a model of democratic propriety and the industrial core of the now thriving Second Republic.

The immediate aftermath of Nazi rule was one of almost indescribable confusion and uncertainty. For weeks after the German capitulation mobs of refugees, foreign workers, and concentration camp inmates roamed the streets of the shattered city, plundering warehouses, river barges, shops, wine cellars, and private homes. Many were the victims of Nazism, and their plight evoked the sympathy of the American occupiers who, more often than not, refused to intervene except to break up fistfights or other disturbances that appeared to be getting out of hand. Adding to the lawlessness, especially on the outskirts of the city, were nearly 18,000 armed Hungarian troops whose continued presence in the countryside during the spring and early summer kept farmers from the normal cultivation of their crops. The breakdown of law and order also led to a crisis of food distribution in which caloric consumption in Linz fell from 1500 in May to 762 in mid-July, leaving much of the population vulnerable to infectious disease, especially typhus, typhoid, diphtheria, and tuberculosis. Transcending and compounding the general distress was the physical devastation of the war itself. Not only were large parts of the town reduced to rubble, but the damage to the network of water mains, sewers, and gas, electricity, and telephone lines was so extensive that basic services virtually no longer existed.[1]

In coping with the chaos of the immediate postwar period the municipality relied on its own meager resources and the aid of the American military government. In contrast to the situation after the First World War, neither federal nor provincial authorities were at first in a position to exert much influence in Linz: in the first instance the Western Powers refused to recognize the jurisdiction of the Renner government outside Vienna; in the second, the Americans were reluctant, despite the wishes of local democratic elites, to permit the establishment of an autonomous regime in Upper Austria.

As early as February 1945, Social Democratic and Christian Social politicians had agreed to the restoration of a liberal provincial order on a consociational basis, proposing Dr. Alois Oberhummer, former editor of the Socialist *Tagblatt*, as governor and Dr. Josef Zehetner, a functionary of the Patriotic Front, as his deputy. This coalition the Americans refused to accept, preferring instead a ban on all political activity in favor of a managerial government of their own choosing. Such a government was duly constituted on 17 May, but it ran into trouble three months later when one-third of its members, including the provisional governor, Dr. Adolf Eigl, were taken into custody for investigation of their Nazi past.[2]

It was at this juncture that Lord Mayor Ernst Koref emerged as the outstanding figure in postwar Linz. A former gymnasial professor of English, a much-respected member of the National Assembly before 1934, and an energetic administrator with a spotless anti-Nazi past, Koref was ideally suited to work with the American occupation authorities in reconstructing the life of the city. Despite tactical disagreements, he was able to win the confidence of military government largely because his own goals of denazification, democratic reform, and economic growth coincided almost perfectly with American policy in Central Europe after World War II.

Upon taking the oath of office, Koref appointed an executive committee (*Stadtrat*) of four Social Democrats, four Christian Socials and, in deference to the Russians about to occupy Urfahr on the other side of the Danube, two Communists. Thereafter, he moved effectively to coordinate relief and cleanup procedures with the Americans, so that by September much of the rubble was cleared away and most essential services including street lighting, tramways, and 240 kilometers of gas lines were once again in operation. During the summer the new mayor also made critical decisions affecting the future of the Linz economy. Learning that the Americans were interested in the heavy industrial plant bequeathed by the Germans to supply U.S. forces in Europe, Koref organized a coalition of Social Democrats, Christian Socials—including the former Christian Corporative governor Heinrich Gleissner—trade unionists, Nazi managers and American officers. The group comprised a common front against the efforts of older smokestack concerns in Styria and Vienna to dismantle the installations. At the prodding of the American industrial officer, Colonel Henry B. Engesath, Koref and his associates changed the name of the Göring Works to the United Austrian Iron and Steel Works (VÖEST) and managed to have the plant resume production as early as 18 August. Using gas generated by the coking factory, they also reopened the Nitrogen Works to produce fertilizers for local agriculture.[3]

While Koref had few qualms bowing to economic necessity, he did not oppose the American policy of first purging Linz of its Nazi past. As was so frequently the case in postwar Germany and Austria, his task was, however, complicated by a need for university-trained personnel, many of whom had been National Socialists. Of the 722 party members in the city administration, the mayor reluctantly retained 226 as indispensable and, despite grave personal reservations, eventually rehired all but eighty of the rest under the terms of a general amnesty issued by the Austrian government in 1948. Without the expertise of the administrative, managerial, and technical elites who had supported Hitler, Koref found it nearly impossible to keep the city going or to reconstruct its economic life. For many months after the war, in fact, he was forced to consult the director of the VÖEST not over the table of a board room but through the bars of a prison cell where the latter was awaiting trial as one of Albert Speer's key advisers.[4]

As much as any other figure, Koref also played a key role in the restoration of democratic politics in Linz. The Americans at first prohibited political activity, preferring local administrative structures to support their own authoritarian regime. In the early months of the occupation, military government succeeded admirably in reestablishing public security, in supplying and distributing massive shipments of food, and in taking the first steps to revitalize local economic activity. The military authorities soon discovered, however, that full recovery could not take place without the cooperation of the political parties. Faced with surprising public pressure to resume political life, the Americans gradually relaxed restrictions on trade unions, the press, and public assembly. On 19 September, after the Allied Council in Vienna called for the holding of free elections, they finally agreed to the reestablishment of all non-Nazi political parties.[5]

In reconstituting the Upper Austrian branch of the Socialist party (SPÖ), Koref relied on those surviving elites who before 1934 had comprised the conservative wing of the labor movement. While some had been Revolutionary Socialists, none had been ideologically close to the militants of the First Republic who, with few exceptions, had perished with Richard Bernaschek in Mauthausen. Under Koref's leadership the provincial party emerged in tune with Karl Renner's national organization in Vienna as a democratic reform movement, able to capitalize on the moral legacy of an antifascist past but pledged to the primacy of production over distribution and eager to collaborate with political opponents in fruitful legislation.[6]

While the SPÖ experienced little difficulty reorganizing in Linz after World War II, the Christian Socials encountered some ideological and organizational bottlenecks. Sometime before the arrival of the Americans, Dr. Josef Zehetner had taken the initiative in establishing a shadow apparatus composed of onetime functionaries of the Catholic unions and the provincial Peasants' Association (*Bauernbund*). In light of their authoritarian past, the Catholic elites had to redefine the relationship of their movement to the Church and to the cause of democracy. Their decision was to sever formal ties to the clerical hierarchy and to establish a democratic mass party, the Austrian People's Party (*Österreichishe Volkspartei*—ÖVP). This was easier said than done in Upper Austria, however, since neither Bishop Fliesser nor Felix Kern, the head of the influential *Bauernbund*, acknowledged Zehetner's leadership; they insisted instead on the nomination of Heinrich Gleissner, the governor of the Christian Corporative era. While Gleissner's reemergence placed the ÖVP at a moral disadvantage vis à vis the SPÖ, the former governor, who had been affiliated with the Kreisau Circle of the German resistance during the war, readily renounced his authoritarian principles and extended a conciliatory hand to Koref and the Socialists.[7]

Once the Americans permitted the political parties to rebuild their organizational structures, it was possible to restore provincial government on a more rational basis. At the end of October a proposal by Renner's federal cabinet for proportional reorganization led to the dissolution of Eigl's rump administration and to the formation of a provisional order based on the constitution of 1929. As the leader of the traditionally dominant Catholic party, Gleissner assumed the office of governor and formed a cabinet consisting of four members of the People's Party, three Socialists, and one Communist. He then appointed three deputies, one each from the three parties including the Communists.[8]

The subsequent development of political life in Linz closely paralleled that of the Second Republic. As elsewhere in Austria, the resurrected parties were at first hobbled by military censorship and Western mistrust of the Russian-sponsored federal government in Vienna. A series of provincial conferences in the autumn, however, quickly produced a broadening of the Renner regime, a relaxation of press regulations, and, on 20 October, full Allied recognition. The elections of 25 November 1945 thus took place under favorable circumstances, with the Socialists winning 60 percent of the municipal vote and thirty-six seats of the city council; the People's Party garnered 36 percent with twenty-two seats, and the Communists a mere 4 percent and two seats. In the provincial balloting the results were reversed. As in the First Republic, the Catholics swept the rural districts, capturing 59 percent of the votes and twenty-nine seats in the diet. Trailing them were the Socialists with 38 percent and nineteen seats, and the Communists with 3 percent, though not a single mandate. In the country as a whole the ÖVP captured 50 percent of the ballots, the SPÖ 45 percent, and the KPÖ 5 percent. Overall, the results were a striking demonstration of the persistence of political loyalties in Austria. What was different was the absence of the German Nationalists whose voters either stayed home as disenfranchised National Socialists or threw their support to the ÖVP.[9]

On April 1946 the Linz city council held its first formal session since the end of the war. The councillors unanimously elected Ernst Koref lord mayor and, for the first time, took an oath affirming the Austrian, rather than German, character of the city. Overlooking their absolute majority, the Socialists solicited the support of the other parties in overcoming the serious problems of the day. As on the federal level in Vienna, the majority party organized a proportional coalition based on the municipal statute of 1931 and resting on a broad consensus of denazification, reconstruction, and economic stabilization. For the Socialists this meant subordinating their traditional goals of social justice to the imperatives of economic growth; for the People's Party it meant accepting the necessity of communalization and even limited nationalization. As for the Communists, they too were willing to cooperate, at least until the spread of the Cold War to Linz the following year.[10]

Throughout most of 1946 economic recovery continued at a modest pace. Koref and the municipal administration devoted considerable attention to industrial development, both planning production and, after the National-ization Act of 26 July, coordinating the American transfer of the VÖEST, the Nitrogen Works, and other former German plants to the Austrian govern-ment. With the full support of the Americans and the United Nations Relief and Rehabilitation Administration (UNRRA), tolerable levels of food sup-plies were maintained, and public morale remained comparatively high. This cautious optimism gave way, however, first to dissatisfaction and then to despair as the crippling winter of 1947 brought bitterly cold temperatures, food and fuel shortages, a near collapse of the currency, and in March the complete failure of the Moscow Conference of foreign ministers to reach agreement on an Austrian state treaty. So distraught was the public mood that Koref, who feared a recrudescence of radicalism, took considerable pains to dissociate the economic difficulties of the day from the restored democratic order.[11]

On the global stage, the European crisis of 1947 and the rapid deteriora-tion of East-West relations combined to accelerate the development of the Marshall Plan. The decision of the Austrian government to participate was of enormous benefit to Linz. As one of the few centers of heavy industry outside the Russian Zone, the Danubian city subsequently received massive infusions of American capital for the modernization and expansion of the VÖEST, the Nitrogen Works, and the aluminum refineries at Ranshofen. Between 1948 and 1952 the VÖEST alone accumulated $3 million in Marshall aid, which it used to repair and overhaul its blast furnaces, to construct both a hotstrip mill and a cold rolling mill, and to build a separate converter plant. The concern used these facilities to develop and, in 1952, to put into operation the revolutionary Linz Donawitz (LD) oxygen conversion process of manufacturing low cost, high quality steel from low phosphorous iron. During the same period, the Nitrogen Works expanded its operations by constructing a gypsum sulphuric acid factory and a phosphate fertilizer plant.[12]

Although the Marshall Plan largely bypassed the consumer sector, as well as housing and social programs, both the ÖVP and the SPÖ readily endorsed it. The Socialists, in particular, argued for its acceptance, shrewdly judging that American aid offered the best means of strengthening their own position. They saw in the first place that expansion of the state-owned VÖEST, the Nitrogen Works, and other nationalized firms provided opportunity for party members, organizers, technicians, administrators, and managerial specialists to check the capitalist owners of the means of production. Becoming capitalists themselves, the Socialists also perceived that expanded production and profits would enhance their own dominance of Linz, since the municipality (after 1948) had the legal right of levying a tax on the VÖEST, in effect freeing it from the financial control of the Upper Austrian diet.[13] Unlike their colleagues in the First Republic, Koref and the leadership cadre had good reason to postpone the goals of higher wages and social security in favor of capital investment, modernization, and full employment.

With the adoption of the Marshall Plan, living conditions in Austria improved perceptively, especially after the arrival of 45 percent of the initial outlays in foodstuffs. By 1949, overall industrial output exceeded the last prewar year by 23 percent and two years later by 66 percent.[14] The package deal of currency stability, economic growth, and full employment found broad popular acceptance, even though wages usually failed to keep pace with rising prices. Nevertheless, by the end of the decade, discontent with the inflationary spiral had become sufficient to mount a series of challenges to governmental activity from both the left and the right.

In Linz, as elsewhere, it was the Communists who first took exception to the pro-Western policies of the SPÖ-ÖVP coalition. Following the refusal of the Soviet Union in August 1947 to participate in the European Recovery Program, the KPÖ bitterly assailed the budgetary policies of the city council by demanding the introduction of a municipal luxury tax in lieu of higher rates for gas and utilities. The party's councillors protested currency stabilization measures as harmful to consumers and even organized mass demonstrations against Koref in the streets of Urfahr. Once industrial recovery got under way, they continued to insist on a reversal of priorities, pointing (correctly) to a decline in real wages and demanding both comprehensive communalization and massive funds for public housing. Their pleas fell on deaf ears. With the intensification of the Cold War—the fall of the coalition government in Hungary, the Communist coup in Prague, and the Berlin blockade—few Linzers were willing to consider their arguments. In

City Hall the SPÖ and ÖVP thus reflected public opinion when they closed ranks to exclude the KPÖ from the decision-making process. Accusing the Communists of plotting the establishment of a People's Democracy in Linz, Koref went so far as to stigmatize them both as "fascists" and the "Russian party."[15]

Although hardly clear at the time, the tiny KPÖ really presented fewer difficulties for the restored democratic order in Linz than the remnants of the German Nationalist *Lager*, especially the former National Socialists. The Austrian government had at first planned to distinguish higher Nazi officials and leaders from the great mass of nominal members, fully intending to punish those guilty of atrocities and to integrate the rest into the fold of society as quickly as possible. Allied insistence on the registration of every party member, however, coupled with mandatory penalties for minor offenders disrupted these plans and created a bureaucratic nightmare. As actually implemented, denazification tended to deflect attention from major offenders, to create a "community of suffering" among Hitler's former followers, great and small, and to evoke public sympathy, even among non-Nazis. When a general amnesty restored full citizenship rights in 1948, most former Nazis were ready to throw their support to a new protest party, the League of Independents (VdU).[16]

In the municipal, provincial, and national elections of 9 October 1949 the VdU scored a stunning upset in Linz. Mobilizing large numbers of former Nazis, Sudeten German refugees, war veterans, and disgruntled young voters, it captured 28 percent of the ballots, thus surpassing the ÖVP (24 percent) and the KPÖ (5 percent) as the second largest party on the city council. Two weeks later the VdU repeated its show of strength by winning an absolute majority in shop steward elections at the Nitrogen Works and Elektrobau AG, a plurality at the VÖEST, and, in a separate ballot, 34 mandates in the municipal Chamber of Labor. The success of the new party at the expense of the left in no way threatened the democratic order in Linz, but it did have a brief disruptive impact on municipal affairs. In the constituent meeting of the city council, for example, the VdU refused to endorse the unanimous reelection of Koref and denounced what its spokesman, Dr. Alfred Mold, tendentiously called the "Demokratur" of the "monopoly" parties. After a bitter exchange reminiscent of the First Republic, Mold and his colleagues fell in line, however, to support the municipal budget.[17]

The discontent spawning the VdU increased significantly when the outbreak of the Korean War in June 1950 produced a drastic cut in American aid and a sharp rise in the cost of living. To counter the inflationary spiral the Austrian government, the chambers, and the trade unions grudgingly negotiated a wage and price agreement that raised wages but sharply reduced food and fuel subsidies. As the rank and file of organized labor was largely ignored in the negotiating process, the announcement of the terms on 25 September provoked a wave of demonstrations, strikes, and riots that swept through Vienna, Linz, and other industrial cities for over a week. The disturbances were largely spontaneous, but the participation of large numbers of Communists at the height of the Cold War conveyed the impression of a well-orchestrated Leninist coup.[18]

In Linz and Upper Austria, despite the presence of Russian forces in the occupied Mühlviertel, it was indisputably the Independents who played the leading role in the September strikes.[19] On 26 September VdU shop stewards took the initiative in downing tools at the VÖEST and five other major enterprises. Supported by the Communists, they succeeded in mobilizing 15,000 demonstrators—including the municipal tramway workers—on the main square by the Danube. The strikers then forced their way into City Hall and onto the balcony, where VdU and KPÖ speakers took turns addressing the throng. The next day about a thousand demonstrators stormed the Chamber of Labor building and, at the threat of defenestration, brutally forced the elderly president of the chamber to resign. That was the climax of the riots. With the cooperation of American military authorities, municipal and provincial officials rushed police reinforcements to Linz and restored order. Deliberately blaming the Soviets for the disturbances, Socialist organizers appealed to the anti-Communist sentiments of the workers, especially those who were refugees from the Sudetenland, in order to regain control of the factory floor. By Wednesday, 4 October, the workers were back on the job.[20]

The mass strikes of 1950 constituted the only outburst of radicalism experienced in Linz—and Austria—in the postwar period. Thereafter economic conditions stabilized, and in 1952 prices even dropped slightly. The following year a brief recession ensued that saw unemployment rise to 9 percent. At the end of 1953, however, the economy took off, launching Austria on a course of remarkably steady growth and high employment that has persisted, at least in relation to other countries, right up to the present.[21] Among the immediate consequences of the boom in Linz was a final stabilization of the democratic order, made manifest by the decline of the VdU and the absorption of most of its electorate by the two major parties. By 1967 the German Nationalist movement, which had so significantly shaped the city's history over the past century, could mobilize no more than 10 percent of the urban vote. As for the KPÖ, it too gradually faded into oblivion, losing all but one of its seats in 1967 on the city council. The Socialists and People's Party, by contrast, continued to narrow the political, ideological, and social cleavages dividing them. While party leaders still resorted to verbal invective in electoral contests, they rarely permitted serious disagreement to mar their collaborative efforts in City Hall. The improved financial status of the municipality based on revenue from the

VÖEST encouraged cooperation and facilitated compromise on such thorny issues as housing, taxation, and communalization. That the two parties also reached agreement on ideological matters such as the municipalization of funeral facilities and communal aid to parochial schools was perhaps of even greater significance.[22]

CONCLUSIONS

Viewing the Linz of Hitler's lifetime in the larger context of Central European history, it is abundantly clear that the town's political culture was molded in large part by the socioeconomic trends of the late nineteenth century. Shortly before the Führer's birth, the Long Depression of 1873 to 1896 enabled the newly enfranchised middle strata of Upper Austria to mount an effective counter attack against the liberal doctrines of laissez faire capitalism. The rural *Mittelstand* under the Church hierarchy was the first to organize a mass protest movement, which in the form of the Catholic People's Association demanded protection from foreign competition and sought to restore bans on division and alienation of peasant holdings. The farmers were soon joined by the urban petite bourgeoisie who in the famous Linz Program of 1882 called for progressive taxation, extension of the franchise, and, above all, protection of artisanal manufacturers. Despite an obvious congruence of interests, rural and urban middle strata did not join forces, partly because of a natural antipathy between town and country, but more fundamentally because of a deep-rooted anticlerical tradition in Linz that encompassed nearly all classes of society. It was thus the German Nationalists—rather than the Christian Socials—who mobilized the city's *Bürger* und *Kleinbürger* behind a program of small-firm protection, anti-Semitism, and, after the turn of the century, anti-Marxism.

In the decade before World War I the gap between the Catholic party and the German Nationalists in Upper Austria widened considerably, especially after the People's Association began cooperating with the nascent Social Democrats in undermining the curial franchise. Catholic peasants and Socialist workers still remained ideological foes, but their leaders endorsed a kind of corporate or consociational pluralism that found expression in frequent bargaining and interest group conciliation. By the time of the collapse of the Habsburg monarchy, interelite collaboration in Linz had become a semi-institutional feature of the local political scene. In the revolutionary turmoil and confusion of the next several years this provided the social framework of all three *Lager*—including the German National-ists—to subsume their differences in effective crisis management.

The interwar period was generally unfavorable to the cause of democracy in Austria. Although the Revolution of 1918–19 gave birth to a democratic Republic based on universal suffrage, few Austrians accepted the new state or believed in its economic viability. After an initial period of cooperation, the predominant leaders withdrew into their respective *Lager*, preferring confrontation to collaboration and placing allegiance to their subcultures above allegiance to the state. In Linz and Upper Austria, however, a political culture existed that preserved a modicum of cooperation and proved remarkably resilient in regulating local political conflict. The proportional system functioned effectively on the regional level partly because of common misery but also because of a tradition of interelite collaboration, shared cultural values, and the ability of party leaders to control their respective political organizations. That there was also an unstated consensus on economic matters was less fortunate and ultimately injurious to the democratic order. Despite bitter disagreement on the organization and distribution of productive resources, elites of all three *Lager* in Linz eschewed policies of economic growth in favor of protection for their constituents. The Social Democrats, therefore, advocated a redistribution of wealth and income for the wage-earning classes; the Christian Socials demanded tariff shelter for local agriculture and artisanal manufacturing; and the German Nationalists insisted on higher salaries for civil servants and teachers. Even the members of the Linz business community shied away from industrialization, partly out of habit and partly out of fear of eventually strengthening the forces of organized labor. The result was economic stagnation and eventual polarization of the political landscape.

In the shattering storm of the Great Depression the consociational order of Linz at first withstood the upsurge of political radicalism in Central Europe surprisingly well. Deflation and economic decline, however, gradually eroded consensus and intensified the anxiety of the rural and urban middle strata to the point of driving many of the former into the ranks of the *Heimwehr* and most of the latter into the arms of the National Socialists. When the town's working classes took up arms against the Dollfus dictatorship, they intended to preserve a system in which they had a very real stake but which by that time no longer existed. The subsequent Christian Corporative interlude constituted something more than a throwback to an earlier era. It was also an attempt to stabilize the capitalist system by favoring the old *Mittelstand* of landowners, peasants, and small producers, and by engaging the masses in an Austroclerical form of nation building. Precisely because the authoritarian order offered so little to the new *Mittelstand* of white-collar employees, let alone to the industrial working classes, it attracted only a minimum of support, actually alienating the population to the point of welcoming Hitler's homecoming in 1938.

Without doubt, it was the German occupation of Linz that marked the decisive turning point in the city's development. The *Anschluss* enabled a new generation of German Nationalists with little sentimental attachment to the preindustrial world of the past to recover the power lost by their fathers in 1918. Under Hitler's tutelage they carried out a program of secularization and industrialization that transformed the life of the city. In seven short years the Nazis curtailed the power of the church hierarchy, destroyed the guild-bound dominance of traditional manufacturing, and through the construction of a massive iron, steel, and nitrogen complex generated thousands of jobs for the town's aspiring new middle class. The dazzling economic performance of National Socialism in Linz unified the community as no other system in recent history, though its sense of common purpose did not extend to the countryside where Nazi social, economic, and above all, religious policies provoked widespread discontent and resentment. In Hitler's hometown the National Socialist consensus survived, however, until shortly before the end of World War II, when aerial bombardment and looming defeat eventually induced municipal opinion to reject what was at last regarded foreign rule. It was only at this point that the notion of an independent Austrian state, once espoused primarily by traditional elites, became a viable alternative to most city dwellers including many disillusioned Nazis.

After 1945 a constitutional regime was established in Austria on the basis of Austrian patriotism and liberal democracy. In Linz and Upper Austria the local order was patterned after Hauser's consociational system of crisis management and interest reconciliation. In contrast to the interwar period, however, the Socialist and Catholic politicians who resurrected the democratic order in Linz agreed on more than a desire to avoid conflict. This time there was consensus on a wide variety of issues including the viability of Austria, the nationalization of heavy industry, currency stability, and full employment. The cooperation of the two major parties—both on the local and federal level—made it possible with American aid to reconstruct the damaged German industrial complex, thus completing and consolidating the Nazi economic revolution. Acceptance of the reorientation of the Austrian economy also made it imperative to forego protection, *nolens volens* linking municipal fortunes to economic growth and foreign competition. The subsequent expansion and modernization of industrial production in Linz gave the two major parties an enormous stake in economic prosperity and social stability. Invariably, the process narrowed the difference between them, creating a genuine social partnership known in the Koref era as the "Upper Austrian climate" and regarded today as paradigmatic of Austrian political culture. That the achievement of social peace was also the consequence of the successful integration into the community of the wage-earning new middle class of employees, technicians, and younger managers was equally important. As part of a larger historical process it represented a development that embraced more, however, than Linz, Austria, or Central Europe.

NOTES

INTRODUCTION

1. Harry R. Ritter, "Recent Writing on Interwar Austria," *Central European History*, vol. 12, no. 3 (September 1979): 247–311.

2. David Schoenbaum, *Hitler's Social Revolution: Class and Status in Nazi Germany* (New York, 1967), especially pp. 273–88; Ralf Dahrendorf, *Society and Democracy in Germany* (New York, 1967), pp. 381–91; Geoffrey Barraclough, "A New View of German History," *New York Review of Books*, 16 November 1972, pp. 25–31; and Radomir Luža, *Austro-German Relations in the Anschluss Era* (Princeton, 1975). For slightly different perspectives see Henry A. Turner, "Fascism and Modernization," in *Reappraisals of Fascism*, ed. Henry A. Turner (New York, 1975), pp. 117–39 and Horst Matzerath and Heinrich Volkmann, "Modernisierungstheorien und Nationalsozialismus," in *Theorien in der Praxis des Historikers*, ed. Jurgen Kocka (Göttingen, 1977), pp. 86–116.

1. UNDER THE DOUBLE-EAGLE, 1908–1918

1. Adolf Hitler, *Mein Kampf* (New York, 1939), p. 25. On Hitler's childhood in Linz see August Kubizek, *The Young Hitler I Knew* (Cambridge, 1955), Franz Jetzinger, *Hitler's Youth* (London, 1958), and Bradley F. Smith, *Adolf Hitler His Family, Childhood and Youth* (Stanford, 1967).

2. Kubizek, *The Young Hitler I Knew*, p. 8; Erwin Stein, ed., *Das Buch der Stadt Linz a.D* (Berlin, 1927), pp. 18–28; *Encyclopedia Britannica*, 9th ed. (Philadelphia, 1882), vol. 14, pp. 684–85, 11th ed. (Cambridge, 1911), vol. 16, p. 737; and E.A. Gutkind, *Urban Development in the Alpine and Scandinavian Countries* (New York, 1965), pp. 40–44.

3. C.V. Wedgewood, *The Thirty Years War* (New York, 1961), pp. 206–9 and Stein, *Das Buch der Stadt Linz*, p. 25.

4. Lady Wallace, *The Letters of Wolfgang Amadeus Mozart* (New York, 1866), pp. 191–92.

5. Stein, *Das Buch der Stadt Linz*, pp. 191–204; Gutkind, *Urban Development*, p. 44.; and Erich Maria Meixner, *Männer, Mächte, Betriebe* (Salzburg, 1952), pp. 11–16, 288–330 passim.

6. Gustav Otruba, "Der gesellschaftliche und wirtschaftliche Strukturwandel der Stadt Linz und dessen Auswirkungen auf kulturelle Institutionen," *Linzer Aspekte* (1970), pp. 21–23 and Josef Fendt, "Die Textilindustrie Oberösterreichs: Untersuchung über die Entwicklung, Bedeutung und strukturelle Verhältnisse eines Industrie-Zweiges (diss., Vienna, 1975), p.71 passim.

7. According to an Imperial Patent of 1859 the medieval guilds in Austria were dissolved and replaced by free associations (*Genossenschaften*). In 1883, under strong pressure from the still powerful handicraft industries, the patent of 1859 was modified to restore certain corporate rights such as the privilege of training apprentices and the mandatory certificate of skill. In Upper Austria even the Liberal-dominated Chamber of Commerce agitated for these changes. Franz Pisecky, *Wirtschaft, Land und Kammer in Oberösterreich 1851–1976* (Linz, 1976), vol. 1, pp. 237–43 and Erich Maria Meixner, "Die Entwicklungstendenzen von Industrie, Gewerbe, und Handel in Linz, 1858–1958," *Statistisches Jahrbuch der Stadt Linz—1958* (Linz, 1959), pp. 37–53.

8. Hans-Hubert Schönzeler, *Bruckner* (New York, 1970), pp. 37–51; Werner

Wolff, *Anton Bruckner: Rustic Genius* (New York, 1942), pp. 37–63; and Stein, *Das Buch der Stadt Linz*, p. 136 passim.

9. Schönzeler, *Bruckner*, pp. 37–51, *The Catholic Encyclopedia* (New York, 1913), vol. 9, pp. 273–76, and Arthur May, *The Habsburg Monarchy* (Cambridge, 1951), p. 48.

10. Cf. William H. Hubbard, "Politics and Society in the Central European City: Graz, Austria, 1861–1918," *Canadian Journal of History* vol. 5, no. 1 (March, 1970), pp. 25–45 and idem, "A Social History of Graz, Austria, 1861–1914" (diss., Columbia University, 1973), pp. 246–344.

11. Kurt Tweraser, "Der Linzer Gemeinderat 1880–1914: Glanz und Elend bürgerlicher Herrschaft," *Historisches Jahrbuch der Stadt Linz* (1979), p. 295.

12. Ibid., pp. 295–96 and Richard Bart and Emil Puffer, *Die Gemeindevertretung der Stadt Linz vom Jahre 1848 bis zur Gegenwart* (Linz, 1968), pp. 22–23. On liberalism in Linz and Upper Austria see Kurt Wimmer, *Liberalismus in Oberösterreich 1869–1909* (Linz, 1979) and Harry Slapnicka, *Oberösterreich—Unter Kaiser Franz Joseph 1861–1918* (Linz, 1982), pp. 177–79.

13. On the concept of the three "camps" see Adam Wandruszka's famous essay "Österreichs Politische Struktur: Die Entwicklung der Parteien und politischen Bewegungen" in *Geschichte der Republik Österreich*, ed. Heinrich Benedikt (Munich, 1954), pp. 289–485.

14. John W. Boyer, *Political Radicalism in Late Imperial Vienna: Origins of the Christian Social Movement 1848–1897* (Chicago, 1981).

15. Kurt Tweraser, "Carl Beurle and the Triumph of German Nationalism in Austria," *German Studies Review*, vol. 4, no. 3 (October 1981) pp. 403–26 and Hubbard, "Politics and Society in the Central European City," pp. 38–45.

16. On Schönerer and German Nationalism in Austria see Andrew Whiteside, *The Socialism of Fools: Georg Ritter von Schönerer and Austrian Pan Germanism* (Berkeley, 1975).

17. Tweraser, "Carl Beurle," p. 418.

18. Fritz Mayrhofer, "Franz Dinghofer: Leben und Wirken (1873 bis 1956)," *Historisches Jahrbuch der Stadt Linz* (1969): pp. 11–152.

19. Tweraser, "Carl Beurle," pp. 422–23.

20. Actually, religious services had been conducted in Czech since 1853, when they were instituted at the request of the Linz garrison commander. The number of Czechs in Upper Austria in 1890 was 3,709; in 1900, 3,535; and in 1910, 1,953. Harry Slapnicka, "Linz, Oberösterreich und die tschechische Frage," *Historisches Jahrbuch der Stadt Linz* (1978), pp. 210–13 and idem, *Oberösterreich—Unter Kaiser Franz Joseph*, pp. 41–61.

21. Eleanore Kandl, "Hitlers Österreichbild" (diss., Vienna, 1963), p. 2.

22. Whiteside, *The Socialism of Fools*, pp. 268–69 and Andre Banuls, "Das völkische Blatt 'Der Scherer': Ein Beitrag zu Hitlers Schulzeit," *Vierteljahrshefte für Zeitgeschichte*, vol. 18 (1970) pp. 196–203.

23. Slapnicka, *Oberösterreich—Unter Kaiser Franz Joseph*, pp. 188–224 and Kurt Tweraser, "How Mass Politics Came to Upper Austria: A Preliminary Report," paper presented at the Sixth Annual Conference of the Western Association for German Studies, El Paso, Texas, 9 October 1982. Also Wilhelm Salzer, *Vom Untertan zum Staatsbürger: Oberösterreich von 1848 bis 1918* (Linz, 1970), pp. 122–53.

24. Cf. Boyer, *Political Radicalism in Late Imperial Vienna*, especially pp. 410–21 and Slapnicka, *Oberösterreich—Unter Kaiser Franz Joseph*, pp. 206–07.

25. On the Social Democrats in Upper Austria see Anton Weiguny, *Erinnerungen*

eines Alten aus den Anfängen der oberösterreichischen Arbeiterbewegung (Linz, 1911); Helmut Konrad, *Die Anfänge der Arbeiterbewegung in Oberösterreich* (Vienna, 1981); Slapnicka, *Oberösterreich—Unter Kaiser Franz Joseph*, pp. 225–39; and Salzer, *Von Untertan*, pp. 153–256.

26. Harry Slapnicka, *Von Hauser bis Eigruber: Eine Zeitgeschichte Oberösterreichs* (Linz, 1974), p. 32.

27. Josef Honeder, *Johann Nepomuk Hauser: Landeshauptmann von Oberösterreich* (Linz, 1973), pp. 5–23 and Harry Slapnicka, *Oberösterreich—die politische Führungsschicht 1918 bis 1938* (Linz, 1975), pp. 119–24.

28. The provincial electorate in Upper Austria was divided into four curiae: 1) estate owners who paid a poll tax of 100 gulden and elected ten seats in the diet, 2) notables of cities, markets, and industrial towns who were those eligible to vote in the first two curiae in communal elections and elected seventeen deputies to the diet, 3) members of the Chambers of Commerce and Trade who were entitled to three mandates, 4) primary voters (*Urwähler*) of rural communes who were those eligible to vote in the first or second curia of villages and elected nineteen dietal deputies. In addition to the elected mandates an individual ex officio seat was reserved for the bishop of Linz. Slapnicka, *Oberösterreich—Unter Kaiser Franz Joseph*, pp. 91–96.

29. Honeder, *Hauser*, pp. 27–28 ff. Despite the addition of a fifth curia, no more than 21 percent of the provincial population actually possessed the right to vote before 1919. Slapnicka, *Oberösterreich—Unter Kaiser Franz Joseph*, p. 25.

30. Tweraser, "Der Linzer Gemeinderat 1880–1914," pp. 294–98; Bart and Puffer, *Gemeindevertretung*, pp. 28–33; and Mayrhofer, "Franz Dinghofer."

31. Honeder, *Hauser*, pp. 27–28 ff. Even before Hauser's appointment as governor, Catholic politicians had thrown their support to Social Democratic candidates in the runoff elections of 1907 to the *Reichsrat*. Slapnicka, *Oberösterreich—Unter Kaiser Franz Joseph*, p. 238.

32. Tweraser, "Der Linzer Gemeinderat 1880–1914," pp. 309–10.

33. Mayrhofer, "Franz Dinghofer," pp. 71–73. In contrast to Linz, a similar process of reform was effectively stymied by the German Nationalists on the city council of Graz. See Hubbard, "A Social History of Graz," pp. 301–10.

34. Robert Mateja, "Oberösterreich im I. Weltkrieg" (diss., Innsbruck, 1948), pp. 15–16.

35. Ibid., pp. 80–85, 98–156.

36. Ibid., pp. 98–106, 161–62 and Arthur J. May, *The Passing of the Hapsburg Monarchy, 1914–1918* (Philadelphia, 1966), pp. 329–34.

37. Mateja, "Oberösterreich im I. Weltkrieg," pp. 85–86, 98–100 ff.

38. Ibid., pp. 105, 129–32ff.

39. Ibid., pp. 161–62; May, *Passing of the Hapsburg Monarchy*; and Charles A. Gulick, *Austria from Habsburg to Hitler* (Berkeley, Cal., 1948), vol. 1, pp. 40–42.

40. Gulick, *Austria*, vol. 1, pp. 35–39 and May, *Passing of the Hapsburg Monarchy*, pp. 335–39.

41. Quoted in Slapnicka, *Von Hauser*, p. 11.

42. Ibid., p. 39 and Mateja, "Oberösterreich im I. Weltkrieg," pp. 86–88.

43. Mateja, "Oberösterreich im I. Weltkrieg," pp. 61–63 and Kurt Tweraser, "Der Linzer Gemeinderat 1914–1934: Krise der parlamentarischen Demokratie," *Historisches Jahrbuch der Stadt Linz* (1980), p. 215.

44. Mateja, "Oberösterreich im I. Weltkrieg," pp. 61–63 and Honeder, *Hauser*, pp. 30–32, 62–65.

45. Mateja, "Oberösterreich im I. Weltkrieg," pp. 210–26.
46. Ibid., pp. 86–89 and Slapnicka, *Von Hauser bis Eigruber*, pp. 39–40.
47. Hellmut Andics, *Der Untergang der Donau Monarchie: Österreich-Ungarn von der Jahrhundertwende bis zum November 1918* (Vienna, 1974), p. 264 and Gulick, *Austria, vol. 1, pp. 58–59.*

2. REVOLUTION BY CONSENSUS, 1918–1920

1. F. L. Carsten, *Revolution in Central Europe 1918–1919* (Berkeley, 1972), pp. 78–126, 223 ff., Klemens von Klemperer; *Ignaz Seipel Christian Statesman in a Time of Crisis* (Princeton, 1972), pp. 94–109; and Bruce F. Pauley, *The Habsburg Legacy 1867–1939* (New York, 1972), pp. 60–99.
2. Hans Hautmann, *Die Verlorene Räterepublik: Am Beispiel der Kommunistischen Partei Deutschösterreichs* (Vienna, 1977), p. 76.
3. Karl W. Deutsch, *Nationalism and its Alternatives* (New York, 1969), p. 27.
4. Gulick, *Austria*, vol. 1, p. 84.
5. Honeder, *Hauser*, p. 81–82.
6. Carsten, *Revolution*, p. 26–27; Slapnicka, *Von Hauser*, p. 25; and Anton Staudinger, "Die Ereignisse in den Ländern Deutschösterreichs im Herbst 1918," in Ludwig Jedlicka, *Ende und Anfang: Österreich 1918–19: Wien und die Bundesländer* (Salzburg, 1969), pp. 78–79.
7. Staudinger, "Ereignisse," p. 78.
8. Linz *Tagespost*, 2 November 1918.
9. Ibid.; Carsten, *Revolution*, p. 27; Slapnicka, *Von Hauser*, p. 49–50; Mateja, "Oberösterreich im I. Weltkrieg," pp. 65–66; and Slapnicka, *Führungsschicht*, p. 76.
10. Linz *Tagespost*, 2 November 1918.
11. Mateja, "Oberösterreich im I. Weltkrieg," pp. 63–65; Carsten, *Revolution*, pp. 26–27; and Slapnicka, *Von Hauser*, pp. 25–35.
12. Honeder, *Hauser*, pp. 32–34; Carsten, *Revolution*, p. 27; Slapnicka, *Von Hauser*, p. 86; and Gulick, *Austria*, vol. 1, p. 87.
13. Honeder, *Hauser*, p. 35.
14. Mateja, "Oberösterreich im I. Weltkrieg," pp. 67–68 and Franz Langoth, *Kampf um Österreich: Erinnerungen eines Politikers* (Wels, 1951), p. 20 passim.
15. Slapnicka, *Von Hauser*, pp. 52–67.
16. Richard Kutschera, *Johannes Maria Gföllner: Bischof dreier Zeitenwenden* (Linz, 1972), p. 25.
17. Mateja, "Oberösterreich im I. Weltkrieg," pp. 68–69.
18. Österreichisches Staatsarchiv, Abteilung Allgemeines Verwaltungsarchiv (AVA), Vienna: Bundeskanzleramt (Bka), Inneres (I), 22/0 Oest, box 5099, doc. 870–918: Upper Austrian Provisional Government to State Office of the Interior, 4 November 1918.
19. Slapnicka, *Von Hauser*, pp. 20–21.
20. Ibid., pp. 49–53; Mateja, "Oberösterreich im I. Weltkrieg"; and Carsten, *Revolution in Central Europe*, p. 92.
21. Carsten, *Revolution in Central Europe*, pp. 90–91 and Slapnicka, *Von Hauser*, pp. 49–53.
22. Carsten, *Revolution in Central Europe*, pp. 16–17, 108–9.
23. Slapnicka, *Von Hauser*, p. 42.
24. Slapnicka, *Führungsschicht*, pp. 145–46. Interestingly, Kelischek later became a Nazi and served as mayor of Königswiesen between 1938 and 1945.
25. Carsten, *Revolution in Central Europe*, pp. 110–11, 115.

26. Otto Bauer, *The Austrian Revolution* (London, 1925), p. 86.

27. Carsten, *Revolution in Central Europe*, p. 115, and Staudinger, "Ereignisse," p. 79.

28. Slapnicka, *Von Hauser*, p. 42. Carsten, *Revolution*, p. 111 gives the number of Communists as thirteen.

29. Carsten, *Revolution in Central Europe*, p. 115.

30. Otto Stöber, *Die Moor-Stöber* (Linz, 1975), pp. 250–251.

31. Slapnicka, *Von Hauser*, pp. 23–24.

32. Bauer, *Austrian Revolution*, p. 104 and Gulick, *Austria*, vol. I, p. 84.

33. Slapnicka, *Von Hauser*, pp. 142–43.

34. Carsten, *Revolution in Central Europe*, pp. 91–92 and Gerhard Botz, *Gewalt in der Politik: Attentate, Zusammenstösse, Putschversuche in Österreich 1918–1934* (Munich, 1976), p. 40.

35. Langoth, *Kampf um Österreich*, p. 21.

36. AVA, Bka, I, 22/0 Oest, box 5099, doc. 6930–19: Report of Police Commissioner Otto Steinhäusel, 22 February 1919. Slapnicka reports damage to over three hundred shops, an exaggerated estimate in light of the official figure of sixty-six indicated by a lengthy investigation. AVA, Bka, I, 22/0 Oest, box 5099, doc. 15617/21.

37. Botz, *Gewalt in der Politik*, p. 41.

38. Langoth, *Kampf um Österreich*, p. 20 passim and AVA, Bka, I, 22/0 Oest, box 5099, doc. 7893–19: Relation 20 February 1919.

39. Carsten, *Revolution in Central Europe*, p. 93.

40. Ibid., p. 115; Mateja, "Oberösterreich im I. Weltkrieg"; and Gulick, *Austria*, vol. 1, pp. 88–89.

41. Slapnicka, *Von Hauser*, pp. 145–46.

42. Tweraser, "Der Linzer Gemeinderat 1914–1934," pp. 219–20.

43. Stadler, *Austria*, pp. 106–7.

44. On the other hand, voter participation outside Linz was greater in February than May. (See table 1.)

45. Mateja, "Oberösterreich im I. Weltkrieg," p. 68.

46. Slapnicka, *Von Hauser*, p. 105 and passim.

47. Mateja, "Oberösterreich im I. Weltkrieg," p. 64.

48. Ibid., pp. 69–76; Institut für Zeitgeschichte (IfZ), Vienna: Oswald Gruber, "Die Stellung der politischen Parteien und Räte Oberösterreichs in den Jahren 1918–19" (unpublished paper, SE 850); and Slapnicka, *Von Hauser*, pp. 80–121.

49. On 1 November 1918 Gföllner issued a proclamation urging support of the new German-Austrian state, but he remained unreconciled to it. Kutschera, *Gföllner*, pp. 24–28.

50. Some party zealots took the slogan more seriously than Hauser, demanding virtual autonomy for the province. Slapnicka, *Von Hauser*, pp. 87–90 and Gulick, *Austria*, vol. I, p. 89.

51. Slapnicka, *Von Hauser*, p. 133.

52. Ibid., p. 92.

53. Linz *Tagespost*, 18 February 1919.

54. Adopted in October 1920. For an exhaustive analysis of Upper Austrian constitutional questions see Slapnicka, *Von Hauser*, pp. 105–32.

55. Bart and Puffer, *Gemeindevertretung*, pp. 33–37.

56. Carsten, *Revolution in Central Europe*, p. 322.

57. On 17 April 1919 Viennese Communists organized a mass demonstration on the Ringstrasse that led to the storming of parliament. Several fires were set inside

the building, but they were extinguished and the riot quelled by the *Volkswehr*. See: Carsten, *Revolution in Central Europe*, pp. 228–229; Gulick, *Austria*, vol. I, p. 76; Botz, *Gewalt in der Politik*, pp. 48–53; and Hautmann, *Die Verlorene Räterepublik*, pp. 143–52.

58. Carsten, *Revolution in Central Europe*, pp. 92–94, 232 and AVA, Bka, I, 22/0 Oest, box 5099, doc. 26220–19: Upper Austrian provincial government to Ministry of the Interior, 19 July 1919.

59. The official date of founding was 26 February 1919, but meetings were being held as early as 22 December 1918. Cf. Slapnicka, *Führungsschicht*, pp. 219–20 and AVA, Bka, I, 22/0 Oest, Box 5100, doc. 21643–22: Upper Austrian provincial government to Ministry of the Interior, 24 March 1922.

60. AVA, Bka, I, 22/0 Oest, Box 5099: "Relation über die Erhebung bezüglich der Vorfälle vom 10 Mai 1920 in Linz" and Carsten *Revolution in Central Europe*, p. 237.

61. Slapnicka, *Von Hauser*, p. 44; Langoth, *Kampf um Österreich*, pp. 21–22; and AVA, Bka, I, 22/Gen., doc. 16635–90: Abschrift (n.d.) and doc. 18369–920: Presidium of the Upper Austrian provincial government to the Ministry of Interior, 30 April 1920.

62. Unlike their German counterparts, the Austrian Social Democrats retained party unity during the revolution by refusing to expel the Communists. In this way they not only avoided civil war, but also prevented the KP from becoming a mass movement.

63. Botz, *Gewalt in der Politik*, p. 78; Langoth, *Kampf um Österreich*, pp. 22–24, and AVA, Bka, I, 22/Gen., doc. 28476/20, Linz Communist Unrest on 10 May 1920. Also doc. 19635–920.

64. Langoth, *Kampf um Österreich*, pp. 23–24 and AVA, Bka, I, 22/Gen., doc. 31354–920, State Attorney's Office Linz to Attorney General's Office in Vienna, 7 August 1920.

65. Inez Kykal and Karl Stadler, *Richard Bernaschek: Odysee eines Rebellen* (Vienna, 1976), pp. 18–25.

3. A MODERATE POLITICAL CULTURE, 1920–1927

1. Kurt Steiner, *Politics in Austria* (Boston, 1972), pp. 409–11 and Walter B. Simon, "Democracy in the Shadow of Imposed Sovereignty: The First Republic of Austria," in *The Breakdown of Democratic Regimes: Europe*, ed. Juan L. Linz and Alfred Stepan (Baltimore, 1978), pp. 80–84. Also see the perceptive comments by Hans Mommsen in *Die Ereignisse des 15. Juli 1927: Protokoll des Symposiums in Wien am 15 Juni 1977*, ed. Rudolf Neck and Adam Wandruszka (Vienna, 1979), p. 233.

2. Since political associations were not required to report the names of members to the police after 1918, it is difficult to reconstruct party membership for the First Republic. My own sociography is based on lists published in the Linz press as well as the biographies of city councillors in Bart and Puffer, *Die Gemeindevertretung der Stadt Linz*, pp. 99–290.

3. Otto Stöber, *Die Moor-Stöber*, p. 260.

4. Slapnicka, *Von Hauser*, pp. 45–46.

5. Tweraser, "Structural Changes," p. 14.

6. Slapnicka, *Führungsschicht*, pp. 59–60 and Stöber, *Die Moor-Stöber*, p. 291.

7. Slapnicka, *Führungsschicht*, pp. 195–206 and *Oberösterreichische Lehrerzeitung*, vol. 1, no. 3 (March 1927).

8. *Bericht über die Tätigkeit der sozialdemokratischen Partei Oberösterreichs für die Zeit vom 1. Jänner bis 31. Dezember 1927* (Linz, 1928), p. 24.

9. Kutschera, *Gföllner*, pp. 47–58.

10. Honeder, *Hauser*, pp. 48–58.

11. There is as yet no hard data on the Christian Social party in Vienna after 1918, but see Alfred Diamant, *Austrian Catholics and the First Republic: Democracy, Capitalism and the Social Order, 1918–1923* (Princeton, 1960), pp. 77–78, 89–94.

12. Boyer, *Political Radicalism in Late Imperial Vienna*, especially pp. 297–300 and 411–21.

13. Kurt Tweraser, "How Mass Politics Came to Upper Austria," pp. 16–19.

14. See the excellent appraisal of Hauser in Slapnicka, *Von Hauser*, pp. 156–66.

15. Ibid., p. 136 passim; Honeder, *Hauser*, pp. 32–44; and Slapnicka, *Führungsschicht*, pp. 49, 129–30, 192–93, 204–6.

16. *Volksvereinsbote*, no. 3 (March 1924) and no. 6 (5 July 1930).

17. Honeder, *Hauser*, pp. 48–58, 121–24.

18. Ibid., pp. 48–50 and Kutschera, *Gföllner*, pp. 7–28.

19. Kutschera, *Gföllner*, pp. 23–31.

20. Ibid., pp. 29–42 and Honeder, *Hauser*, pp. 48–58.

21. Honeder, *Hauser*, pp. 48–58, 120–24.

22. Ibid., pp. 57–58.

23. Kutschera, *Gföllner*, pp. 47–50 and Heidrun Deutsch, "Franziska Fürstin Starhemberg" (diss., Vienna, 1967), p. 176 passim and Slapnicka, *Führungsschicht*, pp. 90–94.

24. Kutschera, *Gföllner*, pp. 57–64 and *Linzer Diözesanblatt*, vol. 67 (1921), no. 2–3; vol 69 (1923), no. 2, pp. 18–22; vol. 71 (1925), no. 1; vol 72 (1926), no. 6; vol. 74 (1928), nos. 4, 9, pp. 91–97.

25. *Oberösterreichische Arbeiterzeitung*, 23 July 1927: "Wenn wir auch als Christliche Arbeiterbewegung der Heimwehr nicht offiziell angehören, so stehen wir sehr sympatisch gegenüber und freuen uns wenn ihr recht viel christliche Arbeiter und Angestellte angehören."

26. Diamant, *Austrian Catholics*, p. 123.

27. *Mitteilungen des Handelsgremiums der Landeshauptstadt Linz*, no. 9 (September 1929).

28. *Mitteilungen des oberösterreichischen Handels und Gewerbebundes*, vol. 2, no. 10 (October 1930).

29. Tweraser, "Structural Aspects," p. 47.

30. F.L. Carsten, *Fascist Movements in Austria: From Schönerer to Hitler* (London and Beverly Hills, 1977), pp. 89–90.

31. Slapnicka, *Von Hauser*, pp. 89–90.

32. Ibid.

33. Tweraser, "Structural Aspects," pp. 11–12, 16; Carsten *Fascist Movements*, pp. 93–96; and *Mitteilungen des d.v. Turnvereines Urfahr*, 15 Ostermond (sic) 1926, p. 3 and passim. The social composition of the German Populist Gymnastic Association of Urfahr in the 1920s was strikingly similar to that of the Gymnastic Association of Prague in the late 1880s. See Cohen, *The Politics of Ethnic Survival*, pp. 192–93.

34. On the problems of education in interwar Austria see Gulick, *Austria*, vol. 1, pp. 544–82.

35. Cf. the Socialist *Oberösterreichische Lehrerzeitung: Monatschrift der freien Lehrergewerkschaft Landesgruppe Oberösterreich*, vol. 1, no. 1, (May 1926), p. 2; vol. 2, no. 12 (December 1927); and the German Nationalist *Zeitschrift des O Oe Landes-Lehrerverein 1867* (Linz, 1937).

36. See Langoth's memoirs, *Kampf um Österreich*, pp. 11–26 and Slapnicka, *Führungsschicht*, pp. 163–65.

37. Langoth, *Kampf um Österreich*, p. 21.

38. See, for example, Langoth's inflated account of his role in the days following the burning of the Viennese Palace of Justice. Ibid., pp. 31–33.

39. Johann Goudsblom, *Dutch Society* (New York, 1967), pp. 32–33 passim; Arend Lijphardt, "Consociational Democracy," *World Politics*, vol. 21, no. 2 (January 1969), pp. 206–25; and Steiner, *Politics in Austria*, pp. 48–172, 266, 409ff.

40. Slapnicka correctly emphasizes this point in his excellent evaluation of the Hauser era. Slapnicka, *Von Hauser*, pp. 156–66.

41. Unlike many deputies in the National Assembly whose skeptical views of democracy were molded by the memory of the highly volatile and fragmented prewar *Reichsrat*, Upper Austrian politicians regarded their experience in the provincial diet as salutary and rewarding. Kurt Tweraser, "Der Linzer Gemeinderat 1914–1934: Krise der parlamentarischen Demokratie," *Historisches Jahrbuch der Stadt Linz* (1980): p. 208 and Adam Wandruszka, "Die Krisen des Parlamentarismus 1897 und 1933. Gedanken zum Demokratieverständnis in Österreich," in *Beiträge zur Zeitgeschichte: Festschrift Ludwig Jedlicka zum 60. Geburtstag*, ed. Rudolf Neck and Adam Wandruszka (St. Pölten, 1976): p. 77.

42. Slapnicka, *Von Hauser*, pp. 156–66.

43. Tweraser, "Der Linzer Gemeinderat 1914–1934," pp. 208–9.

44. The data assembled by Gerhard Botz suggest that Linz and Upper Austria experienced relatively fewer incidents of violence than other big cities and at least half of the other provinces of interwar Austria. Botz, *Gewalt in der Politik*, pp. 246–49.

45. On the problems of legitimacy and authority in new democratic societies see the pertinent observations of Juan Linz (based on Max Weber) in Juan Linz, *The Breakdown of Democratic Regimes: Crisis, Breakdown, and Reequilibration* (Baltimore, 1978), pp. 16–23 and 45–49.

46. AVA, BKA, I, 22/ O Oest, box 5100, doc, 167.823–8: Bundesdirektion Linz to BKA, 14 October 1928.

47. Ernst Barker, trans. and ed., *The Politics of Aristotle* (Oxford, 1958), p. 225.

48. Bart and Puffer, *Gemeindevertretung*, pp. 33–37.

49. Kulczycki, "Dametz," pp. 185–87 and Slapnicka, *Führungsschicht*, pp. 59–60.

50. Tweraser, "Linzer Gemeinderat 1914–1934," pp. 220–22.

51. Ibid., pp. 224–26.

52. Slapnicka, *Oberösterreich zwischen Bürgerkrieg und Anschluss*, (Linz, 1975), p. 21 and National Archives (NA), Washington, D.C., microcopy T 120 (Records of the German Foreign Office), roll 4626, frame K 281688: Deutsche Passstelle Linz an das Auswärtiges Amt, 29 March 1922.

53. Tweraser, "Linzer Gemeinderat 1914–1934," pp. 225–26.

54. Ibid., pp. 226–29, *Linzer Volksstimme*, 27 June 1923 and A St Linz, "Sitzungsprotokolle des Gemeinderates Linz," 6 July 1923.

55. See Bruce F. Pauley, *Hitler and the Forgotten Nazis: A History of Austrian National Socialism* (Chapel Hill, 1981), especially pp. 16–36, and Evan B. Bukey, "The Nazi Party in Linz, Austria: A Sociological Perspective, *German Studies Review*, vol. 1 (October 1978), pp. 302–26.

56. A St Linz, "Stizungsprotokolle der Stadt Linz," 3. Sitzung, 27 March 1925.

57. Gulick, *Austria*, vol. 1, pp. 383, 491.

58. Tweraser, "Linzer Gemeinderat 1914–1934," pp. 231–38.

59. Ibid.

60. *Statistisches Jahrbuch der Stadt Linz* (1946), pp. 20–22; Otruba, "Der gesellschaftliche und wirtschaftliche Strukturwandel der Stadt Linz"; Friedrich Katzwedel, "Die wirtschaftliche Bedeutung der Landeshauptstadt Linz" in Stein, *Das Buch der Stadt Linz*, pp. 195–205; Frederick Hertz, *The Economic Problem of the Danubian States: A Study in Economic Nationalism* (New York, 1970), p. 137; and *Statistisches Jahrbuch der Stadt Linz* (1947), pp. 76ff.

61. Hubbard, "A Social History of Graz," pp. 342–44.

62. Meixner, *Männer, Mächte, Betriebe*, pp. 307–14 passim; idem, *Linz, 1945–1960: Industrie, Gewerbe, Handel, Verkehr, Fremdenverkehr, Geldwesen* (Linz, 1962), pp. 19–27; Fendt, "Textilindustrie," p. 152; and Rudolf Kropf, *Oberösterreichs Industrie (1873–1938): ökonomisch-strukturelle Aspekte einer regionalen Industrieentwicklung* (Linz, 1981), pp. 171–81.

63. On the other hand, demographic growth was certainly better in Linz than in Vienna or in Austria as a whole, where stagnation was more literal. Cf. B. R. Mitchell, *European Historical Statistics 1750–1970* (New York, 1975), p. 26 and *Statistisches Jahrbuch für Österreich* (1938), p. 13.

64. Tweraser, "Structural Aspects," p. 14.

65. Meixner, *Linz*, p. 21.

66. Otruba, "Der gesellschaftliche und wirtschaftliche Strukturwandel der Stadt Linz," p. 24.

67. Meixner, *Linz*, p. 21.

68. Slapnicka, *Von Hauser*, p. 143; Katzwedel, "Die wirtschaftliche Bedeutung der Landeshauptstadt Linz," pp. 191–205; and Kammer für Arbeiter und Angestellte, *Verzeichnis jener Betriebe in Oberösterreich (Gewerbe, Handel, und Bergbau) welche über 5 Arbeiter und Angestelltenbeschäftigen, gereiht nach Branchen, Bezirkshauptmannschaften und Ortsgemeinden nach dem Stande vom 1. Juli 1935* (Linz, 1935), n.p.

69. Growing out of the wartime Control Stations, the town's municipal enterprises included the gas and water works, the municipal slaughter house, a dairy, a bakery, a communal bath, the fire department, and an institute of essential services (*Wirtschaftshof*) that collected garbage, maintained sewers and streets, did moving and storage, serviced city vehicles, and even buried the dead. Phip Imhof, "Die Unternehmungen der Stadtgemeinde Linz," in Stein, *Das Buch der Stadt Linz*, pp. 341–52.

70. Fendt, "Textilindustrie," pp. 130–45.

71. Katzwedel, "Wirtschaftliche Bedeutung," pp. 191–205 and Meixner, *Männer, Mächte, Betriebe*, pp. 299–306.

72. Langoth, *Kampf um Österreich*, p. 23 and AVA, BKA, 20/0 Oest, box 4204, doc. 154.555.25; box 4205, doc. 116.573, Personal Standes Verzeichnis der Bundespolizeidirektion Linz: Nach dem Stande vom 1. Jänner 1928; and box 4218, doc. 240.233: Dr. Viktor Bentz an das Bundeskanzleramt, 13 September 1934.

73. AVA, BKA, 20/0 Oest, box 4218, doc. 240.233: Dr. Viktor Bentz an das Bundeskanzleramt, 13 September 1934 and AVA, Militärverband der Republik Österreich, box 5, doc. 494/27: Letter of Militärverband in Linz to Vienna, 10 May 1927, presumably by Richard Bernaschek.

74. Gulick, *Austria*, vol. 1, p. 751.

75. See the correspondence of Richard Bernaschek with the Verbandleitung der Militärverbandes Wien at AVA, Militärverband der Republik Oesterreich, boxes 4 and 5, especially 4 May 1926; 8 October 1926; 5,6,13,29 April 1927; 10 May 1927; 20 July 1927; and 20 July 1928.

76. Walter B. Simon provides slightly different figures. Walter B. Simon, "The Political Parties of Austria," (diss., Columbia, 1957), pp. 153, 159, 171.

77. IfZ: Helmut Gamsjäger, "Dr. Josef Schlegel. Landeshauptmann von Oberösterreich und Präsident des Rechnungshofes," unpublished paper, SE 244.

4. HOLDING THE FASCIST TIDE, 1927–1932

1. The literature on the July riots and the burning of the Palace of Justice is extensive. For descriptions of the actual events see Gulick, *Austria*, vol. I, pp. 717–71; Botz, *Gewalt*, pp. 141–60; and Hellmut Andics, *Der Staat den keiner wollte: Österreich von der Gründung der Republik bis zur Moskauer Deklaration* (Vienna and Munich, 1976), pp. 119–47. For an exceptionally astute analysis of these events see Anson Rabinbach, *The Crisis of Austrian Socialism: From Red Vienna to Civil War* (Chicago, 1983), pp. 32ff. Also see: Botz, *Gewalt*, pp. 141–60; idem, "Der '15. Juli 1927' seine Ursachen und Folgen," in *Österreich 1927 bis 1938: Protokoll des Symposiums in Wien 23. bis 28. Oktober 1972*, ed. Rudolf Neck and Adam Wandruszka (Munich, 1973), pp. 31–42 and the essays in *Die Ereignisse des 15. Juli 1927: Protokoll des Symposiums in Wien am 15. Juni 1977*, ed. Rudolf Neck and Adam Wasdrunzka (Vienna, 1979). Figures on the dead and wounded vary. Carsten (*Fascist Movements*, p. 111) reports seventy-seven demonstrators and seven policemen killed and "many more wounded." Botz (*Gewalt*, p. 154) gives the figures as eighty-five rioters and four policemen killed. The number of wounded, Botz argues, will never be known, since many fleeing to avoid arrest did not report their injuries.

2. C. Earl Edmonson, *The Heimwehr and Austrian Politics*. (Athens, Georgia, 1978).

3. IfZ: Dagmar Lack, "Die Entwicklung der Heimwehr in Oberösterreich, 1927–1931," (unpublished seminar paper, 1969), pp. 1–9.

4. Anton Staudinger, "Christlichsoziale Partei und Heimwehren bis 1927," in *Die Ereignisse des 15. Juli 1927*, ed. Neck and Wandruszka, p. 115.

5. Andics, *Der Staat den keiner wollte*, p. 62.

6. Ludger Rape, *Die österreichischen Heimwehren und die bayerische Rechte 1920–1923* (Vienna, 1977), pp. 177–78.

7. Carsten, *Fascist Movements*, pp. 45–46.

8. NSDAP Hauptarchiv (Hoover Institution Microfilm Collection), roll 34, folder 37: "Bericht über die Verhandlungen in Oberösterreich, 24 April 1920." Rape incorrectly cites Krazer's visit as having occurred on 22 April 1920.

9. Rape, *Die österreichischen Heimweheren*, pp. 180–81.

10. Carsten, *Fascist Movements*, p. 54 and Slapnicka, *Zwischen Bürgerkrieg*, pp. 18–19.

11. Slapnicka, *Zwischen Bürgerkrieg*, p. 19 and Rape, *Die österreichischen Heimwehren*, p. 182.

12. IfZ: Lack, "Entwicklung," p. 2.

13. National Archives (NA), Washington, D.C. microcopy T 120 (Records of the German Foreign Office), roll 4626, frame K281688: Deutsche Passstelle Linz an das Auswärtiges Amt, 29 March 1922.

14. IfZ: Lack, "Entwicklung," p. 2.

15. Carsten, *Fascist Movements*, p. 53.

16. Ibid., pp. 53–55, IfZ: Lack, "Entwicklung," pp. 7–8; Rape, *Die österreichischen Heimwehren*, p. 182; and *Heimatschutz in Österreich* (Vienna, 1934), pp. 73–74.

17. Heidrun Deutsch, "Franziska Fürstin Starhemberg," p. 207.

18. Edmonson, *Heimwehr*, p. 37. As an experienced politician Hauser never categorically disavowed the *Heimwehr*, and he may have said something to that effect to Princess Starhemberg. That he suddenly threw his full support to armed reactionaries after so many years of democratic commitment and achievement, as she claimed, is highly improbable.

19. Slapnicka, *Zwischen Bürgerkrieg*, p. 24 and IfZ: Lack, "Entwicklung," p. 8.

20. IfZ: Lack, "Entwicklung," pp. 7–8.

21. IfZ: Peter Huemer, "Die Ereignisse in den Bundesländern nach dem Brand des Wiener Justizpalastes," (unpublished seminar paper, SE 291), pp. 58–60 and Carsten, *Fascist Movements*, p. 111.

22. Edmondson, *Heimwehr*, p. 46; IfZ: Huemer, "Ereignisse," p. 60; and Slapnicka, *Zwischen Bürgerkrieg*, p. 227.

23. Barbara Berger, "Ernst Rüdiger Fürst Starhemberg: Versuch einer Biographie" (diss., Vienna, 1967), p. 29ff.; Ernst Rüdiger Prince Starhemberg, *Between Hitler and Mussolini* (New York, 1942), pp. 1–19; and Carsten, *Fascist Movements*, pp. 131–33.

24. Carsten, *Fascist Movements*, pp. 131–33 and IfZ: Lack, "Entwicklung," pp. 11–13.

25. AVA, BKA, I, 22 O Oest, box 5101, doc. 219.259/31 ("Heimatschutzbewegung in Oberösterreich"), 6 November 1931. Edmonson (*Heimwehr*, pp. 108–9) states that Starhemberg commanded twenty-three *Jäger* battalions in 1930 and was supported by "forty thousand activists." Police records, however, indicate rather lower figures. The exact number of active Upper Austrian *Heimwehr*, given these conflicting sources and the fluctuating nature of paramilitary organizations in general, is simply not clear. Carsten's estimate of 20,000 men with considerably less equipment is as good as any. Carsten, *Fascist Movements*, p. 114.

26. Carsten, *Fascist Movements*, p. 132.

27. AVA, BKA, I, 22 O Oest, box 5101: doc. 219.251/32 ("Heimatschutzbewegung in Oberösterreich"), 6 November 1931.

28. AVA, BKA, I, 22 O Oest, box 5100, doc. 119.552, 6 May 1927.

29. *Heimwehr* percentages in Linz were 11.4; in Upper Austria, 8.98; and in Linz County (excluding Linz), 13. Linz *Tagespost*, 10 November 1930.

30. Ernst Fischer, *An Opposing Man* (New York, 1974), p. 181.

31. AVA, BKA, I, 22 O Oest, box 5100, doc. 119.552/27, 6 May 1927.

32. Data on Linz derived primarily from lists of candidates presented in federal, provincial, and municipal elections and from police reports at AVA, Vienna. Data on Upper Austria from Gerhard Botz, "Faschismus und Lohnabhängige in der Ersten Republik: Zur "sozialer Basis" und propagandistischen Orientierung von Heimwehr und Nationalsozialismus," *Österreich in Geschichte und Literatur*, vol. 21, pp. 2, 107.

33. Carsten, *Fascist Movements*, pp. 45, 66.

34. Ibid., p. 133; Slapnicka, *Zwischen Bürgerkrieg*, pp. 26, 30; and IfZ: Lack, "Entwicklung," pp. 21–22.

35. Lack, "Entwicklung," pp. 21–23 and Slapnicka, *Zwischen Bürgerkrieg*, pp. 30–31.

36. IfZ: Gamsjäger, "Schlegel," pp. 28–29.

37. On the *Schutzbund* see Christine Vleck, "Der republikanische Schutzbund in Österreich: Geschichte, Aufbau, und Organisation," (diss., Vienna, 1971) and Ilona Duczynska, *Workers in Arms: The Austrian Civil War of 1934* (New York, 1978).

38. For biographical data see Hans Sperl, "Richard Bernaschek," in Norbert Leser, *Werk und Widerhall: Grosse Gestalten des österreichischen Sozialismus*

(Vienna, 1964), pp. 76–84; Slapnicka, *Führungsschicht*, pp. 42–45; and the excellent study by Kykal and Stadler, *Bernaschek*.

39. Kykal and Stadler, *Bernaschek*, pp. 35–39; Slapnicka, *Zwischen Bürgerkrieg*, pp. 13–27; and AVA, BKA, I, 22 O Oest, box 5100: doc. 147.537/27 ("Republikanischer Schutzbund in Oberösterreich").

40. AVA, BKA, I, 22 O Oest, box 5100, docs. 18798/23 and 70559/23 (Dr. Hobelsberger, Industriellerverband Oberösterreich-Salzburg an die Landesregierung Oberösterreichs, 20 October 1922).

41. *Linzer Volksstimme*, 17 November 1923 and Kykal and Stadler, *Bernaschek*, p. 37.

42. On the debates between Körner and Republican *Schutzbund* commander Alexander Eifler over strategy and tactics see Ducynska, *Workers in Arms*, pp. 82–139; Vleck, "Der republikanischer Schutzbund," p. 267 passim; and Eric C. Kollman, *Theodor Körner: Militär und Politik* (Munich, 1973), pp. 191–228.

43. AVA, BKA, I, 22 O Oest, box 5100, doc. 135.894/30 ("Organisation und Stärke des republikanischen Schutzbundes in Oberösterreich") and Kykal and Stadler, *Bernaschek*, pp. 39–40.

44. Kykal and Stadler, *Bernaschek*, pp. 48–52.

45. Carsten, *Fascist Movements*, p. 120 and Botz, *Gewalt*, p. 163.

46. AVA, BKA, I, 22 O Oest, box 5100, doc. 167.823/8 ("Heimatwehr O Oe in Linz"), 14 October 1928. Also Carsten, *Fascist Movements*, p. 131.

47. AVA, BKA, I, 22, O Oest, box 5100, doc. 122.336/29 ("Bericht"), 8 May 1929.

48. *Jahrbuch der Bundespolizeidirektion in Linz a. D. mit statistischen Daten aus den Jahren 1927 bis 1931* (Linz, 1932), pp. 20–28.

49. AVA, BKA, I 22 O Oest, box 5100, doc. 177.678 ("Bezirkshauptmannschaft Urfahr-Umgebung an das Amt der O Oe"), 21 October 1929.

50. See, for example, the police reports from November 1929 through January 1930 at AVA, BKA, I, 22 O Oest, box 5100, docs. 190.403/29; 191.339/29; 191.915/29; 192.179/29; 194.835/29; 207.250/29; 208.819/29; and 100.957/30.

51. Slapnicka, *Zwischen Bürgerkrieg*, pp. 40, 44.

52. AVA, Vienna: I, 22 O Oest, box 5102, doc. 124.738/32 ("Politische Parteien und Wehrverbände in Linz: Mitgliederbewegung"), 17 February 1932.

53. The principal work on the German Workers' Party is Andrew G. Whiteside, *Austrian National Socialism Before 1918* (The Hague, 1962).

54. Bruce F. Pauley, "Fascism and the *Führerprinzip*: The Austrian Example," *Central European History*, vol. 12, no. 3 (September, 1979), p. 277.

55. Karl Dietrich Bracher, *The German Dictatorship: The Origins, Structure, and Effects of National Socialism* (New York, 1970), pp. 50–57.

56. Ernst Hanisch, "Zur Frühgeschichte des Nationalsozialismus in Salzburg (1913–1925)," *Mitteilungen der Gesellschaft für Salzburger Landeskunde*, vol. 67, pp. 371–410.

57. *Deutscher Volksruf: Alpenländisches Wochenblatt für die arbeitenden Stände*, 18 August 1918, 25 August 1918, 3 November 1918, and 12 January 1919.

58. Linz *Tagespost* 13 March 1941. Proksch in a 1931 deposition before the Nazi party court in Munich (U. Schl. A.) claimed the date was April 1919. Berlin Document Center (BDC), Berlin, Oberste Parteigericht (OPG): Alfred Proksch an den U. Schl. A. Reichsleitung der NSDAP, 10 March 1931. I am grateful to Gerhard Botz for calling my attention to this document and for making a copy available to me.

59. Linz *Tagespost*, 2 October 1920. Hitler's hometown visit is confirmed by Werner Maser, *Hitler's Letters and Notes* (New York, 1974), p. 99 and Alexander Schilling Schletter, "Das Parteileben bis zum Zusammenbruch," in *Deutscher Geist*

in *Österreich: Ein Handbuch des völkischen Lebens der Ostmark*, ed. Karl Wache (Vienna, 1933).

60. According to the *Deutscher Volksruf* of 20 August 1921 those National Socialists in attendance numbered 180 from German-Austria, 25 from Germany (including Feder and Julius Streicher), and 18 from Czechoslovakia. Also see Carsten, *Fascist Movements*, p. 75.

61. *Linzer Volksstimme*, 27 June 1923.

62. Although the records of the Nazi party in Linz were collected and maintained after 1938 by an Upper Austrian *Gauarchiv*, most of them were lost or destroyed in 1945. In identifying party activists I have relied on a variety of disparate sources. Chief among them are: 1) police reports among the files of the Generaldirektion für öffentliche Sicherheit, Bundeskanzleramt, at AVA, Vienna; 2) personnel files of the BDC, Berlin; 3) C.I.C. Files, 1945, Record Group 407, National Records Center, Suitland, Maryland; 4) lists of electoral candidates published in the *Linzer Volksstimme*, 1923–1931; 5) Bart and Puffer, *Gemeindevertretung*, and 6) Erich Stockhorst, *Fünftausend Köpfe; Wer war was im Dritten Reich* (Velbert, 1967). These sources provide a fairly accurate impression of Nazi social structure in Linz between 1919 and 1939, but they are not without flaws since they do not constitute a complete statistical universe or even a random sample. Information on occupation, for example, is fairly complete and easy to determine, while data on religion, date of birth, and education are rather sparse. Similarly, the records of the Berlin Document Center are not always reliable, since after 1938 Austrian Nazis frequently altered their resumes or backdated their memberships to qualify for the Golden Party Badge or other honors. For some sobering thoughts on these matters see the remarks by Gerhard Botz in *Das Jahr 1934; 25 Juli: Protokoll des Symposiums in Wien am 8 Oktober 1974*, ed. Ludwig Jedlicka aud Rudolf Neck (Munich, 1975), pp. 84–87.

63. Bart and Puffer, *Gemeindevertretung*, passim. According to the census of 1923, some 7,424 inhabitants or 7.8 percent of the municipal population of Linz were born in Bohemia-Moravia. Archiv der Stadt Linz (A St Linz) Statistischer Vierteljahresbericht, 1923.

64. Data on the Viennese, Austrian, and Bavarian parties are tabulated in Juan J. Linz, "Some Notes toward a Comparative Study on Fascism in Sociological Historical Perspective," in *Fascism: A Reader's Guide; Analyses, Interpretations, Bibliography*, ed. Walter Laquer (Berkeley, 1976), table 9, p. 71; table 10, p. 74.

65. Of a total of 65, at least 47 (72.3 percent) depended on wages or salaries, while 32 (49.2 percent)—including teachers—received their payments from the state. Only a fifth of the group (3 shopkeepers, 6 professionals, and 5 artisans) derived their incomes in traditional ways.

66. Linz *Tagblatt*, 17 November 1923 and A St Linz, "Sitzungsprotokolle des Gemeinderates Linz, 1925," 14. Sitzung (July 1925). As late as 1931 the NSDAP in Linz was still regarded as a Sudeten German party. See Sumetinger to Hitler, 24 February 1931, BDC OPG (Alfred Proksch). Quote from Gideon Hausner, *Justice in Jerusalem* (New York, 1966), p. 28.

67. *Linzer Volksstimme*, 14 April, 25 April, 6 June, 25 July 1923 and A St Linz: "Sitzungsprotokolle," 3. Sitzung, 20 February 1924; 4. Sitzung, 14 March 1925; 11. Sitzung, 30 October 1925.

68. Botz, "Faschismus und Lohnabhängige," pp. 121–23. *Linzer Volksstimme*, 30 May 1923, 31 July 1931.

69. *Linzer Volksstimme* 26 September 1925, 21 August 1926; E. März and E. Weissel, "Die Bedeutung und Entwicklung der Arbeiterkammern in der ersten Republik," in *Verbände und Wirtschaftspolitik in Österreich*, ed. Theodor Pütz

(Berlin 1966), p. 400; and Slapnicka, *Von Hauser*, pp. 192–93. That so many white-collar employees should have supported the DNSAP in Linz is not unusual and confirms the observations and studies throughout Austria and Germany of many journalists, sociologists, and historians during the past half century. Caught between propertied businessmen above and organized labor below, suffering from inflation and status anxiety, and seeking greater job security from the government, salaried nonmanual employees were particularly prone to succumb to fascist or quasi-fascist movements. For the most recent assessment see Michael H. Kater, *The Nazi Party: A Social Profile of Members and Leaders*, 1919–1945 (Cambridge, Mass., 1983).

70. *Linzer Volksstimme*, 5 July 1924 and Linz *Tagespost*, 17 October 1932.

71. BDC/PK: Marie Werbik and Fritz Werbik; Bart and Puffer, *Gemeindevertre-tung*, pp. 279–80; *Linzer Volksstimme*, 14 February 1925, 8 April 1931; and A St Linz: Marie Werbik to Wilhelm Rausch, 20 November 1966.

72. Karl Marx perceptively defined and analysed the behavior of what might be called the "old" petty bourgeoisie—artisans, shopkeepers, and small merchants of a preindustrial society. Lenin accepted and expanded the concept but refused to acknowledge the emergence of the "new" petty bourgeoisie of salaried white-collar workers as anything more than a "disguised" proletariat. As dogma this view has severely crippled Communist perceptions of Nazism and Fascism. See Alfred G. Mayer, *Leninism* (New York, 1957), pp. 245–46.

73. NA, microcopy T 580, Nonbiographical Records of the Berlin Document Center, Roll 62; Proksch to *Reichsleitung*, 22 May 1929.

74. Carsten, *Fascist Movements*, pp. 87–102.

75. Slapnicka, *Zwischen Bürgerkrieg*, pp. 17–24.

76. *Amtsblatt der Landeshauptstadt Linz*, 15 April 1924; *Linzer Volksstimme*, 12 April 1924; and AVA, BKA, I, 22 O Oest, box 5099, doc. 63.288-24 ("Vorfälle bei der Smetnafeier in Linz"), 30 March 1924.

77. Carsten, *Fascist Movements*, pp. 80–83; Bruce F. Pauley, "From Splinter Party to Mass Movement: The Austrian Nazi Breakthrough," *German Studies Review*, vol. 2, no. 1 (February 1979) p. 8; and Schilling, "Parteileben," pp. 74–84.

78. Proksch was so discouraged by the Salzburg meeting that he briefly relinquished control of the Upper Austrian party to a certain Karl Breitenthaler. The latter was so inept that in 1925 Proksch reassumed command. BDC/OPG: Proksch an den U. Schl. A, 10 March 1931, p. 2.

79. The most lucid account of these labyrinthine machinations is Pauley, *Hitler and the Forgotten Nazis*, pp. 36–51. But also see Carsten, *Fascist Movements*, pp. 141–48; Wache, *Deutscher Geist in Österreich*, pp. 250–56; Langoth, *Kampf um Österreich*, pp. 29–30; and BDC/OPG: Proksch an den U.Schl. A., 10 March 1931. Karl Schulz published his own bitter recollection of the Passau "mini-Anschluss" in his newspaper, *Deutsche Arbeiter Presse*, 14 January 1934.

80. NA, T 580, Roll 63, Ordner 306, II, "Rundschreiben," 6 October 1926.

81. *Linzer Volksstimme*, 1 August 1926 and 26 March 1927. The fusion list of 1927 was primarily the work of Christian Social Chancellor Ignaz Seipel. It did *not* include the entire Nazi party, as implied by Seipel's biographer Klemens von Klemperer. Klemperer, *Seipel:* pp. 260–61. Only the splinter group around Walter Riehl in Vienna agreed initially to join the coalition, while the majority of the NSDAP remained opposed. Proksch's decision to collaborate came at the last moment, and, although approved by the Munich leadership, it aroused the full fury of the other Austrian *Gauleiter*. Cf. Wache, *Deutscher Geist*, p. 261; the anonymous broadside (typescript) "Hitler oder Schulzpartei" at AVA, BKA, I, 22 O Oest, box 5101, doc.

212.599/32; and NA, T 580, Roll 63, "Parteiamtlich wird verlautbart . . . ," 1 April 1927.

82. NA, T 580, Roll 62, "Rundschreiben," no. 1, 7 April 1927; no. 2, 31 May 1927; no. 3, 7 July 1927; no. 4, 5 September 1927; and Proksch to Strasser, 28 September 1928; Roll 63, Ordner 305, II, Strasser to Konrad Habl, 23 July 1928.

83. Pauley, *Hitler and the Forgotten Nazis*, pp. 54–55.

84. BDC/OPG: Proksch an den U. Schl. A, 10 March 1931, p. 5.

85. NA, T 580, Roll 62, Ordner 305, I, Franz Woldrich to Gregor Strasser, 30 September 1930.

86. *Linzer Volksstimme*, 10 July 1930.

87. NA, record group 238, interrogation of August Eigruber, 6 February 1946 and T 580, Roll 63, Ordner 306, I, Rolf West to Strasser, 22 March 1930. Also Carsten, *Fascist Movements*, pp. 158–63.

88. NA, T 580, Roll 63, Frauenfeld to Strasser, 22 March 1930 and "Rundverfügung," Nr. 21, 11 January 1930. Also AVA, BKA, I, 22 O Oest, box 5101, doc., 128.597, 27 February 1932 and Carsten, *Fascist Movements*, p. 162.

89. NA, T 580, Roll 62, Proksch to Strasser, 20 January 1930 and 31 January 1930. "Rundverfügung," Nr. 21, 11 January 1930.

90. NA, T 580, Roll 62, Proksch to Strasser, 22 March 1930; AVA, BKA, I, 22 O Oest, box 5100, doc. 211.779/30, 27 October 1930; and Carsten, *Fascist Movements*, pp. 162–63. The negotiations are also sketched in Starhemberg, *Between Hitler and Mussolini*, pp. 36ff.

91. Wache, *Deutscher Geist*, p. 270 and the following police reports at AVA, BKA, I, 22 O Oest, box 5100: docs. 202.022/30, 2 October 1930; 203.827/30, 7 October 1930; 205.661/30, 11 October 1930; 206.849/30, 15 October 1930; 208.164/30, 17 October 1930; 210.691/30, 24 October 1930; 211.779/30, 27 October 1930; 207.893/30, 17 October 1930; 215.409/30, 6 November 1930; and 215.778/30, 8 November 1930.

92. *Linzer Volksstimme*, 15 November 1930.

93. Pauley, "From Splinter Party to Mass Movement," pp. 14–15 and idem, *Hahnenschwanz und Hakenkreuz: Der steirische Heimatschutz und der öster-reichische Nationalsozialismus* (Vienna, 1972), pp. 98–105.

94. NA, T 580, Roll 63, Ordner 306 II, Frauenfeld to Strasser, 17 November 1930; Leopold to Strasser, 20 March 1930; Suske to Strasser, 27 September 1930; and Karl Pischtiak, "Denkschrift über die Entwicklung der Parteikrise in Österreich."

95. AVA, NS Parteistelle, box 6: Schirach to Frauenfeld, 9 March 1931.

96. Pauley, "Fascism and the *Führerprinzip*," p. 288.

97. This is a figure quite low when compared to police estimates ranging from 700 to 1,500 in Linz and from 7,000 to 8,000 in Upper Austria. For the same period Nazi records indicate membership in other provinces as follows: Carinthia 6,592; Lower Austria 13,434; Styria 5,453; Salzburg 488; Tyrol 1,188; Vienna 15,284. Cf. NA, T 580 Roll 61, Ordner 303, I, "Mitgliederstand" and Radomir Luža, *Austro-German Relations in the Anschluss Era*, (Princeton, 1975), p. 376. Also, AVA, BKA, I, 22 O Oest, box 5101: docs. 113.646/32, 23 January 1932; 212.599/32, 21 September 1932; box 5103, doc. 122.341/33, 18 February 1933. Whatever the true figure, Linz and its hinterland was clearly below the Austrian average. Carsten (*Fascist Movements*, p. 198) makes the rather unhelpful observation, "It is difficult to account for the small membership in the western *Länder*—Salzburg, Tyrol, and Upper Austria—close to the German frontier and in general very much influenced by developments there."

98. Hans Hautmann and Rudolf Kropf, *Die österreichische Arbeiterbewegung vom Vormärz bis 1945: Sozialökonomische Ursprünge ihrer Ideologie und Politik*

(Vienna, 1974), pp. 154–58 and Hertz, *The Economic Problem of the Danubian States*, p. 148.

99. See the chart in Hertz, *The Economic Problem of the Danubian States*, p. 147.

100. Simon, "Political Parties," p. 294.

101. Simon, "The First Republic of Austria," pp. 100–103.

102. Unemployment figures for Linz derived from the scattered and often inconsistent data in *Amtsblatt der Landeshauptstadt Linz*, 1922–38; A St Linz, Statistiche Vierteljahresberichte der Stadt Linz, 1922–32; Tweraser, "Der Linzer Gemeinderat, 1914–1934," p. 231; and *Oberösterreichische Arbeiterzeitung*, 1931–34. For Upper Austria (Arbeitsamt Linz) and Austria see Bundesamt für Statistik, *Statistisches Handbuch für die Republik Österreich*, vols. 1–18 (Vienna, 1920–38); Hertz, *The Economic Problem of the Danubian States*, p. 148; and Slapnicka, *Zwischen Bürgerkrieg*, pp. 209–16.

103. *Statistisches Handbuch für die Republik Österreich* (Vienna, 1932), vol. 13, p. 162.

104. AVA, BKA, I, 22 O Oest, box 5101, doc. 191.136/31, 28 August 1931.

105. Slapnicka, *Zwischen Bürgerkrieg*, p. 213.

106. K. W. Rothschild, *Austria's Economic Development Between the Wars* (London, 1947), pp. 51–65.

107. AVA, BKA, I, 22 O Oest, box 5101, doc. 191.682/31, 28 August 1931.

108. AVA, BKA, I, 22 O Oest, box 5102, doc. 226.482/32 ("Periodische Berichterstattung der Landesgendarmeriekommandos an das Bundeskanzleramt Generaldirektion für die öffentliche Sicherheit"), 24 October 1932.

109. AVA, BKA, I, 22 O Oest, box 5101, doc. 208.056/31, 12 October 1931.

110. See the newspaper clippings from the *Linzer Volksblatt*, *Neueste Zeitung*, Linz *Tagespost*, and *Kremser Zeitung* at AVA, SD Parteistelle, box 64: Sozial Demokraten Affairen 1931–32: Fall Walla-Mehr.

111. Simon, "Political Parties of Austria," pp. 332–35. For the official Communist version see Autorenkollektiv der Historischen Kommission beim ZK der KPÖ, *Geschichte der Kommunistischen Partei Österreichs: 1918–1955—Kurzer Abriss* (Vienna, 1977), pp. 77–89.

112. AVA, BKA, I, 22 O Oest, box 5100, doc. 113.317/30, 3 February 1930.

113. AVA, BKA, I, 22 O Oest, box 5101, doc. 176.094/30, 16 July 1930 ("Kommunistischebewegung im ersten Halbjahren 1930").

114. AVA, BKA, I, 22 O Oest, box 5101, doc. 190.940/31, 27 August 1931.

115. AVA, BKA, I, 22 O Oest, box 5102, doc. 153.820/32, 23 April 1932 and 201.255/32, n.d.

116. AVA, BKA, I, 22 O Oest, box 5102, doc. 201.255/32, 19 August 1932. The same police report, however, estimated KP strength in Steyr at 650.

117. Data derived form police reports at AVA, BKA, I, 22 O Oest in boxes 5100–5103.

118. AVA, BKA, I, 22, O Oest, box 5102, doc. 151.187/32, 18 April 1932.

119. AVA, BKA, I, 22, O Oest, box 5102, docs. 201.797/32, 23 August 1932 and 230.883, 17 November 1932.

120. Slapnicka, *Zwischen Bürgerkrieg*, pp. 50–56.

121. One needs an Ariadne as a guide through the labyrinth of *Heimwehr* politics in 1930. But see Edmondson, *Heimwehr*, pp. 91–121.

122. Ibid., p. 122.

123. The Viennese and Tyrolean *Heimwehr* leaders Emil Fey and Richard Steidle broke with Starhemberg in January 1931 because of the prince's abysmal performance as a member of the federal cabinet. Facing serious financial problems,

Starhemberg then alienated the proclerical conservative wing of the Christian Social party by running his own slate of candidates in Upper Austria. In consequence even his own mother disavowed him and gave up her position in the CSP. As for Starhemberg, his poor electoral performance on 19 April caused him to take a "leave of absence" from the *Heimwehr* in order to untangle his financial affairs. Edmondson, *Heimwehr*, pp. 129–30.

124. IfZ: Gerda Ziervogel, "Die Landtagswahlen in Oberösterreich 1931" (unpublished seminar paper, 1969, SE 558).

125. Slapnicka, *Zwischen Bürgerkrieg*, pp. 50–55 and Edmondson, *Heimwehr*, p. 137.

126. For accounts of the farcical Pfrimer putsch see Edmondson, *Heimwehr*, pp. 130–49; Carsten, *Fascist Movements*, pp. 181–84; and Pauley, *Hahnenschwanz*, pp. 117–20.

127. Pauley, "Fascism and the *Führerprinzip*," pp. 288–89; idem, "From Splinter Party to Mass Movement," pp. 15–19; and Carsten, *Fascist Movements*, pp. 183–84, 194–207.

128. AVA, BKA, I, 22 O Oest, box 5102, doc. 203.966/32, 29 August 1932.

129. Carsten, *Fascist Movements*, p. 194.

130. Ibid., p. 183.

131. Ibid., p. 184.

132. AVA, BKA, I, 22 O Oest, box 5101, doc. 225.655/31, n.d, and Carsten *Fascist Movements*, p. 195.

133. Simon, "The First Republic of Austria," p. 109; idem, "The Political Parties of Austria," pp. 321–31; and Pauley, "From Splinter Party to Mass Movement," pp. 17–19.

134. AVA, BKA, I, 22 O Oest, box 5102, doc. 151.662, 16 April 1932.

135. *Linzer Volksstimme*, 8 November 1931.

136. Ibid., 5 March 1932.

137. AVA, BKA, I, 22 O Oest, box 5102, doc. 161.852/32, 10 May 1932: "Vorwärts! Wir greifen an!"

138. The Nazis in the *Volksstimme* of 11 June 1932 claimed 10,000 participants, but police estimates put the figure at 5,191. AVA, BKA, I, 22 O Oest, box 5102, doc. 169.028/32, 4 June 1932.

139. AVA, BKA, I, 22 O Oest, box 5102, docs. 169.028/32, 4 June 1932; 170.072/32, 7 June 1932; and 170.075/32, 5 June 1932.

140. *Amtsblatt der Landeshauptstadt Linz an der Donau*, Nr. 14 (14 July 1932).

141. AVA, BKA, I, 22 O Oest, box 5102, doc. 169.028/32 "Nationalsozialistische und Sozialdemokratische Veranstaltungen am 4. und 5. Juni 1932."

142. According to a police report of 22 December 1932, the SA in Linz numbered 236 men, the SS only 26. No doubt, the number rose over the next six months but not enough to counter the thousands of *Schutzbündler* in the city. AVA, BKA, I, 22 O Oest, box 5102, doc. 251.167/32.

143. Botz, *Gewalt*, pp. 198–99 and AVA, NS Parteistelle, box 6, Habicht an die Gauleiter, 30 May 1932.

144. Slapnicka, *Zwischen Bürgerkrieg*, p. 41.

145. IfZ: Lack, "Entwicklung," p. 33.

146. Kutschera, *Gföllner*, pp. 73, 92–97 and *Linzer Diözesanblatt*, vol. 72, no. 6; 92, vol. 75, no. 8, p. 101.

147. Linz *Tagespost*, 17 October 1932.

148. Rural opposition to Nazi agitation in Upper Austria was especially striking at a time when hundreds of thousands of peasants and farmers in Schleswig-Holstein,

Lower Saxony, Thuringia, Carinthia, and Styria were flocking to Hitler's banner. In the words of the newsletter of the National Socialist Farmers Association of Austria (NSBOe): "The development of the NSBOe is quite good in the district of Lower Austria, satisfactory in Styria and Carinthia, but lags far behind in the western districts, especially Upper Austria. The latter suffers from 'Bachingenier,'" (a grudging tribute to Franz Bachinger, Federal Minister of Internal Administration and chief of the German Nationalist *Landbund* in Upper Austria). AVA, NS Parteistelle, box 7, Nationalsozialistische Bauernschaft Oesterreichs L.L.F., Rundschreiben Nr. 4, Linz, 28 April 1932.

149. AVA, BKA, I, 22 O Oest, box 5102, doc. 212.599/32, 21 September 1932; box 5103, docs. 102.830/33, December 1933 and 251.167/32, 22 December 1932.

150. The eventual loss was $420,000. For more details see Slapnicka, *Zwischen Bürgerkrieg*, pp. 92–96; *New York Times*, 24 August 1933; and the indignantly anti-Semitic police report at AVA, 22 Gen., doc. 193.854/SD O Oe, 1 August 1933.

151. *Amtsblatt der Stadt Linz*, no. 23 (1 December 1932), pp. 221–33.

152. Pauley, *Hahnenschwanz*, pp. 159–61 and Slapnicka, *Zwischen Bürgerkrieg*, p. 188.

153. Isabella Ackerl, "Das Kampfbündnis der Nationalsozialistischen Deutschen Arbeiterpartei mit der Grossdeutschen Volkspartei vom 15. Mai 1933" in *Das Jahr 1934 :25 Juli*, ed. Ludwig Jedlicka and Rudolf Neck (Vienna, 1975), pp. 21–35.

154. On the other hand, the Nazis did not attract many members of the old *Mittelstand*, who appear to have remained loyal to the Christian Socials and after 1934 supported the Dollfuss-Schuschnigg dictatorship.

155. *Amtsblatt der Stadt Linz*, no. 14, 14 July 1932, p. 126. In response, Starhemberg formally expelled Steinsky and fifty-seven of his "Styrian" followers from his organization. AVA, BKA, I, 22 O Oest, box 5102, doc. 196.268/32, 6 August 1932.

156. Slapnicka, *Zwischen Bürgerkrieg*, p. 188 and Ackerl, "Kampfbündnis," pp. 21–35. Text of the agreement in Langoth, *Kampf um Österreich*, pp. 101–2.

157. In Styria the *Heimatschutz* officially joined the NSDAP on 9 March 1933. Pauley, "From Splinter Party to Mass Movement," p. 26.

158. In his memoirs (p. 245) Langoth emphatically denied joining the NSDAP before 1938. His files at the BDC (PK and SS, "Lebenslauf," 15 May 1938) indicate the date was March 1933.

159. Although no bargains were struck, both Christian Socials and Starhemberg's *Heimwehr* negotiated with Habicht in April and May 1933. Jürgen Gehl, *Austria, Germany, and the Anschluss* (New York, 1963), pp. 52–57; Andrew G. Whiteside, "Austria," in *The European Right: A Historical Profile*, ed. Hans Rogger and Eugen Weber (Berkeley and Los Angeles, 1966), p. 342; and Gulick, *Austria*, vol. 2, p. 1063.

160. Gehl, *Austria, Germany and the Anschluss*, p. 56 and Extracts from the Minutes of the Conference of Ministers on 26 May 1933 in *Documents on German Foreign Policy* (DGFP), series C., vol. 1, no. 262 (Washington, D.C., 1957), p. 490.

161. For more details see Gulick, *Austria*, vol. 2, p. 1040 and passim.

162. AVA, BKA, I, 22 O Oest, box 5103, doc. 151.300/33, 30 April 1933.

163. In Mattighofen near Braunau, *Schutzbündler* attacked a Nazi meeting on 4 March and severely wounded five National Socialists. Botz, *Gewalt*, p. 274.

164. AVA, BKA, I, 22 O Oest, box 5103, docs. 151.300/33, 30 April 1933 and 163.691/33, 27 May 1933. For an account of Nazi inspired violence in Vienna see Rudolf Neck, "Simmering, 16 October 1932: Vorspiel zum Bürgerkrieg" in *Vom Justizpalast zum Heldenplatz*, ed. Ludwig Jedlicka and Rudolf Neck (Vienna, 1975), pp. 94–102.

165. Kutschera, *Gföllner*, p. 93.

166. Ibid., p. 94.

167. Slapnicka, *Zwischen Bürgerkrieg*, p. 261.

168. Kutschera, *Gföllner*, p. 100. The official police report on the incident is at AVA, BKA, I, 22 O Oest box 5103, doc. 14.471/33, 21 April 1933. According to it, the author of the limerick was the fifty-five-year-old Arnold Dietrich Pollack, a longtime editor of the virulently anti-Semitic *Linzer Fliegende Blätter*.

169. NA, T 120, roll 4638, frame K285018-21: Langen to Foreign Office, Berlin, 22 April 1933.

170. Ibid.

171. Carsten, *Fascist Movements*, pp. 333–34.

5. CRISIS AND CIVIL WAR, 1932–1934

1. On the collapse of Austrian democracy see Peter Huemer, *Sektionschef Robert Hecht und die Zerstörung der Demokratie in Österreich: Eine historisch-politische Studie* (Munich, 1975). For a provocative general analytic framework see Linz, "Crisis, Breakdown, and Reequilibration," *The Breakdown of Democratic Regimes*, pp. 3–124.

2. For an up to date survey of the literature on the establishment of the Dollfuss regime see Gerhard Botz, "Die Ausschaltung des Nationalrates und die Anfänge der Diktatur Dollfuss im Urteil der Geschichtsschreibung von 1933 bis 1973," in *Vierzig Jahre danach: Der 4. März im Urteil von Zeitgenossen und Historikern*, ed. Anton Benya (Vienna, 1974).

3. This point has been made many times by such prominent scholars as Martin Broszat, Ernst Nolte, and Karl Dietrich Bracher, but it needs to be reiterated.

4. Tweraser, "Der Linzer Gemeinderat 1914–1934," p. 239.

5. *Linzer Volksblatt*, 18 September 1931.

6. Tweraser, "Der Linzer Gemeinderat 1914–1934," pp. 242–43 and A St Linz, "Sitzungsprotokolle der Stadt Linz," 1 July 1932.

7. Slapnicka, *Zwischen Bürgerkrieg*, pp. 98, 81–89, 105–9.

8. Alfred Diamant has carefully shown how the Austrian hierarchy construed the encyclical to justify the dominance of business interests and the establishment of an authoritarian bureaucratic order. For his part, Pfeneberger correctly contended that *Quadragesimo Anno* did not call for the creation of vocational estates in place of parliamentary institutions. In his view, estates were autonomous intermediate bodies that should be represented by an association subordinate to the political parliament. Cf. Diamant, *Austrian Catholics and the First Republic*, pp. 153–207 and Slapnicka, *Zwischen Bürgerkrieg*, pp. 90–91.

9. Anton Staudinger, "Christlichsoziale Partei und Errichtung des 'Autoritären Ständestaates' in Österreich," in *Vom Justizpalast zum Heldenplatz: Studien und Dokumentationen*, ed. Ludwig Jedlicka and Rudolf Neck (Vienna, 1975), p. 68 and Walter Goldinger, ed., *Protokolle des Klubvorstandes der Christlichsozialen Partei 1932–1934* (Vienna, 1980), pp. 22–23.

10. Staudinger, "Christlichsoziale Partei," pp. 69–74; Huemer, *Sektionschef Robert Hecht*, p. 165; and Erika Weinzierl, "Aus der Notizen von Richard Schmitz zur österreichischen Innenpolitik im Frühjahr 1933," in *Geschichte and Gesellschaft*, ed. Gerhard Botz et. al. (Vienna, 1974), pp. 122–29. For a complete transcript of the proceedings see Goldinger, *Protokolle des Klubvorstandes*, pp. 139–73.

11. Felix Kern, *Oberösterreichischer Bauern und Kleinhäuslerbund* (Ried, 1956), p. 1243.

12. Ibid., pp. 1207–17 and Staudinger, "Christlichsoziale Partei," pp. 69–74, 80.

13. Langoth, *Kampf um Österreich*, pp. 94–101.

14. Slapnicka, *Zwischen Bürgerkrieg*, p. 58.

15. Ibid. and Langoth, *Kampf um Österreich*, pp. 101–5.

16. Slapnicka, *Zwischen Bürgerkrieg*, pp. 112–17 and Huemer, *Sektionschef Robert Hecht*, p. 165.

17. See, for example, Dollfuss's confidential remarks to the Christian Social Parliamentary Club on 12 January 1934 in Goldinger, *Protokolle des Klubvorstandes*, pp. 326–27.

18. Staudinger, "Christlichsoziale Partei," pp. 78–80 and Huemer, *Sektionschef Robert Hecht*, pp. 272–74.

19. Slapnicka, *Zwischen Bürgerkrieg*, pp. 112–14 and Erika Weinzierl-Fischer, *Die österreichischen Konkordate von 1855 und 1933* (Munich, 1960), pp. 226–27.

20. Gulick, *Austria*, vol. 2, p. 1198.

21. Cf. Kern, *Oberösterreichischer Bauern und Kleinhäuslerbund*, pp. 1246–47 and Boyer, *Political Radicalism in Late Imperial Vienna*, pp. 122–83.

22. Slapnicka, *Zwischen Bürgerkrieg*, p. 114.

23. Staudinger, "Christlichsoziale Partei," p. 80; Slapnicka, *Zwischen Bürgerkrieg*, pp. 118–21; and idem, *Führungsschicht*, pp. 31–33.

24. Julius Braunthal, *History of the International* (New York, 1967), vol. 2, p. 406.

25. Richard Bernaschek, "Die Tragödie der österreichischen Sozialdemokratie" in *Österreich Brandherd Europas* (Zürich, 1934).

26. Norbert Leser, *Zwischen Reformismus und Bolschewismus: Der Austromarxismus als Theorie und Praxis* (Vienna, 1968), p. 462ff. and Huemer, *Sektionschef Robert Hecht*, p. 207.

27. Huemer, *Sektionschef Robert Hecht*, pp. 203–8.

28. Tweraser, "Der Linzer Gemeinderat 1914–1934," pp. 244–46 and A St Linz: "Sitzungsprotokolle der Stadt Linz," 12 May 1933. For Koref's own account see Ernst Koref, *Die Gezeiten meines Lebens* (Munich, 1980), pp. 164–221, especially his evasive comment on p. 182 on the failure to respond with force on 31 March 1933.

29. Kykal and Stadler, *Bernaschek*, pp. 61–62.

30. Ibid., pp. 63–68, 229–42.

31. Ibid., pp. 68–69.

32. Dokumentationsarchiv des österreichischen Widerstandes (DÖW), Vienna, doc. 12.064, Testimony of Ludwig Bernaschek, June 1934.

33. Kykal and Stadler, *Bernaschek*, pp. 63–68 and Ducyznska, *Workers in Arms*, pp. 53–57.

34. Carsten, *Fascist Movements*, pp. 231–32.

35. Braunthal, *History of the International*, vol. 2, p. 409.

36. Kykal and Stadler, *Bernaschek*, pp. 53–77.

37. Ibid., p. 65.

38. Rabinbach, *The Crisis of Austrian Socialism*, p. 194.

39. AVA, BKA, I, 22 O Oest, box 5104, docs. 205.712/33, 30 August 1933; 219.278/33, 29 September 1933; 237.397/33, 13 November 1933; 242.664/33, 27 November 1933.

40. AVA, BKA, I, 22 O Oest, box 5104, doc. 223.408/33, 13 October 1933.

41. AVA, BKA, I, 22 O Oest, box 5104, doc. 100.946/34, 30 December 1933.

42. Edmondson, *Heimwehr*, pp. 204–15 and Carsten, *Fascist Movements*, pp. 233–34.

43. Carsten, *Fascist Movements*, pp. 234–35, Edmondson, *Heimwehr*, pp. 215–16, and Slapnicka, *Zwischen Bürgerkrieg*, pp. 122–24.

44. Slapnicka, *Zwischen Bürgerkrieg*, p. 124 and Carsten, *Fascist Movements*, p. 234.
45. Slapnicka, *Zwischen Bürgerkrieg*, p. 125.
46. Ibid.
47. AVA, Vienna, BKA, I, 22 O Oest, box 5105, doc. 106.778, 12 January 1934.
48. Kykal and Stadler, *Bernaschek*, p. 83.
49. Ibid., pp. 84–85 and Bernaschek, "Tragödie," p. 276. Jetzinger later disavowed any responsibility for the outbreak of the Austrian civil war, disingenuously placing the entire blame on Bernaschek.
50. Kykal and Stadler, *Bernaschek*, pp. 86–87 and DÖW, doc. 12.064, testimony of Ludwig Bernaschek.
51. DÖW, Vienna: doc. 12.064.
52. Ibid., Kykal and Stadler, *Bernaschek*, and Bernaschek, "Tragödie," p. 276.
53. Kykal and Stadler, *Bernaschek*, pp. 89–92; Bernaschek, "Tragödie"; and DÖW, docs. 12.064, testimony of Ludwig Bernaschek; 12.061, testimony of Franz Schlagin; and 12.833, testimony of Otto Huschka.
54. Reproduced in Kykal and Stadler, *Bernaschek*, pp. 92–93 and in part in Fischer, *An Opposing Man*, p. 228. Both General Theodor Körner and Secretary of the Free Trades Union Schorsch were to receive copies of the letter.
55. See for example his filial pietistic explanation in Bernaschek, "Tragödie," pp. 272–73.
56. Gulick, *Austria*, vol. 2, p. 1349.
57. Slapnicka, *Zwischen Bürgerkrieg*, p. 128. Bernaschek's flagrant disregard of established procedures and usurpation of executive privilege in the Upper Austrian party is overlooked by the otherwise incisive Rabinbach, who credits the Linz commander with greater control of the provincial party apparatus than he actually exercised. Rabinbach, *The Crisis of Austrian Socialism*, pp. 189–94.
58. Bernaschek's testimony in Kykal and Stadler, *Bernaschek*, pp. 290–291 and Bernaschek, "Tragödie," is rather ambiguous on this point; that of Ferdinand Hüttner and Ludwig Bernaschek indicates a showdown was not anticipated for Monday. According to Otto Huschka, "we received word from Vienna that the situation would be unresolved until the middle of the next week when all provincial diets were to convene." See DÖW, docs. 12.064, 12.833, and 12.070.
59. Kykal and Stadler, *Bernaschek*, pp. 285–86.
60. DÖW, docs. 12.064 and 12.833, Polizeiakte über die Vorgeschichte des 12. February 1934 in Linz.
61. Kykal and Stadler, *Bernaschek*, p. 95.
62. Martin Kitchen, *The Coming of Austrian Fascism* (London and Montreal, 1980), pp. 202, 230. The transcript of the conversation, first discovered by Karl R. Stadler, is at AVA, BKA, I, 22 O Oest, box 5105, doc. 123.845, 18 February 1934.
63. Kykal and Stadler, *Bernaschek*, p. 95.
64. Duczynska, *Workers in Arms*, p. 156 and AVA, BKA, I, 22 O Oest, box 5105, doc. 123.845, 18 February 1934.
65. Kykal and Stadler, *Bernaschek*, p. 90.
66. Kitchen, *The Coming of Austrian Fascism*, pp. 203–204.
67. DÖW, doc. 12.833, testimony of Otto Huschka.
68. Kitchen, *The Coming of Austrian Fascism*, p. 204; Bernaschek, "Tragödie," pp. 280, 282; and Kykal and Stadler, *Bernaschek*, pp. 95–96.
69. DÖW, doc. 12.064, testimony of Johann Waldburger.
70. Most versions of the fighting at the Hotel Schiff hold that "it is not clear who fired the first shot," thus Kitchen, *The Coming of Austrian Fascism*, p. 204. Actually,

both sides agreed the Socialists opened fire first. According to the testimony of *Schutzbund* prisoners, it was the cabinetmaker, Rudolf Kunst, who commenced hostilities with a machine gun burst. In the view of Police Commissioner Dr. Franz Petrich, however, the first shots came from a pistol. Since Kunz was killed in the fighting, conveniently serving as a scapegoat for the defeated workers, Petrich's account may be the more accurate. DÖW, docs. 12.065, testimony of Dr. Franz Petrich, and 12.845, Strafsache gegen Kornhuber und Genossen.

71. Rudolf Walter Litschel, *1934—Das Jahr der Irrungen* (Linz, 1974), pp. 42–46.

72. See Kitchen, *The Coming of Austrian Fascism*, p. 13 and Duczynska, *Workers in Arms*, pp. 122–28.

73. AVA, BKA, I, 22 O Oest, box 5104, doc. 227.853/32, 26 October 1932, "Republikanischer Schutzbund in Linz." Also see Winfried Garscha amd Hans Hautmann, *Februar 1934 in Österreich* (Berlin, 1984), p. 117.

74. For a comprehensive account of the fighting in Linz see Helmut Fiereder, "Der Republikanische Schutzbund in Linz und die Kampfhandlungen im Februar 1934," *Historisches Jahrbuch der Stadt Linz* (1978).

75. Shuffling into the streets, hands on their heads, the workers passed two obscure members of the victorious government forces. One was Lieutenant Robert Bernardis, who would hang as a conspirator in the 20 July 1944 plot against Hitler; the other was Patrolman Franz Stangl, future commandant of Treblinka. Litschel, *Das Jahr der Irrungen*, p. 48 and Gitta Sereny, *Into That Darkness: From Mercy Killing to Mass Murder* (New York, 1974), p. 28.

76. Litschel, *Das Jahr der Irrungen*, pp. 50–52 and DÖW, doc. 12.094, testimony of Josef Lang, 11 May 1934.

77. Kitchen, *The Coming of Austrian Fascism*, pp. 204–5.

78. Arnold Reisberg, *Februar 1934: Hintergründe und Folge* (Vienna, 1974), p. 40.

79. Litschel, *Das Jahr der Irrungen*, pp. 54–56.

80. Kitchen, *The Coming of Austrian Fascism*, p. 209 and Litschel, *Das Jahr der Irrungen*, p. 52.

81. Litschel, *Das Jahr der Irrungen*, pp. 58–61.

82. Ibid.

83. AVA, B/839: Die Bundesgendarmerie in den Tagen des Aufstandes/Aktion in Linz und Umgebung.

84. Ibid.

85. Kitchen, *The Coming of Austrian Fascism*, pp. 221–22.

86. Slapnicka, *Zwischen Bürgerkrieg*, pp. 140–41 and *Linzer Tagblatt*, 12 February 1946.

87. Kykal and Stadler, *Bernaschek*, pp. 101–21.

6. CHRISTIAN CORPORATIVE INTERLUDE, 1934–1938

1. Slapnicka, *Zwischen Bürgerkrieg*, pp. 156–64.

2. Kitchen, *The Coming of Austrian Fascism*, p. 288.

3. For conflicting assessments of the Christian Corporative regime see ibid. pp. 277–88; R. John Rath, "Authoritarian Austria," in *Native Fascism in the Successor States*, 1918–1945, ed. Peter Sugar (Santa Barbara, 1971), pp. 24–83; Pauley, *Hitler and the Forgotten Nazis*, pp. 155–71; Gulick, *Austria*, vol. 2, pp. 1403–1858, especially 1454–56; Grete Klingenstein, "Bemerkungen zum Problem des Faschismus in Österreich," *Österreich in Geschichte und Literatur*, vol. 14, no. 1 (1970), pp. 1–13; Carsten, *Fascist Movements*; pp. 229–48, 271–92; Edmondson, *The Heimwehr and Austrian Politics*, pp. 232–37; R. John Rath and Carolyn Schum, "The

Dollfuss-Schuschnigg Regime: Fascist or Authoritarian?" in Stein Ugelvik Larsen et al., *Who Were the Fascists?: Social Roots of European Fascism* (Bergen, 1980), pp. 249–56; Emmerich Talos and Wolfgang Neugebauer, eds., *"Austrofaschismus:" Beiträge über Politik, Ökonomie und Kultur 1934–1938* (Vienna, 1984); and Ulrich Kluge, *Der österreichische Ständestaat 1934–1938: Entstehung und Scheitern* (Vienna, 1984).

4. Carsten, *Fascist Movements*, pp. 237–38 and Huemer, *Sektionschef Robert Hecht*, pp. 252–59. Also see Heinrich Heffter, *Die Deutsche Selbstverwaltung im 19. Jahrhundert: Geschichte der Ideen und Institutionen* (Stuttgart, 1950), pp. 325–27.

5. Slapnicka, *Zwischen Bürgerkrieg*, pp. 165–71.

6. Bart and Puffer, *Die Gemeindevertretung der Stadt Linz*, pp. 42–45.

7. Gerhard Jagschitz has coined the term *Agrartechnokrat* to characterize Dollfuss. Gerhard Jagschitz, *Der Putsch: Die Nationalsozialisten 1934 in Österreich* (Graz, 1976), p. 15.

8. Slapnicka, *Führungsschicht*, pp. 97–99.

9. Georg Grill, *Das Linzer Bürgermeisterbuch* (Linz, 1959), p. 117; Slapnicka, *Fürhungsschicht*, pp. 51–52; and Wilhelm Bock, "Wir und die Judenfrage," *Der christlich-deutsche Student: Mitteilungsblatt des christlich-deutschen Studentenbundes für Oberösterreich*, 20 December 1930. Also interview by the author of Dr. Josef Stöger, 26 June 1975.

10. Slapnicka, *Zwischen Bürgerkrieg*, pp. 173–76.

11. Data compiled from Bart and Puffer, *Die Gemeindevertretung der Stadt Linz*, pp. 89, 104 and passim.

12. Tweraser, "Structural Changes," p. 17.

13. *Nachrichtendienst des DHV-V.D.W.A.* (Kreisleitung Oberösterreich-Linz), vol. 1, nos. 16, 17, 28 February 1934, 2 May 1934.

14. AVA, BKA, I, 22 O Oest, box 5106, docs. 170.330, Lackney to BKA-I, 11 May 1934; 192.275, Jahresbericht 1933 Industriellenverband Oberösterreich; 211.712, 27 July 1934.

15. Meixner, *Linz, 1945–1960*, p. 21.

16. Gulick, *Austria*, vol. 2, pp. 1936–1941.

17. Kutschera, *Gföllner*, pp. 79–86; *Linzer Diözesanblatt*, vol. 80 (1934), no. 7, pp. 154–57; no. 8, 166–80; no. 10, 187–91; vol. 82 (1936), no. 7, 151–54; and *New York Times*, 24 March 1937.

18. Carsten, *Fascist Movements*, pp. 237–40 and Pauley, *Hitler and the Forgotten Nazis*, pp. 159–63. The most comprehensive analysis of the Patriotic Front is Irmgard Bärnthaler, *Die Vaterländische Front: Geschichte und Organisation* (Vienna, 1971).

19. Slapnicka, *Zwischen Bürgerkrieg*, p. 280.

20. Although *Heimwehr* chieftans such as Heinrich Wenninger and Count Peter Revertera were given posts in the Upper Austrian provincial government, their regional power base remained small. As the Patriotic Front gradually extended its influence throughout Upper Austria, local *Heimwehr* leaders sensed their movement was being coopted. After the assassination of Dollfuss, in particular, Revertera lashed out against the "vaticanization of the state," urging his followers to root out clerical influence. The subsequent establishment of an official government militia, the *Ostmärkische Sturmscharen*, also aroused the ire of the Heimwehr but not sufficiently to provoke open resistance. Never exceptionally influential, the Upper Austrian *Heimwehr* diminished in importance until the national organization was dissolved by Schusschnigg on 10 October 1936. AVA, BKA, I, 22 O Oest, box 5109, doc. 321.097, Heimatwehr, O Oe öffentliche Versammlung, 27 March 1935, and Edmondson, *Heimwehr*, p. 262.

21. AVA, BKA, I, 22 O Oest, box 5110, doc., 328.272. Gendarmerieabteilung-skommando Linz, no. 1, March 1935 and Carsten, *Fascist Movements*, p. 273.

22. AVA, BKA, I, 22, O Oest, box 5115, doc. 319.337, 23 March 1937.

23. AVA, BKA, I, 22, O Oest, box 5117, doc. 349.026, July 1937.

24. Carsten, *Fascist Movements*, pp. 272–73.

25. Oberösterreiches Landesarchiv (OÖLA), Linz, Politische Akten, box 77, Amtswalter der VF Oberösterreich 1935.

26. Cf. Stephen Fischer-Galati, "Fascism in Eastern Europe" in *Who Were the Fascists?*, ed. Larsen, pp. 350–417 and Anthony James Joes, *Fascism in the Contemporary World: Ideology, Evolution, Resurgence* (Boulder, 1978), pp. 97–119. Also see Stanley Payne's taxonomy of fascist and "new right" dictatorships in *Who Were the Fascists?* ed. Larsen, pp. 418–22.

27. Most insistently perhaps by R. John Rath, "Authoritarian Austria," pp. 34–35.

28. Barrington Moore, Jr., *Social Origins of Dictatorship and Democracy* (London, 1967), p. 447.

29. Pauley, *Hitler and the Forgotten Nazis*, pp. 155–71 and Elizabeth Barker, *Austria*, (Coral Gables, 1973), pp. 100–102.

30. AVA, BKA, I, 22 O Oest, box 5106, doc. 162.130, 27 April 1934.

31. Josef Buttinger, *In the Twilight of Socialism: A History of the Revolutionary Socialists of Austria* (New York, 1953), pp. 305–6.

32. Slapnicka, *Zwischen Bürgerkrieg*, pp. 178–79 and AVA, BKA, I, 22 O Oest, box 5106, docs. 129.555, 23 February 1934 and 229.800, 26 February 1934.

33. AVA, BKA, I, 22 O Oest, box 5109, docs. 810.298 and 351.997, 9 July 1935.

34. DÖW, doc. 6629, Bundespolizeidirektion Linz an die GDföS, 28 December 1934.

35. AVA, BKA, I, 22 O Oest, box 5109, doc. 308.803, 29 January 1935.

36. AVA, BKA, I, 22 O Oest, box 5107, doc. 183.452/34: *Rote Rebellen Kampfblatt des K.J.V.*, June 1934.

37. AVA, BKA, I, 22 O Oest, box 5109, doc. 303.169, 12 June 1935.

38. AVA, BKA, I, 22 O Oest, box 5108, doc. 249.967, 23 September 1934.

39. Buttinger, *Twilight of Socialism*, pp. 305–6.

40. AVA, BKA, I, 22 O Oest, box 5110, docs. 351.997, 9 July 1935 and 322.021, 2 April 1936. Also Slapnicka, *Zwischen Bürgerkrieg*, p. 179.

41. Everhard Holtmann, *Zwischen Unterdrückung und Befriedung: Sozialistische Arbeiterbewegung und autoritäres Regime in Österreich 1933–1938* (Munich, 1978), p. 231.

42. Thus Revertera in Slapnicka, *Zwischen Bürgerkrieg*, p. 180.

43. Slapnicka, *Führungsschicht*, pp. 173–175.

44. Ibid., and idem, *Zwischen Bürgerkrieg*, p. 180–81.

45. Gulick, *Austria*, vol. 2, pp. 1512–32 and Slapnicka, *Zwischen Bürgerkrieg*, p. 182.

46. Gulick, *Austria*, vol. 2, pp. 1527–32 and the collection of documents at AVA, BKA, 22 O Oest, box 5111, doc. 304.112/36.

47. Hautmann and Kropf, *Die österreichische Arbeiterbewegung*, pp. 165–66. Norbert Schausberger, *Der Griff nach Österreich* (Munich, 1978), pp. 475–82.

48. Slapnicka, *Zwischen Bürgerkrieg*, p. 210.

49. Cf. Statistisches Amt der Stadt Linz, *Statistisches Jahrbuch der Stadt Linz (1946)*, pp. 112–17 and Meixner, *Linz, 1945–1960*, p. 20.

50. *Amtsblatt der Landeshauptstadt Linz*, Nr. 4, 15 February 1936, p. 42.

51. Slapnicka, *Zwischen Bürgerkrieg*, p. 212.

52. Hautmann and Kropf, *Die österreichische Arbeiterbewegung*, pp. 164–65 and Schausberger, *Der Griff nach Österreich*, pp. 478–82.

53. AVA, BKA, I, 31 O Oest, box 5517, Gesetz vom 29 April 1936.

54. The provincial budget fell from 58.6 million schillings in 1931 to 46.2 million schillings in 1934. It increased only slowly thereafter to 48.9 million schillings for 1938. The municipal budget, on the other hand, was balanced only in 1930, 1933, 1934, and 1935. Cf. Slapnicka, *Zwischen Bürgerkrieg* p. 68 and *Statistisches Jahrbuch der Stadt Linz*, 1947–48, p. 148.

55. Kropf, *Oberösterreichs Industrie*, pp. 139–44; Slapnicka, *Zwischen Bürgerkrieg*, pp. 213–15; and Meixner, *Männer*, p. 380.

56. DÖW, doc. 1449, Geheime Staatspolizei Linz to RSHA, Berlin, 30 December 1940.

57. Linz *Tagespost*, 14 June 1933.

58. During a stormy session of the Linz city council on 16 June 1933, the German Nationalist councillor Otto Foltz rose to denounce the Dollfuss regime, to demand new federal elections, and to propose immediate negotiations with Hitler. He also proclaimed melodramatically that the GDVP in Upper Austria had taken up the fallen Nazi standard. Linz *Tagespost*, 16 June 1933 and *Amtsblatt der Landeshauptstadt Linz an der Donau*, vol. 13, 1 July 1933, pp. 142–49.

59. Langoth, *Kampf um Österreich*, pp. 124–63; Kitchen, *The Coming of Austrian Fascism*, pp. 155–56; and Wolfgang Rosar, *Deutsche Gemeinschaft: Seyss Inquart und der Anschluss* (Vienna, 1971), pp. 65–67.

60. AVA, BKA, I, 22 O Oest, box 5103, doc. 114.096, 27 January 1934 and Slapnicka, *Zwischen Bürgerkrieg*, pp. 189–90.

61. Slapnicka, *Zwischen Bürgerkrieg*, pp. 189–90 and AVA, BKA, I, 22 O Oest, box 5103, docs. 115.628, n.d., 252.516, 29 November 1933, and 112.557, 28 January 1934.

62. AVA, BKA, I, 22 O Oest, box 5103, doc. 114.461, 28 January 1934.

63. Slapnicka, *Zwischen Bürgerkrieg*, pp. 178–79.

64. Carsten, *Fascist Movements*, pp. 257–58.

65. Pauley, *Hitler and the Forgotten Nazis*, pp. 124–28. The most nearly definitive account of the July putsch is Jagschitz, *Der Putsch*.

66. AVA, BKA, I, 22 O Oest, box 5109, doc. 301.835, report of the federal police commissioner in Wels, 7 January 1935.

67. Ibid., and Langoth, *Kampf um Österreich*, pp. 166–76.

68. DÖW, doc. 60.155, Bundesdirektion Linz an den Staatsanwalt beim Militärgericht in Linz, 19 August 1934.

69. Ibid.

70. AVA, BKA, I, 22 O Oest, box 5108, doc. 238.538, Bentz an den Staatsanwalt beim Militärgericht in Linz, 5 September 1934.

71. Ibid.; AVA, BKA, Präsidium, Juli Putsch 1934, doc. E., Nr. 2580, Die österreichische Bundesgendarmerie in den Julitagen 1934; Bundeskanzleramt für Heimatdienst, *The Death of Dollfuss: An Official History of the Revolt of July 1934 in Austria* (London, 1935); and Jagschitz, *Der Putsch*, pp. 157–61.

72. On 22 August 1934 a motley cache of pistols, hand grenades, dynamite, carbines, and rifles was uncovered outside Linz. Whether the weapons were to be used for terrorist activities or for a general insurrection is unknown. Ironically, the policeman credited with the discovery was Franz Stangl, future commandant of Treblinka. Sereny, *Into That Darkness*, p. 28. For an inventory of the weapons see AVA, BKA, I, 22 O Oest, box 5108, doc. 238.538.

73. Pauley, *Hitler and the Forgotten Nazis*, pp. 131–33; Jagschitz, *Der Putsch*, pp. 157–67; and AVA, BKA, I, 22 O Oest, box 5109, 7 January 1935.

74. Carsten, *Fascist Movements*, p. 265.

75. Rosar, *Deutsche Gemeinschaft*, p. 76.

76. Barker, *Austria*, pp. 97–106; Pauley, *Hitler and the Forgotten Nazis*, pp. 156–59; and Carsten, *Fascist Movements*, pp. 271–88.

77. Rosar, *Deutsche Gemeinschaft*, pp. 75–82; Pauley, *Hitler and the Forgotten Nazis*, pp. 148–50; and Gerhard Jagschitz, "Zwischen Befriedung und Konfrontation: Zur Lage der NSDAP in Österreich 1934 bis 1936," in *Das Juliabkommen von 1936: Hintergründe und Folgen: Protokolle des Symposiums in Wien am 10. und 11. Juli 1976*, ed. Ludwig Jedlicka and Rudolf Neck (Munich, 1977), pp. 163–65.

78. Langoth, *Kampf um Österreich*, pp. 210–13 and Maurice Williams, "Delusions of Grandeur: The Austrian National Socialists," *Canadian Journal of History*, vol. 14, no. 3, pp. 417–36; and idem, "Aid, Assistance, and Advice: German Nazis and the Austrian *Hilfswerk*," *Central European History*, vol. 14, no. 3 (September 1981), pp. 230–42.

79. Langoth, *Kampf um Österreich*, p. 179 and W. R. Houston, "Ernst Kaltenbrunner: A Study of an Austrian SS and Police Leader" (diss., Rice, 1972), pp. 46–47.

80. Gehl, *Austria, Germany and the Anschluss*, p. 109.

81. Jagschitz, "Zwischen Befriedung und Konfrontation," p. 170.

82. For a measure of the resentment felt by the "old fighters" in Linz see NA, R.G. 238: interrogation of August Eigruber, 3 November 1945.

83. Ludwig Jedlicka, "Gauleiter Josef Leopold," in *Geschichte und Gesellschaft: Festschrift für Karl R. Stadler zum 60. Geburtstag* (Vienna, 1974), pp. 143–61.

84. NA, RG 238: interrogation of August Eigruber, 3 November 1945; Bart and Puffer, *Die Linzer Gemeindevertretung*, pp. 139, 286; BDC, PK, and SS (Sepp Wolkerstorfer); and *Österreichischer Beobachter*, 9 April 1938.

85. Peter Merkl, *Political Violence Under the Swastika: 581 Early Nazis* (Princeton, 1975), p. 14.

86. Interview of Josef Wolkerstorfer by the author, 28 July 1978.

87. NA, RG 238, interrogation of August Eigruber, 3 November 1945. On Kaltenbrunner's role in the Austrian Nazi underground see Peter R. Black, *Ernst Kaltenbrunner: Ideological Soldier of the Third Reich* (Princeton, 1984), pp. 69–103.

88. *Österreichischer Beobachter*, 9 April 1938, pp. 9–11 and AVA, BKA, I, 22 O Oest, box 5114, doc. 324.957, 8 April 1935: Versuchte Wiederaufrichtung der SA und PO in Oberösterreich.

89. Rosar, *Deutsche Gemeinschaft*, p. 96.

90. Ibid., pp. 94ff. and John A. Bernbaum, "Nazi Control in Austria: The Creation of the Ostmark, 1938–1940" (diss., University of Maryland, 1972), pp. 38–40.

91. Comment by Gerhard Botz in *Das Juliabkommen von 1936*, p. 429.

92. AVA, BKA, I, 22 O Oest, box 5113, docs. 356.107, 7 September 1936 and 165.352, 27 October 1936.

93. For a measure of the pride felt by Revertera at his double game see DÖW, doc. 2.162, Bericht des Grafen Revertera am 13 April 1946. Also see Black, *Ernst Kaltenbrunner*, pp. 90–91.

94. Wolkerstorfer interview, 28 July 1978.

95. DÖW, doc. 14.601: Dr. Alfred Persche, "Erinnerungen aus der Geschichte der nationalsozialistischen Machtergriefung in Österreich: Jahre 1936–1938: Niedergeschrieben von einen Alten Kämpfer der NSDAP," unpublished MS, p. 39.

96. On this notion see Charles S. Maier, *Recasting Bourgeois Europe: Stabilization in France, Germany, and Italy in the Decade After World War I*, (Princeton, 1975), pp. 3–15.

7. ANSCHLUSS IN LINZ, 1938–1939

1. Probably the best, or at least the most vivid, description of the Anschluss in Linz is in the *New York Times*, 13 March 1938. But also see *The Times*, 14 March 1938, the *Manchester Guardian*, 15 March 1938; and Dieter Wagner and Gerhard Tomkawitz, *Anschluss: The Week Hitler Seized Austria* (New York, 1971), p. 87. Also Gerhard Botz, "Hitler's Aufenthalt in Linz in März 1938 und der Anschluss," *Historisches Jahrbuch der Stadt Linz* (1971), pp. 185–214; Langoth, *Kampf um Österreich*, p. 236; and Heinz Guderian, *Panzer Leader* (New York, 1952), p. 52.

2. The literature on the background of the Anschluss is immense. The most comprehensive, up-to-date account is Schausberger, *Der Griff nach Österreich*.

3. Interview of Josef Wolkerstorfer by Gerhard Botz, 15 March 1971 in A St Linz, Tonband Sammlung, Reel 87 and *Österreichischer Beobachter*, 9 April 1938, pp. 7–8.

4. *Österreichischer Beobachter*, 28 July 1936, 1 October 1936, July 1937, 9 April 1938 and DÖW, doc. 2.162: Bericht des Grafen Reverteras, 13 April 1946.

5. Although Gleissner wanted to put an end to government subsidies, Austrian Foreign Minister Guido Zernatto insisted on maintaining them, presumably as a means of appeasing the National Opposition.

6. For example, Martin Fuchs, *Showdown in Vienna: The Death of Austria* (New York, 1939), pp. 220–26; Gulick, *Austria*, vol. 2, p. 1813; Wagner and Tomkawitz, *Anschluss*, p. 87; and John Lukacs, *The Last European War* (New York, 1976), p. 9.

7. Pauley, *Hitler and the Forgotten Nazis*, p. 92 and Slapnicka, *Zwischen Bürgerkrieg*, pp. 197–98, 288.

8. BDC, PK: Arnulf Maschek, "Personal Fragebogen" and *Völkischer Beobachter* (Wiener Ausgabe), 16 October 1938.

9. AVA, BKA, I, 22 O Oest, box 5114, docs. 312.249, 15 February 1937; 326.531, 20 April 1937, Revertera to GDföS; and 289.193, 1 March 1937, Dirndlabend im Gasthaus Otto Hönes.

10. DGFP, D, I, p. 454; Franz von Papen, *Memoirs* (New York, 1953), p. 398; AVA, BKA, I, 22 O Oest, box 5117, doc. 341.785, 26 June 1937, Soldatentreffen in Wels; and *Linzer Volksblatt*, 29 November 1937.

11. Carsten, *Fascist Movements*, p. 319; Anton Fellner, "Die Machtergreifung im Gau Oberdonau," *Österreichischer Beobachter*, March 1939, pp. 9–12; and Wagner and Tomkawitz, *Anschluss*, p. 77.

12. Carsten, *Fascist Movements*, p. 319; Fellner, "Machtergreifung," pp. 9–12; Botz, "Hitler's Aufenthalt," pp. 201–2; Wagner and Tomkawitz, *Anschluss*, p. 95; and Josef Hofer, *Weggefährten: Von österreichischen Freiheitskampf, 1933–1945* (Vienna, 1946), pp. 12–15.

13. Fellner, "Machtergreifung," p. 11 and Botz, "Hitler's Aufenthalt," p. 203.

14. NA, R.G. 238, interrogation of August Eigruber, 3 November 1945, p. 17 and Botz, "Hitler's Aufenthalt," pp. 204–5. The fears of the Austrian Nazis were well founded since the German invasion was directed as much against them as against Schuschnigg. The truth was that Hitler did not want to lose control of the situation to men who had caused him so much trouble in the past. Pauley, *Hitler and the Forgotten Nazis*, pp. 192–215 and Radomir Luža, *Austro-German Relations*, p. 47.

15. Botz, "Hitler's Aufenthalt," p. 189 and idem, *Die Eingliederung Österreichs*

in das Deutsche Reich: Plannung und Verwirklichung des politisch-administrativen Anschlusses (1938–1940) (Vienna, 1976), p. 39.

16. As quoted in Wagner and Tomkawitz, *Anschluss*, p. 200.

17. Botz, "Hitler's Aufenthalt," p. 210.

18. Harry Slapnicka, *Oberösterreich als es "Oberdonau" hiess (1938–1945)* (Linz, 1978), p. 279 and passim.

19. Luža, *Austro-German Relations*, p. 60.

20. Ibid., p. 376.

21. NA, R.G. 238, Eigruber interrogation, 5–6 February 1946; BDC, PK: Eigruber "Lebenslauf"; DÖW, doc. 1401: Persche, "Erinnerung," pp. 39–41; and Slapnicka, *Oberdonau*, pp. 452–54.

22. NA, R.G. 238, Eigruber interrogation and interview of Josef Wolkerstorfer by the author, 28 July 1978.

23. See Eigruber's address of 14 July 1941 in August Eigruber, *Ein Gau wächst ins Reich: Das Werden Oberdonaus im Spiegel der Reden des Gauleiters August Eigruber* (Wels, 1941), pp. 192–96.

24. Slapnicka, *Oberdonau*, pp. 452–54.

25. See the extensive records on this matter at DÖW, doc. 2947. Also see Slapnicka, *Oberdonau*, pp. 497–98. Ironically, Kaltenbrunner interceded on Wolkerstorfer's behalf two years later, when the hapless municipal official faced charges of criminal negligence in his new position at the Hermann Göring Works. Despite Kaltenbrunner's efforts, Wolkerstorfer was convicted and fined RM 3,000. Black, *Ernst Kaltenbrunner*, pp. 124–25.

26. Personnel data at BDC are not entirely complete. For the *Gauleitung* I found information on 20 out of 28 cases, for the *Kreisleitung* on only 12 out of 25. Data on the city council (48 cases), collected by Bart and Puffer and augmented at the BDC, are virtually complete.

27. For purposes of comparison some of the following tables include data from Lerner's famous analysis of the Nazi elite in Germany. Daniel Lerner, "The Nazi Elite," in Harold D. Laswell and Daniel Lerner, *World Revolutionary Elites: Studies in Coercive Ideological Movements* (Cambridge, Mass., 1965), pp. 195–318.

28. That is to say from a preindustrial strata of society consisting of peasant-proprietors, artisans, self-employed businessmen, civil servants, and professionals to an industrial middle class which also included public and private employees and those employed by the state who were not tenured officials.

29. It is not clear what Lerner means by "high school," given the wide variety of secondary schools in Central Europe. I suspect that he may mean only *Gymnasia* and *Realgymnasia*. In Linz 27 percent of the city councillors attended *Realschulen*.

30. Lerner, "The Nazi Elite," pp. 195–318.

31. "A man who deviates from a substantial number and variety of predominant attributes in his society may be regarded as a 'marginal man.'" In this sense the Nazi movement was led and followed by "marginal men." Ibid., p. 288.

32. On the other hand, few of Langoth's older generation of German Nationalists actually shared power with the Nazis. Most of the Greater Germans received minor positions or honorary titles; Franz Dinghofer, for example, took early retirement. Slapnicka, *Oberdonau*, pp. 57–58.

33. Wolfgang Sauer, "National Socialism: Totalitarianism or Fascism?" *The American Historical Review*, vol. 73 (1967), pp. 417–18.

34. Bukey, "The Nazi Party in Linz, Austria, 1919–1939," pp. 302–26. The Salzburg historian Gerhard Botz has reached parallel conclusions in his analysis of the

Nazi movement in Austria, "The Changing Patterns of Social Support for Austrian National Socialism (1918–1945)" in *Who Were the Fascists?* ed. Larsen, pp. 202–25 and "Strukturwandlungen des österreichischen Nationalsozialismus (1904–1945) in *Politik und Gesellschaft im alten und neuem Österreich: Festschrift für Rudolf Neck zum 60. Geburtstag,* ed. Isabella Ackerl et al., (Munich, 1981), vol. 2, pp. 195–218. On the upwardly mobile character of the German Nazi party see Kater, *The Nazi Party,* especially p. 160.

35. Luža, *Austro-German Relations,* pp. 116–25 and Slapnicka, *Oberdonau,* pp. 55–57.

36. "Mehr als die Hälfte waren Nazi," Linz *Volksblatt,* 30 March 1946; Luža, *Austro-German Relations,* pp. 118–25; and Botz, "The Changing Pattern of Support for Austrian National Socialism," pp. 217–22.

37. Gerhard Botz, *Wien vom "Anschluss" zum Krieg: Nationalsozialistische Machtübernahme und politisch-soziale Umgestaltung am Beispiel der Stadt Wien 1938–39* (Munich, 1978), p. 115.

38. Ibid., pp. 115–89; Luža, *Austro-German Relations,* pp. 62–72; and John A. Bernbaum, "Nazi Control in Austria: The Creation of the Ostmark, 1938–1940" (diss., University of Maryland, 1972), pp. 88–105.

39. A St Linz, Tagesereignisse.

40. Max Domarus, *Hitler: Reden und Proklamationen 1932–1945* (Wiesbaden, 1973), vol. 1, pt. 2, p. 847.

41. Botz, *Wien vom "Anschluss" zum Krieg,* pp. 117–27 and Luža, *Austro-German Relations,* p. 64.

42. Rudof Zinnhobler, "Die Haltung Bischof Gföllner gegenüber dem Nationalsozialismus," in Rudolf Zinnhobler, *Das Bistum Linz im Dritten Reich* (Linz, 1979), pp. 61–68.

43. Slapnicka, *Oberdonau,* p. 52.

44. Ibid.

45. Ibid., pp. 281–83 and Hautmann and Kropf, *Die österreichische Arbeiterbewegung,* p. 106.

46. Botz, *Wien vom "Anschluss" zum Krieg,* pp. 129–45.

47. Bernbaum, "Nazi Control in Austria," p. 91 and Luža, *Austro-German Relations,* pp. 192–94.

48. A St Linz, Tagesereignisse (March–April, 1938). Franz Langoth headed the NSV in Austria from 1938 to 1944, but his memoirs provide little information on the subject.

49. Slapnicka, *Oberdonau,* p. 52.

50. Hofer, *Weggefährten;* Sereny, *Into That Darkness,* p. 39; *New York Times,* 14 March 1938; *Österreichischer Beobachter,* 9 April 1938; *Völkischer Beobachter* (Wiener Ausgabe), 14 May 1939; and Slapnicka, *Oberdonau,* p. 183.

51. Linz *Tagespost,* 15 March 1938.

52. OÖLA, Pol. Akten, box 20, doc. 180/18 (1938): Gestapo Linz an die Oberösterreichische Landeshauptmannschaft, 20 May 1938.

53. Felix Kern, "Fahrt nach Dachau," Linz *Volksblatt,* 18 June 1946.

54. Approximately fifty Upper Austrian Social Democrats and labor militants were picked up by the Gestapo on 7 September 1944. They were sent to Mauthausen where most, including Richard Bernaschek, were murdered. Linz *Tagblatt,* 27 April 1946.

55. Gerhard Botz, "Comments," *Austrian History Yearbook,* vol. 14 (1978), pp. 179–80 and idem, *Wien vom "Anschluss" zum Krieg,* p. 58.

56. Slapnicka, *Oberdonau,* p. 53.

57. Ibid., and OÖLA, Pol. Akten, box 20, doc. 183/18/1938: Mildner an alle Gemeindeämter, 24 March 1938.

58. Slapnicka, *Oberdonau*, pp. 53–54, 343; Linz *Tagblatt*, 27 November 1946; and Luža, *Austro-German Relations*, p. 70. For other examples of Nazi electoral intimidation see the scanty but interesting collection of documents in DÖW, *Widerstand und Verfolgung in Oberösterreich 1934–1945: Eine Dokumentation* (Vienna, 1982), vol. 2, pp. 264–69.

59. But see the speculative conclusions reached by Botz, *Wien vom "Anschluss" zum Krieg*, pp. 175–83.

8. HITLER'S HOMETOWN, 1939–1945

1. While Austrian historians have acknowledged the popular enthusiasm that welcomed the Anschluss, they have generally finessed the problem of collaboration by emphasizing the domination of Austrian society by Reich German officials, and, more recently, by publishing evidence of widespread suffering, discontent, and even resistance to the Hitler regime. Except for the outstanding work by Ernst Hanisch, *Nationalsozialistische Herrschaft in der Provinz: Salzburg im Dritten Reich* (Salzburg, 1983), the literature taking this approach is endless. It includes the works of the otherwise sophisticated Gerhard Botz, whose extensive use of quantitative data and theoretical models occludes the very real power wielded outside Vienna by the native-born NSDAP. Cf. Botz, *Wien vom "Anschluss" zum Krieg*, pp. 355–64, 487–505; idem, "Comments," *Austrian History Yearbook*, vol. 14 (1978), pp. 167–82; Hanisch, *Nationalsozialistische Herrschaft in der Provinz*, pp. 129–48ff.; and idem, "'Gau der Guten Nerven': Die Nationalsozialistische Herrschaft in Salzburg 1939–40," in Ackerl, *Politik und Gesellschaft im Alten und Neuen Österreich*, vol. 2, pp. 195–218, especially 202–8. For a sample of the ongoing emphasis on discontent and resistance see the publications of the DÖW: *Widerstand und Verfolgung in Wien 1934–1945: Eine Dokumentation*, 3 vols. (Vienna, 1975); *Widerstand und Verfolgung in Burgenland 1934–1945: Eine Dokumentation* (Vienna, 1979); and *Widerstand und Verfolgung in Oberösterreich 1934–1945: Eine Dokumentation*, 2 vols. (Vienna, 1982). To date no one has systematically tackled the problem of collaboration in the Ostmark, but see Bernbaum's pioneering dissertation, "Nazi Leadership in Austria" as well as his article, "The New Elite: Nazi Leadership in Austria, 1939–1945" in *Austrian History Yearbook*, vol. 14 (1978), pp. 145–60. Also see Hanisch, *Nationalsozialistische Herrschaft in der Provinz*. For a balanced introductory assessment see Peter J. Katzenstein, *Disjoined Partners: Austria and Germany Since 1815* (Berkeley, 1976), pp. 163–76.

2. Luža, *Austro-German Relations*, p. 60.

3. Botz, "Comments," loc. cit., pp. 167–82.

4. "Oberösterreichische Nazibonzen auf der vierten Kriegsverbrecherliste," Linz *Tagblatt*, 6 June 1946; Slapnicka, *Oberdonau*, pp. 341, 480, 476; Sereny, *Into That Darkness*, pp. 32–39; DÖW, *Widerstand und Verfolgung in Oberösterreich*, vol. 2, pp. 492–93; and DÖW, doc. 14.899 a–f: Verfahren des Volksgerichts Linz, 1947–49.

5. DÖW, doc. 8359: Unveröffentliche Manuskripte für das Bundesregierung herausgegebende rot/weiss/rot Buch: Bericht verschiedener Gendarmerieposten-kommandos in Oberösterreich.

6. BDC, SS-Führer, Hans Feil: Ernst Kaltenbrunner to v. Herff, 14 December 1944.

7. Slapnicka, *Oberdonau*, p. 98.

8. Botz, "Comments," pp. 177–81.

9. Ibid. and Slapnicka, *Oberdonau*, p. 62.

10. Botz, "Comments," pp. 177–81.

11. Hanisch, "Gau der Guten Nerven," pp. 202–8; Luža, *Austro-German Relations*, pp. 231–63, 317–32; and idem, "Nazi Control of the Austrian Catholic Church, 1939–1941," *The Catholic Historical Review*, vol. 63 (1977), pp. 537–72, especially 537–39 and 547–51.

12. *Amtskalender für das Gau Oberdonau*, vol. 70 (Linz, 1939), pp. 51–60; vol. 82, pp. 319–20; Slapnicka, *Oberdonau*, pp. 55–60; NA, T 175, S 124, R 124, frames 599664–71: Malz to Ohlendorf, 25 November 1942 and Himmler to Bormann, 14 January 1943. Eigruber's ruthless vigor earned him the admiration not only of Hitler, Goebbels, and Speer but also of Franz Ziereis, commandant of the nearby Mauthausen concentration camp. With Ziereis, the *Gauleiter* was in fact on a "du" basis. Fred Taylor, ed., *The Goebbels Diaries, 1939–1941* (New York, 1983), 265–66; Louis P. Lochner, *The Goebbels Diaries, 1942–1943* (New York,) 433; A St Linz, Tonbandsammlung, Reel 33: Interview of Rudolf Jirkowsky by Wilhelm Rausch, 9 March 1965; and Bundesarchiv, Koblenz, R3/1577, fol. 1–93, Speer to Eigruber, 11 November and 29 December 1944. I am grateful to Siegwald Ganglmair for calling my attention to the Speer correspondence and for making copies available to me.

13. Most notably Ludwig Jedlicka, *Der 20. Juli in Österreich* (Vienna, 1966). On the problem of Austrian views of the Nazi past see Harry Ritter, "Recent Writing on Interwar Austria, pp. 306–11 and Katzenstein, *Disjoined Partners*, pp. 163–76. Also see the conflicting articles by Bernbaum ("The New Elite") and Maurice Williams ("The Aftermath of Anschluss: Disillusioned Germans or Budding Austrian Patriots?") as well as the comments by Peter Burian, Herbert Steiner, Ernst Hanisch, and Gerhard Botz—all published as "The Nazi Interlude" in *Austrian History Yearbook*, vol. 14 (1978), pp. 127–86.

14. Avrid Fredborg, *Behind the Steel Wall: A Swedish Journalist in Berlin* (New York, 1944), p. 187; Slapnicka, *Oberdonau*, pp. 281–82 and passim; DÖW, doc. 4081: Gestapo Linz to RSHA, 3 December 1940; *Mitteilungsblatt des Gaupropagandaamtes*, Folge 6 (6 July 1941); OÖLA, Pol. Akten, box 69, doc. 12/20, Bericht des SD Linz, 27 June 1941; and Lukacs, *The Last European War*, p. 176. Although hardly an impartial observer, even Goebbels was struck by the popularity of the Nazi order in Linz and Upper Danube. Taylor, *The Goebbels Diaries, 1939–1941*, pp. 265–66.

15. Hautmann and Kropf, *Die österreichische Arbeiterbewegung*, p. 106.

16. A St Linz, Tagesereignisse; *Linzer Volksstimme*, 4, 9, 13 July and 3 September 1938; Albert Speer, *Inside the Third Reich*, p. 99; and *Amtsblatt der Stadt Linz* (1938), no. 7, p. 74.

17. Luža, *Austro-German Relations*, pp. 192–94.

18. Ibid., p. 193.

19. *Völkischer Beobachter* (Wiener Ausgabe), 16 September 1938; Meixner, *Männer, Mächte, Betriebe*, p. 383; and Slapnicka, *Oberdonau*, p. 160.

20. Franz Stadlbauer, *Ein Jahr Deutsche Arbeitsfront* (Berlin, 1939).

21. *Statistisches Jahrbuch der Stadt Linz* (1946), p. 126. Both Luža and Bernbaum have shown that inflationary pressure in Vienna under the Nazis was considerable and aroused a good deal of resentment. In Linz this seems not to have been the case, as the tables published by the statistical office of the city and cited here reveal. On the other hand, data marshaled by Slapnicka indicates that food prices in Upper Danube as a whole rose from 110 to 300 percent between 1937 and 1941; the cost of

meal rose 10 percent, fat 42 percent, veal and pork 50 percent, pressed sausage 73 percent, cheese and eggs 80 percent, peas 88 percent, potatoes and cabbage 150 percent, margarine 209 percent, and apples 300 percent. It is difficult to square these figures with those published by the city of Linz *after* World War II except to note that the cost of living index, especially for food and clothing, did rise substantially during the first year of the Anschluss, but remained comparatively stable thereafter. It is also important to recall that Nazi price controls benefitted urban dwellers, largely at the expense of rural producers, from the very beginning. Luža, *Austro-German Relations*, pp. 201, 301–4; Bernbaum, "Nazi Control in Austria," p. 173; and Slapnicka, *Oberdonau*, pp. 252–60.

22. Slapnicka, *Oberdonau*, pp. 281–82 and DÖW, *Widerstand und Verfolgung in Oberösterreich*, vol. 1, pp. 196–97, 239.

23. Bernbaum, "Nazi Control in Austria," pp. 151–55; Hautmann and Kropf, *Die österreichische Arbeiterbewegung*, pp. 176–90; DÖW, *Widerstand und Verfolgung in Wien*, vols. 2 and 3; Karl Stadler, *Österreich 1938–1945 im Spiegel der NS-Akten* (Vienna, 1966), pp. 53–59 and passim; Fredborg, *Behind the Steel Wall*, p. 187; and Karl R. Stadler, *Austria*, (New York, 1971), p. 175. In light of Kater's quantitative discovery of increasing blue collar identification with Hitler's regime during World War II, the question of working-class attitudes toward National Socialism remains far from settled. For conflicting conclusions see Kater, *The Nazi Party*, pp. 117–19, 160, 346–47 and Timothy W. Mason, *Arbeiterklasse und Volksgemeinschaft: Dokumente und Materialen zur deutschen Arbeiterpolitik 1936–1939* (Opladen, 1975), especially pp. 171–73. Also see Ian Kershaw, *Popular Opinion and Political Dissent in the Third Reich: Bavaria 1933–1945* (Oxford, 1983), pp. 303–15. In Upper Danube blue-collar opinion was usually rooted in specific geographical and historical circumstances. Dissent was most evident on the floor of the Steyr armaments plant; it was also widespread among railwaymen and miners elsewhere in the *Reichsgau*. In Linz, on the other hand, even the Nazis were struck by the absence of blue-collar discontent. When in 1943 dissent did emerge in the town's vast Hermann Göring Works, it was confined to Italian, Czech, and French, rather than Austrian, wage earners. DÖW, *Widerstand und Verfolgung in Oberösterreich*, vol. 1, pp. 183–335, especially doc. 15 on p. 239.

24. Ian Kershaw, "The Persecution of the Jews and German Popular Opinion in the Third Reich," in Leo Baeck Institute, *Yearbook XXVI* (London, 1981), pp. 261–89.

25. According to available statistics, the numbers of Jewish inhabitants in Linz were: in 1869, 391 (1.3 percent); in 1880, 553 (1.3 percent); in 1923, 1,238 (1.2 percent); and in 1934, 650 (0.60 percent). *Encyclopedia Judaica*, vol. 11, p. 262.

26. Tweraser, "Carl Beurle and the Triumph of German Nationalism in Austria," pp. 403–26 and Slapnicka, *Oberdonau*, p. 178.

27. The letter infuriated the Nazis, as we have seen, but it is today remembered in Austria for its anti-Semitism. See Pelinka, *Stand oder Klasse*, p. 216.

28. Harry Slapnicka, "Zum Antisemitismus Problem in Oberösterreich," *Zeitgeschichte*, 11/12 (1974), pp. 264–66 and Karl Stuhlpfarrer, "Antisemitismus, Rassenpolitik und Judenverfolgung in Österreich nach dem Ersten Weltkrieg" in Anna Drabek et al., *Das österreichische Judentum: Voraussetzungen und Geschichte* (Vienna, 1974), especially p. 143.

29. Karl Schwager, "Geschichte der Juden in Linz" in Hugo Gold, *Geschichte der Juden in Österreich: Ein Gedenkbuch* (Tel Aviv, 1971), pp. 58–60.

30. Slapnicka, "Antisemitismus," p. 266.

31. *Österreichischer Beobachter*, 2 Junifolge 1938, pp. 9–11 and A St Linz,

Tagesereignisse. On the Nazi persecution of the Jews in Austria see Jonny Moser, *Die Judenverfolgung in Österreich 1938–1945* (Vienna, 1966) and Herbert Rosenkranz, *Verfolgung und Selbstbehauptung: Die Juden in Österreich 1938–1945* (Vienna and Munich, 1978).

32. OÖLA, Pol. Akten, box 20, Ferngespräch des Sicherheitsdirektor Dr. Laine vom 18.3.1938. Also quoted by Slapnicka, *Oberdonau*, p. 183.

33. BDC, SS, Kaltenbrunner: Wolf to Kaltenbrunner, 14 July 1938. According to Bloch's daughter Trude Kren, Hitler made inquiries about Bloch during the Anschluss, wistfully regretting that more Jews could not be like him. See Kren's emotional letter in *Der Spiegel*, vol. 32, no. 7 (13 February 1978), p. 8.

34. OÖLA, Pol. Akten, box 20, Orders from Gestapo Linz, 31 March, 21 June, and 24 June 1938. Also A St Linz, Tagesereignisse (31 March 1938).

35. Slapnicka, *Oberdonau*, pp. 184–86; Schwager, "Geschichte der Juden in Linz," pp. 60–62; Rosenkranz, *Verfolgung und Selbstbehauptung*, p. 160; A St Linz: Chronik der Judenschule; and DÖW, doc. 3522, Herbert Sperling an den SD-Führer des Oberabschnittes Donau, November 1938, also reproduced in *Widerstand und Verfolgung in Oberösterreich*, vol. 2, pp. 378–79.

36. Erika Weinzierl, *Zu wenig Gerechte: Österreicher und Judenverfolgung 1938–1945* (Graz, 1969), pp. 39, 62, 158.

37. On 24 July 1942 Hitler confided to his intimates at Führer Headquarters that he "rejoiced that at least Linz is completely clear of Jews." By that time, approximately six hundred Upper Austrian Jews, including Dr. Bloch, had already fled Nazi occupied Europe; the remaining 166 had presumably perished in death camps in the East. So far as it is known, only one man, Michael Hauser, stayed behind to die a natural death as a 73-year-old pensioner on 23 May 1944. Slapnicka, *Oberdonau*, pp. 188–89; Schwager, "Geschichte der Juden," p. 62; and A St Linz, Tagesereignisse (23 May 1944).

38. OÖLA, Pol. Akten, box 29, Gendarmerieposten Kommando Hörsching Nr. 913 an die Bezirkshauptmannschaft in Linz, 30 April 1938.

39. DÖW, doc. 3522: Sperling an den SD Führer, November 1938.

40. DÖW, *Widerstand und Verfolgung in Oberösterreich*, vol. 2, doc. 5, p. 378.

41. Additional evidence of popular support of the Nazi persecution of the Jews in Linz and its environs can be found in Slapnicka, *Oberdonau*, pp. 177–93; Weinzierl, *Zu wenig Gerechte*, pp. 39, 62, 158; and NA, T 175, R 261, F 755761: "Meldungen aus dem Reich," 2 February 1942. Despite the presence of nearby Mauthausen, few people in Linz appear to have had an inkling of the ultimate fate of the Jews. For evidence of persisting anti-Semitism in the Danubian city see Stuhlpfarrer, "Antisemitismus, Rassenpolitik und Judenverfolgung in Österreich nach dem ersten Weltkrieg," p. 143.

42. Slapnicka, *Oberdonau*, p. 282.

43. Ibid., pp. 252–60 and Kershaw, *Popular Opinion and Political Dissent in the Third Reich*, pp. 34–65, 282–96.

44. Slapnicka, *Oberdonau*, pp. 252–60.

45. Ibid., pp. 162–66, 210–11 and OÖLA, Pol. Akten, box 69, doc. O Oe 12/34: Rubesch an das Polizeipräsidium, 27 April 1940.

46. Quoted in Slapnicka, *Oberdonau*, p. 281.

47. Evidence of agricultural discontent in Upper Danube is amply and convincingly documented in DÖW, *Widerstand und Verfolgung in Oberösterreich*, vol. 2, pp. 293–317.

48. OÖLA, Pol. Akten, box 69, doc. O Oe 12/24: SD Abschnitt Linz, 7 March 1941.

49. Luža, *Austro-German Relations*, p. 182; Slapnicka, *Oberdonau*, pp. 194–200; idem, "Die Kirche Oberösterreichs zur Zeit des Nationalsozialismus" in *Das Bistum Linz im Dritten Reich*, ed. Rudolf Zinnhobler (Linz, 1979), pp. 1–12; Kutschera, *Gföllner*, pp. 108–9; *Linzer Volksstimme*, 26 August 1938; and *Völkischer Beobachter* (Wiener Ausgabe) 8 November and 13 December 1938.

50. Even before the signing of the Reich Concordat of 1933, Gföllner's unbending resistance to Nazism had provoked the resentment of Cardinals Buchberger of Regensburg and Faulhaber of Munich-Freising. In a letter to Cardinal State Secretary Pacelli on 10 April 1933, Faulhaber complained that Gföllner's hostility was causing "great damage to clerical authority." Rudolf Zinnhobler, "Die Haltung Bischof Gföllners gegenüber dem Nationalsozialismus" in Zinnhobler, *Das Bistum Linz im Dritten Reich*, pp. 61–73.

51. Kutschera, *Gföllner*, p. 106 and passim.

52. Ibid., p. 113 and *Linzer Volksstimme*, 17 October 1938.

53. Luža, *Austro-German Relations*, p. 188.

54. Slapnicka, "Die Kirche Oberösterreichs zur Zeit des Nationalsozialismus," pp. 14–16.

55. Ibid., p. 15.

56. AVA, Reichskommissar für die Wiedervereinigung Österreichs mit dem Deutschen Reich, box 134, folder 266: Eigruber to Bürckel, 3 November 1938; Luža, "Nazi Control of the Austrian Catholic Church," p. 547; Slapnicka, *Oberdonau*, p. 22 passim; and Kutschera, *Gföllner*, pp. 108–9.

57. Ferdinand Klostermann, "Katholische Jugend im Untergrund," in Zinnhobler, *Das Bistum Linz im Dritten Reich*, p. 144.

58. Ibid., pp. 194–96.

59. Luža, "Nazi Control of the Austrian Catholic Church," pp. 553–59 and idem, *Austro-German Relations*, p. 190.

60. Fliesser to Prelate Jakob Fried, 8 November 1946 in Zinnhobler, *Das Bistum Linz im Dritten Reich*, pp. xv–xvi.

61. Anton Naderer, "Dr. Josef Cal. Fliesser: Bischof von Linz" (diss., University of Vienna, 1972), p. 89 and passim; idem, "Bischof Fliesser und der Nationalsozialismus" in Zinnhobler, *Das Bistum Linz im Dritten Reich*, pp. 87–90; and Slapnicka, *Oberdonau*, pp. 223–24.

62. Slapnicka, *Oberdonau*, pp. 214–19, 223 and idem, "Die Kirche Oberösterreichs zur Zeit des Nationalsozialismus," p. 27.

63. Guenter Lewy, *The Catholic Church and Nazi Germany* (New York, 1964); Ernst Christian Helmreich, *The German Churches under Hitler: Background, Struggle and Epilogue* (Detroit, 1979), pp. 237–301, 347–67; John S. Conway, *The Nazi Persecution of the Churches 1933–45* (New York, 1968), pp. 61–71, 91–92, 125 and passim; and Anthony Rhodes, *The Vatican in the Age of the Dictators 1922–1945* (New York, 1973), pp. 141–53, 161–209 and passim. That the Catholic Church endured greater hardship in Austria, the Sudetenland, and other incorporated areas of Greater Germany than in the Old Reich is mentioned but not thoroughly explored by both Helmreich, pp. 350–52 and Conway, pp. 224–26. Also see Luža, "Nazi Control of the Austrian Catholic Church," pp. 537–72.

64. Gordon C. Zahn, *In Solitary Witness: The Life and Death of Franz Jagerstätter* (New York, 1964), p. 165.

65. Kubizek, *The Young Hitler I Knew*, pp. 89–97.

66. Ibid.

67. Ibid., p. 278.

68. Ibid., p. 86.

69. Jost Dülfer, Jochen Thies, and Josef Henke, *Hitlers Städte: Baupolitik im Dritten Reich* (Cologne, 1978), pp. 254–81.

70. Slapnicka, *Oberdonau*, pp. 66–67.

71. *Hitler's Table Talk*, p. 445 (28 April 1942). For a succinct summary of Hitler's plans for Linz see Robert R. Taylor, *The Word in Stone: The Role of Architecture in the National Socialist Ideology* (Berkeley, 1974), pp. 49–52.

72. In his memoirs Giesler claims to have been entrusted with the entire Linz project. In view of Hitler's habits, it seems more likely that Giesler was one of two or three rivals appointed to carry out the same assignment. That he was charged with revamping the shoreline is indisputable. Cf. Hermann Giesler, *Ein Anderer Hitler: Bericht seines Architect: Erlebnisse, Gespräche, Reflexionen* (Leoni am Starnberger See, 1978), p. 213 and Slapnicka, *Oberdonau*, pp. 62–72.

73. Slapnicka, *Oberdonau*, p. 77.

74. Giesler, *Ein anderer Hitler*, pp. 90–99, especially pp. 96–97 for photographs of wooden models of Hitler's plans.

75. Ibid., pp. 215–16.

76. Speer, *Inside the Third Reich*, p. 99.

77. *Hitler's Table Talk*, p. 322 (20 February 1942).

78. Giesler, *Ein Anderer Hitler*, pp. 98–99 and Slapnicka, *Oberdonau*, pp. 75–77.

79. Giesler, *Ein Anderer Hitler*, pp. 99–103; Slapnicka, *Oberdonau*, pp. 75–77; and Taylor, *The Word in Stone*, pp. 49–52.

80. DÖW, doc. 8363: Gauleitertagung am 7 Mai 1943, 16:00. The transcript of this conference is also available at OÖLA, Pol. Akten, box 66: Vorträge des Gauleiters Eigruber vor dem Führer in Angelegenheit der Planung der Stadt Linz.

81. Giesler, *Ein Anderer Hitler*, pp. 99–103; Slapnicka, *Oberdonau*, pp. 75–77; and Taylor, *The Word in Stone*, pp. 49–52.

82. DÖW, doc. 8363: Besprechung in München am 27 April 1942. Only a fragment of this conversation is published in *Hitler's Table Talk*, p. 447.

83. Slapnicka, *Oberdonau*, pp. 66–78.

84. On this whole subject see Hildegard Brenner, "Der Führerauftrag Linz," in idem, *Die Kunstpolitik des Nationalsozialismus* (Hamburg, 1963), pp. 154ff.

85. Speer, *Inside the Third Reich*, p. 179.

86. Slapnicka, *Oberdonau*, pp. 80–85.

87. Meixner, *Linz*, pp. 9–19. On the Nazi economic integration of the *Ostmark* see Hermann Freudenberger and Radomir Luža, "National Socialist Germany and the Austrian Industry, 1938–1945" in *Austria Since 1945*, ed. William E. Wright (Minneapolis, 1982), pp. 73–100; Luža, *Austro-German Relations*, pp. 192–214; and Felix Butschek, *Die österreichische Wirtschaft 1938 bis 1945* (Stuttgart, 1978). Also see Mason, *Arbeiterklasse und Volksgemeinschaft*, pp. 101–19.

88. Meixner, *Linz*, pp. 9–19.

89. Albert Speer, *Spandau: The Secret Diaries* (New York, 1976), p. 174.

90. Meixner, *Linz*, pp. 18–19.

91. Slapnicka, *Oberdonau*, pp. 125–33.

92. Ibid., pp. 131–34 and Speer, *Spandau*, p. 174. On the Göring Works see Freudenberger and Luža, "National Socialist Germany and the Austrian Industry, 1938–1945," pp. 77–80, 84–87 and Helmut Fiereder, *Die Reichswerke Hermann Göring in Österreich 1938–1945 (Vienna and Salzburg, 1983)*.

93. Slapnicka, *Oberdonau*, pp. 139–40, and Meixner, *Linz*, p. 30.

94. Slapnicka, *Oberdonau*, pp. 174–75.

95. Ibid., pp. 170–74; Meixner, *Männer, Mächte, Betriebe*, p. 396; and idem, *Linz*, pp. 28–31, 59.

96. Meixner, *Linz*, pp. 28–31, 59.

97. Maurice Duverger, *Modern Democracies: Economic Power versus Political Power* (Hillsdale, 1974), p. 110.

98. Slapnicka, *Oberdonau*, pp. 162–66.

99. Ibid., pp. 170–73 and Meixner, *Männer, Mächte, Betriebe*, p. 395.

100. Slapnicka, *Oberdonau*, pp. 164–76.

101. OÖLA, Pol. Akten, box 69, doc. O Oe 12/34: memorandum, 1 July 1940.

102. On Mauthausen see Evelyn Le Cheyne, *Mauthausen: The History of a Death Camp* (London, 1974); Hans Marsalek, *Die Geschichte des Konzentrationslagers Mauthausen* (Vienna, 1974); Gisela Rabitsch, "Das KL Mauthausen" in *Studien zur Geschichte der Konzentrationslager*, ed. Martin Broszat (Stuttgart, 1970); and *Encyclopedia Judaica*, vol. 11, pp. 1137–38.

103. Slapnicka, *Oberdonau*, pp. 226–28.

104. Ibid., pp. 240–46.

105. In this respect, Nazism's impact in Linz was considerably different from neighboring Bavaria. See Kershaw, *Public Opinion and Political Dissent in the Third Reich*, p. 376ff.

106. For an overview see Slapnicka, *Oberdonau*, pp. 279–94. For selected excerpts of the opinion surveys see DÖW, *Widerstand und Verfolgung in Oberösterreich*, vol. 1, pp. 195–99, 364–68; vol. 2, pp. 260–65, 293–99, and 321–30.

107. Slapnicka, *Oberdonau*, pp. 281–82 and DÖW, docs. 4081: Gestapo Linz to Gestapo Berlin, 1 September 1938 and 1449: Gestapo Linz to RSHA, 3 December 1940. Also see Radomir V. Luža, *The Resistance in Austria*, 1938–1945, (Minneapolis, 1984), p. 138.

108. Both quotations in Slapnicka, *Oberdonau*, p. 286. Also see DÖW, doc. 4081.

109. OÖLA, Pol. Akten, box 69, doc. O Oe 12/24: SD Abschnitt Linz, 7 March 1941.

110. NA, T 175, R 258, F 751115: Meldungen aus dem Reich, 27 March 1940.

111. A St Linz, Tonband Sammlung, no. 87, Interview of Josef Wolkerstorfer by Gerhard Botz, 15 March 1971.

112. *Mitteilungsblatt des Gaupropagandaamtes*, Folge 6 (6 July 1941).

113. Slapnicka, *Oberdonau*, pp. 288–89 and OÖLA, Pol. Akten, box 69, doc. 12/20, Bericht des SD Linz, 27 June 1941.

114. Slapnicka, *Oberdonau*, pp. 289–90. A relatively complete file of opinion surveys for the winter 1942–43 can be gleaned from NA, T81, R6–7.

115. On Jägerstätter's life and death see Zahn, *In Solitary Witness*.

116. Fredborg, *Behind the Steel Wall*, p. 187. For another glimpse of the prevailing favorable mood in Linz see Luža, *The Resistance in Austria*, p. 138.

117. Luža, *Austro-German Relations*, pp. 330–39 and Walter Maass, *Country Without a Name: Austria Under Nazi Rule* (New York, 1979), pp. 62–67.

118. For example both works cited in ibid, as well as Hellmuth Andics, *50 Jahre Unseres Lebens: Österreichs Schicksal seit 1918* (Vienna, 1968).

119. Fredborg, *Behind the Steel Wall*, p. 187.

120. Slapnicka, *Oberdonau*, p. 290.

121. NA, T 175, R 265, F 2760052–54: Meldungen aus dem Reich, 2 August 1943.

122. DÖW, docs. 12.316: Akte des Eisenwerke Oberdonau and 1950: Katharina Nöbauer to Herbert Steiner, 22 November 1963.

123. Of the many documents of dissatisfaction, suffering, and persecution published by the DÖW in *Widerstand und Verfolgung in Oberösterreich* comparatively few can be regarded as evidence of organized or systematic opposition. See, however, vol. 1, pp. 119–204. 234–84, and vol. 2, pp. 279–92.

124. For example, compare Kershaw's conclusions in *Popular Opinion and Political Dissent in the Third Reich*, pp. 373–85 to the material organized and analyzed by Botz in DÖW, *Widerstand und Verfolgung in Oberösterreich*, especially vol. 1, pp. 351–544.

125. There are numerous examples of denunciations to the Gestapo by neighbors, workmates, family members, and even lovers in DÖW, *Widerstand und Verfolgung in Oberösterreich*, especially vol. 1, pp. 351–544 and vol. 2, pp. 482–86.

126. DÖW, doc 9337: Urteil des Landesgerichtes, 3 August 1938. The Nazis tried and convicted Gruber for "sexual perversion."

127. DÖW, docs. 9343: Strafsache gegen Anton Baumgartner and 4081: Bericht des SD Linz, 1 September 1938.

128. On the especially significant role played by the Communists in the Austrian Resistance as a whole see Luža, *The Resistance in Austria*, pp. 99–155 and passim.

129. Maass, *Country Without a Name*, pp. 35–36; Slapnicka, *Oberdonau*, p. 262; and DÖW, *Widerstand und Verfolgung in Oberösterreich*, vol. 2, pp. 279–87; and Luža, *The Resistance in Austria*, p. 52.

130. NA, T 175, R 258, F 751018, 11 March 1940.

131. Slapnicka, *Oberdonau*, p. 264.

132. DÖW, docs. 2127 and 2129: Die Linzer Widerstandsgruppe GB; Slapnicka, *Oberdonau*, pp. 265–66; and Luža, *The Resistance in Austria*, pp. 171–73.

133. Kykal and Stadler, *Bernaschek*, pp. 211–16 and Hofer, *Weggefährten*, pp. 18–20ff.

134. DÖW, doc. 2129. According to this document, an account of Italian resistance at the Göring Works was published after the war by three of the principal participants, Marco Cortelazzo, G.B. Bianchini, and W. Guidi, *FG-IMI* (Carrara, 1946). I have been unable to obtain a copy of this book or to corroborate its existence.

135. DÖW, doc. 2199.

136. DÖW, *Widerstand und Verfolgung in Oberösterreich*, vol. 1, pp. 199–205.

137. Ibid., vol. 1, pp. 270–76; Slapnicka, *Oberdonau*, pp. 269–70; and Luža, *The Resistance in Austria*, pp. 201–4.

138. A St Linz, Tagesereignisse and Slapnicka, *Oberdonau*, pp. 310-11ff.

139. Luža, *Austro-German Relations*, p. 341.

140. DÖW, *Widerstand und Verfolgung in Oberösterreich*, vol. 2, doc. 34, p. 330. Also Slapnicka, *Oberdonau*, pp. 292–94.

141. Slapnicka, *Oberdonau*, p. 390.

142. NA; RG 238, Eigruber interrogation. The celebrated Alpine Redoubt was to be a fortified rectangle in western Austria and northern Italy to include the industrial cities of Linz and Steyr. Although the defense system was never constructed, Eigruber appears to have believed in it as much as Eisenhower and the Americans.

143. See Sebastian Haffner, *The Meaning of Hitler* (New York, 1979), pp. 152–53.

144. Slapnicka, *Oberdonau*, pp. 321–40 and Gabriele Hindinger, *Das Kriegsende und der Wiederaufbau demokratischer Verhältnisse in Oberösterreich im Jahre 1945* (Vienna, 1968), pp. 18–27.

145. For example, hear the recollections of former *Gaupropagandaleiter* Rudolf Jirkowsky, A St Linz, Tonbandsammlung, Reel 32, 9 March 1965.

146. Hindinger, *Kriegsende*, pp. 18–19 and Maass, *Country Without a Name*, pp. 147–48.

147. Langoth, *Kampf um Österreich*, pp. 265–67.

148. Hindinger, *Kriegsende*, pp. 39–41; Slapnicka, *Oberdonau*, pp. 338–40; and Franz Danzer, "Die Ersten Maitage des Jahres 1945 in Linz," *Historisches Jahrbuch der Stadt Linz* (1965), pp. 464–65.

149. Danzer, "Die Ersten Maitage," pp. 367–75; Langoth, *Kampf um Österreich*, pp. 268–85; and National Records Center (NRC), Suitland, Maryland, record group 407, entry 427, box 16060: A/A 11th Armored.

150. NRC, RG 407, E 427, box 16060: *The Story of the Eleventh Armored Division* (pamphlet, n.d.): Danzer, "Die Ersten Maitage," pp. 475–77; Langoth, *Kampf um Österreich*, pp. 288–89; Slapnicka, *Oberdonau*, pp. 339–40; and Hindinger, *Kriegsende*, pp. 46–49.

151. Langoth, *Kampf um Österreich*, pp. 288–91 and Hindinger, *Kriegsende*, pp. 59–64.

9. EPILOGUE

1. On conditions in postwar Linz see Hindinger, *Kriegsende*, pp. 85–91; Koref, *Die Gezeiten meines Lebens*, pp. 268–81; Wilhelm Rausch, *Linz 1945* (Linz 1975); Medical Department, U.S. Army, *Preventive Medicine in World War II* (Washington, D.C., 1976), vol. 8, pp. 513–21 passim; and NRC, RG 427, boxes 11245, 11248, 11258, 12465, 12466, 12525, 12505, and 16060.

2. Hindinger, *Kriegsende*, pp. 71–84.

3. Ibid., pp. 91–94; Rausch, *Linz 1945*, pp. 21–32; and Koref, *Die Gezeiten meines Lebens*, pp. 326–29.

4. Kurt Tweraser, "Der Linzer Gemeinderat, 1934–1962: Ständestaat, NS-Regime und die Ära Koref," *Historisches Jahrbuch der Stadt Linz* (1983), p. 173 and Koref, *Die Gezeiten meines Lebens*, pp. 283, 326–29.

5. On the clumsy American occupation of Linz and its limited impact on the city's development see Kurt Tweraser, "Neither Revolution nor Restoration: Linz and Upper Austria under American Occupation, 1945–48," paper presented at the Eighth Annual Conference of the German Studies Association, Denver, Colorado, 12 October 1984.

6. Tweraser, "Linzer Gemeinderat, 1934–1962," p. 174.

7. Ibid.; Naderer, "Dr. Josef Cal. Fliesser," pp. 202–10; and Luža, *The Resistance in Austria*, p. 188. On the difficulties experienced by Koref in convincing rank and file Socialists to accept Gleissner's conversion to democracy see Koref, *Die Gezeiten meines Lebens*, p. 328.

8. Hindinger, *Kriegsende*, pp. 161–69.

9. Ibid., pp. 161–69; *St. Jahrbuch der Stadt Linz 1946*, pp. 185–92 and John Mair, "Austria," in Survey of International Affairs, *Four Power Control in Germany and Austria 1945–1946* (Oxford, 1956), pp. 319–24.

10. Tweraser, "Linzer Gemeinderat, 1934–1962," pp. 182–83.

11. Ibid., pp. 184–88.

12. On the American role in the revitalization of heavy industry in Linz see *Military Government in Austria: Report of the United States Commissioner*, no. 1 (Nov. 1945), pp. 88–97; no. 2 (Dec. 1945), pp. 64–65; no. 3 (Jan. 1946), p. 64; no. 4 (Feb. 1946), p. 71–72; no. 5 (Mar. 1946), pp. 82–87; no. 6 (Apr. 1946), p. 96; no. 13 (Nov. 1946), pp. 134–47 and Federal Chancellery, Vienna, *Austria and the ERP*, Eighth Quarterly Report (1950), pp. 28, 50; Ninth Q. R. (1950), pp. 13–17; Tenth Q. R. (1950), pp. 17–21; Eleventh Q. R. (1951), pp. 17–19; Twelfth Q. R. (1951), pp. 11, 13; Thirteenth Q. R. (1951), pp. 12–15; Seventeenth Q. R. (1952), pp. 12–13; Eighteenth Q. R. (1952–53), pp. 13–15; and Nineteenth Q. R. (1953), p. 19.

13. Tweraser, "Linzer Gemeinderat, 1934–1962," pp. 188–93, 211–12.

14. Stephan Koren, "Monetary and Budget Policy," in *Modern Austria*, ed. Kurt Steiner (Palo Alto, 1981), p. 176.

15. Tweraser, "Linzer Gemeinderat, 1934–1962," p. 189–90.

16. Ibid., pp. 194–95 and Luža, *Austro-German Relations*, pp. 354–58. On the VdU see Max E. Riedelsperger, *The Lingering Shadow of Nazism: The Austrian Independent Party Movement Since 1945* (Boulder, 1978).

17. Tweraser, "Linzer Gemeinderat, 1934–1962," pp. 196–99.

18. Whether the October strikes constituted the birth pangs of an aborted Communist coup remains an open question, but see Richard Hiscocks, *The Rebirth of Austria* (Oxford, 1953), pp. 224–32 and William B. Bader, *Austria Between East and West* (Stanford, 1966), pp. 155–83. For a more balanced assessment see Manfred Rauchensteiner, *Der Sonderfall: Die Besatzungszeit in Österreich 1945 bis 1955* (Graz, Vienna, and Cologne, 1979), pp. 288–97.

19. This is reluctantly conceded by the fiercely anti-Communist Koref, *Die Gezeiten meines Lebens*, pp. 300–301. For a full account of the leading role of the VdU in the disturbances in Linz see Tweraser, "Linzer Gemeinderat, 1934–1962," pp. 200–206.

20. Hiscocks, *The Rebirth of Austria*, pp. 226–27 and Tweraser, "Linzer Gemeinderat, 1934–1962," pp. 200–206.

21. On economic developments in postwar Austria see K. W. Rothschild, *The Austrian Economy Since 1945* (London, 1950); Franz Heissenberger, *The Economic Reconstruction of Austria 1945–1952* (Washington, D. C., 1953); Gottfried Haberler, *Austria's Economic Development: A Mirror of the World Economy* (Washington, D.C., 1980); and the essays by Eduard März, Felix Butschek, Ferdinand Lacina, Stephan Koren, and Maria Szecsi in Steiner, *Modern Austria*, pp. 121–201.

22. Tweraser, "Linzer Gemeinderat, 1934–1962," p. 212.

BIBLIOGRAPHY

1. DOCUMENTS AND MANUSCRIPTS

Allgemeines Verwaltungsarchiv (AVA), Vienna
    Bundeskanzleramt (BKA), Inneres (I),
        20/0 Oest, boxes 4204–6, 4217–18, 4227, 4229.
        22/0 Oest, boxes 5099–5119.
        31/0 Oest, box 5517.
        VIe Justiz/NSDAP, boxes 9208/4, 9241/3.
        Militärverband der Republik Österreich, boxes 4–5.
        N S Parteistelle, boxes 6–7.
        Reichskommissar für die Wiedervereinigung Österreichs mit dem Deutschen
            Reich, box 134.
        SD Parteistelle, boxes 33–4, 36, 64–5.
Archiv der Stadt Linz (A St Linz), Linz
    Chronik der Judenschule.
    Sitzungsprotokolle des Gemeinderates der Landeshauptstadt Linz,
        1923–1938.
    Statististische Vierteljahresberichte, 1922–1932.
    Tagesereignisse.
    Tonband Sammlung, reels 32–3, 87.
Berlin Document Center (BDC), West Berlin
    Nationalsozialistische Kartei.
    Oberste Parteigericht (OPG).
    Parteikanzlei-Korrespondenz (PK).
    SS-Führer (SS).
Dokumentationsarchiv des österreichischen Widerstandes (DÖW), Vienna
    Documents 12, 118, 316, 441, 1321, 1401, 1449, 1460, 1549, 1950, 1952,
        2127, 2129, 2162, 2507, 2574, 2883, 2923, 2947–8, 3165, 3522, 3678,
        3691, 3732, 4081, 4294, 4401, 4660, 4716, 1996, 5028, 5281, 5322, 6029,
        6155, 6165, 6173, 6365–76, 6629, 6688, 6720, 6744, 6895, 7323, 7343,
        7356, 7510, 8328, 8357–63, 8367, 8381, 8384, 8387, 8409, 8414, 8440,
        9281, 9307–29, 9336–37, 9340, 9343, 11.080, 11.473, 12.055–130,
        12.200, 12.316, 12.637, 12.833–4, 12.845, 12.893, 13.110, 14.899.
National Archives (NA), Washington, D.C.
    Microcopy T-580, Non Biographical Records of the Berlin Document Center,
        Schumacher Material, reels 60–63.
    Record Group 238, interrogation of August Eigruber.
    World War II Collection of Seized Enemy Records:
        a) Records filmed at Alexandria, Virginia,
            microcopy T-81, Records of the National Socialist German Labor
                Party, reels 6–7
            microcopy T-175, Reichsführer SS and the German Police, reels 10,
                72, 124, 258–66.
        b) Records filmed at Whaddon Bucks, England,
            microcopy T-120, Records of the German Foreign Office, reels 3394,
                4621, 4626, 4633, 4638.
National Records Center (NRC), Suitland, Maryland
    Record Group 407, Records of the Adjutant General's Office, entry 427, box
        16060.

Oberösterreichisches Landesarchiv (OÖLA), Linz
  Politische Akten, 1933–1945, boxes, 20–22, 29, 66, 69, 74–77.
Stanford University, Palo Alto
  Hoover Institution Microfilm Collection, NSDAP Hauptarchiv, reels 33–34.

2. NEWSPAPERS AND CONTEMPORARY PERIODICALS

*Der christlich-deutsche Student: Mitteilungsblatt des christlich-deutschen Stu-
  dentenbundes für Oberösterreich*, 1930–33.
Deutsche Arbeiter Presse, 14 January 1934.
Deutscher Volksruf: Alpenländisches Wochenblatt für die arbeitenden Stände,
  1914–23, 1927–30.
*Kaufmannische Nachrichten für den Wirtschaftsbezirk Oberdonau: Mitteilungs-
  blatt der Abteilung Handel der Wirtschaftskammer Oberdonau*, 1932–42.
Linzer Diözesanblatt, vols. 65–85, 1919–39.
Linzer Heimatblatt: Parteiamtliches Blatt der NSDAP, 1938–39.
Linz, Tagblatt, 1919–34, 1945–46.
Linz, Tagespost, 1919–38.
Linzer Volksblatt, 1945–46.
Linzer Volksstimme (after 1926, *Die Volksstimme*), 1923–32, 1938.
Manchester Guardian, 15 March 1938.
Mitteilungen des d.v. Turnvereines Urfahr, 1925–38.
Mitteilungen des Handelsgremiums der Landeshauptstadt Linz.
Mitteilungen des oberösterreichischen Handels und Gewerbebundes, vols. 1–3,
  1929–31.
Mitteilungen für die Vertrauensleute des katholischen Volksvereines, 1930.
Mitteilungen: Wohlfahrtsvereinigung der Glasenbacher, 1957–78.
Mitteilungsblatt des Gaupropagandaamtes, 1941–42.
Nachrichtendienst des DHV-V.d.w.A.: Kreisleitung Oberösterreich, Linz, I, 1934.
New York Times, 24 August 1933, 13–14 March 1938.
*Oberösterreichische Arbeiterzeitung: Wochenblatt des katholischen Ar-
  beiterbundes und der Landeskommission der christichlen Gewerkschaften
  Oberösterreichs*, 1926–34.
*Oberösterreichische Lehrerzeitung: Monatsschrift der freien Lehrergewerkschaft
  Landesgruppe Oberösterreich*, vols. 1–8, 1926–33.
Österreichischer Beobachter: Organ der NSDAP in Österreich, vols. 1–4,
  1936–40.
*Starhemberg Jäger: Kampforgan der Heimatwehr Oberösterreichs und der
  heimattreuen Österreicher aller Bundesländer*, vols. 1 and 2, 1930–31.
The Times, 14 March 1938.
Vaterländische Front: Mitteilungsblatt der VF Oberösterreich, 1935–37.
*Verhandlungsschriften der Vollversammlungen der Kammer für Handel, Gewerbe
  und Industrie in Linz*, 1931–35.
Völkischer Beobachter (Wiener Ausgabe), 1938–40.
Volksvereinsbote, 1924–35.
Zeitschrift des O Oe Landes-Lehrerverein 1867, vols. 61–65, 1929–33.

3. INTERVIEWS

Dr. Josef Stöger, 26 June 1975.
Josef Wolkerstorfer, 28 July 1978.

4. GENERAL

Ackerl, Isabella. "Das Kampfbündnis der Nationalsozialistischen Deutschen Arbeiterpartei mit der Grossdeutschen Volkspartei vom 15. Mai 1933." In *Das Jahr 1934: 25 Juli*, edited by Rudolf Neck and Adam Wandruszka (Vienna, 1975), pp. 21–35.

Amtskalender für das Gau Oberdonau, vols. 80–82 (Linz, 1939–42).

Andics, Hellmut. *50 Jahre unseres Lebens: Österreichs Schicksal seit 1918* (Vienna, 1968).

———. *Der Stadt den Keiner wollte: Österreich von der Gründung der Republik bis zur Moskauer Deklaration* (Vienna and Munich, 1976).

———. *Der Untergang der Donau Monarchie: Österreich-Ungarn von der Jahrhundertwende bis zum November 1918* (Vienna, 1974).

Austria. *Austria and the ERP* (Vienna, 1950–53).

———. Bundesamt für Statistik. *Statistisches Handbuch für die Republik Österreich*, vols. 1–18 (Vienna, 1920–38).

———. Bundeskanzleramt für Heimatdienst, *The Death of Dollfuss: An Official History of the Revolt of July 1934 in Austria* (London, 1935).

Autorenkollektiv der Historischen Kommission beim ZK der KPÖ. *Geschichte der Kommunistischen Partei Österreichs—Kurzer Abriss* (Vienna, 1977).

Bader, William B. *Austria Between East and West* (Stanford, 1966).

Banuls, Andre. "Das völkische Blatt der Scherer: Ein Beitrag zu Hitlers Schulzeit." *Vierteljahrshefte für Zeitgeschichte*, 18 (1970): 196–203.

Bärnthaler, Irmgard. *Die Vaterländische Front: Geschichte und Organisation* (Vienna, 1971).

Barker, Elizabeth. *Austria* (Coral Gables, 1973).

Barraclough, Geoffrey. "A New View of German History." *New York Review of Books*, 16 November 1972: 25–32.

Bart, Richard and Puffer, Emil. *Die Gemeindevertretung der Stadt Linz vom Jahre 1848 bis zur Gegenwart* (Linz, 1968).

Bauer, Otto. *The Austrian Revolution* (London, 1925).

Berger, Barbara. "Ernst Rüdiger Fürst Starhemberg: Versuch einer Biographie" (diss., Vienna, 1967).

Bernaschek, Richard. "Die Tragödie der österreichischen Sozialdemokratie." In *Österreich: Brandherd Europas* (Zurich, 1934): pp. 257–99.

Bernbaum, John A. "Nazi Control in Austria: The Creation of the Ostmark, 1938–1940" (diss., University of Maryland, 1972).

———. "The New Elite: Nazi Leadership in Austria, 1939–1945." *Austrian History Yearbook* 14 (1978): 145–60.

Black, Peter R. *Ernst Kaltenbrunner: Ideological Soldier of the Third Reich* (Princeton, 1984).

Bock, Wilhelm. "Wir und die Judenfrage." *Der christlich-deutsche Student: Mitteilungsblatt des christlich-deutschen Studentenbundes für Oberösterreich*, 20 Dezember 1930.

Botz, Gerhard. "Die Ausschaltung des Nationalrates und die Anfänge der Diktatur Dollfuss im Urteil der Geschichtesschreibung von 1933 bis 1973." In *Vierzig Jahre Danach: Der 4. März im Urteil von Zeitgenossen und Historikern*, edited by Anton Benya et al. (Vienna, 1974), pp. 31–59.

———. "The Changing Patterns of Social Support for Austrian National Socialism (1918–1945)." In *Who Were the Fascists? Social Roots of European Fascism*, edited by Stein Ugelvik Larsen et al. (Bergen, 1980), pp. 202–25.

———. "Comments." *Austrian History Yearbook* 14 (1978): 179–80.

_____. *Die Eingliederung Österreichs in das Deutsche Reich: Plannung und Verwirklichung des politisch-administrativen Anschluss* (1938–1940) (Vienna, 1976).

_____. "Faschismus und Lohnabhängige in der Ersten Republik: Zur "sozialer Basis" und propagandistischen Orientierung von Heimwehr und Nationalsozialismus." *Österreich in Geschichte und Literatur* 21, 2 (March–April 1977): 102–28.

_____. "Der '15. Juli 1927' seine Ursachen und Folgen." In *Österreich 1927 bis 1938: Protokoll des Symposiums in Wien 23. bis 28. Oktober 1972,*" edited by Rudolf Neck and Adam Wandruszka (Munich, 1972), pp. 31–42.

_____. *Gewalt in der Politik: Attentate, Zusammenstösse, Putschversuche in Österreich 1918–1934* (Munich, 1976).

_____. "Hitlers Aufenthalt in Linz in März 1938 und der Anschluss." *Historisches Jahrbuch der Stadt Linz* (1971), pp. 185–214.

_____. "Strukturwandlungen des Österreichischen Nationalsozialismus (1904–1945)." In *Politik und Gesellschaft im alten und neuen Österreich: Festschrift für Rudolf Neck zum 60. Geburtstag,* edited by Isabella Ackerl et al. (Munich, 1981), vol. 2, pp. 195–218.

_____. *Wien vom "Anschluss" zum Krieg: Nationalsozialistische Machtübernahme und politisch-soziale Umgestaltung am Beispiel der Stadt Wien 1938–39* (Munich, 1978).

Boyer, John W. *Political Radicalism in Late Imperial Vienna—Origins of the Christian Social Movement 1848–1897* (Chicago, 1981).

Bracher, Karl Dietrich. *The German Dictatorship: The Origins, Structures, and Effects of National Socialism* (New York, 1970).

Braunthal, Julius. *History of the International,* 2 vols. (New York, 1967).

Brenner, Hildegard. "Der Führerauftrag Linz." In *Die Kunstpolitik des Nationalsozialmus,* edited by Hildegard Brenner (Hamburg, 1963).

Bukey, Evan B. "Hitler's Hometown under Nazi Rule: Linz, Austria, 1938–1945." *Central European History,* 16, 2 (June 1983): 171–86.

_____. "The Nazi Party in Linz, Austria, 1919–1939: A Sociological Perspective." *German Studies Review,* 1 (October 1978): 302–26.

Bund der österreichischen Industriellen, Landesverband für Oberösterreich. *Bericht über das Jahr 1936* (Linz, 1936).

Bundespolizeidirektion Linz. *Jahrbuch der Bundespolizeidirektion in Linz a. D. mit Statitischen Daten aus den Jahren 1927 bis 1931* (Linz, 1932).

Butschek, Felix. *Die österreichische Wirtschaft 1938 bis 1945* (Stuttgart, 1978).

Buttinger, Josef. *In the Twilight of Socialism: A History of the Revolutionary Socialists of Austria* (New York, 1953).

Carsten, F.L. *Fascist Movements in Austria: From Schönerer to Hitler* (London and Beverly Hills, 1977).

_____. *Revolution in Central Europe 1918–1919* (Berkeley, 1972).

The Catholic Encyclopedia (New York, 1913).

Christlicher Landesverein für Oberösterreich. *60 Jahre Christlicher Landeslehrerverein für Oberösterreich, 1898–1958* (Reid, 1958).

Conway, John S. *The Nazi Persecution of the Churches, 1933–45* (New York, 1968).

Dahrendorf, Ralf. *Society and Democracy in Germany* (New York, 1967).

Danzer, Franz. "Die Ersten Maitage des Jahres 1945 in Linz." *Historisches Jahrbuch der Stadt Linz* (1965): 464–77.

Deutsch, Heidrun. "Franziska Fürstin Starhemberg" (diss., Vienna, 1967).

Deutsch, Karl W. *Nationalism and its Alternatives* (New York, 1969).

Diamant, Alfred. *Austrian Catholics and the First Republic: Democracy, Capitalism and the Social Order, 1918–1923* (Princeton, 1960).

Doblhamer, Gerhard. *Die Stadtplanung in Oberösterreich von 1850 bis 1938* (Vienna and New York, 1972).

Dokumentationsarchiv des österreichischen Widerstandes. *Widerstand und Verfolgung in Burgenland 1934–1945: Eine Dokumentation* (Vienna, 1979).

————. *Widerstand und Verfolgung in Oberösterreich 1934–1946: Eine Dokumentation*, 2 vols. (Vienna, 1982).

————. *Widerstand und Verfolgung in Wien 1934–1945: Eine Dokumentation*, 3 vols. (Vienna, 1975).

Domarus, Max. *Hitler: Reden und Proklamationen 1932–1945*, 4 vols. (Wiesbaden, 1973).

Duczynska, Ilona. *Workers in Arms: The Austrian Civil War of 1934* (New York, 1978).

Dülfer, Jost; Thies, Jochen; and Henke, Joseph. *Hitlers Städte: Baupolitik im Dritten Reich* (Cologne, 1978).

Duverger, Maurice. *Modern Democracies: Economic Power versus Political Power* (Hillsdale, 1974).

Edmondson, C. Earl. *The Heimwehr and Austrian Politics* (Athens, Georgia, 1978).

Eigruber, August. *Ein Gau wächst ins Reich: Das Werden Oberdonaus im Spiegel der Reden des Gauleiters August Eigruber* (Wels, 1941).

Encyclopedia Britannica, 9th and 11th editions.

Encyclopedia Judaica, 16 vols. (Jerusalem, 1971).

Fendt, Josef. "Die Textilindustrie Oberösterreichs: Untersuchung über die Entwicklung, Bedeutung und strukturelle Verhältnisse eines Industriezweiges" (diss., Vienna, 1975).

Fiereder, Helmut. *Die Reichswerke Hermann Göring in Österreich (1938–1945)* (Vienna and Salzburg, 1983).

————. "Der Republikanische Schutzbund in Linz und die Kampfhandlungen im Februar 1934." *Historisches Jahrbuch der Stadt Linz* (1978).

Fischer, Ernst. *An Opposing Man* (New York, 1974).

Fischer-Galati, Stephen. "Fascism in Eastern Europe." In *Who Were the Fascists? Social Roots of European Fascism*, edited by Stein Ugelvik Larsen et al. (Bergen, 1980), pp. 350–417.

Fredborg, Avrid. *Behind the Steel Wall: A Swedish Journalist in Berlin* (New York, 1944).

Freudenberger, Hermann and Luža Radomir,. "National Socialist Germany and the Austrian Industry, 1938–1945." In *Austria Since 1945*, edited by William E. Wright (Minneapolis, 1982), pp. 73–100.

Fuchs, Martin. *Showdown in Vienna: The Death of Austria* (New York, 1939).

Gamsjäger, Helmut. "Dr. Josef Schlegel: Landeshauptmann von Oberösterreich und Präsident des Rechnungshofes" (unpublished seminar paper (SE224) IfZ, Vienna).

Garscha, Winfried and Hautmann, Hans. *Februar 1934 in Österreich* (Berlin [East], 1984).

Gauleitung der NSDAP Oberdonau. *Politischer Informationsdienst* (Linz, 1940–41).

Gedye, G.E.R. *Betrayal in Central Europe, Austria and Czechoslovakia: The Fallen Bastions* (New York, 1939).

Gehl, Jürgen. *Austria, Germany and the Anschluss* (New York, 1963).

Giesler, Hermann. *Ein Anderer Hitler: Bericht seines Architect: Erlebnisse, Gespräche, Reflexionen* (Leoni am Starnberger See, 1978).

Goldinger, Walter, ed. *Protokolle des Klubvorstandes der Christlichsozialen Partei 1932–1934* (Vienna, 1980).

Goudsblom, Johann. *Dutch Society* (New York, 1967).

Grill, Georg. *Das Linzer Burgermeisterbuch* (Linz, 1959).

Gruber, Oswald. "Die Stellung der politischen Parteien und Räte Oberösterreichs in den Jahren 1918–19" (unpublished paper, SE850, IfZ, Vienna).

Guderian, Heinz. *Panzer Leader* (New York, 1952).

Gulick, Charles A. *Austria from Habsburg to Hitler*, 2 vols. (Berkeley and Los Angeles, 1948).

Gutland, E.A. *Urban Development in the Alpine and Scandinavian Countries* (New York, 1965).

Haberler, Gottfried. *Austria's Economic Development: A Mirror of the World Economy* (Washington, D.C., 1980).

Haffner, Sebastian. *The Meaning of Hitler* (New York, 1979).

Hanisch, Ernst. "'Gau der Guten Nerven': Die Nationalsozialistische Herrschaft in Salzburg 1939/40." In *Politik und Gesellschaft im alten und neuen Österreich: Festschrift für Rudolf Neck zum 60. Geburtstag*, edited by Isabella Ackerl (Munich, 1981), vol. 2, pp. 195–218.

_____. *Nationalsozialistische Herrschaft in der Provinz: Salzburg im Dritten Reich* (Salzburg, 1983).

_____. "Zur Frühgeschichte des Nationalsozialismus in Salzburg (1913–1925)." *Mitteilungen der Gesellschaft für Salzburger Landeskunde*, 117: 371–410.

Hausner, Gideon. *Justice in Jerusalem* (New York, 1966).

Hautmann, Hans. *Die Verlorene Räterepublik: Am Beispiel der Kommunistischen Partei Deutschösterreichs* (Vienna, 1977).

Hautmann, Hans and Kropf, Rudolf. *Die österreichische Arbeiterbewegung vom Vormärz bis 1945: Sozialökonomische Ursprünge ihrer Ideologie und Politik* (Vienna, 1974).

Heffter, Heinrich. *Die Deutsche Selbstverwaltung im 19. Jahrhundert: Geschichte der Ideen und Institutionen* (Stuttgart, 1950).

Heimatschutz in Österreich (Vienna, 1934).

Heissenberger, Franz. *The Economic Reconstruction of Austria 1945–1952* (Washington, D.C., 1953).

Helmreich, Ernst Christian. *The German Churches under Hitler: Background, Struggle and Epilogue* (Detroit, 1969).

Hertz, Frederick. *The Economic Problem of the Danubian States: A Study in Economic Nationalism* (New York, 1970).

Hindinger, Gabriele. *Das Kriegsende und der Wiederaufbau demokratischer Verhältnisse in Oberösterreich im Jahre 1945* (Vienna, 1968).

Hiscocks, Richard. *The Rebirth of Austria* (Oxford, 1953).

Hitler, Adolf. *Mein Kampf* (New York, 1939).

Hofer, Josef. *Weggefährten: Von österreichischen Freiheitskampf 1933–1945* (Vienna, 1946).

Holtmann, Everhard. *Zwischen Unterdrückung und Befriedung: Sozialistische Arbeiterbewegung und autoritäres Regime in Österreich 1933–1938* (Munich, 1978).

Honeder, Josef. *Johann Nepomuk Hauser: Landeshauptmann von Oberösterreich* (Linz, 1973).

Houston, W. R. "Ernst Kaltenbrunner: A Study of an Austrian SS and Police Leader" (diss., Rice University, 1972).

Hubbard, William H. "Politics and Society in the Central European City: Graz, Austria, 1861–1918." *Canadian Journal of History* 5, 1 (March, 1970): 25–45.

――――. "A Social History of Graz, Austria, 1861–1914" (diss., Columbia University, 1973).

Huemer, Peter. "Die Ereignisse in den Bundesländern nach dem Brand des Wiener Justizpalastes" (unpublished paper, SE 291, IfZ, Vienna).

――――. *Sektionschef Robert Hecht und die Zerstörung der Demokratie in Österreich: Eine historisch-politische Studie* (Munich, 1975).

Jagschitz, Gerhard. *Der Putsch: Die Nationalsozialisten 1934 in Österreich* (Graz, 1976).

――――. "Zwischen Befriedung und Konfrontation: Zur Lage der NSDAP in Österreich 1934 bis 1936." In *Das Juliabkommen von 1936: Hintergründe und Folgen: Protokolle des Symposiums in Wien am 10. und 11. Juli 1976*, edited by Ludwig Jedlicka and Rudolf Neck (Munich, 1977).

Jedlicka, Ludwig. "Gauleiter Josef Leopold." In *Geschichte und Gesellschaft: Festschrift für Karl R. Stadler zum 60. Geburtstag*, edited by Gerhard Botz et al. (Vienna, 1974), pp. 143–61.

――――. *Der 20. Juli in Österreich* (Vienna, 1966).

Jetzinger, Franz. *Hitler's Youth* (London, 1958).

Joes, Anthony James. *Fascism in the Contemporary World: Ideology, Evolution, Resurgence* (Boulder, 1978).

Kandl, Eleanore. "Hitlers Österreichbild" (diss., Vienna, 1963).

Kater, Michael H. *The Nazi Party: A Social Profile of Members and Leaders, 1919–1945* (Cambridge, Mass., 1983).

Katzenstein, Peter J. *Disjoined Partners: Austria and Germany Since 1815* (Berkeley, 1976).

Kern, Felix. *Oberösterreichischer Bauern und Kleinhäuslerbund*, 2 vols. (Ried, 1956).

Kershaw, Ian. "The Persecution of the Jews and German Popular Opinion in the Third Reich." In *Yearbook XXVI*, edited by the Leo Baeck Institute (London, 1981), pp. 261–89.

――――. *Popular Opinion and Political Dissent in the Third Reich: Bavaria 1933–1945* (Oxford, 1983).

Kitchen, Martin. *The Coming of Austrian Fascism* (London and Montreal, 1980).

Klemperer, Klemens von. *Ignaz Seipel: Christian Statesman in a Time of Crisis* (Princeton, 1972).

Klingenstein, Grete. "Bemerkungen zum Problem des Faschismus in Österreich." *Österreich in Geschichte und Literatur* 14, 1 (1970): 1–13.

Klostermann, Ferdinand. "Katholische Jugend im Untergrund." In *Das Bistrum Linz im Dritten Reich*, edited by Rudolf Zinnhobler (Linz, 1979), pp. 138–92.

Kluge, Ulrich. *Der österreichische Ständestaat: Entstehung und Scheitern* (Vienna, 1984).

Kollman, Eric C. *Theodor Körner: Militär und Politik* (Munich, 1973).

Konrad, Helmut. *Die Anfänge der Arbeiterbewegung in Oberösterreich* (Linz, 1980).

Koref, Ernst. *Die Gezeiten meines Lebens* (Munich, 1980).

Koren, Stephan. "Monetary and Budget Policy." In *Modern Austria*, edited by Kurt Steiner (Palo Alto, 1981), pp. 173–83.

Kreissler, Felix. *Der Österreicher und seine Nation: Ein Lernprozess mit*

Hindernissen (Vienna, Cologne, Graz, 1984).

Kren, Trude. "Letter to the Editor." *Der Spiegel* 32, 7 (13 February 1978): 8.

Kropf, Rudolf. *Oberösterreichs Industrie (1873–1938): Ökonomisch-strukturelle Aspekte einer regionalen Industrieentwicklung* (Linz, 1981).

Kubizek, August. *The Young Hitler I Knew* (Cambridge, 1955).

Kulczycki, Werner. "Burgermeister Josef Dametz." *Historisches Jahrbuch der Stadt Linz* (1976): 183–219.

Kutschera, Richard. *Johannes Maria Gföllner: Bischof dreier Zeitenwenden* (Linz, 1972).

Kykal, Inez and Stadler, Karl. *Richard Bernaschek: Odysee eines Rebellen* (Vienna, 1976).

Lack, Dagmar. "Die Entwicklung der Heimwehr in Oberösterreich" (unpublished paper, IfZ, Vienna).

Langoth, Franz. *Kampf um Österreich: Erinnerungen eines Politikers* (Wels, 1951).

Le Cheyne, Evelyn. *Mauthausen: The History of a Death Camp* (London, 1974).

Lerner, Daniel. "The Nazi Elite." In *World Revolutionary Elites: Studies in Coercive Ideological Movements*, edited by Harold D. Laswell and Daniel Lerner (Cambridge, Mass. 1965).

Leser, Norbert. *Zwischen Reformismus und Bolschewismus: Der Austromarxismus als Theorie und Praxis* (Vienna, 1968).

Lewy, Guenter. *The Catholic Church and Nazi Germany* (New York, 1964).

Lijphardt, Arend. "Consociational Democracy." *World Politics*, 21, 2 (January 1969): 206–25.

Linz, Juan L. "Some Notes toward a Comparative Study of Fascism in Sociological Historical Perspective." In *Fascism: A Reader's Guide: Analysis, Interpretations, Bibliography* (Berkeley, 1976), pp. 3–121.

———. *The Breakdown of Democratic Regimes: Crisis, Breakdown, and Reequilibration* (Baltimore, 1978).

Linz (Austria). *Amtsblatt der Landeshauptstadt Linz.*

———. *Kammer für Arbeiter und Angestellte. Verzeichnis jener Betriebe in Oberösterreich (Gerwerbe, Handel, und Bergbau) welche über 5 Arbeiter und Angestelltenbeschäftigen gereiht nach Branchen Bezirkshauptmannschaften und Ortsgemeinden nach dem Stande vom 1. Juli 1935* (Linz, 1935).

———. *Statistisches Jahrbuch der Stadt Linz* (1946–59).

———. *Die Wohnverhältnisse in Linz: Beiträge zur Statistik der Gauhauptstadt Linz* (Linz, 1943).

Litschel, Rudolf Walter. *1934—Das Jahr der Irrungen* (Linz, 1974).

Lochner, Louis, ed. *The Goebbels Diaries, 1942–1943* (New York, 1948).

Lukacs, John. *The Last European War* (New York, 1976).

Luža, Radomir. *Austro-German Relations in the Anschluss Era* (Princeton, 1975).

———. "Nazi Control of the Austrian Catholic Church, 1939–1941." *The Catholic Historical Review*, 63 (1977): 537–72.

———. *The Resistance in Austria, 1938–1945* (Minneapolis, 1984).

Maass, Walter. *Country Without a Name: Austria Under Nazi Rule* (New York, 1979).

Maier, Charles S. *Recasting Bourgeois Europe: Stabilization in France, Germany and Italy in the Decade after World War I* (Princeton, 1975).

Mair, John. "Austria." In *Four Power Control in Germany and Austria 1945–1946: Survey of International Affairs* (Oxford, 1956).

März, E., and Weissel, E. "Die Bedeutung und Entwicklung der Arbeiterkammern in der Ersten Republik." In *Verbände und Wirtschaftspolitik in Österreich*, edited by Theodor Pütz (Berlin, 1966).

Maser, Werner. *Hitler's Letters and Notes* (New York, 1974).

Matzerath, Horst and Volkmann, Heinrich. "Modernisierungstheorien und Nationalsozialismus." In *Theorien in der Praxis des Historikers* (Göttingen, 1977), pp. 86–116.

Marsalek, Hans. *Die Geschichte des Konzentrationslagers Mauthausen* (Vienna, 1974).

Mason, Timothy W. *Arbeiterklasse und Volksgemeinschaft: Dokumente und Materialen zur deutschen Arbeiterpolitik 1936–1939* (Opladen, 1975).

Mateja, Robert. "Oberösterreich im I. Weltkrieg" (diss., Innsbruck, 1948).

May, Arthur. *The Hapsburg Monarchy* (Cambridge, 1951).

――――. *The Passing of the Hapsburg Monarchy 1914–1918*, 2 vols. (Philadelphia, 1966).

Mayrhofer, Fritz. "Franz Dinghofer: Leben und Wirken (1873 bis 1956)." *Historisches Jahrbuch der Stadt Linz* (1966): 11–152.

Meixner, Erich Maria. "Die Entwicklungstendenzen von Industrie, Gewerbe und Handel in Linz, 1858–1958." *Statistisches Jahrbuch der Stadt Linz—1958* (Linz, 1959).

――――. *Linz, 1945–1960: Industrie, Gewerbe, Handel, Verkehr, Fremdenverkehr, Geldwesen* (Linz, 1962).

――――. *Männer, Mächte, Betriebe* (Salzburg, 1952).

Merkl, Peter. *Political Violence under the Swastika: 581 Early Nazis (Princeton, 1975)*.

Moore, Barrington, Jr., *Social Origins of Dictatorship and Democracy* (London, 1967).

Moser, Jonny. *Die Judenverfolgung in Österreich 1938–1945* (Vienna, 1966).

Naderer, Anton. "Dr. Josef Cal. Fliesser: Bischof von Linz" (diss., Vienna, 1972).

――――. "Bischof Fliesser und der Nationalsozialismus." In *Das Bistum Linz im Dritten Reich*, edited by Rudolf Zinnhobler (Linz, 1979), pp. 74–107.

Neck, Rudolf. "Simmering—16. Oktober 1932: Vorspiel zum Burgerkrieg." In *Vom Justizpalast zum Heldenplatz*, edited by Ludwig Jedlicka and Rudolf Neck (Vienna, 1975), pp. 94–102.

Neck, Rudolf and Jedlicka, Ludwig, eds. *Das Jahr 1934: 25. Juli: Protokoll des Symposiums in Wien am 8. Oktober 1974* (Munich, 1975).

Neck, Rudolf and Wandruszka, Adam, eds. *Die Ereignisse des 15. Juli 1927: Protokoll des Symposiums in Wien am 15. Juli 1977* (Vienna, 1979).

NSDAP. *Heimatblatt: Parteiamtliches Blatt der NSDAP für Linz, das Mühlviertel und den Böhmerwald* (1940).

NSDAP, DAF Gauverwaltung Oberdonau. *Leistungskampf der deutschen Betriebe, 1940–41* (Linz, 1941).

NS Lehrerbund, *Der Erzieher im Gau Oberdonau* (Linz, 1939).

Oberösterreichischer Landeslehrerverein. *70. Jahre Oberösterreicher Landeslehrerverein 1867* (Linz, 1937).

Otruba, Gustav. "Der gesellschaftliche und wirtschaftliche Strukturwandel der Stadt Linz und dessen Auswirkungen auf kulturelle Institutionen." *Linzer Aspekte* (1970): 21–24.

Otruba, Gustav and Möller, Hano. "Der Wandel des Wirtschaftsgefüges der Städte Wien, Linz, Innsbruck und Graz in den letzten hundert Jahren." *Wiener Geschichtsblätter*, 28 (1973): 48–55.

Papen, Franz von. *Memoirs* (New York, 1953).

Pauley, Bruce F. "Fascism and the *Führerprinzip*: The Austrian Example."
    Central European History, 12, 3 (September 1979): 272–96.

_____. "From Splinter Party to Mass Movement: The Austrian Nazi Break-
    through." *German Studies Review* 2, 1 (February, 1979): 7–29.

_____. *The Habsburg Legacy 1867–1939* (New York, 1972).

_____. *Hahnenschwanz und Hakenkreuz: Der steirische Heimatschutz und der
    österreichische Nationalsozialismus* (Vienna, 1972).

_____. *Hitler and the Forgotten Nazis: A History of Austrian National Socialism*
    (Chapel Hill, 1981).

Perz, Elfriede. "12. Februar 1934: Verlauf der Kampfhandlungen in Oberöster-
    reich und Steiermark" (unpublished paper, SE 154, IfZ, Vienna).

Pisecky, Franz. *Wirtschaft, Land und Kammer in Oberösterreich 1851–1976*, vol.
    I: *Das 19. Jahrhundert-die Zeit des Liberalismus* (Linz, 1976).

Rabinbach, Anson. *The Crisis of Austrian Socialism: From Red Vienna to Civil
    War 1927–1934* (Chicago, 1983).

Rabitsch, Gisela. "Das KL Mauthausen." In *Studien zur Geschichte der
    Konzentrationslager*, edited by Martin Broszat (Stuttgart, 1970).

Rape, Ludger. *Die österreichischen Heimwehren und die bayrische Rechte
    1920–1923* (Vienna, 1977).

Rath, R. John. "Authoritarian Austria." In *Native Fascism in the Successor States,
    1918—1945*, edited by Peter Sugar. (Santa Barbara, 1971).

Rath, R. John and Schum, Carolyn. "The Dollfuss-Schuschnigg Regime: Fascist or
    Authoritarian?" In *Who Were the Fascists? Social Roots of European
    Fascism*, edited by Stein Ugelvik Larsen et al. (Bergen, 1980), pp. 249–56.

Rauchensteiner, Manfred. *Der Sonderfall: Die Besatzungszeit in Österreich 1945
    bis 1955* (Graz, Vienna, and Cologne, 1979).

Rausch, Wilhelm. *Linz, 1945* (Linz, 1975).

Reisberg, Arnold. *Februar 1934: Hintergründe und Folge* (Vienna, 1974).

Rhodes, Anthony. *The Vatican in the Age of the Dictators 1922–1945* (New York,
    1973).

Riedelsperger, Max E. *The Lingering Shadow of Nazism: The Austrian Indepen-
    dent Party Movement Since 1945*. (Boulder, 1978).

Ritter, Harry R. "Recent Writing on Interwar Austria." *Central European History*
    12, 3 (September 1979): 297–311.

Rosar, Wolfgang. *Deutsche Gemeinschaft: Seyss Inquart und der Anschluss*
    (Vienna, 1971).

Rosenkranz, Herbert. "*Reichskristallnacht*" 9. November 1938 in Österreich*
    (Vienna, 1968).

_____. *Verfolgung und Selbstbehauptung: Die Juden in Österreich 1938–1945*
    (Vienna and Munich, 1978).

Rothschild, K.W. *The Austrian Economy since 1945* (London, 1950).

_____. *Austria's Economic Development between the Wars* (London, 1947).

Salzer, Wilhelm. *Vom Untertan zum Staatsburger: Oberösterreich von 1848 bis
    1918* (Linz, 1970).

Sauer, Wolfgang. "National Socialism: Totalitarianism or Fascism?" *The American
    Historical Review*, 73, 2 (December 1967): 404–24.

Schausberger, Norbert. *Der Griff nach Österreich: Der Anschluss* (Vienna and
    Munich, 1978).

Schilling, Alexander. *Dr. Walter Riehl und die Geschichte der Nation-
    alsozialismus* (Leipzig, 1933).

Schilling-Schletter, Alexander. "Das Parteileben bis zum Zusammenbruch." In

Deutscher Geist in Österreich: Ein Handbuch des völkischen Lebens der Ostmark, edited by Karl Wache (Vienna, 1933), pp. 78–115.

Schoenbaum, David. *Hitler's Social Revolution: Class and Status in Nazi Germany* (New York, 1967).

Schönzeler, Hans-Hubert. *Bruckner* (New York, 1970).

Schwager, Karl. "Geschichte der Juden in Linz." In *Geschichte der Juden in Österreich: Ein Gedenkbuch* (Tel Aviv, 1971), pp. 58–60.

Sereny, Gitta. *Into that Darkness: From Mercy Killing to Mass Murder* (New York, 1974).

Simon, Walter B. "Democracy in the Shadow of Imposed Sovereignty: The First Republic of Austria." In *The Breakdown of Democratic Regimes: Europe*, edited by Juan L. Linz and Alfred Stepan (Baltimore, 1978), pp. 80–121.

Slapnicka, Harry. "Die Kirche Oberösterreichs zur Zeit des Nationalsozialismus." In *Das Bistum Linz im Dritten Reich*, edited by Rudolf Zinnhobler (Linz, 1979): 1–12.

_____. "Linz, Oberösterreich und die tschechische Frage." *Historiches Jahrbuch der Stadt Linz* (1978): 210–13.

_____. *Oberösterreich als es "Oberdonau" hiess (1938–1945)* (Linz, 1978).

_____. *Oberösterreich—Die politische Führungsschicht 1918 bis 1938* (Linz, 1976).

_____. *Oberösterreich—Unter Kaiser Franz Joseph 1861–1918* (Linz, 1982).

_____. *Oberösterreich Zwischen Bürgerkrieg und "Anschluss" 1927–1938* (Linz, 1975).

_____. *Von Hauser bis Eigruber: Eine Zeitgeschichte Oberösterreichs* (Linz, 1974).

_____. "Zum Antisemitismus Problem in Oberösterreich." *Zeitgeschichte* 11–12 (1974): 264–66.

Smith, Bradley F. *Adolf Hitler His Family, Childhood and Youth* (Stanford, 1967).

Social Democratic Party. *Bericht über die Tätigkeit der sozialdemokratischen Partei Oberösterreichs für die Zeit vom 1. Jänner bis 31. Dezember 1927* (Linz, 1928).

Speer, Albert. *Inside the Third Reich: Memoirs* (New York, 1970).

_____. *Spandau: The Secret Diaries* (New York, 1976).

Sperl, Hans. "Richard Bernaschek." In *Werk und Widerhall: Grosse Gestalten des Österreichischen Sozialismus*, edited by Norbert Leser (Vienna, 1964), pp. 76–84.

Stadlbauer, Franz. *Ein Jahr Deutsche Arbeitsfront* (Berlin, 1939).

Stadler, Karl. *Austria* (London, 1971).

_____. *Österreich 1938–1945 im Spiegel der NS-Akten* (Vienna, 1966).

Starhemberg, Ernst Rüdiger. *Between Hitler and Mussolini* (New York, 1942).

Statistisches Amt für die Reichsgaue der Ostmark. *Statistische Übersichten für den Reichsgau Oberdonau* I-II (Vienna, 1941–42).

Staudinger, Anton. "Christlichsoziale Partei und Errichtung des 'Autoritären Ständestaates' in Österreich." In *Vom Justizpalast zum Heldenplatz*, edited by Ludwig Jedlicka and Rudolf Neck (Vienna, 1975), pp. 65–81.

_____. "Christlichsoziale Partei und Heimwehren bis 1927." In *Die Ereignisse des 15. Juli 1927: Protokoll des Symposiums in Wien am 15. Juli 1977*, edited by Rudolf Neck and Adam Wandruszka (Vienna, 1979), pp. 110–36.

_____. "Die Ereignisse in den Ländern Deutschösterreichs im Herbst, 1918." In *Ende und Anfang: Österreich 1918/19: Wien und die Bundesländer*, edited by Ludwig Jedlicka (Salzburg, 1969).

Stein, Erwin, ed. *Das Buch der Stadt Linz a.D.: Die Städte Deutschösterreichs I: Linz* (Berlin, 1927).

Steiner, Kurt, ed. *Modern Austria* (Palo Alto, 1981).

———. *Politics in Austria* (Boston, 1972).

Stöber, Otto. *Die Moor-Stöber* (Linz, 1975).

Stockhorst, Erich. *Fünftausend Köpfe: Wer war was im Dritten Reich* (Velbert, 1967).

Stuhlpfarrer, Karl. "Antisemitismus, Rassenpolitik und Judenverfolgung in Österreich nach dem ersten Weltkrieg." In *Das österreichische Judentum: Voraussetzungen und Geschichte.* edited by Anna Drabek et al. (Vienna, 1974), pp. 141–64.

Talos, Emmerich and Neugebauer, Wolfgang, eds. *"Austrofaschismus": Beiträge über Politik, Ökonomie und Kultur 1934–1938* (Vienna, 1984).

Taylor, Fred, ed. *The Goebbels Diaries 1939–1941* (New York, 1983).

Taylor, Robert R. *The Word In Stone: The Role of Architecture in the National Socialist Ideology* (Berkeley, 1974).

Trevor-Roper, H.R., ed. *Hitler's Table Talk, 1941–1944* (London, 1953).

Turner, Henry A. "Fascism and Modernization." In *Reappraisals of Fascism,* edited by Henry A. Turner (New York, 1975), pp. 117–39.

Tweraser, Kurt. "Carl Beurle and the Triumph of German Nationalism in Austria." *German Studies Review* 4 (October, 1981): 403–26.

———. "How Mass Politics Came to Upper Austria: A Preliminary Report" (unpublished paper prepared for the Western Association for German Studies, El Paso, 1982).

———. "Der Linzer Gemeinderat 1880–1914: Glanz und Elend bürgerlicher Herrschaft," *Historiches Jahrbuch der Stadt Linz* (1979): 293–340.

———. "Der Linzer Gemeinderat 1914–1934: Krise der parlamentarischen Demokratie." *Historiches Jahrbuch der Stadt Linz* (1980): 199–274.

———. "Der Linzer Gemeinderat 1934–1962: Ständestaat NS-Regime und die Ära Koref." *Historisches Jahrbuch der Stadt Linz* (1983): 153–243.

———. "Neither Revolution nor Restoration: Linz and Upper Austria under American Occupation, 1945–48" (paper prepared for the German Studies Association, Denver, Colorado, 12 October 1984).

Wagner, Dieter and Tomkowitz, Gerhard. *Anschluss: The Week Hitler Seized Austria* (New York, 1971).

Wallace, Lady. *The Letters of Wolfgang Amadeus Mozart* (New York, 1866).

Wandruszka, Adam. "Die Krisen des Parlamentarismus 1897 und 1933: Gedanken zum Demokratieverständnis in Österreich." In *Beiträge zur Zeitgeschichte: Festschrift für Ludwig Jedlicka zum 60. Geburtstag*, edited by Rudolf Neck and Adam Wandruszka (St. Pölten, 1976).

———. "Österreichs Politische Struktur: Die Entwicklung der Parteien und politischen Bewegungen." In *Geschichte der Republik Österreich,* edited by Heinrich Benedikt (Munich, 1954), pp. 289–485.

Wedgewood, C.V. *The Thiry Years War* (New York, 1961).

Weiguny, Anton. *Erinnerungen eines Alten aus der Anfängen der oberösterreichischen Arbeiterbewegung* (Linz, 1911).

Weinzierl, Erika. "Aus der Notizen von Richard Schmitz zur österreichischen Innenpolitik im Frühjahr 1933." In *Geschichte und Gesellschaft,* edited by Gerhard Botz et al. (Vienna, 1974), pp. 122–29.

———. *Die österreichischen Konkordate von 1855 und 1933* (Munich, 1960).

———. *Zu wenig Gerechte: Österreicher und Judenverfolgung 1938–1945* (Graz,

1969).

Whiteside, Andrew. *Austrian National Socialism Before 1918* (The Hague, 1962).

_____. "Austria." In *The European Right: A Historical Profile* (Berkeley and Los Angeles, 1966), pp. 303–63.

_____. *The Socialism of Fools: Georg Ritter von Schönerer and Austrian Pan Germanism* (Berkeley, 1975).

Williams, Maurice. "The Aftermath of Anschluss: Disillusioned Germans or Budding Austrian Patriots?" *Austrian History Yearbook*, 14 (1978): 127–86.

_____. "Aid, Assistance and Advice: German Nazis and the Austrian Hilfswerk." *Central European History* 14, 3 (September, 1981): 230–43.

_____. "Delusions of Grandeur: The Austrian National Socialists." *Canadian Journal of History*, 14, 3: 417–36.

Wimmer, Kurt. *Liberalismus in Öberösterreich 1869–1909* (Linz, 1979).

Wolff, Werner. *Anton Bruckner: Rustic Genius* (New York, 1942).

Vleck, Christine. "Der Republikanische Schutzbund in Österreich: Geschichte, Aufbau, und Organization" (diss., Vienna, 1971).

United States. *Military Government in Austria: Report of the United States Commission* (1945–46).

United States Army Medical Department. *Preventive Medicine in World War II* vol. 8 (Washington, D.C., 1976).

United States Department of State. *Documents on German Foreign Policy, 1918–1945* (DGFP) series C, vol. 1 (Washington D.C., 1949–59).

Zahn, Gordon C. *In Solitary Witness: The Life and Death of Franz Jägerstätter* (New York, 1964).

Ziervogel, Gerda. "Die Landtagswahlen in Oberösterreich 1931" (unpublished paper, SE 588, IfZ, Vienna).

Zinnhobler, Rudolf. "Die Haltung Bischof Gföllner gegenüber dem Nationalsozialismus." In *Das Bistum Linz im Dritten Reich*, edited by Rudolf Zinnhobler (Linz, 1979), pp. 61–73.

INDEX

EVAN BURR BUKEY is Professor of History
at the University of Arkansas in Fayetteville.